DATE DUE

AP 21 03			

DEMCO 38-296

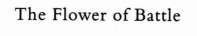

The Flower of Battle

The Flower of Battle

HOW BRITAIN WROTE THE GREAT WAR

Hugh Cecil

STEERFORTH PRESS

SOUTH ROYALTON, VERMONT

The text for this book was composed by Steerforth Press
using a digital version of Bembo.

LIST OF ILLUSTRATIONS:

1. Richard Aldington as an officer, 9th Royal Sussex Regt (*Beinecke Library, Yale University*); 2. Hilda Doolittle (H.D.) in 1913 (*Beinecke Library, Yale University*); 3. Bright Patmore (*Mary Patmore*); 4. V.M. Yeates in R.A.F. uniform (*Yeates family*); 5. Henry Williamson, c. 1923; 6. J.A. Gristwood's letter, about his son's death, to H.G. Wells (*Rare Book and Special Collections Library, University of Illinois, Urbana*); 7. R.H. Mottram with Claims Commission colleagues (*Norwich Public Library*); 8. R.H. Mottram marching to Peterborough, 1914 (*Norwich Public Library*); 9. Wildrid Ewart, c. 1921 (*Anne Butler*); 10. Dollie Rawson, c. 1916; 11. Sybil Keable in middle age (*Mrs D. Trewolla-Hulme*); 12. Robert Keable and Jolie Buck, Tahiti, c. 1923 (*Dr Anthony Keable-Elliott*); 13. Gilbert Frankau, portrait by Flora Lion; 14. Ford Madox Ford as a soldier; 15. C.E. Montague as a conducting officer, c. 1917; 16. Ronald Gurner as Head Master of Whitgift, Armistice Day 1928 (*Whitgift School*); 17. Ronald Gurner in uniform, c. 1916 (*Leon Gurner*); 18. Rosalie Gurner, Whitgift (*Whitgift School*); 19. Herbert Read, c. 1917 (*Benedict Read*); 20. Oliver Onions, c. 1916 (*Jane Oliver*); 21. Pamela Hinkson, c. 1932; 22. Jacket of *The Victors*, with illustration by Eric Kennington; 23. Richard Blaker as an undergraduate (*Mrs. Phyllis Blaker*); 24. Mamie Blaker (*Betty Ingleby*); 25. Louis Golding, May Owen and Mamie Blaker at the launch of *The Needle Watcher*, 1934; 26. 'Forward Observation Post': sketch by Richard Blaker.

Library of Congress Cataloging-in-Publication Data
Cecil, Hugh (Hugh P.)
The flower of battle : how Britain wrote the Great War / Hugh
Cecil. -- 1st North American ed.
p.   cm.
Includes bibliographical references and index.
ISBN 1-883642-05-1
1. English fiction--20th century--History and criticism. 2. World
War, 1914-1918--Great Britain--Literature and the war. 3. War
stories, English--History and criticism. I. Title.
PR830.W65C43   1996
823'.91209358--dc20   96-5030   CIP

Manufactured in the United States of America

FIRST EDITION

To Simon Head

Contents

The Flower of Battle

The summer twilight gently yields
To star-sown luminous night and close
The flowers in these Flemish fields
Are folded, still the leaves repose;

But, as the colour leaves the sky,
And darkness wraps a suffering earth,
Clamouring, climbing endlessly
Another blossom springs to birth.

The Flower of Battle, down the wide
Horizon mantles, tendrils spread,
Its far-hung petals brilliant dyed,
Yellow, and blinding white, and red.

Fed with our bodies at its root,
Fed with our hearts its living flame,
It sways in wonder absolute,
The Flower of Battle is its name . . . .

Men will gaze, awestruck, men will strive
To reach its glowing heart . . . and some
May turn away while yet alive,
But few from out its shade may come!

R. H. MOTTRAM, *London Mercury*
January 1926

I

The Flower of Battle

This book is about a war – the "Great War" of 1914–18 – and about people who lived through it. It focuses closely on eleven men and one woman and how they tried to cope, through their literary efforts, with the raw experience of horror, and with separation, dislocation, and grief. These writers, British and Irish, were among the first wave during the 20th century who attempted to resurrect for readers the terrible nightmare of living through the extreme experience of modern war on a modern battlefield. They sought words to describe the vast man-made catastrophe they had witnessed, as others, later, have tried to absorb, to understand, and somehow to transcend the other extreme experiences of the century – the great terror of Stalin's Russia, the Second World War, and the Holocaust.

War, of course, is as old as history, and it has always been filled with horror. What made the Great War different was its huge scale and the intensity of the violence on the battlefield. The machine gun and the massing of artillery turned the Western Front into a five-hundred-mile-long killing ground, from the North Sea to the border of Switzerland. What sane purpose could possibly be served by the killing and maiming of millions of men for years on end? For those at the "sharp end" it seemed as if the world had gone mad. The challenge of the war for those who survived was to learn to believe again in life, in reason, in the meaning of sacrifice, in the sanity and goodwill of the governments that had sent their own children into battle; to reassure themselves, if it were possible, that the suffering they had experienced and witnessed had been *for* something. Without some way to "explain" and "understand" the war its violence was as pointless as a car crash. Most of the millions who went home kept their answers, if any, to themselves, but some few, including the dozen treated here, found words for the war in novels, plays, poems, and stories. It would be a hard heart which would trade a book for a life; but when the life is already gone, sometimes a book – indeed, only a book – can rescue it from the unredeemed sorrow of loss. This was the first goal for those who wrote: to take back from the war, or to learn to live with, their all too frequent loss of their schoolchild's faith that no sacrifice can be too great.

But once that is granted, these writers are all very different, both in what they did and in what became of it. Some of them, at the time, enjoyed massive sales, because they briefly caught a public mood. Now, save the best known, Herbert Read and Richard Aldington, they are nearly all forgotten – in common with most First and Second World War authors. Neither this, however, nor any limitations they had as authors, are reasons to despise their testimony; indeed the very fact that a few once reached a very large readership makes the consideration of their books in the debate about war all the more interesting, however remote they may now seem.

This book is not a work of literary criticism. It is a contribution to the social history of our century. These writers were talented and praised in their lifetime, but nobody would claim that any of them, save two or three at their very best, approached the artistry of the finest war writers such as Siegfried Sassoon or Wilfred Owen, although occasionally their vision was quite as penetrating. What they had in common with the literary giants was that they, too, had confronted the same terrifying mayhem and tried to tell the truth about it. The alternative was to be silent; but silence, which many of their contemporaries chose, would have been, for these writers, defeat. The very fact that they managed to write of their ordeal was their triumph. For that, if for nothing else, they deserve attention.

No one person's experience of war is ever quite the same as another's. There were those, as at any time, who tried to find some fragment of hope in the shellshock, loss of friends, panic and horrible sights; and

there were others who despaired of doing so. There were some who
tried to reach out to those who had not been through the fighting and
the sorrow and there were others who gave up the attempt as impossible.

Most difficult, and at the same time most important for them to convey, was the actual experience of battle: those who fought, such as
Richard Aldington, Victor Yeates, and Herbert Read, sought to express
the overwhelming, indescribable sensations which they had felt "in the
cannon's mouth" as well as describing the unique world of the soldier's
life behind the lines.

A common preoccupation among war writers, in their novels, letters,
memoirs, or poetry, was isolation from their compatriots at home, and
with the soldier's return after the war to a diminished homeland, where
old attitudes still reigned, and where neither the older, nor the younger
generation could understand what it was like to have passed through the
terrors of war. This was something that one author, Oliver Onions, a
sympathetic witness on the sidelines, movingly illustrated in *Peace in Our
Time,* as related in a subsequent chapter of this book. The lives and works
of all such writers provide us with a special insight into the impact of
war in Britain.

Central in the minds of those who looked back on the First World
War was the memory of Britain before the war – the Britain, with a century of supremacy behind it, that disappeared forever during the conflict,
both materially and spiritually. R. H. Mottram, one of the authors described in this volume, evoked, in his memoirs, the assured tranquility of
the old city life of Norwich; Richard Blaker at the start of his novel
Medal Without Bar, the sedate confidence of a prewar London lawyer's office; Pamela Hinkson, in *The Ladies' Road,* the still unsevered tie between
Britain and Ireland. Because the war represented the great divide between Britain's century-long preeminence in the world, and its
diminished status thereafter, it has particular resonances for the British
nation, over and above the tragic loss of life. Britain has never recovered
from that decline in the way that France and Germany, for example, have
eventually been able to do. Looking back from today to before the First
World War, Victorian England, forever gone, seems for all its harshness
and inequities, like some broad fertile plain, teeming with creative and
commercial energy.

For the United States, the nearest equivalent to the Great War of 1914–18, in terms of emotional significance, is the Civil War, though in that case the victory of the North, with the danger of secession averted, brought *greater* national power. But for both nations, following these two devastating events, the memory of battle, brotherhood in arms and loss of comrades continued to resound over more than sixty years. For the United States there were the rallies of the Grand Army of the Republic, calling up memories of the Civil War for long years after it was over. For Britain there have been, to this day, the ceremonies (to remember both World Wars) round the Cenotaph at Whitehall on Remembrance Sunday and the two minutes of silence on Armistice Day, 11th November; and although in the last six or seven years the few survivors of the First World War have been fading away in old people's homes, and boarding houses, the interest in it has been kept alive both in new historical writing, in thoughtful fictional reinterpretations such as Pat Barker's *Regeneration,* and in television comedy and drama, such as Bleasdale's *Monocled Mutineer.*

It was open to me to look at the whole question of memory and experience through two or three outstanding and well-known writers such as Siegfried Sassoon, Ford Madox Ford, and Henry Williamson. This did not appeal, for most had been covered, or were about to be, in forthcoming biographies; or there were difficulties over the use of private papers. An example was the case of the finest British war novelist, Frederic Manning. After I had started work on this book, two excellent studies of him appeared by Verna Coleman and by Jonathan Marwill, which said more than I could possibly say on the subject. It is the duty of the historian to discover as well as to interpret.

I was more interested in searching for the war's meaning among the neglected authors whom I have chosen for this volume. One reason was that all those treated here had elected to write up their experiences partly in fiction, which is still an incompletely explored body of World War I evidence, and merits further investigation. Looking through much unfashionable prose, in a search for a picture of the past, I wondered to myself what manner of people its authors were and why they had varied so much in their message about the war.

It seemed to me this would be worth investigating. The very elusiveness of the evidence was a challenge. Some of their lives were not hard to trace. Others took years of looking up wills, birth, marriage, and death certificates, of writing to solicitors, relations and archivists, and of following many long, cold trails.

The second basis on which I selected these writers reflected the wide range of views on the war that was evident in their books: from utter despair to a strong confidence that their cause had been right – and also the deep feeling of estrangement between war veterans and those who had stayed behind. In every case the story I have found behind a particular work of fiction has been treated in conjunction with the literary evidence.

There was one further thought behind my decision to look chiefly at these lesser known writers, many of whose real-life histories were strange, painful, and grim. It was simply that these lacked a chronicler and might never have one. Had the research been postponed, these vanished lives would never have come to light. For the careers of Victor Yeates, Ralph Mottram, Wilfrid Ewart, Robert Keable, Ronald Gurner, A. D. Gristwood, Oliver Onions, Richard Blaker, and others, this has been a rescue operation. Moreover there seemed to be few people today who took any interest in Herbert Read's war writing, while Richard Aldington, save for his novel *Death of a Hero,* continued to count for little in Britain. It is the Americans and French who have taken this young-spirited antimodernist under their wing; and in this book his war letters – to F. S. Flint – are quoted at length for the first time, in all their ribaldry and vigour. All in all, the careers of the writers in this volume – as clerks, insurance brokers, bank and factory managers, journalists, professors, clergymen, schoolteachers, and cigar merchants – give an unique insight into the impact of the war on the texture of British life. The personal histories of these individuals, retrieved in the nick of time, further our understanding of the war they knew, the society they inhabited, and of modern war experience.

Britain's involvement in this tragic conflict lasted four years and a quarter. Between five and six million of her men and women served in the armed forces and noncombatant services from start to finish.

Of these, close on 700,000 lost their lives and two million were wounded, many of whom became permanent cripples, mentally as well as physically. Compared with the losses suffered by Germany, France, or Russia, these were modest figures. Nevertheless the impact they made on British society was lasting and painful for countless individuals and their families.

Few indeed came out from under "The Flower of Battle": all who survived were marked forever by grief for lost friends and relations; by subjection to the impersonal tyranny of the military machine; by the assault on their nerves as they sheltered in trenches from "the monstrous anger of the guns" in a war where artillery, with gas, shrapnel, and high explosive shell, dominated the battlefield; by the sight of comrades drowned in mud or falling to pieces as they decayed on the barbed wire; by the nightmare landscape that was created on the Western Front. "Here nothing lived, not even the leprous growths that feed on rottenness," wrote J. R. R. Tolkien forty years later, drawing on his memories of war to describe a scene of desolation in his epic, *The Lord of the Rings*.

Most, however, were deeply affected by the companionship with their fellow soldiers, which they felt to have been the most inspiring and precious experience of their lives, and many, probably the majority, were far from looking back on the war as unmitigated hell, however great their miseries at the time and despite, in later years, condemning its needless waste. The positive side of the Great War was widely acknowledged – as a test of courage, adventure, escape from a monotonous or complicated existence, a chance to look after horses, or machines, or people, and to serve their country – as duty demanded. The degree to which these compensated for the horror and tragedy depended on each individual's makeup, what they endured in the war, and the ways in which, reflecting later, they felt that it had changed the course of their lives – for better or for worse. Even while the war was going on, soldiers, sailors, nurses, and war workers with an urge to write were trying to express what they had seen on the printed page, whether of school magazine, newspaper, dramatic script, or book.

Quite apart from the plethora of war reminiscences that resulted, well over four hundred British authors put their memories into novels, short stories, plays, and children's tales. Most of these were closely related to their original experiences, but "the excuse for the novel," wrote Richard Aldington in a letter prefacing his *Death of a Hero,* "is that one can do any damn thing one pleases," and so they used their freedom as novelists to alter settings, elaborate characters (while avoiding actions for libel) and introduce dialogue redolent of trench atmosphere.

In the twenties, fiction was particularly in demand, and it was the obvious way for writers to cash in on any aspect of the war that concerned them. The sheer variety demonstrates this. Quite apart from Western Front themes, there are novels about the Arabs in Palestine (Clement Hankey, *Bottles in the Smoke,* 1931), on Serbia (Stephen Graham, *Balkan Monastery*), Russia (Hugh Walpole, *The Dark Forest,* 1916, reissued 1934), South Africa (L. Patrick Greene, *Tug of War*), Ireland (Pamela Hinkson, *The Ladies' Road,* 1932), Gallipoli (George Blake, *The Path of Glory,* 1929), the Merchant Navy (James Hanley, *Hollow Sea*), the Home Front (Godfrey Waytemore, *The Profiteer*), the eastern Mediterranean (William McFee, *Command,* 1922), the North Sea (William Barnet Logan, *Dress of the Day,* 1930), the air (Capt. W. E. Johns, *Biggles of the Royal Flying Corps*), prisoner-of-war camps in Germany (V. W. W. S. Purcell, *The Other Side of No-Man's Land,* 1929), and the Friends' Ambulance Brigade (W. Olav Stapledon, *Last Men in London,* 1932). There are humorous satires (F. O. Mann, *Grope Carries On,* 1932), thriller fiction (Philip Macdonald, *Patrol,* 1927), spy novels (Oliver Madox Hueffer, *Cousins German,* 1930), school stories in a war setting (Guy Pocock, *Knight's Gambit,* 1929), romances (Herbert Asquith, *Roon,* 1929), animal stories (George Goodchild and Major Maurice Mottram, *Old Sport,* 1919), Marxist interpretations of the war (Robert Briffault, *Europa, Europa in Limbo,* 1936, 1937), feminist novels (Vera Brittain, *Honourable Estate,* 1936), fantasies (Richard Deehan, *The Just Steward,* 1922), and even gay novels (A. T. Fitzroy [Rose Allatini], *Despised and Rejected,* 1918, banned and later reprinted).

Many of these writers wanted only to entertain; others had a serious message, and from 1918 were pleading the cause of pacifists or unemployed soldiers. Some, such as John Brophy (*The World Went Mad,* 1934), or Henry Williamson (*A Chronicle of Ancient Sunlight,* 15 vols., 1954–1960), tried, ambitiously, to fit the war into the history of their times; others celebrated King and country; and an increasing element railed bitterly against the generals and the politicians. The greatest number, wishing simply to record their experience as faithfully as possible, took a neutral line. Many of the better works, such as J. L. Hodson's *Grey Dawn, Red Night* (1929), and Frederic Manning's *The Middle Parts of Fortune* (1929) were of this sort. In much of this war fiction the message was ambiguous: it was the reader or playgoer who decided whether or not a work was "antiwar." R. C. Sherriff's *Journey's End* is a case in point.

On the whole, the novels – even more than the memoirs – that appeared shortly after the war tended to be patriotic and romantic, whether they were full of authentic and disturbing detail, like Gilbert Frankau's *Peter Jackson, Cigar Merchant,* or were sentimental and valedictory, like Ernest Raymond's *Tell England.* There were exceptions, more directly critical of army discipline, for example, such as A. P. Herbert's *The Secret Battle.* Few at that time, however, questioned whether Britain should have been involved in the war at all. One that did, F. A. Voigt's *Combed Out* – a memoir, not a novel – by a writer of German extraction, made hardly any impact when it first appeared in 1920, despite sensational and horrific descriptions of the wounded and dying.

It was only gradually that publishers came around more generally to war reminiscences or fiction of such a controversial nature. C. E. Montague's *Disenchantment,* more essay than memoir, sold widely after it appeared in 1922. This brilliant, mannered work, full of literary allusions, by the former theatre critic of the *Manchester Guardian,* attacked the lies and cynicism at home and at the front that disillusioned soldiers about their military and political masters. Montague had been a 1914 volunteer and later a press officer, so he experienced war propaganda both as a recipient and as one of its agents. Fiction such as his later work, *Rough Justice,* Ford Madox Ford's "Tietjens tetralogy," R. H. Mottram's *Spanish Farm Trilogy,* and Edward Thompson's *These Men Thy Friends,* reinforced the criticism.

It was a decade after the conflict that the trend of disillusionment became a flood. This change in the public appetite came about less because readers had acquired a deepened understanding of the nature of the war than because hopes of a better postwar world had been disappointed. Thereafter – and to this day – the British public came to think of the Great War chiefly through the disenchanted vision of the struggle in the German Erich Maria Remarque's *All Quiet on the Western Front* and in

R. C. Sherriff's play, *Journey's End*. Dating from the same year (1929) these two works made a sensational impact, the one presenting the conflict as the futile waste of a generation, the other as irredeemable tragedy. Remarque's belief that "the regenerative power of our youth had been dissipated in the war" was widely accepted, while for some years after, the army was seriously worried about the effect that *Journey's End* and other works might be having on recruitment.

Other much-praised books that gave a disillusioned view at this time were Richard Aldington's *Death of a Hero;* Henry Williamson's *The Patriot's Progress;* Anthony Bertram's *The Sword Falls;* Charles Yale Harrison's *Generals Die in Bed;* Liam O'Flaherty's *The Return of the Brute;* Peregrine Acland's *All Else is Folly;* and Siegfried Sassoon's *Memoirs of a Fox-Hunting Man* and *Memoirs of an Infantry Officer.* But this avalanche of debunking books did not dent the continuing popularity of *Tell England* and A. S. M. Hutchinson's *If Winter Comes,* though as time went on these patriotic effusions were enjoyed more as romantic tales than as "the truth about the war." The success of Herbert Asquith's *Young Orland* (1927) and *Roon* (1929) showed that some of the public still preferred the war to be handled in a delicate and poetical way. Carroll Carstair's memoir, *A Generation Missing* (1930), describing the experiences of a young American in the Grenadier Guards, had much the same appeal, as did Edward Thompson's novel *In Araby Orion.* Moreover, plenty of new books came out after 1929 that defended the British Army and honest fighting men against accusations of stupidity and blind jingoism. Edward Thompson M.C., poet, Methodist padre, and political radical, who had himself been critical of the High Command in his 1927 war novel, *These Men Thy Friends,* proclaimed the independence and spirit of young British soldiers in a new one, *Lament for Adonis,* set in Jerusalem. In it he described a subaltern as "not one of the minority of neurotics who have furnished war novelists with their officer heroes, nor of the majority of crude (yet vaguely unhappy) beasts who are now supposed to have composed the rank and file of the warring armies." J. B. Morton, the humorous columnist "Beachcomber" of the *Daily Express,* in the 1934 edition of his novel, *The Barber of Putney* (first published in 1918), declared: "It is the object of the self-styled enlightened people to persuade the young that the war was 'futile' that those who fought were silly dupes, swept away by an emotional appeal . . . I see now my book has a moral . . . The more you insist on the agonies and tortures and filth of modern warfare, the more honour you must pay to the men who endured these things. My barber would go out to fight again tomorrow – God between him and any such necessity! – but nobody, having read this book, can call him a bloody militarist. That he had no clear idea of what was at stake for Europe, as his French counterpart had, is due to the English system of education." Despite these patriotic pronouncements, the disillusioned picture of futile slaughter and leadership by incompetents was the one that stuck in the popular imagination. During the late 1920s and '30s the dominant literary view of the war seems to have been antipatriotic; but at the same time, evidently, there were enough successful novels with a contrary message for the public to receive a fairly balanced picture.

Very few of these books were outstanding as literature. Doing "any damn thing one pleases" was unfortunately a license for a good deal of fifth-rate stuff. At the frivolous end, facetious works like Crosbie Garstin's South African frolic *The Sunshine Settlers,* or thrillers like Anthony Hope's *Beaumaroy Home from the War,* have become mere curiosities. An exception must be made for F. O. Mann's *Grope Carries On,* which remains a very amusing satire on bureaucracy, much more effective than Gerald O'Donovan's *How They Did It,* a humourless patriotic rant on the same subject. Although not quite in the same lowly category as O'Donovan's book, Ernest Raymond's *Tell England,* with its account of golden youth going through what he innocently, but appropriately, called "Five Gay Years at School" before meeting their ends in a state of moral purity at Gallipoli, seems now absurd, as do A. S. M. Hutchinson's once admired works. The run-of-the-mill disenchanted books such as Helen Zennor Smith's *Not So Quiet: Stepdaughters of War* make repetitive reading. It is not surprising that before the end of 1929 one reviewer was already writing gloomily of "that extremely rare thing, a good war novel." Even so, there are many honest, carefully written volumes that deserve, and reward, careful study. They are not to be lightly dismissed because of their artistic limitations.

Around 1938, the fashion for Great War books finally tailed off. It did not revive fully until the sixties with the success of the satirical revue,

"Oh What a Lovely War!" and of John Terraine's 1914–18 historical series on television, although Leon Wolff's *In Flanders Fields* (1955) pointed
the way. By then some new novels by veterans had been added to the
pile. Long gestation led to Henry Williamson's masterly "Chronicle" volumes, but was not a guarantee of quality: Stuart Cloete waited till 1969
to produce *How Young They Died,* his vigorous tale of shellfire and forni-
cation. A sensational best-seller, like most of his books, it compares
poorly with his absorbing memoirs, *A Victorian Son* and *The Gambler,* being chiefly a fantasy about the kind of sexual opportunities he missed
when a capable young officer, with Clark Gable looks, fifty years before.
Even so, its insights into the cruder aspects of wartime love have their
place in an understanding of the period and could not have appeared in
print much earlier.

In this seemingly endless catalogue, the very best British war novelists
stand out in showing a power of empathy, a command of memorable detail, vigorous expression worthy of the strong stuff that had to be
communicated, and above all a sensitivity to the tragedy and pity of it all.
The quality of their work should be briefly considered.

Of the finer British First World War novels, Siegfried Sassoon's three-
part work, *The Complete Memoirs of George Sherston,* is probably the best
known. Sassoon served with exceptional courage in the 2nd Royal
Welch Fusiliers, publicly denounced the war and tried to resign his commission. To avoid the scandal of court-martialling a hero, the army put
his behaviour down to shellshock, and after a time in hospital, he returned to the front, determined only not to desert his comrades.
Published between 1928 and 1936 (the complete edition in 1937), his
trilogy is the classic British statement of disenchantment with the war.
It is largely autobiographical, though Sherston, the main character, is
less complex than Sassoon himself. As his friend Desmond MacCarthy
observed, Sassoon "half-liked, despite everything, life at the front." Although attacking the war, the three Sherston novels do not go as far as
books like A. D. Gristwood's *The Somme,* which denigrates the whole experience – companionship, loyalty, and courage included.

Sassoon's gifts as a poet, and his intimacy with great danger and distress, combined to make him a superlative war writer. Few passages, for
example, evoke the suffering of war more terribly than his account of a

patient dying in hospital after action on the Somme: "Sometimes I could catch what he said, troubled and unhappy, and complaining. Someone called Dicky was on his mind, and he kept crying out to Dicky, 'Don't go out Dicky; they snipe like hell!' And then, 'Curse the wood . . . Dicky, you fool, don't go out!' . . . All the horror of the Somme attacks was in that raving; all the darkness and the dreadful daylight."

Other highly regarded British Great War novels include Richard Aldington's *Death of a Hero* and V. M. Yeates' *Winged Victory*, discussed later in this volume, and the two great canvasses of England at war. Ford Madox Ford's "Tietjens tetralogy" deals with the damage done to English society and individuals by the war – the selfishness and incompetence of the military caste and the wanton wastage of the nation's best young men. Henry Williamson's fifteen-volume *A Chronicle of Ancient Sunlight*, presents the conflict as a fratricidal tragedy with Englishman set against German. Of the two, Williamson evokes the sensation of battle more vividly and writes with a greater intensity. Here for example is a description of a young boy's first experience of battle, in October 1914:

Mr. Ogilby was moving his sword from his head toward the right. They were too far to the left. Right incline! shouted Baldwin's voice only just audible in the noise. Right incline! How thin his own voice felt. He could now hear machine guns firing. Each bullet passed with a sharp hissing. He broke into a sweat. Why was Baldwin kneeling down? He seemed to be sick. Then he saw that he was vomiting blood from his mouth. He fell sideways, hands clutching face, fingers streaming bright red jerking blood. Movement thereafter for Phillip became automatic. He was stumbling over brown furrows of a plowed field, near a tall hedge red with hawthorn haws. There were stacks at the far end of the field, and a windmill. Near the windmill was a farm house, with a red roof. He was a walking mass of perspiration. A jumble of memories rose before him, his head was filled with a high singing note, a steel wire seemed to make him go on after each automatic bending down, arms shielding face, from great black metallic-rending crumps in the field.

Graphic as Williamson could be, Ford Madox Ford's mind was the subtler: at work in the Tietjens books was a powerful intellect, penetrating the illusions and deceptions of English life in a far more sophisticated manner than Williamson with his simplistic interpretations of economic and social phenomena. However, the fabric of both these works is so rich in colour and vitality that the war comes over as infinitely fascinating, and in all its facets, hellish and exciting alike, so valuable an experience that, if one could endure it, to live through it was a privilege. Ford, an influential literary editor before the war, worked, to his subsequent shame, on war propaganda, then was commissioned in the 3rd Battalion, the Welch Regiment, when he was over forty – and overweight. Williamson served through the war from 1914, as a boy private and later an officer, his literary career beginning after the conflict had ended.

Smaller in scale than these two works, but a masterpiece, is *The Middle Parts of Fortune,* by Frederic Manning, a cultivated Australian "fastidious almost to the point of foppishness," who was a private in the King's Shropshire Light Infantry; he did not set out to denounce the war, though his account of "other ranks" during the 1916 Somme battle is tragic and grim in the extreme. Loyalty and love of comrades is a central theme. Nowhere is the "sorrow of war" better conveyed: early in the action, for example, Corporal Tozer tries to comfort a grief-stricken soldier, Pritchard, who has just lost his best friend: "That's all right, Corporal," answered Pritchard evenly. "Bein' sorry ain't going to do us'ns no manner o'good. We've all the sorrow we can bear of our own, wi'out troublin' ourselves wi' that o' other folk. We 'elp each other all we can, an' when we can't 'elp the other man no more, we must just 'elp ourselves. But I tell thee, Corporal, if I thought life was never goin' to be no different, I'd as lief be bloody well dead myself."

Such writers were most successful in conveying the pity and power of war. It should be reemphasised, however, that this present volume was never intended as a comprehensive literary history or work of criticism and as these four authors have been, or are about to be, covered in biographies and writings, I have chosen to deal with other, lesser-known figures. There are many studies to which readers can turn: for Sassoon, John Stallworthy's forthcoming biography and Paul Fussell's penetrating observations in *The Great War and Modern Memory;* for Williamson, there is Richard and Anne Williamson's new life, tapping the rich source of his private papers, and Daniel Farson's affectionate portrait; for Ford, Alan Judd's excellent recent biography; for Manning, Jonathan Marwill's fascinating investigation, in the great tradition of Symons' *The Quest for Corvo,* and Verna Coleman's indispensable critique, *The Last Exquisite.* On aspects of all four (as well as for insights on many other novelists and playwrights), John Onions' thought-provoking and undeservedly neglected survey of British fiction and the Great War should be required reading.

Without therefore ignoring these well-known authors, the present volume looks at others who were less accomplished, on the whole, but no less true to what they had known of war. Although most of those described in the chapters that follow served on the Western Front, their responses were by no means the same. The marked differences between their works, as well as their similarities, arose of course from the nature of their individual wartime experience – the morale of the units to which they belonged, the intensity of the fighting involved, their age, responsibility, and home attachments at the time of their service; but it arose partly, too, from their expectations of life and their psychological stability before the conflict. Their judgments on the war were also profoundly affected by their lives after it was over, involving, in two cases at least, mental illness, in another, literary disappointments, and, in several, unhappy marriages.

Their novels and their careers present intriguing contrasts: one was over military age and only served at home; another, of aristocratic birth, took part in some of the fiercest fighting in the war. One served as a private throughout, one as a padre, one as an airman, two as gunners; one, a professed pacifist, became a hero; one was a schoolgirl until 1917. Three died violently, two of these by their own hand. All except two had successful careers. All were haunted by the war.

There was nothing strange in that. To be haunted by the war was the common fate of millions. What distinguished these twelve writers was their effort to hold on to the pain they felt, to see it whole, to retain their humanity, to bear witness. The long argument over the war that has not ended yet – whether it was mad and futile, or a triumph of selflessness over fear – was the direct result of their refusal to let the war go. The horror of the war threatened to crush the spirit of those it did not kill. These writers would not submit to that, even in those sorrowful cases where the war can be said to have killed them in the end. Writing the war was their way of holding on to life and hope. The saddest truth of the century is the number of other, later writers who were forced to face the same challenge again – to suffer, to survive, to decline the invitation to despair, and to find the words that redeem.

PART ONE

❦

WAR UNREDEEMED

The rain teems down. The writhen waste is dumb,
Defiled, defaced, shamed in its hopelessness.
This is the ultimate Hell, the Wilderness
To which all Youth, Laughter and Love must come . . .

—from Robert Nichols, "Yesterday" (for Siegfried Sassoon),
3. -"Burial Party at Passchedndaele"

❧

2

A Wounded Lion
Richard Aldington
1892 - 1962

There are perhaps certain men who can never begin to recover as long as they have a vivid memory," wrote Richard Aldington's friend, Frédèric-Jacques Temple: "Never healed, they become outcasts, even untouchables, pariahs, if they are compelled, like Richard Aldington, to proclaim their truth." Richard Aldington was the author of one of the most bitter and rebellious British novels about the Western Front, *Death of a Hero* (1929).

The often intemperate passion of Aldington's writing throughout much of his career was largely the result of his sufferings in the First World War. In old age, still full of the enjoyment of life, Temple recollected, Aldington had nonetheless the look of an animal that has been wounded.

His appearance however did not immediately suggest someone vulnerable. In a *roman à clef* by a friend, John Cournos, he was likened to "a great beautiful clean sensual beast," and even though army life and, later, good living, thickened his powerful frame, his looks remained impressive into old age. He dressed with style. As a young poet before the Great War, he sported a cloak and velvet jacket, his face with pointed beard and peaked eyebrows giving him the appearance of a faun from one of the Greek poems he translated. The beard was abandoned in favour of a small moustache, the romantic poet's attire in favour of harlequin sweaters, tweed jackets, and suits; but the leonine look was still there. When he was in his sixties, another friend, the novelist Lawrence Durrell, urged him unsuccessfully to go on English television: "At a blow you could alter the Aldington image (people seem to think you are both grumpy and cantankerous and "superior") – the young I mean. And with your film-star physique you'd have them bowled."

In Britain today, however, Aldington still has a reputation as a curmudgeon. Only those who grew up before the Second World War know much of his work beyond *Death of a Hero* (1929) and his life of Lawrence of Arabia (1955), the first English work of scholarship to debunk that imperial idol. Thanks to the bad press he received when the Lawrence book appeared, he is remembered as a sour old man denouncing Britain from self-imposed exile in France.

Critics cite also the satirical manner in which he wrote about former friends – T. S. Eliot, Ezra Pound, Ford Madox Ford, D. H. Lawrence, and Norman Douglas – in his memoirs and fiction. His mocking attack on Eliot, *Stepping Heavenwards,* has been condemned for the fun he made of that poet's alleged neglect of his wife – which, because of Mrs. Eliot's mental illness in real life, was a painful subject.

Finally there are many who have seen him as a caddish male chauvinist, discarding his wives and mistresses callously and blaming women for ruining his life.

He deserves better. He was one of Britain's most prolific twentieth-century men of letters. His output over fifty years included seven works of biography or personal reminiscence, eight novels, nearly thirty volumes of translations from the French, Italian, Latin, and Greek, seventeen books of poetry, nine major critical works, and an uncountable number of reviews, editions, and introductions – quite apart from the various collections of his work, which appeared repeatedly under different titles. The French literary world regards him highly for his promotion of Voltaire and Laclos, de Gourmont, Lautréamont, Marivaux, and many other writers.

In the U.S.A. he is also esteemed, not least because his reputation is inextricably bound up with the early 20th century Imagist movement – a set of poets based largely in England who rivalled "Bloomsbury" for their soap-opera interest. They included Hilda Doolittle ("H.D.") – Aldington's wife – and Ezra Pound, two major influences in the development of modern American literature, and other, lesser names: F. S. Flint, John Gould Fletcher, and John Cournos. On the edge of this set, there hovered also the powerful figures of Ford Madox Ford, Amy

Lovell, and D. H. Lawrence. Several were the subjects of *romans à clef* by the various participants in that energetically bohemian world.

But Aldington was not only a clever writer, with a fine literary palate. He was humorous and life-enhancing. His generosity, both with time and money – though he was often poor – was well-known. Much of the apparent bitterness in his books was only his exuberant sense of the mischievous.

He expected too much of life. Romantic and impulsive, he made some disastrous mistakes and was easily disappointed. When he quarrelled, more often than not it was – as in Eliot's case – the result of others taking advantage of him or snubbing him. (Eliot, the beneficiary of much constructive assistance from Aldington before they quarrelled, was later to admit that he himself had been at fault.)

Aldington's life rarely ran on an even keel, and his strong capacity for happiness was often disturbed. He put some of his difficulties down to childhood miseries, which, it seems fairly certain, he exaggerated. In his early years, his family was not poor. His father, Alfred Aldington, a solicitor, was a cultivated man with a huge library and was fond of his son. His mother, May Aldington (*née* Godfrey), an enterprising if untalented writer with a number of successful sentimental novels to her name, came, it is said, from a lower social background. She was temperamental, and in later life a heavy drinker, but she cannot have been unsympathetic to her son's literary efforts since she took the trouble to send a copy of his first published poem (while he was in his teens) to Bernard Shaw. According to Aldington, however, she had very conventional notions of a successful career for him, which would have been the end of his poetical inspiration. She lacked tact or discrimination; her books embarrassed him; most irritating to him of all, but like a good mother, she was constantly urging him to take a practical line, evidently perceiving that his romantic side might be his undoing, as seems to have been the case several times in his relations with women. Indeed, it seems he really recognised the need for such assaults on his fantasy life, and once, in verse, expressed the desire to have a parrot (female, significantly) in attendance to rebuke him for his follies and conceit:

> Parrot, when I'm half-successful,
> When I think I'm rather good,

> When I'm half-inclined to purchase
> Half-indulgences from God,
> *Snap loud, parrot.*

What May Aldington underestimated was his capacity for hard work, not evident during the school life he so much hated. In fact, he owed his drive very largely to her – through inheriting her energy and through her work ethic, which always made him feel guilty about missing a day's writing.

In any case, however oppressive he may have thought his parents, they evidently failed to deflect him from his chosen path, in a period when parents could exercise much greater sway over their children than today. His partial rejection of them was in keeping both with his bohemian image of himself and with the anti-Victorian reaction, as expressed in the widely-read works of Samuel Butler and Edmund Gosse, which made it increasingly fashionable to pour contempt on the older generation. He blamed his parents for years spent in the stifling ugliness of Dover:

> The bitterness, the misery, the wretchedness of childhood
> Put me out of love with God.
> I can't believe in God's goodness;
> I can believe
> In many avenging gods.
> Most of all I believe
>
> In gods of bitter dullness,
> Cruel local gods
> Who seared my childhood.

However, this was by no means the whole story. Before he was eight, the Aldingtons moved to the country, and though he still went to school in Dover, he spent a great deal of time wandering over the chalkland of South Kent. He was a solitary child, absorbed in the study of natural history, which developed into an intense aesthetic response to the countryside and to English literature. The precocious development of his talents, a spell at London University, his entry into London literary life and his marriage to the beautiful American poet "H. D.," represented the apogee of his happiness in its most unalloyed form, when he had escaped the constricting atmosphere of home and before the Great War cut across his life.

When he was nineteen, having had to leave London University beause his father was financially ruined, he was swept into a London literary circle dominated by the charlatan-genius from the American Midwest, Ezra Pound. Then in his twenties, Pound had red-haired narcissistic good looks and a power to enthuse his companions. He saw himself as an iconoclast, challenging the clichés and wordiness of the late Victorian and Georgian poets. In the new poetical efforts of his circle, he identified a revolutionary approach – concentration on a central image only, terse expression and the verse rhythms following freely the music of the phrase rather than any conventional metre or rhyme scheme. He called this school of writing "Imagism" and under his auspices a volume of Imagist poetry, including Aldington's, appeared in February 1914 as *Des Imagistes* (the use of French was pure affectation on Pound's part).

This was followed by further anthologies, in addition to other books of verse by imagists writing independently. Quite soon, however, Pound lost interest, being more concerned to launch new movements such as "Vorticism" than to stay with this particular poetic form.

Though some imagist poets achieved a fresh directness and beauty in their verses, their importance lay not so much in what they produced as in the fact that they broke with formal tradition, and in that sense, constituted an early "modern" movement. Today, however, many of the images themselves seem to belong to the far side of the line that divides the romantic era from the modern. The poems of Aldington and his wife Hilda Doolittle were largely of fauns and dryads; and the pre-war bohemia that they inhabited, for men, in beards and cloaks, or, for women with Grecian "filets" round their brows, gushing of oreads and thyrsi over tea and buns in cafés near the British Museum, seems quaint, theatrical, and utterly remote – a world the guns blasted away forever.

Hilda Doolittle, whom Aldington married in 1913, was an ultra-refined, high-strung Philadelphian with a greater poetic talent than her husband – as he recognised without resentment. She had been introduced to him by the beautiful Mrs. Patmore, an early lover of his. It had been Ezra Pound who had spotted H. D.'s talent. Nobody seeing her could doubt she was a poet. Her dryad loveliness appeared to fit her ideally for partnership with the Arcadian Aldington. A powerful intellect showed in her high forehead, deep, melancholy gaze, and firm moulded chin. Though she held herself awkwardly, she had a tall, graceful figure. Her personality was compelling and provocative. With her cryptic smile and studied disregard for convention, she seemed to Aldington like a wild spirit of the woods. She dressed carelessly, and her fervent, complex discourse was punctuated with girlish giggles.

Their relationship was intensely romantic. It was based on shared poetic aims and a love of Ancient Greece, as well as a strong physical attraction. H. D. and her husband were perfectly in tune with a prewar aesthetic ideal that went with Pan pipes, the Greek Anthology, afternoon fauns and neopaganism. H. D.'s poems were rarified and haunting, the very best in an attenuated genre. Aldington's were more sensual, and inspired largely by the Ancient Greek poet Meleager.

By the time the war broke out he was recognised as a promising poetic talent and had recently become literary editor of an avant-garde journal, *The Egoist*. His instinctive reaction to the news of war, like that of most young Englishmen from his background, had been to try to join the army. Turned down because of an earlier hernia operation, he tried, again unsuccessfully, in late 1915, to enter an officer training unit. By this time he was beginning to have second thoughts.

H. D. was distressed about the possibility of his going into the army, and Aldington was aware that the war would damage both their relationship and his poetical inspiration. Early in 1916 they decided to leave London. T. S. Eliot, Pound's discovery, and destined to eclipse all of them, took over the *Egoist*. The Aldingtons went to live, at the suggestion of John Cournos, a fellow writer, deep in the rural Devon countryside close to Cournos's friends, Carl Fallas and his wife Flo.

Fallas was in his mid-twenties, a short, guileless, rumbustious man, who had spent his early years travelling round the world. He had literary ambitions, but achieved little success. Late in life, he wrote a lyrical, moving war novel, *St. Mary's Village Through the Eyes of an Unknown Soldier Who Lived On,* recalling his service in the 6th Leicesters. It shows his resilience and simple optimism about human nature. In 1915, however, "Pénis," as Aldington referred to him, was far from wishing to be a soldier, which accorded ill with his *Wandervogel* nature-spirit ideas; and he and Flo were under the influence of a pacifist friend, John Mills

Whitham. Aldington himself had now concluded that the war was pointless. All his friends agreed with him, he told one of the closest of them, the imagist poet Frank Flint, but the public had no wish to listen. What were a handful of poets against the vulgar press, such as Horatio Bottomley's *John Bull* or the "arse-licking, stinking" Northcliffe's *Daily Mail,* which gave people what they wanted to hear?

The Aldingtons spent much time with Carl and Flo, joining them on country picnics, bathing naked together and drinking German wine, which because of the war was not a popular item at hotels and was going cheap. The conversation was relaxed, bawdy, and somewhat below H.D.'s level. Richard admired Flo's full figure, writing to Flint of her *"cuisses spongeuses, le ventre joli – tres joli! – et un entre-jambes fort alléchant!"*

He and H.D. had agreed, unrealistically as it turned out, that their marriage must be an open one, held together by love and not by conventional rules. Despite an assurance to Flint that *"j'ai renoncé à faire la bête à deux dos"* with Flo, out of consideration for H.D., in the end Aldington, naively hoping that his wife would not really mind, obeyed his senses. He found Flo easy to persuade. In fact H.D. resented this infidelity deeply, although it was not a serious entanglement.

She intimated her confused feelings about Richard to John Cournos and became, in her turn, overinvolved with her confidant, who took her expressions of devotion for encouragement. Subsequently disillusioned, Cournos wrote a spiteful picture of the Aldington marriage some years later: the novel *Miranda Masters.*

Aldington was losing his way in his relationship with H. D. and could not understand clearly what she expected of him. Despite his protestations, he was also plagued with conscience about staying out of the war. In the end he and Carl Fallas decided to wait until both were called up as privates in the Devonshire Regiment under the second Military Service Act of May 1916.

On 24 June 1916, accordingly, Aldington and Fallas enrolled in the 11th Devons, based at Wareham in Dorset. H. D. moved to the ancient Dorset village of Corfe Castle so that she could see her husband regularly, while settling down to write poetry. However Richard felt urgently that she should get away from war-torn England and her ever-present anxieties about him. He tried to persuade her to go back to the U.S.A. or, as he accurately predicted, the strain on both would be too great: "To feel you are making other people wretched by your own inconsiderable demise is a torture," he explained to Flint; "it won't help me to stand knee deep in mud under shrapnel if I know H. D. is in an agony of apprehension in England." To persuade her further, he warned her that the government might conscript the female population as labour. Essentially he felt he could cope with the soldier's life if he did not have too strong an emotional pull the other way. "It's devilish difficult to leave her at 8 o'clock," he complained to Flint, "to return to this filthy hut full of fellows who swear and converse in the most idiotic and obscene fashion." When she did leave Corfe Castle, however, it was to return to London where she substituted for him as assistant director of the *Egoist*. She sought the company of Cournos, to make up for her husband's attention being largely absorbed by his military duties. The stage was set for the destruction of their marriage, though the process took nearly three more years.

Death of a Hero, with all its bitterness, arose largely out of Aldington's army experience. This began badly. First, by starting in the ranks he had to perform more degrading tasks than he had ever imagined. Swabbing greasy kitchen floors with filthy cloths reduced him to tears. During the first weeks, he told Flint, "I was just an unhappy being, suffering and unimaginably low." Secondly, he was temperamentally unsuited to institutional existence or enforced companionship. Self-disciplined and used to running his life in his own way, he resented putting his time and energies into the often mindless keeping of others. A highly educated middle-class private, he was isolated from the supportive camaraderie that working-class civilian soldiers rapidly created. He thought his fellow-soldiers' existence pitiable: "The young learn to drink and fornicate with disgusting '*horizontales*.' The old quickly become foul-mouthed animals."

On the other hand he was at times genuinely touched by them – in particular by the way that they spent a part of their Saturdays solemnly gathering wildflowers to decorate their tables. Moreover he was quite convinced he had to accept his fate: "So many better men have perished in this foolish contest that I have no sainted right to claim or hope for exemption for myself."

As a soldier, he fortunately had some advantages. His powerful physique gave him a natural standing in a world where strength and stamina were important, and where being a poet might need some living down. He was also practical. The tasks required of him as an N. C. O. and later an officer came fairly easily. He was courageous and through a habit of self-control, he, like many others, did not break down nervously until the war was over. Gradually, he came to admire many of the military qualities that he assumed he would despise – discipline (though not "bull"), not losing face, battalion spirit. In time, too, he warmed to the companionship of the front. Deep down he thought poorly of many men of his age who had managed to evade that experience, and he always felt a link with those who had been through it.

His training went on throughout 1916. Promoted to lance-corporal after impressing his superiors with his ability to name, without hesitation, the parts of a rifle, he remained on the Dorset coast for some months. In November he was at the grim barracks at Verne Citadel on the Portland peninsula, built by convict labour from cyclopean blocks of local stone. The scene matched his feelings of imprisonment: "the icy wind shoots, as if through a funnel, across the parade ground and freezes face, hands & feet until we almost weep with the pain .... Far below is the dismal, curdled sea, and beyond, the grey, sickly greenish line of "England," its edges lapped by a foul, desolate marsh! Complete the picture by a few long, black warships at anchor, and numbers of oil-tankers along the shore ... "

At last, he set off for France, on 21 December, now assigned to the 11th Leicesters, a transfer that unfortuntely meant losing his corporal's stripe. Early on, he told Flint of an incident that amused him and could have come straight from the pen of Captain Bruce Bairnsfather, the cartoonist who most caught the humour of the British Expeditionary Force. The battalion had reached a village that had been battered out of existence by bombardment: "We were passing what had been a row of shops. Everyone was tired & trudging along in silence. Then a broad Midland voice exclaimed: 'Bill, business don't seem to be very brisk in these parts.'"

He listened with amusement also to the soldiers' songs and jingles as they made their way along French roads:

Marching, marching, marching,
Always bloody marching,

From Reveille to Tattoo.
When the war is over
We shall be marching still.

And again: "Are we downhearted?" "NO!" "Shall we win?" "YES!"
"Shall we have a good dinner?" "NO!" Aldington agreed that the British
Army cooking would have disgraced a tribe of bushmen, but now that
they were over in France, there was a chance of the occasional civilised
meal. One thing was lacking, he told Flint, whom he reproved for not
writing. *"Ne crois pas que je veux de tes nouvelles; c'est que je manque diable-*
ment de torche-culs. C'est un manque dont M. le Commissaire-Génèrale ne s'est
point aperçu, sans doute."

His habit of writing to Flint in French came up against officialdom,
which banned the practice, presumably feeling that it would put too
much of a strain on the officers censoring letters from the front. "That
robs me of half my rhetoric," he lamented, "and all my pornography,
so you'll get dull letters from me." He was happy with his battalion however, had plenty to eat, not too much work, and fairly good billets. "So as
the saying is, I've clicked!" he reported cheerfully. At first, he beheld
the scenes of battle without undue nervousness: "It is emphatically
worth seeing if only as a kind of Pompeii with the eruptions not yet
terminated."

Though less despondent than he expected to be, he was homesick for
the world of books: "How I long for the dear musty smell of old vellum
& the crisp rustle – like banknotes, yet how much more precious – of
those unreadable Aldines I collected with such gusto. When oh when
this armed strife is o'er I shall retire to Rome for a season, grow hy-
acinths in my shrapnel helmet – which I intend to purchase or abduct as
a "souvenir" – and browse about in the Vatican library. Also wander
about that city with H. D. whose gusto for antiquities fits so gloriously
with mine."

He cheered himself up with thinking about the verses and translations
that he was getting published that year and contemplating the bird and
animal life that miraculously survived the gunfire: "I had a talk with a
field mouse in the trenches the other day," he wrote to Flint. "We got on
splendidly!"

His separation from the English literary scene, however, and the feeling that his own work was now off the central stage, was a constant source of anxiety, and he vented his feelings with humorous ferocity in his letters to Flint, as his collaborator in translation and fellow-imagist. He looked forward to composing a new Dunciad, in the manner of Pope's abusive satire. He was furious with "that fatted imbecile of destruction, Eliot," for dismissing the Greek epigrams that they had translated as belonging to epigraphy rather than literature. It was too much for Aldington to read of his beloved Meleager thus belittled by "this festering lunatic, this bunion on the soul of Pound, this comPound, this insult to God." It was a foretaste of his rollicking irreverence in *Death of a Hero*.

In April 1917 his battalion carried out Pioneer duties on the La Bassée-Cambrai front, against the background of the great Battle of Arras. In time he became desensitised to the horrors; but the destruction of so many young people preyed on his mind. Once, coming on a mud-caked cross in a trench, he scraped away the filth, and was able to read its inscription: "Here lis [*sic*] the remains of two unknown British soldiers. Heroes both!" A mile away he found a similar motto on a German cross. He was moved to write to Flint: "All wasted youth, broken hope, lost effort touches me deeply – and – you will think me very inhuman – I don't mind when I see older men 'clipped' & hear them moaning – it's the boys, the dear heart of youth stabbed – that's what hurts."

Returning to England for officer training in July 1917, he was commissioned in the 9th Battalion, the Royal Sussex Regiment. The long strain of the past months now told on him. Happy in camp at Lichfield, with H. D. staying in a hotel in the city square that September, and with a sleeping-out pass every weekend, he dreaded the moment of return to France. "I've got the wind up horribly. I think I shall just lie down & sob if I get into another artillery barrage."

He vented his feelings on civilians and Europe's bourgeois masters, treating frivolously the rumour that Oxford Street had been bombed to ruins: "a bloody good job if it were. We are apparently assisting at the death agonies of civilisation, & the quicker it gets through them the better . . . I do wish the capitalists would rise in revolt & give us the job of quelling them. I would use a Lewis gun not a rifle!"

One of his obsessive preoccupations was that the war had prematurely destroyed his freshness of response and poetical sensibilities. He found the devastation and horror drained away his earlier inspiration. "We have become old before our time," he wrote later to H. D. "I did not think it would come so soon to me; I hope it has not come to you. But directly we cease to live in ecstasy, youth has gone."

The coarsening of his sensibilities, though in fact far from total, was enough, it seemed, too, to widen the gulf between him and his wife, a gulf that yawned between those who fought and the noncombatants. His feelings about poetry and about H. D. were indeed inseparable. For him, she was the embodiment of the poetic muse in its highest form: her standards were the ones to which he reached out. Not to meet her approval was to fail to be one of the Gods. Her powerful, confused soul would not yield at all to his changed circumstances and made him always feel, while in the army, that he was falling short of what she expected of him. She was appalled by the idea of him sweating, unclean, muddy, crude – all those things that soldiers must be. When he returned from the front in 1917, and seeing him, stripped, walking round the room, or talking loudly, she was repelled by the change that had come over him. It was, for her, the transformation she had dreaded, as she described in *Bid Me to Live,* published many years after:

> . . . his voice seemed coarser, his throat and body hardened and his moods more violent . . . . A great oversexed officer on leave, who had thrown off his tunic . . . . His body was harder, he was as they say well set-up, his head was bronze on the less bronze shoulders, he was perfectly proportioned, a little heavy – [Roman, she thought, rather than Greek:] "A bronze late-Roman image had got out of the wrong department of the Louvre or the British Museum."

It was not that she did not understand something of what he was going through at the front. He spared her the details of battle but he continually spoke of the assault on his senses, of his loss of poetical feelings. She hated but could forgive, though she did not want to see, how much of a soldier he had become. She heard him speaking of having "them [the Germans] on the run," and giving other indications that there was a side of military life he relished. What she found unbearable was that having adjusted to the fact of losing him for the duration, in body and in spirit, she saw him trying to get back on the old terms of poet and poet, talking together in a way that the war made impossible. Moreover, since he had come back from the fighting his sexual demands had become too much for H. D. in her nervous state.

Given these circumstances it would have been very hard for the relationship to have survived intact. When John Cournos (once again creating an awkward situation) asked if they would look after Arabella Yorke, a young woman he had long loved, who had taken over his rooms in Mecklenburgh Square, London, what followed was almost a foregone conclusion. Cournos himself was away in Russia on a Foreign Office mission during 1917. Arabella was alluring and "running a little wild." When Aldington joined his wife there, he felt violently attracted to this new friend, and she to him. H. D., with a curious mixture of guilt, jealousy, hatred, and generosity, allowed – almost encouraged – matters to take their course. The two began to sleep together under the same roof as H. D., and though H. D. made her jealousy plain Aldington found he could not bear to give up his new "star-performer" mistress. Arabella, who was a straightforward, amiable character, was equally upset by the hold H. D. retained over him; "You tyrannise his spirit," H. D. makes the "Arabella" character say in her novel Bid Me to Live.

He did not go out to France until April 1918. A younger subaltern in the regiment, Lieutenant Bate (later awarded the Military Cross – "M.C." – the officer's medal for valour, rated below the Victoria Cross and Distinguished Service Orders), rated him a good officer and companion. To him Aldington, 25 and married, seemed sophisticated – a man, not a half-child like so many.

Their battalion, part of the 24th Division, had been involved in very heavy fighting during the March 1918 retreat, when the German army forced the Allies back – in this case nearly fifty miles from their original positions at Hesbecourt. The 9th Royal Sussex had lost many men. By the time he arrived, on 8th April, with a draft of 365 other ranks, his battalion were training, before going north to Maroc, near Loos, a sector of evil repute, in the devastated mining heartland of Northern France. He had been in the same part of the line near there the year before, and from the notorious "Hill 70" had watched British howitzers bombarding the town of Lens, with two thousand women and children still living there.

The new soldiers who accompanied Aldington seemed at first a sorry lot. The number of needless casualties in the weeks in the line near Loos that followed, when there was no major offensive action involving the battalion, demonstrates how unprepared these hapless recruits were. There were twenty-five injuries or deaths in twenty-nine days, several of which were accidents – through what is now termed "friendly fire" and mishandled or dirty firearms – and one of which was from a self-inflicted wound. In *Death of a Hero,* Aldington has described Winterbourne's dismay at the lamentable quality of the new drafts: "The gaps had been filled chiefly by raw, half-trained boys of eighteen and a half, many of whom were scared stiff by the mere thought of going into the trenches."

Clearly too, these youths had little understanding of how to act during a gas attack. On the night of 31 May the enemy fired about 420 large gas projectiles, producing a heavy concentration of gas. Twenty-one other ranks were killed or put out of action. Aldington described a similar incident in his novel: "Two mustard shells fell just outside the parapet of a fire-step with six men on it. They ducked down when the shells burst, and then stood stupidly looking at the bright yellow shell-hole, wondering what the funny smell was. Three of them were gassed, and two died."

Although not mentioned in battalion diaries until 1919, when his demobilisation is listed, Aldington, as a seasoned serviceman, evidently had a vital function in getting this nervous rabble to function effectively. It must have been disheartening, and exhausting, for the experienced soldiers were all having to do other men's work as well as their own. Several officers successfully applied for transfers to the R.A.F. Further officers and about 250 other ranks succumbed to the epidemic of P.U.O. (pyrexia of unknown origin, a virulent strain of trench fever) between 11 and 23 June.

Fortunately the enemy opposite them (the 1st Bavarian Reserve Division) were not in very good heart either. Fortunately too, the presence of a Canadian division in the sector ensured that there was some backbone in the defence. Moreoever the efforts of Lieut-Colonel W. R. Corrall M. C., the temporary Commanding Officer, and others like Aldington, to make the battalion more efficient seem to have had some effect, though Corrall, a martinet, was very unpopular. A successful raid on 3 June provided a much needed boost to morale, and three Military Crosses, five mentions in despatches, one Distinguished Conduct Medal, and three Military Medals ensued from this and other exploits. Clearly, however, an intensive spell of training was needed, especially now that the Allies were preparing to take the offensive. Aldington was among the first to go to the Corps training course, on 6 June. The Corps Commander, inspecting the battalion on 13 July, was very pleased with it and the way that training was being organised. Fresh drafts of men and the arrival of an outstanding officer, Lieut-Col. M. V. B. Hill D.S.O., M.C., to resume command on 26 July, gave further confidence.

As a soldier, Aldington was still far from demoralised, though his nerves were very taut. He may not have believed in the purposes of war; but he had faith in the army and even in the competence of the generals. By September, the battalion was in far better shape, even though it remained in the unpleasant area around Loos and Lens. There were few casualties, and training had proceeded effectively. At last the Germans were beginning to retreat. "Of course it's hell in the line," Aldington wrote to Frank Flint, who had finally been conscripted, "but there are compensations. There is something great about the expeditionary force – Whitman would call it 'abrupt, huge, hairy, testicular.' It is specifically male, as opposed to the eunuch-like composition of sedentary townsmen."

He was always protective towards his friend Flint, who was sensitive, poor, unhealthy, and married – too vulnerable, Aldington felt, for the rough soldier's life. He helped him out with money, passing on to him what he earned from the newly refurbished American literary journal, the *Dial*. In the first issue, which they devoted exclusively to verse, the editors had included one of Aldington's war poems. When Frank Flint had first received notice that he would be conscripted Aldington did all he could to cheer him: "I wish I could save you many inevitable bumps some of which you cannot foresee. Yet in a strange way, I believe the miseries and deprivations and melancholies you will undergo, will benefit you as they have benefited me," he had written at the end of the previous year, 1917. "You will realise then how much you now enjoy. And also you will come to hate and perhaps to love men, as never before. With death imminent and threatening you will find courage to support terror & in the gaps of liberty allowed you, to grasp at life with a zest you never before had."

Back in the line six months later Aldington was unhappy himself and in June could only express indignation at his friend's fate: "You don't need military service – it's not good enough for you – you've suffered enough in life. You need liberty more than you need discipline and pleasure more than you need pain." Several weeks after, he added, "You know it makes me mad to have you pushed into a front line mob, when sods like Pound & Eliot & Whitall go scot free . . . This is no ordinary war, Oscar, & next year – when presumably you will be out here – will be a bugger."

He was delighted, however, when Flint proved happy enough in the Rifle Brigade, and in the end, much to Aldington's relief, was spared the ordeal of combat, finishing the war with an army clerk's job.

If, as a soldier, Aldington tried to be as positive as he could, he saw no reason to keep his antiwar feelings out of his war poems. His first war anthology, *War and Love,* appeared early in 1918. A more important selection was published as *Images of War,* in the following year: "I have spoken of the war more frankly than almost any other Englishman – & the result is that I could not get my poems published & am in the forefront of the battle," he told Flint. "Do you doubt for an instant that if I had chosen to adopt the official point of view I could not have got a 'cushy' job like MacGill, like Nash, like so many others? Say what you will, I have kept my integrity here. Though I may seem absurdly vain in claiming it, I believe them to be the most sincere war-poems yet written in English." Siegfried Sassoon's *Counter-Attack* had not yet burst on the public, nor Herbert Read's *Naked Warriors.*

Aldington's sixty-odd verses evoke memorable images of gunfire or horror, quiet places behind the line, or fellow-soldiers. Taken singly, they are not great poetry. Their effect is cumulative. As he claimed, they are indeed sincere, despite their theatrical language. For his finest war writing, readers would have to wait over ten years. Despite their shortcomings, these verses convey a desolation of spirit and the clash between the writer's poetical, romantic yearnings and the brutal present. Many of Aldington's poems, as in "Vicarious Atonement," dwell on the cruelty and wastage, though in this poem and in others, archaisms and imagery from the translated Greek Anthology lessen the immediacy of his message:

> If our wasted blood
> Make bright the page
> Of poets yet to be;
> If this our tortured life
> Saved from destruction's nails
> Gold words of a Greek long dead;
> Then we can endure,
> Then hope,
> Then watch the sun rise
> Without utter bitterness.
>
> But, o thou old and very cruel god,
> Take, if thou will, this bitter cup from us.

More effective is "Machine Guns," which explored a theme that preoccupied him — the ineradicable impress of his pubic school education, which required him to act like an officer and a gentleman (the emphasis is on the word *act*), and of which he was partly ashamed and partly proud. This poem is fundamental to the ambiguous nature of *Death of a Hero*:

> Gold flashes in the dark,
> And on the road
> Each side, behind, in front of us,
> Gold sparks
> Where the fierce bullets strike the stones.
>
> In a near shell-hole lies a wounded man,
> The stretcher-bearers bending over him;

And at our feet
Cower shrinkingly against the ground
Dark shadowy forms of men.

Only two stand upright;
All differences of life and character smoothed out
Save that one foolish tie of caste
That will not let us shrink.

His "Two Epitaphs" – as eloquent in their pathos as any verse written
in the Great War – bore witness to Aldington's generosity of nature, not
least the second, "E.T. Killed May, 1917":

You too are dead,
The coarse and ignorant,
Carping against all that was too high
For your poor spirit to grasp,
Cruel and evil-tongued –
Yet you died without a moan or whimper.
O, not I, not I should dare to judge you!
But rather leave with tears your grave
Where the sweet grass will cover all your faults
And all your courage too.

Brother, hail and farewell.

"Battlefield" above all, expresses Aldington's despair in a blighted
world:

The wind is passing chill
And blows fine grains of snow
Over this shell-rent ground;
Every house in sight
Is smashed and desolate.

But in this fruitless land,
Thorny with wire

And foul with rotting clothes and sacks,
The crosses flourish –
Ci-gît, ci-gît, ci-gît ...
"Ci-gît soldat Allemand
Priez pour lui."

Poignant in the context of his disordered emotional life was his memory of his honeymoon with H.D. before the war, "Time's Changes":

Four years ago to-day in Italy
I gathered wild flowers for a girl –
scented broom, wild sword flowers,
The red anemones that line the ways
And the frail-throated freezia
Which lives beneath the orange boughs
And whose faint scent to me
Is love's own breath to kiss ...

To-day in sunless barren fields
I gather heads of shells,
Splinters of shrapnel, cartridges ...
What shall I gather
Four years from to-day?

The complications of Aldington's marital life did much to intensify his nervous stress at the front. His wartime letters to H. D. have largely disappeared. Those left cover the later months of 1918 only. They reveal a man desperately unhappy about the state of his marriage, something he was not prepared to confess to Flint. Several times, he told H. D., he had attempted suicide by deliberately putting himself in the line of fire, like Winterbourne in *Death of a Hero*.

He was very reluctant to let either Arabella or H. D. go. "I love you, I desire *l'autre,*" he told H. D. in a letter. H. D. remained, and would always remain, his ideal, in terms of poetical inspiration and intellectual partnership. Arabella however wanted him sexually, and offered not only excitement but comfort. Had H. D. been less ambiguous in her feelings there is little doubt he would have given up Arabella; but H. D., deeply upset by what had happened, still wanted to distance herself from him.

She fell in love, a little, with D. H. Lawrence when he and his wife Frieda took refuge with her in London. They had had to leave Cornwall, a coastal area where enemy ships might be active, under suspicion of being enemy agents (Frieda was German). Lawrence, albeit fond of H. D., did not respond in any satisfactory way. Later she let herself be seduced by a young musician, Cecil Gray. Though she could not reciprocate his feelings, she became pregnant by him during the summer of 1918.

The news was far from welcome to Aldington, though he cannot have been exactly surprised, and indeed in one letter long before, commending her to Flint's care, had written to his friend: "if you can devise some sort of affair *pour passer le temps,* so much the better. She'll be a grass widow a while longer yet." Now, despite his extreme perplexity and low spirits, he tried to hold himself together by being as constructive and optimistic as possible. He continued to declare his love and to remind her of the closeness of their sexual as well their intellectual relationship in time past. In case her pregnancy might be a false alarm, he encouraged her to make love to herself – in the hope of bringing on a period: "Don't forget to have a tremendous affair with yourself *at once* – the excitement of the spasms may start you. Have as many orgasms as you can, even if you don't want them – go to bed after lunch, say, and do it then. If that doesn't do any good, you can pretty certainly decide you are *enceinte.* Don't talk to your flower too often – it is a strain on the nerves. What I mean you to have is a sort of orgy straight off to stimulate you. Otherwise only do it once or twice a week – & don't forget to think of me. I think of you when I have mine."

After discussing the possibility of their separating, he finally persuaded himself that if Gray would not take responsibility for the child he himself would at least give it his name, and in the end perhaps he and H. D. could come back together. "I don't want to lose my Astraea," he told her.

Late in the summer of 1918 the British Army was engaged in a war of movement. The 24th Division was involved initially in dislodging the German forces from Lens. By 1 September they were on the outskirts of the town and the Germans were evacuating it. Aldington's battalion was repeatedly shelled. He himself was one of the officers responsible for keeping communications open between command and the forward line. Between 6 September and 8 October, he was withdrawn for a course of training as a signals officer.

Meanwhile the battalion was engaged in the big final push against the Germans. On 4 October, they left the town of Mondicourt, near Doullens, and began to advance east. By 9 October, they were at the front of the attack on Cambrai. In the five days that followed they lost ten killed and mortally wounded, fifty-four wounded, and twenty-nine gassed. The battalion signals officer was among the casualties and Aldington took over as acting captain and Signals and Intelligence Officer. His nerves, as *Death of a Hero* shows, were almost worn away, but it was despair as much as fear that gripped him. Like most of his fellow-soldiers he was convinced that the struggle would go on well into 1919 or even 1920 and these closing days of the war seemed to him like a dark meaningless nightmare that would never end.

The fact that the British army was moving forward did not reassure him. There had been other moves and countermoves in the war. The Germans fought every inch. Advancing across old battlefield areas could sometimes be a horrific rather than an exhilarating experience. Stumbling over the vast graveyards of Germans killed on the Somme during their successful March 1918 offensive against the Allies, he told a friend forty years later, was something he could never forget:

> Having seen that, I know what Death is. In that desolation nothing lived. Even the rats had been killed by the gas, and if the birds drank the water of the shell-holes, poisoned with mustard gas, they died. There stood smashed guns and broken tanks like wrecks in that ocean of shell-holes. As had been the case a month or more before, on the old battle-line, the ground was covered with a bewildering chaos of abandoned German equipment—camouflaged German helmets, rifles, entrenching tools, bombs, gas masks, water-bottles, overcoats, hairy packs, cartridges. Here and there, occasionally, the equipment of one of ours, dumped by the stretcher-bearers or the burying parties. The utter silence . . . the utter desolation, the ugliness, the sense of misery, the regret of all our lost comrades.

At this point, when it became known that the Germans were requesting an armistice, he finally allowed himself to hope; but his feeling of elation was overwhelmed by a sense of loss:

> I went out & stood leaning my head on the cross over a dead German's grave and cried, yes cried like a weakling. It is too much. O my God, if only it is true.
>
> They speak of what they have lost. A brother, money, a mistress. I say nothing – I have lost my dreams, only my dreams. Yet I am thankful. Oscar Wilde came out of prison broken, penniless, almost friendless. I shall leave (if this peace comes) this harsher prison, no less broken than he, but with a good heart, a great heart. It does not matter if I must hold out my hand for bread to my inferiors, if I must be a beggar. At least I shall be free & perhaps my lost dreams will come home to me. O to see with clear unafraid eyes once more the calm light upon calm waters, sun, wind, & trees and the ecstasy of beauty, the presence of the gods. It will not matter if I be lonely & friendless & poor, shamed some ways & desolate, if only once more we have peace, if only once more we can feel the gods near, and the divine dreams return.

Cruelly, however, the war was not yet over and many lives were to be lost, including Wilfred Owen's, in the same offensive. The climax of action for the 9th Royal Sussex came on 4 November, when they were involved in a massive assault on German positions on the Sambre Canal and the Rhonelle river. In the raw, black early morning, so misty they could not see what lay ahead, they advanced on the village of Wargnies-le-Grand, bayonets fixed, beneath a thunderous British barrage. Although there was no hand-to-hand fighting, the casualties they sustained were devastating: forty-one dead and ninety-five wounded. For the next few days the impetus of the advance carried them forward until they arrived at the Maubeuge-Mons road where the British Expeditionary Force had first gone into action.

The war's ending, for conscripts like Aldington was, however, an exasperatingly protracted business. He was not demobilised until well into 1919. Also it seems as if the noble emotions of self-sacrifice he had felt towards his wife began to dissolve in bitterness as the danger, and the need to keep up a front, evaporated. He became a victim of war exhaustion, then loosely called "shell shock," the disorder caused by the draining of vital reserves of nervous energy, beyond the powers of normal sleep and rest to rectify. The symptoms in his, as in many cases, were tears, feelings of intense anxiety, insomnia, depression, irrational anger, a sense of betrayal, and persecution. It was no mood in which to confront the consequences of the emotional mess that was largely its cause. He violently rejected H. D., feeling, not wrongly, that she had rejected him – that wherever her emotional focus was to be it would never except in a very limited sense be with him in the way that he had believed to be the case before. At the time of the parting of their ways H. D. was already deeply involved with a younger woman, Winifred Ellerman, who made no secret of her strong passion for her. This was not the first of such relationships and it was not so much a sign that H. D. was becoming entirely lesbian (she never did) as that she now looked, as so often in her life, for a new source of emotional support, such as she had found in Aldington and momentarily in John Cournos – and had hoped to find in Lawrence. She was like some wonderfully fine-tuned but brittle machine, which required the careful attention of a skilled mechanic to keep it functioning, though it was actually more resilient than it looked, and often tougher than the chosen attendants. Aldington may have been a casualty of the war, but he was also a casualty of H. D.

Her baby, Perdita, was born on 31 March. Cecil Gray showed no interest in accepting fatherhood. After a while Aldington, too, wanted nothing to do with the little girl and was furious that she was registered in his name, fearing prosecution by the military for perjury. Although he had told H. D. he would give up Arabella, he now felt that there was no reason not to live with his mistress. He did so for nearly ten years, longer than with H. D. or with Arabella's successor, Brigit Patmore. Arabella was effectively "Mrs. Aldington" during the years when he struggled to gain equilibrium; but she never fully replaced H. D., with whom he continued to be half in love.

For almost nine years he worked hard to recover the position he had held in British letters in the early part of the war. Two things conspired against this. First Imagism, that had been at the forefront of modern poetical experiment, was left behind, a mere stage in the revolt against traditional forms, by the modernism of Eliot and Joyce. Eliot and Aldington were outwardly friendly in the early twenties but it was not long before Aldington's verse fell victim to Eliot's often lacerating contempt, while Aldington grew increasingly jealous of Eliot's growing reputation.

Much of Aldington's postwar poetry, as in *Exile and Other Poems* (1923) had a disappointing reception, unsurprisingly, for the latter's appearance almost coincided with Eliot's "The Waste Land" and, in the eyes of some younger critics, seemed passé and ineffective by comparison. It was to prose that his talents were mainly directed thereafter, principally because he needed to earn money. Looking at his vital post-war prose works side by side with the "nymph and faun" prewar verses, it is hard to feel that the drying up of that earlier vein of poetic inspiration was a great loss to literature. Of his later poems, the most famous was *A Dream in the Luxembourg* (1930), which enjoyed considerable acclaim and gave the lie to the view that he had lost the power to delight readers with his verse. *A Dream* celebrates a love affair. Elegant and romantic, it has an artfully casual charm. It is without the voluptuous quality of his prewar verse, and is all the better for being in a more ironic mode. The allusions in it to his prewar imagery, wood nymphs and the like, are a wistful, half-humorous salute to his past. Echoes of the war are still there and inspire some of the most moving lines in the poem:

> Must fair women die?
> I'll not believe it, Death is masculine.
> Death, like a war-lord, wants more man-power,
> And, by God, he gets it, I've seen him get it.
> How many yellow dead men have I seen?
> Carried how many stretchers?
> Stood by how many graves – of young men, too?
> Reported how many casualties?
> But one gets used to it, quite used to it,
> And it seems nothing for men to die,
> Nothing for one to die oneself.
> But for a fair woman to die,
> And that a woman one loves or has loved –
> No, it is incredible, they don't die . . .

Among Aldington's achievements at this time were his incisive and learned contributions to literary criticism, his translations from the French and Greek, and his study of Voltaire (a writer who suited his ironical, disenchanted postwar mood). He was prodigiously industrious, working concentratedly for often eight or ten hours on end. As long as he was making little money from his writing he mastered the art of living frugally. He was proud to feel that he could survive through his own efforts as a writer and even, at a pinch, help out others in difficulty, by putting them in the way of work and, when he could, with a gift of money. Yet he was generally near the edge of indigence himself, which is why he felt so angry with the Australian writer Frederic Manning. Aldington had helped him to complete a book on the understanding that he would be paid; but Manning failed to do so, until threatened with legal action.

His life at Padworth, a secluded Berkshire country village, had its quiet satisfactions, including a love affair with a woman living nearby, but Aldington felt himself unappreciated. He was haunted by the conviction that he had lost forever a life on the slopes of Parnassus. Some of his tensions stemmed from overwork. In the later twenties, teetering on the edge of a breakdown, he decided to kick over the traces and enjoy himself. His promiscuity and hard living of the next year or two was partly a release, partly a symptom of the various poisons in his system coming to a head. Arabella, who had lived patiently with him, found this change a trial.

During 1928 he fell passionately in love with his old friend Brigit Patmore, and on a holiday at Port-Cros in the south of France that autumn, where he went with both women, he changed partners. Arabella threatened and even attempted suicide, but their affair had irrevocably ended.

For the next eight years Brigit was his companion. She was forty-six, nine years older than Aldington, and still had much of the seductive auburn-haired beauty that had made such a strong impression on Ford Madox Ford, Aldington, H. D., and others in their world before 1914. Her warmth and social gifts had helped to weld together the Imagist set into the tight-knit group that they formed in the decade spanning the war, just after which her unhappy marriage, to the grandson of the poet Coventry Patmore, had ended. She was kind, sensual, and a shade naive – so an easy target for the hypercritical, brilliant friends, such as H. D., with whom she mingled. Because she desired so ardently to share in the bohemian life that her marriage prevented her from joining fully, she acquired a reputation for being manipulative and, after her divorce, which plunged her into penury, for sponging. Her worst fault, however, was no more than a lack of wisdom. She was fascinated by artistic success, and staked too much on her romantic feelings. As an adoring mother she was overambitious for her elder son, an aspiring littérateur and interior decorator.

After her marriage collapsed, she worked as a programme seller in Wyndham's theatre. Aldington had seen little of her after the breakup with H. D., whose part she had taken. He was upset to find her so penniless and helped her to find literary work. True to the regular pattern of his life however, he found himself falling under the spell of a passionate woman. "Why do men only thrill to a woman who'll rape them?" complained Lawrence, maliciously, after witnessing the blossoming of the affair at Port-Cros. It was the blossoming of love for her that inspired Aldington in *A Dream in the Luxembourg*.

The ten years from 1929, during much of which he had Brigit's loving support, were those of his greatest success as a writer. This began with his war novel *Death of a Hero,* which was published in 1929. He had tried something of the kind just after the war; but had abandoned the attempt. He resumed work on it in 1928, completing the job in a few weeks after encouragement from Charles Prentice of Chatto. He wrote much of it at Port-Cros. D. H. Lawrence, who was also staying there and in his last illness, was discouraging, warning him he would go mad if he went on with it. It certainly awoke old and hideous memories. Derek Patmore, Brigit's elder son, claims to have seen Aldington weeping on his bed with the emotional strain.

Death of a Hero appeared in 1929 just at the time when the public taste for "disenchanted" war fiction was beginning to grow, but it does not seem as if he was influenced directly by the new fashion in war writing. He was already an admirer of a "literature of revolt," which went back to

Voltaire and included Samuel Butler's *The Way of All Flesh* and Lytton Strachey's *Eminent Victorians*. For his own reasons, however, he shared in a widespread mood of disillusion with postwar England, and his book, consequently, had this feature in common with such works as Graves' *Goodbye to All That*, Williamson's *Patriot's Progress*, and A. M. Burrage's *War is War*.

The success of *Goodbye to All That* and *All Quiet on the Western Front* in the same year helped to boost Aldington's sales. Combining as it did the two themes of love and fighting, and being not only an indictment of war but of English society before, during, and by implication after, the conflict, the novel made an immediate impact. While not really a *roman à clef*, it drew heavily on experience. The theme was the spiritual and physical destruction of George Winterbourne, a sensitive, artistic young man, both by the war and by the complications of his love life.

Winterbourne is torn, as Aldington was himself, between a wife and a mistress — a situation that arises because Winterbourne mistakenly believes that his wife really means it when she tells him that true marriage is open marriage, and that possessiveness has no part in real love. These were, of course, H.D.'s expressed views, and like H.D., Elizabeth, Winterbourne's wife, is unpleasantly surprised to learn of his infidelity. The character of Elizabeth is not however a portrait of H.D.; nor is the mistresss, Fanny, a portrait of either Flo Fallas or Arabella Yorke. This was deliberate. Unlike John Cournos's *Miranda Masters,* where the resemblance of Miranda to H.D. is recognisable and clearly hurtful, Aldington avoided being too close to the life. The often-made accusation that he gratuitously libelled his wife and lover is unfair.

Winterbourne is the victim of others, too: of a tyrannous mother; of the bogus artistic circles of which he is an innocent member; of the hypocritical and stuffy world of his background; and of the politicians who have callously consigned young men to their deaths for dishonourable objectives. Winterbourne is not a rebel, but an innocuous sacrificial lamb offered up to false values in war and peace.

The characters of the men and women who populate the home front are lightly drawn caricatures. Eliot, Ford Madox Ford, and Lawrence appear as Mr. Tubbe, Mr. Shobbe, and Mr. Bobbe. The love theme is treated part-comically. It is only in the army sections that it becomes a serious novel – one of the most powerful accounts of the fighting to come out of war. It contains some of the best descriptions of battle in all literature – for example this account of a 3,000-gun bombardment as British troops, in late 1918, go into action against the German lines:

> The whole thing was indescribable – a terrific spectacle, a stupendous symphony of sound. The devil-artist who had staged it was a master, in comparison with whom all other artists of the sublime and terrible were babies. The roar of the guns was beyond clamour – it was an immense rhythmic harmony, a super-jazz of tremendous drums, a ride of the Walkyrie played by three thousand cannon. The intense rattle of the machine-guns played a minor motif of terror. It was too dark to see the attacking troops, but Winterbourne thought with agony how every one of those dreadful vibrations of sound meant death or mutilation. He thought of the ragged lines of British troops stumbling forward in smoke and flame and a chaos of sound, crumbling away before the German protective barrage and the Reserve line machine-guns. He thought of the German front lines, already obliterated under that ruthless tempest of explosions and flying metal. Nothing could live within the area of that storm except a miraculous hazard. Already in this first half-hour of bombardment hundreds upon hundreds of men would have been violently slain, smashed, torn, gouged, crushed, mutilated. The colossal harmony seemed to roar louder as the drum-fire lifted from the Front line to the Reserve. The battle was begun. They would be mopping-up soon – throwing bombs and explosives down the dug-out entrances on the men cowering inside. The German heavies were pounding M – with their shells, smashing at the communication trenches and cross roads, hurling masses of metal at their own ruined village. Winterbourne saw the half-ruined factory chimney totter and crash to the ground. Two shells pitched on either side of him, and flung earth, stones, and broken bricks all around him. He turned and ran back to his cellar, stumbling

over shell-holes. He saw an isolated house disappear in the
united explosion of two huge shells. He clutched his hands
together as he ran, with tears in his eyes.

There is an exhilaration here, which, in spite of himself, Aldington felt
in the face of battle and this contrasts with the melancholy of his trench
poetry. Even after ten years, Aldington's views on the war were confused,
as were those of many contemporaries, such as Graves and Sassoon. Although he denounced it as the selfish exploitation of young men by
cynical parasites, he acknowledged, as before, the paradox that it could
bring out the best in those who had had to go and fight.

There were moments in the book when he was quite frank in extolling military glory and masculine qualities:

For the first time since the declaration of War, Winterbourne
felt almost happy. These men were men. There was something
intensely masculine about them, something very pure and
immensely friendly and stimulating. They had been where no
woman and no half-man had ever been, could endure to be.

He even held up Winterbourne's company commander, Captain
Evans, for a degree of admiration, though he is the very epitome of the
correct English officer. Despite the absurdity of Evans' conventional
views, his narrowness and lack of imagination, he has a kind of dignity
and integrity, as well as real courage. Although Aldington hated what
public schools stood for, in practice, as he revealed in this book, he shared
many of their values to do with manliness and team spirit.

Bitter though the tone of the book is, it must also be understood in
some ways as a work of comedy. Aldington enjoyed expressing himself
extravagantly, shocking his readers with impermissible sentiments, accusing women of finding the death of their loved ones erotically
stimulating, accusing artists of treating war not as a tragedy but as an opportunity for art. In truth he did not think this of all artists or all women.
Aldington was a good deal more genial than many of his books. Whether
the different moods of the book, the wildly satirical and the sombrely
factual go well together, remains a matter of opinion. It was at any rate
an original form of novel, and it attracted attention. It is not however in

every respect a full satire like Liam O'Flaherty's *The Return of the Brute,* the furious novel written by an Irishman to expunge the shame of having fought for England in the Irish Guards; but Aldington's book was enough of one to be somewhat one-sided in its depiction of English absurdities. "It may enrage you," wrote Arnold Bennett at the time, "It may here and there bore you so you get 'stuck' in it. It is frequently unjust to Richard Aldington's fellow-creatures. And frequently it is too strident. But it has genuine quality. The peaks of it are lofty." Vera Brittain, H. G. Wells, Maxim Gorky, Edmund Blunden, and Wyndham Lewis were among those who also expressed their admiration for its war passages.

During the thirties Aldington wrote other works of fiction, many on the legacy of the war. *Roads to Glory,* a collected edition of his army stories, some effective, appeared in 1930. Two novels in particular were successful. *The Colonel's Daughter* was a tale, cruel though at core sympathetic, of a retired officer and his daughter in a country village, both depleted figures, victims of English upper-middle-class society with its suffocating conventions.

All Men Are Enemies (1933) made a bigger stir. It told the story of a man and a woman, sundered by the war, and apparently blighted by it, who found their way back to an idyll of true love together in Italy. In it, unlike many of his contemporaries, Aldington scorned politics as the solution to the ills of his day, seeing salvation in the values of Europe's ancient culture, at a discount since the war – the message of a hedonist and aesthete. Romantic and sentimental, it lacks the power of *Death of a Hero.* Although artistically superior to most of them, it can be compared with some of the upper-middlebrow novels discussed elsewhere in this volume, such as Robert Keable's *Lighten Our Darkness,* and, like that work, leaves an abiding impression of beauty and tender human feeling.

For a student of the World War, the interest of *Women Must Work* (1934) lies in its reflections on the effects of the conflict on those who go through it. Two victims are a mother who loses a (thoroughly unloveable) son and is broken by it; and a young man, coarsened by military service and danger (Aldington was here writing of his own experience) who wrecks his relationship with the charming young woman he loves.

When he took up with Brigit Patmore, Aldington had decided to give up living in England, and for the rest of his life turned his back angrily on it, feeling that in the twenties its literary circles had failed to appreciate him, and that he could no longer stand the stifling atmosphere of cant and hypocrisy – the objects of his attack in *Death of a Hero* and *The Colonel's Daughter.* He found the French way of life more congenial to his tastes, and most of his own and Brigit's life together was spent in France and Italy.

In 1937 his emotional life took another and sudden turn. At forty-five he fell in love with Brigit's daughter-in-law Netta Patmore, who had recently married the younger of the two Patmore sons, Michael. What precisely caused Aldington to abandon Brigit is not fully clear. Derek Patmore, hardly a disinterested party, took the view that Aldington's success as a novelist had corrupted him. He felt confident for the first time that he could do without Brigit and was ready to boost his ego by successfully courting a younger woman. There may be something in this view but it suggests something that Derek was unwilling to admit, namely that the relationship between his mother and Aldington was less than ideal. It required, however, strong encouragement from Netta for the affair to proceed, though the Patmores successfully sued Richard for alienation of affections. It was a case once again of Aldington being happy to be taken by storm by an ardent female.

Desiring to make a clean break with his earlier life, Aldington decided to start a career in the U.S.A., like Richard Blaker (q.v.). The move was not a success. He found he had to make his way in an even more competitive writer's world and he began to lose his English audience. Staying out of England in time of war cost him in any case more popularity. Though he continued to write with some success (notably a life of the Duke of Wellington) and, when he went to Hollywood, found plenty of work, his marriage brought its problems. The birth of a daughter – the only child – meant fresh financial responsibilities. Michael Patmore obtained a substantial sum from him through the courts and in addition he had pledged a good part of his earnings on all his books to Brigit. However strong his conviction that for Life's sake a man must take a plunge into the romance and adventure it offered, he had been very fond of Brigit and felt bad about the way he had treated her. She never quite recovered and though she lived for over twenty years more, she aged suddenly. The guilt he felt, coupled with literary disappointments and straitened circumstances in the years that followed, may have done as much thereafter to undermine his spirits as any enduring effects of the First World War.

His marriage to Netta petered out in the early 50s. His efforts to make a living in the U.S.A. eventually failed, and their incompatibilities began to show. They returned to France in 1946. After she left him, he lived in Montpellier with his daughter in a few rooms of a fine town villa, Les Rosiers.

Although Aldington worked hard on many projects, and lived as well as his circumstances would allow, his later years in France were clouded by the feeling that he was losing the large reading public he had enjoyed before the war; but both in Montpellier and in his later home with his friend Alister Kershaw at Sury-en-Vaux, in the Sancerre region, his correspondence attests to a life rich in intellectual discovery as well as the industry with which he applied himself to new books. These included a memoir of his old friend Norman Douglas, and one of D. H. Lawrence.

In 1955 he launched himself into print with his most controversial work of all, a life of Lawrence of Arabia challenging the "Lawrence legend" that had made T. E. Lawrence the favourite of so many latter-day imperialists and educators. Originally, Aldington had approached his topic without prejudice. Lawrence's maverick personality was, on the face of it, one to appeal to him. For Lawrence stood outside the herd and was sympathetic to some unorthodox views of the war and authority. Early in his researches, however, Aldington grew to dislike both the man and the legend surrounding him, which seemed to him to encapsulate so much that had always repelled him in English life: self-deception, complacency, priggishness, and snobbery. The portrait he drew was of a contorted liar, desperately compensating for the fact of his bastardy, fantasising and weaving his reputation as his fame grew. Under Lawrence's public mask, Aldington believed, was a homosexual masochist, whose claims to have had a decisive effect on events in the Middle East were widely exaggerated, the lie connived in by British imperialists bent on creating a national symbol.

Even though Aldington had to cut passages to render it acceptable to his publisher, Collins, the book caused a furore. Lawrence's family and his supporters, in particular the eminent military historian Basil Liddell Hart, did their best to ensure its failure. It received unfavourable reviews – or silence. Lawrence enthusiasts, including Robert Graves, Henry Williamson, and the war artist Eric Kennington, wrote defending his reputation. Headmasters and clergy lamented the decline in standards that had led to such attacks on Britain's heroes. Nevertheless the book sold well, and has since gone into further editions. Lawrence's reputation never recovered. Even biographies substantially rehabilitating him have been compelled to face the implications of much of what Aldington raised.

Without doubt Aldington sometimes played unfairly. The book gives Lawrence no credit for his many acts of kindness, his genuine diffidence, and his gentleness. Some of the misogyny of which Aldington accused Lawrence is to be found in his own *Death of a Hero*. Indeed one passage in it about "the lean sinewy bodies" of the soldiers being too good for "miserable French whores" is almost uncannily close to a passage he excoriates in Lawrence's *Seven Pillars of Wisdom*, which contrasts the "clean bodies" of the Arabs with the "raddled meat" of the desert prostitutes. Whatever the rights and wrongs of his general case, and however meticulous his scholarship, his approach, as his letters show, became overemotional.

The Lawrence book preceded by some eight years the nineteen-sixties and -seventies wave of books and theatre that debunked the First World War leadership – though the latter's reputation tended already to be at a discount among the young soldiers in the Second World War, partly thanks, by an irony, to the works of Basil Liddell Hart. The book's appearance heralded therefore no general change of view on the earlier conflict, which, in 1955, was anyway not regarded by publishers as being of interest. But Britain's position in the Middle East was highly topical. The Suez crisis broke the following year and with it came the drastic decline of Britain's influence in the region. Before that, however, her leaders still had the illusion that the Empire was a force in the world, and that even if it did not have the greatest economic power, there was a sense in which it knew best how "the Arab" worked. The Lawrence legend contributed to that idea and its supporters were enraged at it being attacked. In fact, the later fifties saw such a collapse of popular belief in Empire that if Aldington had not shaken Lawrence off his pedestal, another author would have done so a year or two later. It was natural, even so, that Aldington, as the first writer of talent to do so, should have been singled out for hatred. He took this as a compliment and felt that he had met the challenge to tell the truth. But it was a disagreeable experience. Although he believed that his leading antagonists had ruined his career, they only delivered the *coup de grace*. He was already losing his public for other reasons. Though a rebel by temperament, he had begun to seem old-fashioned. His sensibilities were fundamentally those of the pre-First War era. He had never had much time for the Modern Movement, and he was out of touch with most English writing of the 1950s.

His last years, in Sury-en-Vaux, were by no means unhappy or un-productive and he continued to write and plan new projects as he approached his seventies. He always enjoyed good food and drink, nor was he short of company: Alister Kershaw and his wife, who had taken him in hand, rescued him from a reclusive existence.

With H.D., too, he had resumed a close epistolary friendship. She greatly valued his judgment and consulted him particularly on her *roman à clef* about the war and the collapse of their marriage, *Bid Me to Live*. He was an appreciative and generous critic and actually tried, unsuccessfully, to interest English publishers in it. It was well received when it eventually appeared in 1960.

Like H.D.'s other work, it has a subtlety that is lacking in Aldington's own novels. Her fiction, much more than her poetry, enabled her to explore a larger range of imaginative vision. *Bid Me to Live* complemented *Death of a Hero*, giving a deeper insight into the conflicts in Aldington's marital life than his satirical presentation. Her canvas was smaller, centred round her own situation and the effect the war had on it and not attempting a critique of English society and culture. Her gift was for atmosphere, for psychological cross-currents, for fears, obsessions, and feelings of isolation. If there was an element of self-indulgence in all this, it was nonetheless high art, a story told with a delicacy and beauty that make it one of the best novels to describe the 1914–18 period, and the destruction wrought to personal life by the war: "It was all right in the beginning. But as the war crept closer, as it absorbed everything, the thing that bound body and soul together seemed threatened . . . ."

Bid Me to Live, intense and claustrophobic, explains H. D.'s frame of mind during that time, though it merges also with her feelings about the Second World War, when she was also in England. She presented a faithful portrait of Aldington, as she had known him, but it was not unkind; in fact the worst that can be said of the Aldington figure in both her own and in Cournos's books is that he appears weak and something of a victim, though formidable physically and temperamentally. H. D.'s severest judgments were reserved for Arabella (Bella) and Brigit Patmore (Morgan le Fay). She had always suspected Brigit of wanting to share Aldington with her. She was unduly hard on her, as she was on Arabella, depicted as a much more hard-bitten, voracious character than was really the case.

Aldington enjoyed hearing about H. D.'s life. Without the distractions of sex or obligations towards one another, the affection between the two formidable and handsome old people was genuine. When she died, in September 1961, Aldington was overcome with grief.

H. D. had helped him out with a little money – not as much as she might have done, for she was actually very rich; but like many old people she believed herself to be more or less penniless. Aldington on the other hand was far from well-off, the bulk of his earnings from *Lawrence* going into a trust for his daughter Catherine, and a sizeable proportion of such earnings as he made still being assigned to Brigit Patmore. His letters record a steady physical decay – indigestion, tiredness, stiffness in the limbs. He died in his seventy-first year, on 27 July 1962, of a heart attack, following severe head pains.

His collaborator on translation projects at the time, Frédéric-Jacques Temple, has implied recently that Aldington had begun to lose the will to live – that the Great War was finally catching up with him. It may be so; but the pattern of his physical decline was that followed by many strongly made men of outstanding energy and capacity to drive themselves hard. If he suffered from low spirits at times at the end it must in large part have been because the machine had simply worn out.

Richard Aldington packed an exceptional amount of writing into his long literary career. Bold and vital, he was a genuine man of letters who lived for literature and risked poverty rather than do without it. It was

Death of a Hero, by far his best work, that ensured his success in the thirties and raised him to literary prominence after the eclipse that followed the First World War. That eclipse was largely the cause of the bitter tone of the book, as were the difficulties in his first marriage. Had it not been for his emotional and artistic anxieties at that time, indeed, his ordeal in the war, fearful though it was, would not have been so painful, and the military life, which he both detested and admired, would – at least until the last two months – have been easier to bear.

3

"Wingless Victor"
V. M. Yeates
1897 – 1934

In 1918 it was reckoned that if an R.A.F. pilot could survive the air fighting for two weeks, he would learn enough tricks to have a chance of staying alive for several months. That early period in a pilot's career was critical, and many went to a frightful, flaming death before they had been able to teach themselves how to survive.

Twenty-two years later, just before the Battle of Britain, in the late summer of 1940, the youthful airmen waiting to defend their country were desperately aware of their own inexperience, not in flying, but in hunting and survival.

"Johnny" Johnson, who was to be Britain's top-scoring ace during the Second World War, has recalled how frantically members of his squadron searched for anyone or anything that could help them:

> We wanted a man of the calibre of Boelcke or Mannock or Moelders or Malan to explain the unknown and to clear our confused and apprehensive minds, but on this occasion the right senior officer was not present.
>
> Someone told us that an excellent novel published at ten shillings after the First World War was well worth reading because it carried all the lessons of air fighting. So we sent a chap specially to London to search the secondhand bookstalls and get half a dozen copies. The booksellers, it turned out,

knew what we were after, but it was out of print and a recent
heavy demand had pushed up the price to three pounds!

The book was *Winged Victory* by V. M. Yeates, which T. E. Lawrence (of
Arabia) described as "one of the most distinguished histories of the war";
and so it is. Although it only covers the months from February to August
1918, it presents a detailed analysis of the air fighting in those months
from the point of view of an experienced pilot who is being gradually
worn down by the strain of ground-attack missions and aerial combat. It
describes vividly the handling characteristics of the Sopwith Camel, one
of the most effective British fighter planes in use by the R.A.F.; and it
recalls the atmosphere of an R.A.F. officers' mess during a period of intense combat stress. Nobody had done it better. It is a tough, cheeky,
vital, unhappy book that falls emphatically into the "disenchanted"
school of war literature.

The framework of the book is provided by the life of the air squadron and the emerging friendship between two pilots, Cundall and
Williamson, who by August are its longest-serving members, and share
a hut, and later a tent, over a period of seven months. One pilot after
another is killed, is transferred, or falls ill; friendships crash in flames,
conversations are left forever unfinished. Only this pair seem as if they
will survive long enough to reach the time when they will be posted
home – for even in the First World War it was recognised that there was a
limit to the strain that pilots could stand. In the last pages, however, this
strong, unsentimental companionship is destroyed when Williamson is
shot down. Cundall, grief-stricken, is found to be suffering from "Flying
Sickness D" (for "Debility"), which means that he is withdrawn from
flying duties indefinitely. His disillusion at the end is a bitter counter-
point to his earlier feelings of elation when on home leave several weeks
before: "This was England. Wandering lanes, hedged and ditched; casual,
opulent beauty; trees heavy with fulfilment. This was his native land. He
did not care."

Winged Victory sold poorly when it first appeared, in the summer of
1934, though it received excellent reviews in England and North America. For years it was a "rare item" but came back into print in the 1960s
and was revived again in the eighties by a specialist publisher. Considering its importance and quality, its initial failure seems surprising; the

reasons for it are, first, that it came out when enthusiasm for war novels, since the climactic period of 1929–30, was waning. From an artistic point of view it was too long: the author was mortally ill when he wrote it and had insufficient time or energy to step back from the book and revise it more thoroughly. He had some editorial help, but the decisions ulimately had to be his own. Thirdly, he was dead within months of its appearance. Had he lived and prospered as an author, his continuing literary success would have kept the book in the public eye for longer. As it is, he remains relatively unknown.

Victor Yeates was born in West Dulwich, on the southeast outskirts of London, on 30 September 1897. His father, Augustus Yeates, was a tall, thin cashier in the Blackheath branch of Lloyd's Bank. His Irish wife Lavinia (Maslin) was rumoured to have been "in service" as a young woman. In that snobbish minor middle-class milieu, Mrs. Yeates, despite her respectable marriage and her vague allusions to a past career as an opera singer, was regarded as "not out of the top drawer." She was a difficult mother – "an awful old tartar" was one opinion of her. In his unpublished novel "Family Life," Victor introduced a character based on Mrs. Yeates, the mother of his protagonist "who tried to dominate him entirely, using hysteria as a weapon." Victor's sister, Lavinia Augusta, ten years older, clearly found the Yeates home oppressive, for she went off to the U.S.A. as soon as she grew up, only returning to England once. Effectively, therefore, he was an only child throughout much of his boyhood. He insulated himself from his parents through the satirical humour that was one of his most striking characteristics. Another was his handsome appearance. He was very fair, slender – though not weak – in build, with pale, ethereal looks that lasted to the end of his short life.

As a boy, Victor Yeates attended Colfe's Grammar School, Lewisham, very close to his home in 68 Granville Park, Blackheath. Like other older grammar schools, Colfe's conformed closely, in spirit and system, to the public-school model, with its "forms," its house system, its Officer Training Corps, and its sports organisation. Some boys – but not Victor – went regularly for rifle practice at Bisley, as members of a school club. In the twenty years before the First World War, education, particularly at the grammar and public schools, emphasised the Empire and patriotism. The boys at Victor's school came mainly from business and professional backgrounds though there was a sprinkling of upper-working-class boys and the occasional parent was listed as "gentleman" or "independent" in the roll book.

Victor's parents were not well-off; for a time he held a Scholarship giving some remission of fees. This indicated, too, that at least until his midteens he was a satisfactory pupil. In his day, the school had some exceptional boys. F. L. ("Peter") Lucas, the captain of Victor's house, went on to be a leading Cambridge academic, while Dudley Hoys later became an interesting minor novelist and playwright. Victor's most famous contemporary, however, was Henry Williamson, the future war novelist, author of *Tarka the Otter* and champion of Lawrence of Arabia. He arrived a term after Victor, though a year-and-a-half older.

Their friendship, the result of their boyhood together at Colfe's, was central to the writing of *Winged Victory*. Henry (whose chronicle is described in the introductory chapter in this book) was to be among the finest of all the British novelists of the First World War. The Williamson family had lived in the Lewisham area for generations. Henry's father was, like Victor's, a bank clerk. Evidently he felt that this calling was beneath him; and his son Henry, as he grew up, Victor remembered, became ashamed of his background – more because it was unromantic than because it was socially unimportant. His father was a neurotic domestic tyrant in the regular Victorian mould, whose insecurity cut him off from a close relationship with his fascinating, unpredictable son.

Even when so very young, Yeates' friend must have been extraordinary – a graceful, excitable child, with a large-eyed gaze, a purposeful frown, and a light, agile, long-limbed frame. He was not universally popular. His personality was too strong. His whimsical humour and didactic manner irritated some of his schoolfellows, and though sensitive and vulnerable he had a ruthless streak. On the other hand there was a compelling, untamed quality about him, a spirit of adventure and relish for experience, as well as an outstanding knowledge of the natural world, which was later to make him famous. His wild animal's eyes may have betrayed an egotism that went beyond even the ordinary self-centredness of adolescence, but he had an affectionate, generous heart.

Although they played cricket in the same team, Henry and Victor were not as close as they were later to become. Victor's best friend was a boy called Gayton, with whom he maintained contact after the war, from which Gayton emerged a cripple. In their last year at Colfe's, however, Yeates and Williamson were together in the "Special Class" – otherwise known as "the Special Slackers." These boys were not destined for the university and were regarded by the Headmaster, according to Williamson, as "the mediocre half-failures of life." They were left more or less to their own devices, while supposedly equipping themselves as wage earners by learning shorthand, bookkeeping, and commercial French. This suited both Yeates, clever but lazy, who used to read Keats surreptitiously in class, and Henry, who sometimes played truant from the school, unnoticed, on the Saturday mornings officially set aside for study. Yeates joined him and several others on expeditions to private woods at Elmstead and elsewhere in Kent, looking for birds' nest. On one occasion Henry and his companions walked 12 miles and rounded off their day watching the Christy Minstrels at the Hippodrome vaudeville theatre for 6d a seat. Yeates enjoyed these outings more for their illegality than for the thrill of finding birds' eggs, which eluded his own searches. He left school in 1913, aged sixteen, and for the next two and a half years seems to have worked in a bank.

When war broke out, many Old Colfeians volunteered immediately. Altogether some 731 served; of these 124 died on active service. Victor's contemporary Dudley Hoys lost a brother. Hoys himself joined the 10th Bedfords and the Machine Gun Corps, fighting in Mesopotamia, Palestine, and Egypt. This furnished him with the material for several chapters of his novel *The Quiet Men*. It was striking that this melodramatic work, which has for theme the failure of two young men to assert themselves at the right moment, contains an episode where a junior officer is humiliated by a superior – in this case for wasting the lives of his men, though he has merely obeyed the orders of another officer ambitious for glory. This corresponds with similar incidents in both Williamson's and Yeates's books, suggesting that all three, Yeates perhaps the least, felt far from confident in an army where commanding officers could sometimes be overbearing to those they considered "small fry" socially.

While a clerk in the City, Williamson had joined a territorial regiment, the 5th Battalion, the London Regiment (London Rifle Brigade) and was mobilised the day after Britain declared war on Germany, fighting in France and Flanders from the autumn of 1914. That Christmas he took part in one of the numerous truces between British and German regiments along the Western Front, during which they exchanged greetings and souvenirs. This unofficial cease-fire lasted more than a day and finally, as Williamson recorded in a letter to his old school, the British sent the Saxons opposite his section of the line a note saying that their artillery was about to begin and would they please get under cover? He referred to this strange event in almost matter-of-fact tones, yet it was destined to change his whole perception of the war and his political views thereafter.

In 1915 he transferred, as a 2nd Lieutenant, to the 10th Battalion, the Bedfordshire Regiment, and subsequently, the Machine Gun Corps. Thereafter, he returned to the Bedfords until he was demobilised late in 1919. He emerged from the war haunted both by his real experiences and by his conclusions about it.

Victor Yeates only saw Williamson once during the war, when they dined together and drank heavily at the Cafe Royal in Regent Street. They met also the year after it was over, back home in Blackheath, and chatted about literary subjects, chiefly Richard Jefferies, who had done much to inspire both with their love of the countryside. However, their friendship only became of great significance to them both during the early thirties.

Victor himself joined the army in February 1916, when he was eighteen, enrolling in the Inns of Court O.T.C., service being inescapable for unmarried men because of the First National Service Act. He believed sincerely that he was fighting for the defence of his country against "the cruel military discipline of Prussia." Besides, he never had much sympathy with the pacifist position, since he regarded conflict as intrinsic to human nature. On the other hand his rebellious, sceptical side was too strong for him to revere his political or military leaders; and his war experience only confirmed his contempt for their motives.

The following year, 1917, he married, in the emotionally charged mood of those days. His bride, Norah Richards, was five years older than him, and had a wartime job in a bank. She was a sweet-natured, and, as it turned out, courageous girl, but did not share many of her youthful husband's intellectual interests. Both, however, loved music and were deeply devoted to one another. Lavinia Yeates resented her new daughter-in-law. She had found them, while they were still courting, holding hands on a sofa: "What are you doing with this woman old enough to be your mother?" she demanded. She even found racial objections to Norah. She was proud of Victor's blue eyes and was displeased that Norah not only had brown eyes but was inconsiderate enough to pass them on to their children.

They were married at St. Martin's Ruislip, a thirteenth-century parish church of exceptional tranquillity and beauty, west of London. Although Victor had no religion, which he dismissed as antiquated mumbo-jumbo, he was a connoisseur of ecclesiastical architecture. All his life he remained an atheist. This did not prevent him, as a father, from packing his children off to Sunday school to get some peace for writing. His favourite expletive was "God's trousers!" When he joined up, he put down his religion as "Swedenborgian," in order to avoid church parade, knowing that the nearest Swedenborgian church was too far away for the authorities to expect him to attend it. The army was too unimaginative to record this unorthodox detail on their register, whatever private arrangements he may have made, and he is listed in his records as "C. of E."

In May 1917 he had transferred to the Royal Flying Corps, joining as part of the R.F.C. general list rather than being seconded from his regiment. For the next two months he trained with 4th (Officer Training) Squadron. His earliest experience of flying was with an obsolete machine, the Maurice Farman Shorthorn (the "Rumpty") which accustomed pupils to very little they could expect later except being in the air. On the morning of 26 June he flew the plane solo for an hour, taking it round the aerodrome at 500 feet and crashing the ungainly beast without seriously hurting himself – only the first of a long series of narrow escapes, none of which left him with more than superficial injuries.

After four hours solo on this contraption, he graduated to a more responsive aircraft, the Avro 504K, with No. 65 Squadron at Redhill, twelve miles from where Norah was lodging near Croydon. From the beginning flying exhilarated him. One of the best passages in *Winged Victory* records his sensations of flight above the clouds:

> In that passionless bright void, joy abode, interfused among cold atoms of the air. Breath there was keen delight, all earthly grossness purged.
>
> He raced over the craggy plain, now dropping into glens,

now zooming up slopes, leaping over ridges, wheeling round tors. Sometimes he could not avoid a sudden escarpment, and hurtled against the solid-seeming wall that menaced him with destruction: he would hit it with a shockless crash that expunged the wide universe; but in a flash it was recreated after a second of engulfing greyness. And when he had played long enough in the skiey gardens, he would land on a suitable cloud. He throttled down and glided into the wind along the cloud surface, pulling the stick back to hold off and get his tail down. He settled down on the surface that looked solid enough to support him, but it engulfed him as he stalled, and the nose dropped with a lurch into the darkness and almost at once he was looking at the collied world of fields and trees and roads.

Yeates' training over the next months included thirteen hours solo on the obsolete Sopwith Pup scout plane, one of which he crashed on 21 January, and a further thirteen hours on its more advanced successor, the Sopwith Camel. He left training school as a flight lieutenant in February 1918, with fifty-two hours solo flying to his credit, which was rather more than average.

During the second week in February he joined No. 46 (Camel) Squadron in France. The first month was uneventful, the weather being often unsuitable for flying. There were no casualties during that time and only two "kills" by squadron members. New German aircraft were reported, such as the Fokker DVI and DVII biplanes, high-performance scouts, beautifully decorated, as Yeates recorded, in novel colour schemes, irregular polygons of red, yellow, green, and black.

The Camel itself was a neat-looking biplane, eighteen feet long, with a short blunt nose, its "Clerget" engine covered with a rounded cowling. It was an aircraft of brilliant design, which, despite its relatively low forward speed, was so unpredictable in its manoeuvres as to make it a match for more powerful German fighters. With this built-in instability, which gave it such an advantage in combat, the Camel was not a plane a bad pilot could control, in or out of battle: "immediately tail-heavy, so light on the controls that the slightest jerk or inaccuracy would hurl them all over the sky, difficult to land, deadly to crash: a list of vices to emasculate the stoutest courage."

As a flier, Yeates was certainly above average, though he crashed four times in France, and only twice because of enemy action. He was particularly unlucky in his first week of sustained fighting: on 21 March he returned from an early-morning flight with engine trouble after 25 minutes in the air. Two hours later he landed from another mission at Arquèves, a neighbouring airfield, and finished upside down. On 25 March he was shot down by machine-gun fire and three days later, returning from an escort flight, he again turned over as he landed. He was shot down again on 2 April; he got lost on a joyride on 11 April; he had two forced landings in May and a further crash at Szel on 11 May.

Spirited pilots like Yeates loved to dive at people on the ground, particularly staff cars, to "put the wind up them" (the Szel crash may have been the result of such a manoeuvre). Reckless behaviour of this sort was an airman's privilege. Flying carried great prestige and glamour and the dangers, however extreme, were less continuous than those suffered by front-line infantry in battle and the discomforts were appreciably less. Pilots had a bed to come back to every night. As a rule they were dashing both in manner and in combat, though some of the greatest aces, like the Frenchman Guynemer, were quiet and unassuming on the ground. The R.F.C. included some of the best physical specimens in the British armed forces, many of them living, if they survived the war, well into their eighties, despite a frequently uninterrupted regime of gin and sin. Yeates himself, at twenty, cut a handsome figure.

No. 46 Squadron R.A.F. (the Royal Flying Corps, with the Royal Naval Air Service, had become the Royal Air Force since 1 April 1918) was a successful squadron with a good record of "kills" in the air. In the eighteen big air battles in which Yeates was involved, some forty planes were shot down. Morale was always significantly affected by the character of flight leaders and commanding officers. A cheerful, efficient C.O. who kept a fatherly eye on his young pilots could make a great deal of difference in such a small unit with its rapid turnover because of losses; but overzealous officers could cause resentment, particularly as they did not themselves fly continually, their main task being the organisation of the squadron. Flight leaders were even more important. A responsible airman who did not lead his flight into unnecessary trouble, while all the while communicating a sense of *objective,* was crucial in a service asked repeatedly to carry out terrifying, as well as frequently pointless, actions. As compared with the infantry, however, the R.A.F. was very much more an individual's service. Teamwork might be vital, but in the end morale depended on each pilot's personal *élan* and stamina.

Some – those who raised the reputation of the squadron by the number of their kills – were natural hunters, with an instinct for seeking out an enemy, however well sheltered behind a cloud, or however briefly spied in a corner of the field of vision. Such men went out of their way to fight if they had a chance of winning, but were invaluable in a tight corner. Some put their flights badly at risk. This Yeates found to his cost during the highly dangerous and psychologically demanding ground bombing work, for which there were none of the laurels to be gained by shooting down enemy aircraft. In *Winged Victory,* Beal, commander of Tom Cundall's Flight C, was actually a portrait of Capt. S. P. Smith – a "proper hell-fire merchant," but surprisingly without the kind of warlike earnestness that might be expected in such a type – who was in the habit of leading his flight along in a straight line at five hundred feet or below, "Giving the Huns machine-gun practice." Not many of Smith's flights lasted long. Neither did he: he was shot down in flames, the 76th victim, it is claimed, of no less a figure than Manfred von Richthofen.

At the time of the Ludendorff offensive of 21 March 1918, when the Allied armies were forced back many miles towards Paris, 46 Squadron was the only one on the 3rd Army front used exclusively for ground attack. The Camel was a favoured aircraft for these operations because its tail-heavy configuration meant that a slight easing of pressure on the joystick after the bombs were released sent it soaring rapidly out of reach of ground fire. Yeates's first bombing attack took place on 18 March 1918, early in the morning. A mission of this kind might take anything from an hour to an hour and a half. The bombing run itself was a moment of pure fear with none of the release of tension nor exhilaration experienced in the violent manoeuvres of aerial combat. Damage to the aircraft at a few hundred feet could mean loss of control and with it, certain death. Not that serious damage at any altitude gave much cause for optimism. The pilots did not carry the bulky and inefficient parachutes then available. The most merciful death was to be killed by gunfire in the air. If shot down, it was best to be near the ground so that knowledge of imminent death lasted only a second or two. The worst fate was a "flamer." Frying alive for as much as a minute was a pilot's nightmare, and if he thought about it, in the thrill of having scored a "kill," not a fate to wish on a brave enemy.

Yeates was no fire-eater but was recognised as a courageous and competent pilot. He never disgraced himself in his own eyes, though he was privately ashamed of his increasing nervousness. His "bag" was a respectable one. On 3 May 1918 he took a half-share with the Canadian air ace, Capt. D. R. Maclaren, in downing a two-seater German observation plane. On 6 May he joined four others in shooting down another. On 15 May he drove down a Pfalz scout – a less formidable victim – as it blundered earthwards, out of control. Later that month he shot down an LVG two-seater in flames. He had no further kills until August when he was with a patrol that attacked five Fokker biplanes; he personally accounted for one of the three claimed by the squadron. Possibly he had more victories to his credit. On one of the occasions mentioned above he modestly attributed a kill to another officer, Lieut.Vlasto, though that airman insisted thatYeates should take the credit.

Life at the front was hectic for airmen and the casualty rate among inexperienced pilots was so great that in time the old hands who survived became almost indifferent to it. It was always hard, however, to ignore the deaths of longer-serving men, though the squadron did their best with whisky, riotous parties, and endless conversation – either "shop" or, in Yeates's case, arguments about life, women, and the war. He usually drank more moderately than his protagonist, Tom Cundall, in *Winged Victory,* preferring Bordeaux to harder stuff. When the action was at its most intense, however, it is likely that he joined most of the others in thoroughly drowning his tension after the fighting.

The talk was always an important part of his life, and, as a former pilot told Yeates's wife, the conversations recorded in *Winged Victory* were highly evocative for those who had served as airmen in 1918. However, it had been a while before he felt enough at ease in the squadron to enter with gusto into their frenetic arguments: "I am leading a very quiet life out here," he reported to his aunt not very long after he arrived, "amid not very congenial companionship. They are not a bad crowd, but there is no one I could love at first sight, so to speak & no one who might reciprocate such a sentiment." He missed his wife greatly, particularly as they already had a child, Mary, born in 1918. His feelings about home were likely to have been much closer to those of the married pilot, Seddon, in *Winged Victory,* than to those of his protagonist, the footloose bachelor, Tom Cundall, although Cundall's flying experiences were based on his own: "I am afraid she is having a lonely period just now, and she needs companionship above everything . . . at the weekends chiefly," he wrote anxiously to his aunt.

Norah, too, worried about him. He was exceptionally attractive and he missed female company: "What a horrible place a male world would be!" he wrote. Though faithful, he must occasionally have felt tempted. Some of the scenes in his novels, published and unpublished, read like reminiscences: "So he was a very young man again, holding difficult conversation with this grubbily splendid young French woman who sold chocolate and such things. She looked at him in a way that seemed to turn his entrails into warm water. He stood there awkwardly making futile remarks that might or might not be comprehensible to the girl, unable to make out a tenth of her flowing patois, while their eyes talked plainly enough."

Such vignettes were written at a time, twelve years later, when Victor was isolated for days from his family in gloomy T.B. sanatoria, and in a mood to distract himself, with cheerful self-mockery, from his dreary surroundings. The first inklings of the devastating disease that was to ruin his life became known to him after he returned from a month's stay in late June 1918 at a hospital in Wimereux. He had been suffering from yet another feverish complaint widespread along the front that summer, called as usual, "P.U.O." (Pyrexia of Unknown Origin), which, as he commented, was not a bad description of the war itself. When he resumed flying duties, his weakness persisted, and his condition was eventually identified as "Flying Sickness D (for Debility)," the product of prolonged war strain and P.U.O. In theory it was something that would disappear with rest. In practice it often – as in his case – developed into T.B., which in those days was practically a death sentence.

His last operational flight was a low bombing raid over St. Vaast. He had flown over 184 hours in Camels on the Western Front. Returning to England, he completed another thirty hours flying before his demobilisation in February 1919.

As a demobilised flight lieutenant Yeates had to find work. His flying experience was his main asset and because he was technically not disabled by the war, he had no entitlement to a pension. However, aircraft were cheap after the war; huge piles of Camels and SE5s were being destroyed on bonfires, so, like Tom Cundall and many pilots washed up in a postwar world, he contemplated purchasing his own plane and offering joyrides at £5 a go.

Later, this developed into a serious scheme for a commercial service flying between the United Kingdom and Spain, a country with which there was as yet no air network. Another man invited him to join a partnership. Yeates was to be one of the pilots and intended to take his family to Spain, where the warmer weather would suit him. He persuaded his mother, his mother-in-law, and his aunt to put their money into the enterprise. To their horror, his partner absconded with all of it. That left Yeates with still only a smattering of professional training and no possibility of raising a penny more from his relations. By 1922, when he was only 26, he had two more children. He tried commercial travelling, taking a commission on anything he could sell. It was work he hated, mostly driving from one building-site to another, offering unwanted materials at a time when the building trade was in the doldrums. He lacked the commitment and above all the rude health to stand the racketty life and the endless disappointment. For a time after this he set up in partnership as an insurance broker, working from home.

However, he refused to despair, and so escaped the fate of the tragic hero of "Peter Deane's" novel *The Victors,* described elsewhere in this volume, who took his own life after failing to find any employment after he left the army. Yeates' prevailing mood since the war had been that of a character in one of his unpublished novels: "He was apt to accept things at their face value through weariness and cynicism too profound to be sceptical."

Three things saved him. The first was his wife's kind, patient nature, which sustained family life at their home in Blackheath, despite their slender resources. He described his condition on one occasion as that of a respectable pauper. They could not afford to go to the theatre, to buy new clothes, or to take a summer holiday. Their poverty, of course, was relative. There was enough money to survive; but middle-class standards of the day demanded that they keep a maid. They could afford a motor –

a Morgan Three-Wheeler – a dashing open car of which it was said, with a certain exaggeration, that it was the only thing that could get you to 100 m.p.h. for £100. At first he rode a motorcycle; but it was abandoned after Norah Yeates fell off the pillion seat. The Morgan, however, amply fulfilled the romantic, swashbuckling side of Victor's character and made a powerful impression when he drove his children to school in it.

His second asset was that he always enjoyed life and his pleasures were inexpensive. He loved reading, not least the Latin and Greek authors, and enjoyed French literature, notably Molière, Anatole France, and Renan. His taste in English authors was catholic, but above all he enjoyed sardonic and iconoclastic works. He revelled in writers such as Bernard Shaw and Samuel Butler: "Wasn't the Catechism partly responsible for the war?" he once mused; "Never read it, but he'd read *The Way of All Flesh* and that showed you." His love of language, particularly of unusual and improbable words, attracted him to Joyce's *Ulysses,* which was partly the inspiration for his first, unpublished, novel "Adjustment." His passion for nature, for sunlight, open air, and the country drew him to Richard Jefferies. Keats and Shelley satisfied his romantic yearning side.

Britain was then a motorist's paradise, despite some very primitive roads. There were still few enough cars not to spoil the long miles of unblemished landscape, and Yeates himself knew enough about machines to cope with breakdowns. He liked to take his children out to see their uncle, the painter Hain Friswell, who lived at Flatford Mill, Suffolk. There they would gaze at the pastoral scenes that had inspired Constable. Sometimes they would run down through the Kent countryside, which Victor adored. He was usually at his most cheerful on these occasions and was long-suffering in acting as "an Institution for Airing the Aged" when he visited his wife's parents at Mistley on the Stour estuary.

Yeates' third advantage was his fondness for family life. He took a great interest in his children. He would often dress up to amuse them, and would conspire with them to shock guests, whom on one occasion he greeted in his wife's clothes. He retained a boyish love of foolery into his thirties. Doubtless service in the R.A.F., which allowed its young men the privilege of impudent clowning before they went out to court death, encouraged this tendency; and after the war, he and thousands like him who had left the forces were keen to make up for lost time in enjoying themselves. They cheerfully poked fun at their parents' generation and dismissed their social punctiliousness as Victorian priggery.

Even so, Victor accepted a conventional existence. With worsening health, he depended on a steady home life. Another man might have gone to pieces, turned against those who loved him (not uncommon among the chronically ill), or sought refuge in a dream world of escapist pleasures. Affectionate and, at core, contented – despite a romantic imagination – he was in fact a source of strength to his family.

He dressed informally, preferring open-necked shirts and grey flannels, whenever possible, to a suit. His manner was courteous and ironical, his voice pleasant. His pronunciation was correct in the now old-fashioned style: he called a novel a "nuvel," and Coventry "Cuventry." He insisted on his children enunciating their words precisely. He remained youthfully handsome – at thirty, bringing his ten-year-old daughter to school, he was mistaken by admiring older girls for her brother.

He would always take his children's side if they were in trouble with teachers, replying with amiable sarcasm to notes complaining of their conduct in class, or their failure to come to school in the right uniform. He was generally cheerful with the children but could be irascible, a symptom partly of the strain caused by his illness. His tempers however were brief, flaring up and over within a minute.

One thing he lacked was intellectual stimulus from outside. His companions were usually either old schoolmates, like the one-armed Gayton, or chess club acquaintances. One of the latter intrigued him: Arthur Dickinson was a cultivated and touchingly self-important war veteran who still signed himself "Captain," and had been secretary to the Earl of Crawford. A figure of comedy, Dickinson ended tragically, killing both himself, and, because he feared she would be lonely without him, the sister with whom he lived. In his will, he generously rewarded Victor's friendship, leaving Norah Yeates a sum of money, aware that she would be a widow before long.

The inescapable fact was that from 1927 Victor was a seriously sick man and his efforts to earn a living were interrupted by longer and longer periods in hospitals. Thanks to the London County Council, that beneficent governing body, T.B. sufferers were now given some public assistance. This included a hut in the garden so that Yeates could sleep there to get the fresh air. His sanatorium bills (usually for a home in Ventnor, on the Isle of Wight) were paid, too, including dietary supplements such as oranges. The letters that he wrote in the last years of his life chronicle his pathetic existence as he went, with tantalising remissions, from one establishment to another: Colindale (which he called "Pentonville" or "the North Pole"), Colney Hatch ("Wormwood Scrubs," "Brixton," "Dartmoor"), Bournemouth ("I have seldom seen anything so horrible as this place . . . It is green with stagnation. The drawing-room, as it is called, is full of the most mind-scratching junk"), and Eastbourne ("This is an awful life. Here I do nothing but cough, cough, cough"). He remained humorous, but there was a bitter edge to his comic accounts of his fellow patients: "God preserve me from these people who talk. There is a gas fitter in the next room who calls me Nobby and won't leave me alone . . . Once you are friendly to these blokes, there's no end to it." It was flattering that the night nurse at "Wormwood Scrubs" believed him to be only twenty-six, and when he blushed (as he claimed) tried twenty-four; but a death in the ward in the same period had its usual discouraging effect: "Bloke passed out on the red tide in half-a-minute; he entered the same day as I did, so that I was a distinct acquaintance."

For diversion in hospital, there was reading – Boswell and some favourite poets – and visits from his family. There was even a moment of tragedy, which he viewed from his window at Colindale hospital. This was the death of Lord Lytton's cherished and resplendent only son Lord Knebworth, in a crash at Hendon aerodrome on 1 May 1933. As Victor recorded with the sardonic detachment of the R.A.F. man who had been through too much, "I saw the misfortunate Knebworth go up in a cloud of smoke yestere'en." His main preoccupation, however, was with writing; he had toyed for a long time with the idea of a novel about the impact of war. By April 1933, he had completed the manuscript of an 85,000-word Ulyssean meditation, entitled "Adjustment." It was largely an indictment of modern England, its stuffiness and cheap values, through the thoughts of a former R.A.F. officer, Tom Cundall. Full of satirical invective and farcical sexual episode, the action passed from wartime flying scenes to a brave new world of the future and later, to his ancestral past in the fifteenth century, before eventually returning to the squalors of the London café where the novel began. Though disjointed and at times tedious, it demonstrated its author's verve and sense of humour and his ability to evoke the war vividly.

It was at this moment that Henry Williamson once more reentered his life. Henry was now a successful writer who had made a considerable impact with his story of animal life in Devon, *Tarka the Otter* (1927), with his conventionally ironical antiwar novel, *Patriot's Progress,* and with his four-volume novel sequence, *The Beautiful Years* (1921), *Dandelion Days* (1922), *A Dream of Fair Women* (1924), and *The Pathway* (1928), later published as a single book, *The Flax of Dream* (1936). This poetical work describes a boy's early development, fulfilled in his experience of nature and the countryside, but blighted by an unhappy relationship with his father and by his mother's death. The boy grows up, serves in the war, and, disorientated, tries to adjust to a world unsympathetic to his craving for ideal love and a better society. A romantic Shelleyan figure driven by pain and yearning, he finally throws himself into the sea. Williamson was conscious of representing the generation dislocated by war experience. Desperately riding the country on his Norton motorcyle, or seeking peace in farming with a long-suffering wife in the depths of Devon, continually on the edge of poverty and full of ideals for a new world, he gave an impression of being slightly deranged. His heroes were Francis Thompson, the consumptive poet, who had died in 1907; Richard Jefferies, the Wiltshire naturalist and visionary (also a victim of T.B.); Lawrence of Arabia, who had written praising his work and with whom he had a few meetings, until their friendship ended with Lawrence's fatal motorcycle accident in May 1935; and Sir Oswald Mosley, the maverick politician whose talents went to waste on sterile and fanatical Fascist beliefs.

In Chapter 29 of *Dandelion Days,* Henry Williamson paid Yeates a brief tribute by referring to him by name among a crowd of schoolboys; he also described Colfe's School in the same, and the previous volume. This emboldened Victor to write to him asking for his advice about "Adjustment." Williamson thought it unsatisfactory, but was excited by its Air Force passages and urged Yeates to devote a whole book to the subject. To Charles Huntington of Putnam's he praised Yeates' unusual sensibility and gift with words. Huntington, however, told him he thought it bad tactics for an unknown writer at "the most difficult moment ever known in English publishing" (always a stock publisher's phrase) to attempt a book entirely about wartime aviation. Yeates himself resisted the idea, protesting that his memories, however vivid, were of their nature random and inconclusive, hardly the stuff of a novel. Williamson's answer was to suggest a central theme: the close friendship of two pilots, eventually shattered by the death of one in combat. It was sound advice, not the less so for being based on many true examples. Yeates accepted it; but he never seems to have been happy with the form of his book, which certainly does not stand or fall by this linking story. He continued to maintain that plots were obsolete and unlifelike, and resented what he felt to be a prewar literary straitjacket. At least one reviewer later observed that the story was Yeates' only concession to conventional drama.

Williamson subsequently made much of their friendship, and there can be no doubt about his affection for his friend, or that Yeates's debt to him was enormous. Victor reciprocated Williamson's kindness; yet he viewed him detachedly. He had mixed feelings about the *Flax of Dream* novels. He appreciated their lyrical descriptions of nature, of which Williamson remained proud to the end of his days; and he shared many of Henry's rebellious feelings about the hypocrisy and stiffness of modern British society and the profit motive, which seemed to control the destinies of all ordinary people. He himself had expatiated on this theme in "Adjustment," in which, characteristically, he mocked the absurdities of the large subservient class to which his father and Henry's and now, perforce, himself, all belonged. His sarcastic tone reflected his own and his friends' difficulties in finding work after the war:

> Having contributed to their country's useless victory by truly heroic tenacity (partly the result of sterilised imagination) of which they seem to have been time's and the world's greatest exponents, the scarred remnants of this battered band returned to enjoy the fruits thereof, only to find a remarkable dearth of fruit, all the best jobs being in possession of people whose physical weakness, certified medically, had frustrated their military ardour. Many of them accepted such inferior jobs as were available, and the unwanted remnant quietly lapsed into starvation or vile dependence on what was then called charity. Those who were sufficiently damaged in mind

and body to be medically certified as disabled were fobbed off with a pittance, and were left to their broken lives with the assurance that the nation's honour had been vindicated and that their deaths would be the subject of general but subdued satisfaction as helping to balance the budget . . . I ask for a moment your pity for these unfortunate young men, whose sacrifice, often forced upon them, but often made freely for love of England, only resulted in England's worse enslavement by blood-foul money-bugs, after abysmally stupid professional soldiers had indulged to the top of their bent in useless butchery.

In this spirit, Victor therefore relished much of Williamson's impassioned denunciation of English life, especially when delivered in the form of a drunken argument between war veterans in a pub. What he disliked about the *Flax of Dream* books, however, was what he called "the Jesus stuff": "You insist on climbing mental precipices searching for the azure. You are Shelley, you cannot give up hope of that world where moonlight and missive and feeling are one: doomed saint . . . the world is too far gone for saints: they perish, as you admit, and there is no consolation in imagining Shelley's ghost awaiting them." The aspect of Williamson's book that most interested him, naturally, was its theme of adjusting to life after the war.

From this time on, Yeates and his family began to receive frequent visits from Williamson, en route from Devon to Kent, at their home at Mottingham near Lewisham. Victor's illness, his four young children, his lack of a pension, were all too evident to the Yeates's guest, who advised him that the only chance he had of earning a living would be by writing. With typical rashness, he promised him that his reputation would be assured once the air force novel was published.

Williamson's appearances, usually late in the evening, were dramatic. He drove an Alvis, sometimes with a glamorous girl passenger. He dressed like an aviator, in leather coat and flying cap. The children liked him and were impressed by his theatrical presence, his kind remarks, and compelling stare. Mrs. Yeates was more suspicious. She knew he had a wife in Shallowford in the West Country; yet he seemed to be quite open to Yeates about his relationships with girls far younger than himself.

One of these accompanied him to the Yeates home at Mottingham and was introduced as his "secretary" – which was indeed part of her function. Norah Yeates, knowing her own husband's frankly stated theories on sexual freedom (overriden in practice by his strong feelings of affection and loyalty), was afraid that Henry might encourage him to stray. She also feared he might be affected by Williamson's political views.

Since Christmas 1914, when Williamson had claimed he had taken part in one of the truces on the Western Front, he had become convinced (as he regularly told Yeates and his family) that the Allies and the Germans had no quarrel and that all front-line soldiers were thenceforward linked in a brotherhood that must, after the war, resist any attempts to fight one another again. Williamson was as much of a political idiot as his hero Shelley, but his romanticism took him in a more deplorable direction. He had come to believe that Adolf Hitler was a great poet in action, even more creative than T. E. Lawrence, but of the same type. In his 1936 edition of *The Flax of Dream* he was to salute Hitler as an outstanding leader whose achievement was symbolised by the happy children now growing up in Germany. He saw his rise to power as a mighty spiritual struggle against materialism, fear, and laissez-faire – all the forces that he felt had perverted the 19th and early 20th century.

He decided that Sir Oswald Mosley's British Union of Fascists offered the way forward to European partnership, to the comradely spirit of the front-line soldier, and to a better future for British agriculture. None of these were undesirable aspirations. For a long time, however, he refused to acknowledge that there was any evil side of Fascism at home or abroad. Indeed he maintained that the hatreds in Europe came entirely from the prejudices of the pre-1914 mind, which had been revived by fear of the unknown new ideas in Germany.

During the twenties he had believed the *Reaktion* to be the enemy, the diehard, "scarlet majors" in hunting pink. As time went on however, he came to see the British intellectual left and Jewish publicists (Einstein included!) as the real danger to peace. His anti-Semitism, such as it was, was based mostly on the old-fashioned prewar equation of Jewry with capitalist greed, urbanisation, and un-Britishness. This he linked closely with liberal economics, which in his view had undermined farming and created two unnatural classes in society – an enslaved, sickly working class and a spiritually distorted lower middle class. In making these particular connections he was far from unique, but though criticisms of capitalism intensified after the war and a few farsighted spirits campaigned, with scant success, to revive British agriculture, Williamson's highly romantic reaction to all these things had a dated ring. In practice Fascism had little to do with returning to the soil. Hitler's more innocuous monuments are the Volkswagen and the Autobahn, not the revivification of the countryside. Nothing in fact could be further from Richard Jefferies' images of wise, simple countrymen such as "Hodge" and the like, than the hysterical worshippers at the Nuremberg rallies – although there was, as Williamson observed perceptively, something in common between Jefferies' pantheistic confession of faith, *The Story of My Heart,* and Adolf Hitler's *Mein Kampf.* It lay however, not in some shared mystical vision of life, as Williamson believed, but in the element of narcissism behind both statements of personal destiny. This affinity should have put Williamson a little on his guard against his hero Jefferies rather than have caused him to look kindly on Hitler. He was still prepared as late as 1937 to forgive Hitler for what he had come to recognise were bad actions, because he regarded the Fuehrer as being engaged on a great work where the normal moral standards could not apply (an argument used also by the defenders of Stalin). Moreover he felt the overwhelming responsibility of Europeans towards these vital changes was to view them positively and not seek to resist them out of some obsolete instinct about correct behaviour.

For a long time, Williamson was convinced that those Jews who were being persecuted in Germany were a subversive element and that those who had served faithfully in the Great War were receiving better treatment – a view actually put about by Nazi propagandists. It seems to have meant nothing to him, though, that Arnold Zweig, the Jewish author of *The Case of Sergeant Grischa,* a novel banned by the Nazis, was campaigning against exactly the kind of inhuman disregard for individual justice and exploitation of ordinary German soldiers that Williamson himself was most against.

In Williamson's defence, it was clearly a case of self-delusion rather than of spiritual affinity with Hitler and the Nazis. At his most cranky, he never subscribed to the mad racial theories of such as Himmler, and his poetical, wholesome view of the universe was completely at odds with the murky power-hungry resentment that fuelled Nazism. Nor did he extol violence nor practise it himself. Though in unhappy moods he was capable of wounding behaviour, he was far more often wounded by others. His love of the rebel, the casualty, the outcast, such as Francis Thompson, was one of his strongest traits.

Given such feelings, why was he not on the political left, traditionally the position of those who side with the underdog? The answer lay in the sense of social inadequacy that he always felt as a young man, not so much about class, though that came into it, but because his unselfconscious egoism often aroused suspicion. There was a vicious circle. Feeling defensive, he exaggerated his difference from others. All his life he had a compulsive desire to shock and to be an outsider. Hence his identification with other outcasts and his adoption of a political creed that was regarded in thirties Britain as more beyond the pale than communism. His left-footed attempts at practical joking, disarmingly chronicled throughout his works, were of a piece with his perverse political affiliation, so damaging to his reputation.

Despite their close association, Yeates avoided Williamson's political influence. Some of the opinions about financiers that he put into the mouths of the young airmen in *Winged Victory* should not be taken as precisely his own views nor as evidence that he, too, was on the far right. He was afraid of being submerged in the great anonymous mass of those whom he called "the black coats," the ineffectual dependents of a financial system that he blamed for their fate. The experience of soaring above the earth, facing extraordinary dangers, gave to him, as to other aviators, a sense of having been set, for a while, above the ordinary run and intensified his desire to fight for his individuality. His contempt for what he believed to be the creeping elements in society, the caterpillars and the earwigs, might well have led him in a Fascist direction. However, he had too much of a sense of the ridiculous and none of the delusion, the bombast, or the brutality, one or more of which were the invariable ingredients of the Fascist outlook. What he thought of the profit motive and international business was common enough currency among the left at the time, and that was the political direction his rebellious outlook led him; but he was not greatly involved.

On the subject of the war, however, he and Williamson found more to agree. Though both were convinced that it had not been justifiable, neither of them were pacifists. Both, too, recognised moments of fulfilment in that, the most intense experience of their lives. Now Williamson was doing his utmost to help Yeates record it. On this last ground alone, it would have been hard for Yeates to show Williamson the door for sending him, as he did on one occasion, a propaganda postcard of Hitler, with words on the back praising the Fuehrer.

In Williamson's eyes, Yeates had undoubtedly acquired a new glamour. His literary talent coming to fruition; his youthful, handsome appearance; his tragic illness; and his kinship with the gods in the skies above the Western Front: all these qualified him for the status of a Williamson hero. A few years later, in 1937, Williamson was to describe Yeates as one of the few men (T. E. Lawrence, he said, was another) with whom he really could be himself. He had hoped, in fact, to bring these two together, but their deaths had prevented that happening. Perhaps they had become friends in another world, he speculated in characteristic fashion.

At the time that he was reviving his friendship with Yeates, Williamson, as part of his new-found Fascist view of himself, had lately written himself into a novel, *The Gold Falcon,* as a First World War veteran aviator called Manfred Manfred. Though Manfred was an English nobleman, with roots going back to the Norman conquest, the choice of name by the author was a salute to Britain's Teutonic brotherhood with Germany, it being, among other things, the first name of von Richthofen, German's leading air ace. *The Gold Falcon* ends with Manfred's solo flight from the U.S.A. to Britain, after the manner of Charles Lindbergh, another of the "young men of destiny" who espoused Fascist beliefs at this time. Manfred perishes, but his soul, a golden falcon, wings its way back to be united with the spirit of his wife (who has also just died) in Cornwall. The story, verging on the preposterous, is full of self-pity, practical jokes that go wrong, and repeated romantic and sexual failures. Like most of Williamson's books, however, it is all compulsive reading, whether it be about Manfred's paranoid fantasies, a description of a black boy cleaning windows, or a disquisition on war literature. Williamson never attempted in it (and would have derided the attempt) to describe aerial warfare, which he had not himself experienced.

When *Winged Victory* was nearing publication, Williamson was anxious that Yeates should emphasise the connection with the author of *The Gold Falcon,* which he believed would help to sell the new book.

Yeates was sceptical. He was uncomfortable about Williamson's effusive admiration. His friend insisted on calling him "a poet" though he had written almost no verse, other than humorous, and that only for the school magazine. It was, however, how Williamson chose to see *himself,* though he wrote little poetry either; and he felt that the two of them had achieved such felicities in their prose as to qualify them both for the title of poet. He pursued this line after Yeates' death: it had been T.B., the poet's sickness, that killed Yeates as it had killed Keats, Flecker, D. H. Lawrence, and Richard Jefferies; and Yeates had had a poet's pallor, bright hair and eyes, and features sculptured by creative thought. What more need be said?

Yeates was embarrassed by Williamson's hyperbolic fancies. He met them with that air of amused disillusion that made his own book about an aviator so different in character from his friend's self-dramatising work: "Dearest Pussycat," he told his wife, " . . . the poor fellow is as mad as ever, I'm afraid. I tried to hint that he is a genius as well. One should always pay back compliments."

While Williamson was trying to interest the publisher Putnam's in his first manuscript, "Adjustment," Yeates, acting on his friend's advice, tried while in hospital during May 1933 to assemble the records of his war experiences to write the new air-war novel. "There is a lot of material, besides frantic endearments, in the letters I wrote to you from the front," he told his wife. "If you will kindly dig those from France out of the tin in the bottom of the drawer, I will endeavour to extract their materials . . . You might show one to Joy [their second daughter], in case she is afraid I don't love you! and then all aboard for fame and fortune!"

After moving out of the disruptive atmosphere of Colindale Hospital, he made some progress in his writing: "I have written some big words about clouds," he told Norah proudly. He worked first of all in three-penny exercise books. Later, when he had left the sanatorium, he used a typewriter. He sent off each chapter as he wrote it to Williamson. It is quite clear, however, that from the first Yeates resisted, sometimes successfully, Williamson's efforts to determine the shape and content of the book, though he took his advice on many stylistic matters. Williamson's idea that the book should be based on the relationship between two pilots helped to create a climax for the book, but the central theme was the fatigue caused by prolonged danger. The action is seen through the eyes of "Flight Lieutenant Tom Cundall" (who shares much of Yeates' experience, though the book is only partially autobiographical). "Williamson," the other pilot, is not a very clearly-drawn personality other than being robust-minded, civilised, and courageous. Though Yeates chose the name as a compliment to his friend, he did not intend it as a portrait. The introduction of so forceful a personality as the real Williamson would have had a strange effect.

He laboured away at the book – "all hard slogging and chipping words out of my breastbone," he told Williamson. By the spring of 1934 it was virtually complete; it did not seem to him like something he had created but as though it had come "from some great reservoir beyond the varying shores of the world. The individual prism-refraction gives the colour and bias." The question of a title remained for a long time a vexed one. Yeates first called it "This Tassel Gentle" – taking the yearning lines from *Romeo and Juliet,* "Oh for a falconer's voice to bring this tassel gentle back to me." It was another salute to Williamson, using the falcon theme, but Jonathan Cape, whom Williamson had approached, understandably felt it would mystify readers who might not realise that "tassel" meant "hawk." Nonetheless it was under that title that Yeates was given a generous contract in November 1933, which gave a royalty of 12.5% for the first 2000 copies; then 15% for the next 8000, and thereafter, 20%. Encouraged by assurances from Williamson, Cape was hopeful that the book would be a success on the scale of T. E. Lawrence's *Revolt in the Desert.*

In March 1934, again through Williamson's efforts, the novel was given a New York contract by the publishers Smith and Haas; but this time the title had been changed to "A Test to Destruction," Williamson's choice. This was soon abandoned (Williamson later used it for a book of his own about the same period of the war) to be replaced by "Wings of Victory." Yeates thought this "rather horrible," so offered "Aircraft Over Chaulnes" though preferring the more ironical "High Romance" from a line by Keats, "Huge cloudy symbols of a high romance." Neither Norah Yeates nor Cape, however, thought irony appropriate: the public required something simple and direct. So, in the end, despite Williamson's protests that it was banal, the title of the book became *Winged Victory,* as in the Greek mythological image of Victory, the *Nike Pteros.*

Yeates was unwilling to supply a blurb to advertise the book. However he objected with irritation to the one Williamson wrote, which spoke of the author's smiling fortitude and, quite openly, described the novel as a work of collaboration. In his dedication, Yeates made very clear his own view of Williamson's contribution: "To Henry Williamson at whose suggestion this book was begun; with whose encouragement and help it was written and ended."

Williamson was so instrumental in launching the book, and later in keeping interest in it alive, that it is pertinent here to see how far his own view that it was a collaborative effort can be substantiated. What emerges from an examination of original manuscripts is that his advice was nearly always constructive and was often taken; that he attempted very little re-writing, even at the end; and that the cuts he suggested were sensible and greatly improved the book. If Yeates had died earlier, however, leaving the manuscript in his friend's hands, Williamson would doubtless have recast the book extensively, since he was strongly of the opinion that it should have a more "literary" form. On this matter they differed.

"You say I mustn't let these things happen as in life," wrote Yeates. "I MUST. Art is selection not alteration . . . There is no meaning what-ever in events that are not as-in-life, unless we want to use words for rhythm and decoration like late Joyce, but that seems to be plastic art, not literary . . . I am reading *Lord Jim*. It is all so durned literary and his scenes seem all made up to suit his purpose. There is no divine irrele-vance and delight in things for their own mysterious sake. I believe you agree with this eternal getting on with the story: if so the poet in you will keep passing in to describe lovingly the freckled face of the world for its own interest."

To reduce a very bulky work, Yeates was resigned to making many small cuts – amounting to over five thousand words – and some larger ones: in the manuscript of "Wings of Victory," "Phase I, Chapter 18," a long debate on the causes of the war, was entirely removed, because it re-peated a passage in Chapter 7.

He fought harder when other reasons were given for cuts. T. E. Lawrence, who found an advance copy sent him by Williamson in the summer of 1934 "an imperishable pleasure," nonetheless criticised it for having "too many conversations replete with 1932 ideas. In 1918 there were the germs of what we now say aloud – but then they were thought

of only." Williamson, independently, urged Yeates to take out a large discussion about the world's future from his revised "Phase II, Chapter 2,"
insisting, like Lawrence, that the political dialogue was not of war vin-
tage, but of the period 1928-30. Yeates resisted, excising only some
flippant remarks about the need to shoot financiers. On the authenticity
of these debates, he knew that Lawrence and Williamson were wrong. As
one reviewer put it: "This sort of philosophising was of course a commonplace in every Mess of fighting soldiers on the Western Front in the
last stages of the war. It has its place in any narrative with pretension to
an accurate reflection of the war as it was."

Williamson was right, however, about the endless asides in the book –
such as on whether French peasants appreciated Molière, or on the
drawbacks of marriage – which constantly slowed down the story. Airman's banter, he complained, spoiled the tension of prelude to the
mighty German attack of March 1918. He also tried to correct over-
writing: Yeates was sometimes wise enough to listen when Williamson
advised expunging an excessively purple paragraph.

It was not that Williamson objected to heightened prose as such.
He singled out one very bitter passage for its dramatic quality. Often,
however, his friend's eccentric use of words exasperated him, as when
Yeates was describing the German attack on the Somme in March 1918:
"There were swarms of Huns in shell-holes or in the open. They *pullulated* [author's italics]. It was mass attack." Williamson crossed out
"pullulated," commenting that using bizarre words for effect was the sign
of an amateur and in this case distracted attention at a crucial moment.
Yeates was unpersuaded, and "pullulated" (which is curiously effective)
remained. So did other odd concoctions from his Ancient Greek learning, such as "thanatognomonic" (to describe the smoke caused by a
crashing plane) and "rhinoplast" (person with a reconstructed nose)
adding a distinctive if sometimes irritating touch. Williamson, on the
other hand, was keen for him to use the expletive "fucking" in a particularly bitter conversation about the war, maintaining that it was right
artistically, and citing D. H. Lawrence. Yeates agreed, but the publishers
plainly did not, and a blank was substituted.

At times it seems as if Williamson were trying to push Yeates towards
the kind of novel he hoped to write himself. He wanted more historical

touches to be included, such as detailed descriptions of the ground battles as viewed from the air, which he had never seen properly attempted. His own later account of watching the Battle of Loos from "Tower Bridge" (the tall mineworks that dominated that area) was one of the most memorable passages in *A Chronicle of Ancient Sunlight*. He was thrilled by Yeates' success with such scenes and went on pressing for yet more authentic detail: perhaps with Hitler in mind, he was keen for Yeates to bestow a few chivalrous accolades on Germany's heroes. Ever romantic, he suggested that Yeates should refer to the "Red Baron," Manfred von Richthofen, by his full title of "Rittmeister Freiherr!" He begged him to make Tom Cundall encounter the Baron's *Jagdstaffel* in one of his chapters. Yeates ignored most of these appeals, though he allowed his friend to insert a compassionate sentence about the German soldiers at the front towards the end of the war being mainly "half-starved boys of seventeen and eighteen years" – an implied reference to the effects of the Allied blockade, which had had a traumatic effect on that generation of young Germans.

Although Williamson's choice of extra detail was sometimes overweighted in Germany's favour, his plea for illuminating information had a good deal to be said for it, particularly where it replaced irrelevancies. A fault in *Winged Victory* is a degree of self-indulgence, perhaps because Yeates, seriously ill, had a subconscious urge to leave as much of himself behind on his pages as possible.

It was over the final part of the book that Yeates and Williamson came closest to quarrelling. As not many of Yeates' letters to his friend are available for study, the main source for this crucial phase of the book comes from Williamson's introduction to *Winged Victory*. According to this, Yeates' last chapters were deliberately left without a carefully constructed climax. Williamson felt this would not do and rewrote them, telling Yeates that he was going to do so, in a letter he sent in advance. This apparently provoked an agonised protest. Williamson begged Yeates to trust him. The typescript was returned, and, the reader is led to understand, the alterations were accepted.

This account by Williamson leaves the impression that he was effectively the author of the last part. This was certainly not the case. Yeates' manuscripts show that Williamson revised little of the original and that

Yeates rejected many of his minor emendations. The only important passage that looks as if it could have been Williamson's work came to the end of the penultimate chapter, a late addition of some 200 words. It focuses on Tom Cundall's state of mind before the final tragic end:

> His eyes ached. The glass was moving again in his veins. He daren't open his eyes in case the tent was floating and dissolving in brazen sunshine and he was alone in some vacancy beyond the world where he must see the very figure of hideous death that was awaiting him. Seddon had gone, and that queer fellow, what was his name? Grey. And Beal. And how many others. Absorbed into the deathly nihilism of the battlefields. Something seemed drawing him to the same fate. He must open his eyes. Thank God the tent was normal. But he was tired — very tired, numb, insensible. He could not think nor remember. Events sank at once beneath the quicksand surface of things and left no memory. There was no basis to the spinning earth, and death was the only reality.
>
> Then Williamson came in, steadying the round world by his presence.

It was a highly effective piece of writing. One can understand, all the same, why Yeates, if he were not its author, found the last sentence a shade presumptuous!

Otherwise, though the occasional sentence was changed here and there, there was only one really memorable intervention by Williamson, and it was a very subtle one. The final sentence read originally: "It was his native land . . . he did not care." Williamson had an aversion to using dots to create tension, regarding them as a dud writer's device. It was certainly through his influence that in the final version the full bitterness of the words emerges, spat out in bleak staccato: "It was his native land. He did not care." If Yeates felt that Williamson had in some way been untrue to the spirit of *Winged Victory* at the end, he was wrong.

Such alterations were made against a background of depressing sanatorium life, relieved by occasional trips into a spring countryside that seemed unbelievably beautiful by contrast. Round Cranborne, in Dorset, where he went one Sunday in April, he was overwhelmed by the purity of the air and the woods full of violets and primroses. The book's critical reception, when it appeared in July 1934, was enthusiastic. The most rewarding reviews came from veterans of the war, such as H. M. Tomlinson, the former Western Front correspondent and also a war novelist, who called it "one of the real books of the War." In America, Ben Ray Redman, author of *Down in Flames*, who had served as a single-seater scout pilot in the Royal Flying Corps, confirmed the book's authenticity: "Mr. Yeates is the first man to do the whole job and do it perfectly." Another glowing notice came from a new friend, the young airman-poet, Gregory Dunn, who first heard of Yeates from T. E. Lawrence.

In the pacifist climate of the time, imperceptive reviewers tended to admire *Winged Victory* solely as an excellent piece of antiwar propaganda. They failed to see that Yeates' real aim was to record his experience in all its aspects. In doing so, he had drawn a picture of the R.A.F. that was far from the conventional "valiant knights of the air" image, and that showed a wasteful war where fear of nervous collapse stalked every flier. Far from diminishing their heroism, however, this actually made their courage seem the greater.

The book came too late to achieve the success it deserved. It would have rivalled *All Quiet on the Western Front,* James Hilton (author of *Goodbye Mr Chips*) firmly asserted, had it appeared a few years before. It came too late in Yeates's life, too, for him to gain by the new friends and admirers he acquired through it. They included Lord Trenchard, the founding father of the R.A.F., and numerous literary figures, such as the poet Richard Church and John Llewellyn Rhys, the prize-winning writer on flying. It was Yeates' misfortune that, apart from the faithful Williamson, his postwar life so long lacked the enriching cultural contacts that could have stimulated his writing earlier.

His health showed no sign of improving. He was coughing all the time, and running a temperature. In November it was so bad that the doctors urged him to take a whole month's rest at Fairlight, near Hastings. "This is an awful place," he told Norah. "The rain is a solid grey mass here. One can only see two hundred yards . . . No peace for writing & no cure for my bronchitis . . . There are four nurses here, all old & ugly." He sparred with the matron: "was within a touch of packing, but

language, this tribute from Victor's difficult, cranky friend showed his real devotion. In the years that followed Williamson remained Yeates' champion, even while he struggled with the neglected soil of a farm at Stiffkey in Norfolk, a one-man effort at putting the heart back into English agriculture. During the war he fell foul of the British authorities, because of his open Fascist sympathies. He had even daubed the streetside wall of one of his barns with the lightning-flash symbol of Sir Oswald Mosley's party. (It is there to this day.) He was detained briefly as a possible security risk, but was deemed too eccentric and genuinely patriotic to be kept in custody.

Nothing came of the play he had hoped to make of *Winged Victory*. This did not discourage Norah Yeates, who proved resilient in widowhood. For years she continued to hope that her husband's literary reputation would gather strength and bring in money – especially if his unpublished writings could be revised and printed. "Family Life," however, remained incomplete, and the manuscript eventually went to the University of Texas.

Henry Williamson took "Adjustment" away with him, intending to polish it into publishable shape. He may have been distracted by the writing of his greatest work, *A Chronicle of Ancient Sunlight,* but by the time Mrs. Yeates, despairing of his interest, asked for "Adjustment" back, he had turned against the idea. Even so, he proved unwilling to let it go, believing sincerely that it would damage Yeates' reputation to publish a book that fell so far below his best work. Not for the first time his literary judgment was sound.

Winged Victory, however, fared better. In 1961 Jonathan Cape produced a new edition with a new preface and tribute by Henry Williamson, incorporating an earlier introduction based on the obituary he had written in 1935. This was moving, after its fashion, and compared Yeates with other war writers, such as Wilfrid Ewart, whose works Williamson admired. This and another edition of 1972 and the paperback that followed in 1974 did much to revive Yeates as a leading war novelist. By the time of Mrs. Yeates's death she must have felt satisfied that her husband would not be utterly forgotten, even if the financial rewards had been slender.

As a comment on the war, *Winged Victory* has affinities with Richard Aldington's *Death of a Hero* in its combination of bitterness with *élan vi-*

tal. Both are books by men who were happy, at one level, even when they were miserable. Both enjoyed attacking the English bourgeoisie. Both were more than a little proud of their service careers, but Yeates especially so, for his had involved a high degree not only of courage, but also of skill. Perhaps most important was that they, in common with Henry Williamson, were uninhibited personalities. They were not ashamed to admit fear, sexual excitement, humiliation, anger, and even martial feelings. They could clown and they could weep. This is why their war books stay alive.

Unlike Aldington, however, Yeates was not affected by feeling that the war had destroyed his poetical inspiration and wrecked his emotional life. His own tragedy was different, and it was far worse, both for him and his family – the cruel trick of fate that left him a consumptive, doomed to a crippled and brief existence. Had it not been for his love of life and his devoted family, it would have been an even sadder story.

4

The Raw Nerve
A. D. Gristwood
1893 ‒ 1933

What were we all doing out there? That was the question that hammered away always in my mind. The rhetoric of a thousand journalists will never bring home to the civilian a tithe of what war is. The ghastly futility of the thing; its blasphemy of God and human nature; its contemptuous denial of Christianity; its mechanical cold-blooded cruelty - only those who saw these things face to face can measure their horror. And those who know cannot share their knowledge.

Donald Gristwood was one of the earlier English 1914–18 veterans to ask in print the really disturbing questions about the war. His double novel, *The Somme,* including also *The Coward,* appeared in 1927, a year before the main wave of antiwar books. It is one of the bitterest, sparing the reader little. In the opinion of H. G. Wells, what singled out "Mr. Gristwood's unheroic tale," from which the passage above is quoted, was that "he remembers with a courageous clearness. Most of us have the trick of strangling and making away with all our more disagreeable memories; instinctively we destroy the record of how miserable we were or how afraid we were. Mr. Gristwood has the relentless simplicity to recall things as they were." Every schoolboy with a taste for soldiering should be asked to read and ponder the book, Wells urged; for the chances were a thousand to one that Gristwood's path, not that of some famous participant, such as Winston Churchill, would be the one they would be required to follow: therein lay its importance.

The first paragraph of *The Somme* sets the dramatic tone:

> Before the world grew mad, the Somme was a placid stream
> of Picardy, flowing gently through a broad and winding valley
> northwards to the English Channel . . . and then came 1914
> and the pestilence.

The novel tells the story of a futile action in which the central character, Everitt, is wounded. Both in and out of the line he behaves selfishly
and unheroically, but in a manner with which it is hard for the reader not
to identify. *The Coward* is about a man who shoots himself in the hand to
escape the war, during the March 1918 retreat – an offence punishable
by death – and gets away with it. He is haunted however by fear of discovery, and later by shame. Gristwood's main point is that the principal
characters in both stories are more perceptive than their fellow-soldiers
about the true nature of the war. Who therefore can condemn their behaviour? Least of all those who did not fight. As the "coward" himself
says at the end:

> . . . was it, after all, worth while to barter self-respect for
> safety? Often I wish I had risked everything and taken my
> chance with the others. Often I tell myself that it was on the
> knees of the Gods whether in that event I should have
> emerged at all from the struggle; that death on the battlefield
> is merely the crowning absurdity of a life of folly; that self-
> preservation is no crime. Perhaps it is the knowledge of the
> thousands who evaded so successfully the horrors of the War
> – profited by them rather – that reconciles me most of all to
> my own weakness. There is a grim humour in the voluble
> explanations of those who somehow failed to bear the
> burden.

Compared with the other authors described in the present volume,
Gristwood is a shadowy figure. No photographs of him have yet come to
light. All we know of his personality was that he had strong literary interests, a well-developed sense of style, and a mordant wit; he was also what

was then called a "neurasthenic," a victim of nervous trouble, reserved, self-lacerating, and misanthropic.

He was born Arthur Donald Gristwood on 17 May 1893 at 2 Brownhill Villas, Catford, south London, the son of James Arthur Gristwood, a commercial traveller for a City firm, and his wife Margaretta. Later, as their income increased, the Gristwoods moved to a house at 3 Higher Drive, in Purley, a Surrey village that at that time had begun to attract better-off London commuters. Like neighbouring Croydon and Lewisham it was fast becoming absorbed into the metropolis. The name of their mock Tudor, semidetached house was "Chateau d'Oex" (a select Swiss mountain resort), and reflected the romantic pretensions of the Edwardian middle class. Donald Gristwood attended local schools until he was sixteen. Within a year or so he went into the Liverpool and London Globe Insurance Company, in the accounting department. He held the job for fifteen years, and disliked it with increasing intensity.

If the views he expressed in *The Somme* accurately represent those he felt at the outbreak of war, then it seems that when he volunteered, possibly during the summer of 1915, it was more under social pressure than out of clear motives of patriotism. He envied those who could act with conviction, whether conscientious objectors or fire-eaters, though temperamentally he felt nothing in common with either:

> the doubter, the Agnostic, the sitter on the fence, is doubly damned in the hurly-burly. The enthusiasts on either side despise him, and he finds himself committed to an endless balancing of arguments.

The will he left shows that he served in a Territorial unit, the 5th (City of London) Battalion, The London Regiment (London Rifle Brigade), the same that Henry Williamson had enrolled in before the war. It was made up of men who in peacetime had worked in the City of London: clerks, stockbrokers, office employees, bankers, salesmen. All Territorial units were divided into two, mostly at the start of the war. The 2/5th L.R.B., Gristwood's battalion (Williamson was in the 1/5th Battalion), was formed in September 1914. By June of 1915, it was training in Ipswich, Suffolk.

Throughout his time in the battalion Gristwood was in the ranks, as Rifleman 302064. From a letter written by his father it is known that he was severely wounded twice. He has left, in his one book, a vivid and painful account of the ordeal of being stranded in no-man's-land and the hazardous return to the rear. As an "other rank" he gets no mention in battalion diaries and it is difficult to trace his career precisely. But unless he was transferred from another battalion after seeing service earlier, he cannot have taken part in the 1916 Somme battle, which is the setting for the first story in his book, since the 2/5th L.R.B. were not yet in the line at that time. He knew that area, however, because the battalion had gone straight there after landing at Le Havre on 25 January 1917 and so he would have been able to describe it. The actual engagement in which he was first injured could have been any of those in which the 2/5th L.R.B. fought during the spring and early summer of 1917. One may take it that he was temporarily out of the fighting during the later part of 1917: it is highly unlikely that he was involved in the Passchendaele battle, as he would hardly have refrained, given his views, from including that climax of horror in his book. Finally it is probable, if not certain, from the dates given in *The Coward,* that he was wounded for the second time early in 1918, after returning to the front.

His account of the war was deeply disenchanted, firstly because of his scepticism about its purposes; secondly because of his psychological wounds, which blighted his postwar career; thirdly because of his position as a private, which was an uncomfortable one for a well-educated man; and fourthly because of his demoralisation at the front: throughout his book he was at pains to emphasise how widespread this had been in the British army:

> It will be said that here is no trace of the "jovial Tommy" of legend, gay, careless, facetious, facing all his troubles with a grin and daunting the enemy by his light-heartedness. We all know the typical Tommy of the War Correspondents – those ineffable exponents of cheap optimism and bad jokes. "'Alf a mo', Kaiser," is the type in a nutshell. A favourite gambit is the tale of a wounded man who was smoking a Woodbine. Invariably he professes regret at "missing the fun," and seeks

to convey the impression that bayonet fighting is much like a football match, and even more gloriously exciting. It was such trash that drugged men's minds to the reality of war.

This passage by itself proves nothing in particular about the infantry's underlying morale, which showed more in their power of endurance and cooperation than in their outward demeanour. But elsewhere in Gristwood's two stories he reiterates his message that the soldiers around him were obviously disaffected: there was his tale of Forsyth, the soldier who was quite open about his repeated efforts to surrender – a sure sign of lack of battalion spirit:

> His story of the simultaneous surrender of himself and a gigantic Prussian Guardsman is remembered by many to this day – their mutual disappointment and querulous debate, the spinning of a coin to decide the matter, and Forsyth's return with a delighted prisoner.

Again his disturbingly convincing description of an attack during the Somme battle purports to show how often in his experience soldiers were liable to regard discretion as the better part of valour:

> Now was the test of discipline and initiative. The choice lay between organised rushes forward and indefinite delay, and it was not entirely a matter of courage or cowardice, duty or shirking. Against what was evidently overwhelming fire, any advance might well be suicidal folly and in the absence of leadership or encouragement [the platoon commander had been killed], the law of self-preservation swept aside all discipline: since no one seemed to care what happened, men determined to play their own hands. No doubt that moment of hesitation marked the failure of the attack. Hitherto, while there had never been any pretence of enthusiasm, at least the attempt was being made. Now they were fatally quiescent. It is a commonplace of war that a man who takes cover during an advance will never get up again until the battle is over . . .

While none of this was altogether outside the experience of every infantry battalion in the line, Gristwood seemed determined that among the soldiers in his unit there was little of the sustaining comradeship or convictions – realistic or otherwise – that kept troops going. Even in Frederic Manning's far from illusioned work on the same campaign, *The Middle Parts of Fortune*, the private soldiers express a range of views that include strong patriotism and regimental pride as well as an intense bond of friendship with their companions. In Manning's book, the greatest cynic and pessimist among them, "Weeper" Smart, is known to be a good soldier who will always stick by his comrades. Although Gristwood himself clearly felt little of the group spirit that sustained a unit, he did not deny that many men alongside him were trusting and dutiful – out of stupidity and a desire for self-preservation, in his view – nor that some were brave: the tough Scots lieutenant who walked along the parapet calling out (if rather theatrically) words of encouragement that cheered a cowed body of men; the four men from his battalion who carried his stretcher at great hazard to the rear of the line: "If ever man had earned gratitude it was they." Yet the message is fundamentally misanthropic. The honesty with which Gristwood chronicles his protagonist's little acts of cowardice and selfishness in *The Somme* deserves respect – at the same time there is a lack of balance in it too: human nature is too much at a discount, and he is too consumed with self-contempt. His tales are horror stories, but they lack the quality of real tragedy. They were the consequence of a profound despair that it was beyond his power ever to overcome.

How much are his conclusions borne out by what we know of his own battalion, the 2/5th London Rifle Brigade? The evidence is that they were in good heart in 1917, but took some very hard knocks in that year – one reason why his own nerve was so badly broken – and their condition by 1918 may possibly – though not certainly – account for his own very depressed view of the state of the army.

The battalion had more than a year preparing for service overseas. While their sister unit, the 1/5th L.R.B., had been involved in heavy fighting at the battle of the Somme, the 2/5th L.R.B. did not leave for the continent until 24 January 1917. By 1 February, as part of the 58th Division, they were in the trenches at Fonquevillers, the northernmost launching-off point for the previous year's Somme offensive. That February, the weather was bitterly cold, the ground iron-hard with frost.

Over the next month they were in and out of the line close to Arras where a major British offensive began early in April. On 17 May, just after a brief, intense bombardment at 2 a.m., the battalion attacked the German line at Bullecourt, a particularly arduous sector at this time. The action was deemed successful. The shattered village of Bullecourt was captured, though at a cost - in their battalion, an officer and eleven other ranks were killed, three officers were wounded or incapacitated (including one who fell down a well), and 33 other ranks sustained injuries. There was further very heavy fighting around Ecoust-St. Mein from 26 to 30 May, and again at Bullecourt on 31 May to 4 June, and at Mory, with repeated casualties. Five other ranks were awarded the Military Medal for their part in these engagements.

After a brief rest the 2/5th L.R.B. were back in the line on 16 June, in the nearby Croisilles sector. On the following day, two platoons went forward as strong patrols to penetrate the German "Hindenburg Line" and reinforce a remnant of the 173rd infantry brigade, which was still believed to be holding out there. The concentration of enemy fire was so intense they were beaten back. Further actions took place on the same day and over the next two, with the loss of 29 men killed, including an officer, and 78 wounded. From 8 July until 16 July they were in the Beaucamp-Villers-Plouich sector of the line and sustained further casualties. In late August they went into reserve at Reigersburg a mile north of Ypres before being flung into the Third Ypres Battle. From 8 to 12 September they were in the line, suffering 30 casualties including eight killed. From 13 to 19 September the 58th Division trained for a major attack from St. Julien, striking north of the Zonnebeke-Langemarck road. This, the Menin Road Ridge action, was destined to be the climax of the 2/5th L.R.B.'s achievement as a unit.

Zero hour was 5:40 a.m. on 20 September. In the two days' fighting that followed the 58th Division took all their objectives and captured or killed a large number of German soldiers – but paid a price for this highly successful action: in the 2/5th L.R.B., two captains, six lieutenants, and 52 other ranks were killed, two lieutenants and 162 other ranks were wounded, and 25 men were named missing. These losses included many of the battalion runners, which meant that communications during the engagement became very confused. As a result of their success and courage, the Commanding Officer, Lieut-Col. P. D. Stewart, was awarded the D.S.O., and another officer the M.C., while 26 other ranks received the Military Medal and six the Distinguished Conduct Medal. The battalion were allowed to rest for over a month.

From later October until mid-November they were back in the abysmal hell of mud and shelling for which the Passchendaele offensive will be forever notorious. An attack at Poelcapelle on 30 October took place in appalling weather conditions and under heavy shellfire. It was impossible for those fighting to tell what was going on. The following day the attack launched by the battalion halted under withering enemy machine-gun fire and was abandoned. Over the next fortnight they were moved in and out of the line, at Canal Bank, "Kempton Park," and Poelcapelle.

Despite new drafts, losses had been so heavy that platoons had had to be amalgamated to bring them up to strength. By the end of the month, though the battalion's numbers had been substantially restored on paper, it was effectively little more than half its full establishment. After 14 December until mid-January, it continued to go into the line in the Flanders area, but only on working-party duty. On 27 January 1918, the 2/5th L.R.B. was disbanded. Possibly the authorities felt that it was no longer a viable fighting unit; but in any case there was a general reduction of battalions at this period. Its men were assigned to three different Territorial battalions of the London Regiment, the 10th (Hackney), the 1/18th (London Irish), and the 1/28th (Artists' Rifles), the two latter being allocated to other divisions.

It is easy to see that despite initially having the characteristic buoyant demeanour of the volunteer units, the soldiers of the 2/5th L.R.B. had fought in such dangerous actions and suffered such fearful losses that by 1918 they would outwardly at least have seemed battle-worn and pessimistic.

How far did all this tie in with Gristwood's account in his novel? Though morale seems to have been high initially in his battalion, his own was not. If his return to the front, after recovering from his first wound, was (as seems likely) in February or March 1918, he would have found himself in a different battalion, with few faces in it that he recognised. Battalion and divisional spirit was something built up over a period of training and sustained by close companionship in action, but once the unit's identity had been forcibly changed, something would have been lost for ever. By February, now in an unfamiliar battalion and possibly a new *division,* where morale among the uprooted and reallocated remnants of Gristwood's group cannot have been at its best, his own is likely to have been at rock bottom. It was hardly surprising that in summing up the soldiers' outlook in early 1918, just before the Germans' March Offensive, he was moved to write with heavy irony: "It is a damning admission, and one probably unique in the annals of war, but the spirit of the troops was not entirely excellent."

After recovering from his injuries, Gristwood returned to Purley and his insurance company. By 1926 the monotony of the work, and the depleted existence he led as a semiinvalid, had worn him down. Despite the fact that he was well regarded in the firm, promotion was very slow. Eventually he had a nervous breakdown, and though his employers urged him to return when he recovered, he handed in his resignation. On doctors' orders he went abroad in the autumn, to Locarno in Northern Italy, where, in the previous year, leading statesmen had been striving after reconciliation and lasting peace in Europe. Amid that charming lakeland scenery, despite a persistent November drizzle, Donald Gristwood, too, achieved a brief remittance from the long-term effects of the war.

He had decided to turn his back for ever on the world of commerce: "I would do anything," he wrote, with a certain pathetic self-importance, "that did not involve eating out of the public's hand with a view to persuading it to buy my employer's goods. The personalities and rivalries of competitive commerce, & the false heartiness of business 'friends' went far to sicken me of insurance." Most of all he wanted "bookish" work—in a library, a bookshop, or a publishing house. Fortunately, powerful help was at hand.

As a child in the eighteen-seventies, Gristwood's father – who was devoted to him – had attended school at Mr. Morley's Academy in Bromley, Kent, to the south-east of London. One of his friends there had been H. G. Wells, subsequently one of the most important English authors of his day. James Gristwood had seen his illustrious contemporary only once since then.

In 1926, Wells was living at Easton Glebe, Little Easton in Essex, with his wife, who was by then fatally ill. They had made their country home in the Georgian vicarage that he had described with affection in one of the best-known novels of the Great War, *Mr. Britling Sees it Through* (1916). Then in his early sixties, the famous author was a tubby figure with a ragged moustache, only his short stature, sleepy eyes, and vitality recalling the boy whom James Gristwood had known at school. His way of life, with country house, and retreat in Provence (where he stayed for some of each year with his mistress), endless engagements, book projects and international fame, had carried him to quite a different plane from the genteel middle-class commuterland south of the capital. Mr. Gristwood was a reasonably successful member of his own stratum of society. Yet Wells' sophistication, knowledge of the world, social contacts, intellectual milieu, and sheer wealth were far above his, in an early twentieth-century society obsessively aware of social distinctions. His tone towards the eminent writer, consequently, was very deferential.

He confided to Wells about his son's breakdown, and asked for his help: "His heart has always been towards *literature* – he has read widely, & I think with discrimination and he has built up a library which does him credit." Could Wells, he wondered, use his influence to get him a job somewhere in the world of books?

Wells, who looked back on Mr. Morley's inept and Dickensian tuition with an amused horror, was clearly touched by this appeal from his past – and more so when Mr. Gristwood told him quite frankly in his next letter that his son had had a terrible time in the war and that his two wounds had ruined his health. Wells had been a leading war propagandist. Like other distinguished writers who plied their pens in the same cause, he had believed, in those days, that he owed this service to his country and to the soldiers fighting for it; but at the same time he was uneasy about much of what he had let himself say, not all of which he knew in his heart of hearts was the truth; and he was unconvinced that either the narrow nationalism that prevailed in the country during the war years, or the British Empire, or Britain's commercial leaders, were objects for which it had been worth sacrificing countless young lives or his own integrity as a writer. After the war, in common with Galsworthy, Ford Madox Ford, and others, he tried to atone for this betrayal of their calling by taking as much of an antiwar line as he could. In Donald

Gristwood he found a war victim whom he could champion, and with the kindness he often showed, he did his best to help him.

The younger Gristwood was overwhelmed: "You will understand how difficult it is to write to you freely," he explained to Wells in self-abasing tones from his lakeside hotel at Locarno, "& I have spent an hour trying to put together something that did not seem affected, & yet would not too greatly offend your naturally critical eye. The egoism I fear is unavoidable." He had reached, he said, a situation when match-selling seemed preferable to a lifetime spent in balancing debts and credits. He sent Wells a short piece he had written on the scenery of the Somme battle: "I fear you are tortured by similar offerings daily, but if anything could stir a drowsy pen, it would be such a theme, & I should greatly appreciate your most ruthless criticism."

The passage was the core of the one incorporated subsequently into his novel, *The Somme*. It impressed Wells, and he urged Gristwood to persist. Within three months Gristwood had completed *The Somme* and was back in England. He had also decided to offer his book with another manuscript he had written some time before, that of *The Coward*, so that the two could be published together in one volume. Wells was not uncritical. On grounds of taste, he queried, for instance, Gristwood's uncharitable observations about chaplains on the Western Front, which were characteristic of the book's general tone. The line Gristwood took about the army padres was common in war recollections, such as Graves's *Goodbye to All That* and Montague's *Disenchantment*. It may have been true to some people's experience at the Front, but, as will be shown in the chapter on Robert Keable, it was misleadingly one-sided.

> One thing seemed to Everitt extraordinary. Not a Chaplain had he seen since he was wounded. This was notoriously out of keeping with tradition. Everyone knew that no-man's-land during an attack swarmed with Chaplains, administering consolation spiritual and spirituous, and picking up Military Crosses like so many gooseberries. Everitt's experience of these men of God must have been exceptional, for he never saw one of them in front of reserve trenches, and associated them chiefly with Concert Parties and Church Parades. A gramophone was the sole social stock in trade of the

Loamshire's Chaplain. He would deposit this instrument among the men's bivouac when they were out "resting" and lounge near it, smiling foolishly while it blared brazen versions of "Roses are blooming in Picardy" and "Colonel Bogie [*sic*]." For the rest, he made an occasional point of asking men "how they were getting on," and, receiving only colourless and embarrassed answers, retired with obvious relief to the more civilised shelter of the officers' mess . . . On the not infrequent occasions when the battalion's daily duties called it into unpleasant localities, the reverend and gallant gentleman was less in evidence. What he did no one seemed to know. Rumour declared he pressed the Colonel's trousers, but more probably he merely laid low like Br'er Rabbit. At long last he was trepanned by a fire-eating Colonel into a burial party in front of Ypres, and immediately afterwards returned to England for a prolonged rest. But doubtless Everitt's experience was exceptional and unfortunate.

Despite his doubts about this passage, Wells himself had never been one to spare the feelings of parsons in his own books. Indeed it was striking how much Gristwood's book, with its cynical, hypersensitive characters, owed to Wells. *The Somme* and, even more, *The Coward,* have much of the feeling of a Wells book. They are stories of outsiders – like Wells' *Invisible Man,* clever, persecuted, contemptuous of the common herd. There is something of the savagery of the early Wells and the same doom-laden atmosphere.

Gristwood held out against removing the chaplain paragraphs, on the grounds that he must be true to what soldiers felt at the time: "Everitt's thoughts on the matter are not at all garbled, & express a widely felt exasperation," he told Wells, "but in cold blood they seem a little like hitting below the belt. Yet to edit him is to attack his sincerity." He was more concerned that perhaps his periodic pronouncements on the infamy of war were undesirable artistically: "Does the moralising interfere with the story?" he asked Wells anxiously. These parts, however, were also retained, and in the final version only a few excisions were made.

Through Wells' influence, the book found a publisher, Jonathan Cape, and appeared in late October 1927. Wells had written an introduction to it, which gained it such critical attention as it received: "No one book will stand out as the whole complete story," he pronounced, wisely enough, avoiding any claim (as critics were to make for *All Quiet on the Western Front* in 1929) that here at last was the Truth about the war. He recommended that in the future the intelligent popular publisher, when copyright had expired, should assemble a large and representative collection of books and stories on the Great War to give a living, many-sided view of "the immense multiplex experience." By all means let there be the works of leaders like Churchill and Lawrence of Arabia, but "the history will still have something largely hollow about it until we bring in the other less eloquent side of the affair, the feelings and experiences of the directed undistinguished multitude, unwilling either to injure or be injured, caught in the machine."

The book had a fair reception. Captain Cyril Falls in his well-known survey of war books (1930) paid tribute to its considerable skill, though he thought *The Coward* more likely to breed militarists than pacifists in reaction against its loathsome leading character. It received a very hostile review in the *New Statesman* (12 November 1927), which dismissed Gristwood's experiences as recorded in it as, if true, "in no sense typical of the experiences of the ordinary private." It concluded by saying that "they are not likely to be read – and Mr. Gristwood's propagandist journalese certainly does not deserve to be read – by future generations."

"The gentleman seems to have lost his temper with his manners," Gristwood complained.

However much he might object to such comments, Gristwood was prepared to listen to some reviewers about his style, accepting the view that it was sometimes amateurish. But the writing, though sometimes overelaborate, is, in the main, effective and it is not his failure to write well, but the wounded, embittered tone of the book that prevents it from being a great work of war literature – though it is still a fearsomely arresting vision of the war. The book sold around 2,100 copies and was reprinted in 1928. Despite the flood of other war books the following year, however, Cape decided not to keep it in print, and Gristwood's royalties, overall, came to little more than £50, which was in fact the sum Wells had told him to expect.

Inevitably he compared what he had written with other war books appearing at the time. He was not enthusiastic about many of them:

"With all their varied merits," he remarked, "they were bound to mimic one another." He singled out only two, both the work of Germans, as being of exceptional interest: *The Case of Sergeant Grischa* by Arnold Zweig – an outstanding work that combines a powerful war atmosphere with a dramatic debate on important issues of personal liberty – and Fritz von Unruh's *Way of Sacrifice* – an extraordinary attack on war cast in a staccato futurist prose style: "another that stands out from the ruck," commented Gristwood. "It's mannered and exasperating enough no doubt, yet somehow queerly 'right.'" What appealed to him about both books was their rebelliousness and refusal to compromise, which he felt most appropriate to expressing the horrific impact of war.

Never one to waste time, Wells was able to put the hours he had spent on Gristwood's book to his own use. His latest novel *Mr. Blettsworthy on Rampole Island* came out in 1928. In it he included some episodes set in the First World War. The description of a futile attack is closely similar to Gristwood's in *The Somme*: "In a few minutes," Gristwood had written, "they were rather in parallel columns than line, and the warning against bunching was unheeded . . . . There was no attempt to charge: over such broken ground it was almost impossible to run . . . the weight of equipment dragged like an anchor . . . they went forward at a plodding walk." "Our charge was a plodding walk over tumbled ground and under a heavy weight," wrote Wells, " . . . they staggered along, hunched and despondent, looking as though they were running away from something rather than delivering an attack . . . As they dodged along amidst holes and mud puddles they lost alignment and here and there they bunched."

There is also a close similarity between the two authors' descriptions of their protagonists taking refuge in a shell-hole and then being helped by a companion back to the British trenches. In both a man dies in their presence; in both they are terrified of raising their heads because "the bullets continued to raise little spurts of earth around them" (Gristwood), or as Wells put it, "Ever and again the earth on the brim of my basin flew up in little puffs." The bitter remarks of Wells's Mr. Blettsworthy are very much in the spirit of Everitt's in the Gristwood book. Wells received some credit for this effort: "He has made use of all his gifts," wrote one reviewer about *Blettsworthy*, "that gift of rapid, realistic description (there is a chapter on the fighting in France that is actual and terrible . . .)." Gristwood could hardly have objected to this blatant plagiarism after the favour Wells had done him; indeed he may have taken it as a compliment, and perhaps it was intended as such.

Encouraged by his modest success, Gristwood perservered with his writing. He sent Wells a further manuscript in the autumn of 1929:"Nobody loves it," he complained, "but rejection-slips never give reasons, & if you could spare the time for a line or two of criticism, I should be extremely grateful." All that came of this, however, was a visit, shortly afterwards, to Wells's home at Easton Glebe. It was haunted by its owner's memories of his second wife Jane, who had died in 1927. On this occasion, Wells took a kindly interest in poor Gristwood who was embarrassingly tongue-tied and accidentally trod on the writer Philip Guedalla's dog, but enjoyed the beauty of the Essex lanes in the warm October weather. He induced Wells to present a signed photograph as a surprise gift for his father's birthday.

During the next year the elder Gristwood retired finally from the City where he had worked for fifty years. The family, including Donald, moved to Brockham Lane, in Betchworth, a small Surrey village near the town of Reigate, south of Purley. There, on the road leading out towards the towering escarpment that marked the edge of the North downs half a mile away, they lived in a squat, prosaic house, ambitiously named "Avalon." This was one of a string of newly-built dwellings incongruous with their dramatic surroundings. At the time it was still deep Surrey, rural, secluded, a little melancholy, with only the beginnings of suburbanisation. An early Victorian village church built from pale yellow Horsham stone dominated a picturesque green. That then tranquil and intimate countryside, bounded by Leatherhead, Reigate, Horsham, and Pound Hill, had been a retreat for men of letters: at Flint Cottage, Box Hill, two miles from Betchworth, George Meredith, so much embodying the optimistic spirit of pre-1914, had lived out his last years; Pound Hill had been the home of Christopher Stone, of early B.B.C. fame, a novelist both before and after the war, his experience in the 22nd Royal Fusiliers providing part of his material; and at Walton-on-the-Hill was the house of Anthony Hope Hawkins ("Anthony Hope"), famous as the author of *The Prisoner of Zenda*, who during the war had worked, like Wells, for the secret propaganda bureau at Wellington House, and also had made his contribution to war fiction – the best-selling thriller *Beaumaroy Home from the War* (1919).

Gristwood's next surviving letter to Wells, in October 1932, reveals that during the interval his health had deteriorated. He apologised for being slow to thank Wells for a parcel of his books. Since April, Gristwood explained, he had been "muddling about with doctors – hospitals, x-Rays, Nursing Homes and all the rest of the accursed paraphenalia." Until recently, indeed, he had been forced to drop all literary activity, though at last he was now able to do some reviewing for the *Sunday Times*.

Such insights as one has into the Gristwood household at this time show that Donald was a continuous anxiety to his parents. The physician who had looked after him for a long time, Dr. Brice Smith, described him as "a highly nervous man," susceptible to violent nerve storms which were very upsetting for his family. Periodically he went to a nursing home in London. Mrs. Gristwood's worries about him kept her awake at night, reading restlessly through the small hours in her bedroom. She shared this with her niece, Frances Gristwood, who now lived with the family as companion, helping the elderly couple to look after Donald.

On Friday 21 April 1933, Margaretta Gristwood sent for Dr. Brice Smith because, she said, her son was in a very disturbed state of mind. Gristwood told the doctor that he "felt desperate" and when the doctor asked him if he meant that he contemplated suicide, he replied with a nod of the head. Brice Smith prescribed some sedatives and in due course contacted a nerve specialist. Gristwood was in an overwrought state over most of that weekend, but calmed down on Sunday night when he was told that an appointment with the London specialist had been fixed for the next day. Mrs. Gristwood spent some time with him that evening and gave him "Boverine" and a glass of milk. He had some sleeping pills (allonal) to take by his bed. His cousin Frances heard him call out "Good night!" as he always did around 11:30.

The next morning, his mother went into his room after eight o'clock, accompanied by her niece, as usual. He was asleep, breathing heavily, and would not wake up. From 10 o'clock, when the doctor arrived, the most strenuous efforts were made to revive him; but he died at 7:00 the following evening. He was 39.

It was clear that he had been poisoned, and almost certainly by his own hand. But there was a mystery. His sleeping pills were untouched. A postmortem examination revealed that he had taken about 100 grains of veronal, a sleep-inducing drug – two-and-a-half times more than the minimum fatal dose. Where had he obtained such a large quantity? Both his parents denied that he would have had any hidden supplies or kept any secrets from them. They claimed that he had not been to London on his own at all that year, which says something about Gristwood's sadly circumscribed existence. Both denied that their son had made any suicide threats to either of them. Indeed the elder Mr. Gristwood proved unready to offer any explanation for what had happened. The police searched the house and conducted exhaustive enquiries at all the local chemists, but found no clues as to the source of the veronal. Nor could anybody find the glass of water that must have been used by Gristwood to wash it down. It is possible that he had secreted the veronal years before when he had received hospital treatment for his injuries. Only the doctor offered any convincing reason for the suicide, the subject being too painful for the relations. In his view Gristwood's war wounds had affected him mentally: "his whole war experience knocked him off his mental balance." No such explanation was given in the jury's final verdict of suicide, however.

There is little more to record in this melancholy and scantily-documented tale. Only the local press reported the story and made no allusion to Gristwood having written a book or to his connection with a world-famous author. The Gristwoods told Wells of the tragedy very shortly after it occurred, though they did not allude to the cause of Donald's death. They kept up with Wells at least until 1936 when James Gristwood sent him a 70th birthday greeting. They made one more move, to the town of Dorking, nearby, before the elder Gristwood died in 1941. In his will drawn up just after his son died, he left his niece and wife a life interest in his various properties; it was stipulated, however, that after his death these should be sold and the money should go to various soldiers' charities – Papworth Village Settlement, the Ex-Services Welfare Society, and St. Dunstan's Home for Blinded Soldiers in Regent's Park. All Mr. Gristwood's books – which must have included many of Donald's – were to be distributed to libraries, and to Toc H, the servicemen's religious organisation founded in the Great War. All this is eloquent of the feeling of total loss that the elderly parents must have felt at the death of their only, gifted, and unmarried son – and of their knowledge that so much of his brief life had been ruined by his experiences in the war.

Apart from the gravestone in Dorking cemetery, the book is his one monument. It was natural that it aroused the indignation of some ex-servicemen proud of their record like the critic Edward Shanks in the *New Statesman*, for it spoke with the "cold-footed" tones of the trench malingerer, who, unless silenced, could unman his comrades. The strength of the book lies, however, precisely in that unhappy voice, insistent and challenging to orthodox good behaviour. Gristwood spoke out where others dared not, to justify his actions, to attract pity, perhaps, but also to tell the truth as he understood it. The raw honesty of *The Somme* and the author's readiness to abandon reticence and dignity are not enough in themselves to make it a masterpiece, but they liberated the writer from the kind of suffocating conventions that deprive a war book of its force. No book that has *The Somme*'s ability to penetrate to the inner fears of the reader should be altogether discounted. Although Gristwood's style is undistinguished, there is nothing inadvertently comic about it, as there is in some of the First World War best-sellers that have dated; and it is far from dull. The book has a truth to tell about the fighting – the coward's truth. Not easily forgotten once read, it has the baleful quality of a death's-head on a tomb – and is a reminder that the war could not only mutilate a man's body, but wreck his soul as well.

5

❧

Disenchanted Observer
Ralph Hale Mottram
1883 - 1971

Habits, points of view — restraints had been destroyed. Simple
enough for those who, unable ever again to become the citizens they had been, found in the swift death of the battlefield
a halo that endeared them to a generation. But for others
who lived on, through months — years — of shellfire and
bombing, of Army orders and Censorship, not so simple!
They had to alter if not to rebuild themselves.

R H. Mottram was the author of one of the most ambitious
works to be written on the First World War. His view was pessimistic: the British High Command had failed their soldiers
and English civilisation had been undermined by the war. His tone was
quietly ironical rather than bitter. Rooted deeply in Norfolk town life,
he was without Aldington's dislike of the English provincial bourgeoisie,
and although his war was long and arduous, the unusual circumstances of
his service enabled him to take a more unemotional approach.

His most famous work, *The Spanish Farm Trilogy*, consisted of three
interconnected tales of the Western Front. "Highly humanised history"
was the way his literary mentor and friend John Galsworthy described
what was not exactly a novel, nor exactly a chronicle, but a reflective account of the Western Front in fictional form. There is little about the
fighting in it, for what really interested Mottram was the whole world of
the Western Front and how it functioned, rather than the moments of

extreme danger. Much of his own war was spent out of the line, and he always saw himself as an observer. Britain's phenomenal nineteenth-century success and later loss of momentum fascinated him, as did the war's crucial role in that process.

The Spanish Farm, the first of his three volumes, sees the conflict through the eyes of a young farmer's daughter in French Flanders, the shrewd, handsome Madeleine Vanderlynden. The name of her home, *Ferme l'Espagnole*, dates from the wars against the Spanish, fought in Flanders centuries before. In *Sixty-Four, Ninety-Four!* (1925), Madeleine becomes a subsidiary, though important, character in the war career of Lieutenant Skene, an infantry officer. Both characters fade into the background in *The Crime at Vanderlynden's* (1926) in which Mottram's third central figure, Lieutenant Dormer, tries to sort out a compensation claim for the destruction of the family shrine by a British soldier on Mr. Vanderlynden's farm. The Vanderlyndens want money. The French government, who have made the affair a *cause célèbre*, want punishment. But the soldier who perpetrated the "crime" can never be traced. Although told in a satirical tone, the message is serious – the real crime is the war. The desecration of the shrine is symbolic of a general desecration.

Mottram loathed the war not only for its physical destructiveness but also for its interruption of the process of civilised and constructive life. The war taught decent men to kill, to thieve, to drink, to fornicate, and to squander time.

Ralph Mottram, the son of a chief clerk of Gurney's Bank in the city of Norwich, was born in a room above the firm's offices. He described himself later as one of the last of the old city-bred inhabitants, before suburban life became the fate of all the professional classes: "One could live in the middle of a city of a hundred thousand. What an advantage that was. The things we saw! The visit of the Prince of Wales (fat, top-hatted, smiling, in an open carriage, going at a spanking trot), the constant military parades (we were not all sick and tired of khaki), the early bicycle . . . the nightly fights in front of the public houses . . . ."

His confidence in the Britain of his youth did not survive the war. "My firm conviction then," he wrote in 1927, "that, even if I were dying, my father and mother would have sent for the doctor, who (being their doctor) would have stopped death, remains in my mind. How very safe, how naive, how brittle it all was. How dignified, how scrupulous, how civilised. I know better now. I do not ask for it back. But I shall never be able to believe so implicitly in anything as I did in those black-hatted figures, high, safe, old houses, and silent Sundays of that age of gentility."

The Mottram family's adherence to the Unitarians, a dissenting faith with roots stretching deep into the seventeenth century, contributed to his feelings of security. The English and American Unitarians, though their moral precepts were Christian, nonetheless believed that the truth was revealed to a much wider world than simply those of the Christian persuasion. It was a humane religion that, because of its emphasis on intellectual rigour, proved, over the centuries, a seed bed for the development of many remarkable minds. In Norwich, Mottram attended the elegant Octagon Chapel, completed in 1756, where today a plaque commemorates him.

Before the war, though inwardly secure, he was quiet-spoken and lacked the confidence that military experience was to give him. Later, through giving commands and instructions in the army, his voice became more assertive. He was of middle weight, with a slender, wiry frame, an alert, attentive expression, and a large nose. His hair began to recede in his twenties. By the time he joined the army in 1914, he grew, like many young men of his period a neat, thin line of a moustache. His disposition was steady, though not placid. He had a playful sense of humour, all his life amused by absurdities, particularly those of authority, as his famous war novel shows. He loved music and singing.

His parents had married in 1882. His father was an honourable, dutiful man, but set in his ways, and Ralph later reflected sadly on Mr. Mottram's "almost total avoidance of anything spiritual – amounting to a horror of the tragic and heroic." His mother, Fanny, was an energetic, cultured woman eighteen years younger than her husband. When she married him, he was a widower of forty-nine with three daughters. Fanny Mottram had escaped from a stifling middle-class background and had gone to teach in France, eventually finding her way back to a school in Norwich. Although a devoted wife, her attention focused largely on Ralph and his younger brother Hugh. She was a profound moral influence. Active in the life of the Octagon Chapel, she also held classes for the poor in Norwich and was a strong supporter of the Liberal Party's social reforms. Intellectually too, she widened her children's outlook. She loved French literature, and did all she could to encourage Ralph's writing. She organised family holidays in France, which gave him some of his most precious memories. It was his mother's decision that he should leave his Norwich day school, Bracondale, to continue his studies in Lausanne and learn fluent French. This, as he said, "undoubtedly saved my life, fifteen years later."

The Mottram family's connection with Gurney's Bank (from 1896, Barclay's Bank) went back to the eighteenth century and was regarded as hereditary. They shared with their employers, who were leading members of Norfolk's gentry, the same assurance of their position in their local community.

Ralph's father assumed that his son would follow him into the business. Unfortunately, for all his lively curiosity about how the affairs of the world were conducted, the younger Mottram was not interested in this prospect. By 1900, work on the bottom rung was becoming ever more impersonal. His first halting attempts at writing poetry seemed of greater importance. Although he had been brought up to persevere and not to complain and knew that materially he was very fortunate, he worked without enthusiasm and felt guilty about doing so.

His mother, contrasting their family household and its four maids, errand-boy, washerwoman, and atmosphere of affection and security, with that of the Edwardian masses, was afraid that her poetry-loving son would grow up knowing too little of the rougher side of life. She made him take lessons in horsemanship each morning before breakfast, at the local barracks. It was to stand him in good stead in his later wartime army career, though ironically it was she, then, who was to suffer acutely when her son's life really did become dangerous and exposed.

His family's connection with the bank brought him one unexpected stroke of good fortune. His father's responsibilities included looking after the interests of the beautiful Ada Galsworthy; before she married John Galsworthy, she was unhappily wedded to his cousin. She took an interest in the shy young Mottram's poetical efforts, and this was shared by John Galsworthy. Their friendship was to change Ralph's life.

In June 1900 Galsworthy wrote to Mottram asking to see his verses, and giving his views on writing: he dismissed the idea of art for art's sake. Art must be a part of life, he insisted. This view impressed Mottram so deeply "that I got up at five o'clock on one of the last days of June (I was due at the barracks at six) and sitting at my desk booted and spurred, so to speak, I hurriedly made a final revision of such of my verse as was reasonably finished and packed it off to him."

The poems reflected the emotional tension that had built up in their young author. They pleased Galsworthy, who, though not uncritical, encouraged him to believe that even if he had to stay a banker to earn money, he was still doing something worthwhile with his literary talents. It was flattering to be the intimate of a sophisticated couple who had known the anguish of having to conceal from the world, over many years, their love for one another in order to spare Galsworthy's elderly Victorian father the pain of a public divorce case. That, with Galworthy's sense of honour and impeccable bearing, won Ralph's admiration, attached as he was to solid orthodoxies while preserving his own romantic inner nature. Galsworthy was to have a profound effect on his writing, not least *The Spanish Farm Trilogy*.

Yet the two men were unalike. In his maturity Mottram was far from retiring and had a strong public conscience but he did not have Galsworthy's social eminence or the physical energy and presence that gave the author of *The Forsyte Saga* a central position on the literary stage. Galsworthy had what Mottram never attained, an exceptional dramatic power in his writing – one reason why his plays like *The Silver Box* and *The Skin Game* remained for years some of the best in twentieth-century British theatre. Galsworthy's outstanding talent was tempered in the nine tormented, ecstatic years through which he and Ada passed before they could be married. Mottram's own personal life, apart from his ordeal in the war, was secure and uneventful.

Like most young men in 1914, Mottram paid little heed to the build-up to war on the continent. His view, absorbed from the banking community, was that European war would be incompatible with the spirit of progress and could not occur simply because it made no business sense. It was indeed true that no powerful economy at the time was more dependent on peace than Britain's. In no other important European country, either, were its citizens so free of military obligations or so confident of their borders.

When Germany invaded Belgium, however, Mottram and eight of his fellow-clerks at the bank joined up patriotically in the 4th (Territorial)

Battalion of the Norfolk Regiment. His apprehensions were swallowed up in the excitement of being involved in a war of unprecedented scale. This sense of being part of a gigantic, often chaotic, machine, fuelled by popular enthusiasm, and yet so oppressive to the millions who gave it impetus, is one of the most lasting impressions that *The Spanish Farm Trilogy* leaves on its readers.

The letters Ralph Mottram wrote from the front have immediacy, gaiety, and passion. His initial enthusiasm for service at the start, his concern for his mother and the world he had left behind in Norwich, and his affection for the French families with whom he was billeted have a generosity that is both touching and impressive, while his letters to his fiancée reveal an unaffected ardour surprising in a writer later so restrained. Apart from his mother, she was his main correspondent. He had met Margaret ("Madge") Allan at his brother's wedding before the war. Clever and responsive, she was Scottish, and, from 1915, a qualified teacher. Her looks were attractive: fresh and intelligent, with a hint of the resolution that was to show in the testing war years that followed. She and Ralph were amused by the same things; and she was to be his closest critic and guide in his work – as well as his inspiration. She accepted his family readily, but preserved her independence from them. Towards her children she was strongly maternal, yet she always retained a virginal quality – self-contained, mysterious, and elusive – which had drawn Ralph to her originally, and continued to do so throughout a long and happy marriage.

A photograph he gave her at Christmas 1914 showed half of the 4th Norfolks on their way to Peterborough at the beginning of December, with Ralph a competent-looking corporal, pale of face and sharp of feature, carrying a map and seeming more alert than the heavily be-colded officers in front of him. In the sober mood that followed the commencement of the First Battle of Ypres, troops had been moved in great numbers to the Eastern counties to stave off a possible invasion. In the New Year of 1915 the battalion went on to Lowestoft on the coast; Ralph was by then a sergeant.

Though underequipped and having to make do with Japanese rifles of inferior design, the troops still had the high spirits of the early volunteers, which even the marshy atmosphere of Peterborough had failed to quell. "No one falls out," wrote Ralph. "The fellows seem awfully keen & only want to have plenty to do. Today we had to march in our great coats, a most trying proceeding as these garments are meant to sleep in rather than to keep off the rain. But there was no grumbling in our company and we sang as we came home, through icy rain." Ralph's platoon commander at the time was none other than Roland Aubrey Leighton, immortalised as her great love by Vera Brittain, the famous peace campaigner of the 1930s, in her memoir *Testament of Youth*. Ralph enjoyed the exhausting sham battle organised by Lieut. Leighton, which left many others utterly fatigued. He was lucky also to escape the regular plagues of illness that afflicted his fellow-soldiers during that winter.

The chief excitement at Lowestoft occurred early in March when the battalion was called out at nine in the evening to ward off a supposed German invasion: "To my intense disappointment the whole thing fizzled out . . . We think the Germans had a go at the big oil ships & floating dock which are off here somewhere, but we hoped we were going to have a go. I did enjoy it." Ralph was a good shot and proud of it: "If I shoot in battle as I did on Tuesday, out of every five Germans who get in front of me two will be killed and three wounded and none get away."

His fighting spirit and competence made him an obvious candidate for a commission. With John Galsworthy's recommendation he was gazetted as a 2nd Lieutenant that spring. He was given £50 towards buying his equipment, including a revolver and a sword in a leather scabbard, a major expense, which his parents generously subsidised. In April he went on an officer's training course at Harrogate in Yorkshire, most of his fellow trainees being promoted N.C.O.s like himself.

Despite the rigours of those early months, he and his fellows remained very much in the "Vision" stage of volunteer excitement described in C. E. Montague's *Disenchantment*:

> The mental peace, the physical joy, the divinely simplified sense of having one clear aim, the remoteness from all the rest of the world, all favoured a tropical growth of illusion . . . Here were hundreds of thousands of quite commonplace persons rendered, by comradeship in an enthusiasm, self-denying, cheerful, unexacting, sanely exalted, substantially

good . . . Who of all those who were in camp at that time, and are still alive, will not remember till he dies the second boyhood that he had in the late frosts and then in the swiftly filling and bursting spring and early summer of 1915?

Zeppelin scares and the company of fellow-officers provided distractions that Ralph, like all of them, badly needed. Although buoyed up by patriotic feelings, they were highly apprehensive lest their dearest hopes for the future should be snatched away from them. There was a poignant naivety in the way these volunteers foresaw their part in the battles in which they were about to fight; but much of what they said so boldly was to keep up their own spirits and those of their families. From camp in Felixstowe Ralph confided to Madge how important to him now were all the private hours they could spend together: "then you will draw some of the soreness out of my heart I can't tell any living soul about except you . . . I am mortally afraid something should come & upset things at the last moment, but soldiers have to pretend they're not afraid."

In July he went to join the 10th (Service) Battalion of the Royal Norfolk Regiment at Reed Hall Camp, Colchester. The excitement there was intense. Some of the men had been gazetted since the beginning of the war and were straining to get to the front. Round the piano they relieved their feelings by singing rueful versions of well-known hymns:

> We are but little soldiers weak,
> We earn but seven bob a week,
> The more we work, the more we may,
> It makes no difference to our pay.
> Yet Kitchener loves us,
> O Kitchener loves us,
> Still Kitchener loves us,
> The Major tells us so!

In August, Ralph's father suffered a paralytic stroke – increasing Ralph's anxiety about his mother, fearful of her son's imminent departure. He tried to reassure her that the enemy would soon be defeated. He had been tantalised by the knowledge that real Germans were within rifle-fire range when they flew overhead in a Zeppelin one night in mid-August: "If only we had a finer night, we could have done them in."

By September, the pace of training at Reed Hall Camp grew hotter. The ill-fated Allied campaign at Loos began on the Western Front and it was clear that the British Expeditionary Force would soon be calling on the men based on Colchester. When Ralph at last departed for the continent on 4 October, he did not have the heart to tell his mother. It was strange, he reflected, having to leave her at this moment of all moments when his father was close to death.

He went not as part of a draft, but independently, so was liable to be posted to any unit in the 24th Division to which the 10th Norfolks belonged. He ended up with the 9th Norfolks, reporting for duty at a camp near Proven on 12 October. "I was under fire for the first time yesterday – big 16 in. shells bumping about – & I enjoyed it," he wrote.

It had never been a possibility that the Allied offensive at Loos (September-October 1915) could have achieved the desired breakthrough on the Western Front. The German army was still far too strong and the Allied artillery far too weak. What was avoidable, as Gilbert Frankau (q.v.) later argued in *Peter Jackson*, was the failure of the B.E.F. commander to bring up the reserves in time to exploit some considerable local successes achieved by troops along portions of the line. When Ralph reached them, the 9th Norfolks had already suffered 209 casualties out of their total strength of 900 in their three days of action at the end of September. They had had the misfortune to be flung into a big battle almost the moment they had arrived and before they had got used to the conditions.

After a week at the railhead at Poperinghe, spent in a deserted convent, the 9th Norfolks, including Ralph, went up to the front line on 22 October. By this time he was in charge of a platoon and second-in-command of his company. His first reports from France had been cheerful, praising the food, the medical organisation, and "the perfectly charming women" who were running a kind of officers' cafeteria. On 23 October he told Madge: "We have come right up here, into the firing line, all amongst the big guns, at one stretch, carrying the fullest pack possible, so last night, as we crawled into our places, among flying bullets and dropping shells, everyone was very tired and done, and I was the man to take charge of the company for the night, get in the stores and see all safe – It was really not much of a job, we are some way from the enemy, in a piece of country we drove him out of some time ago . . . Really life is not bad up here. The big guns give you a headache, and the rifle & machine gun fire never ceases – but one feels well, the men are cheerful – the stretcher parties are a bit sad, of course – and the country people – here in the dugout some looter has put images of the Virgin – a boy's photo – a dressing table taken from a villa, & a cottage chair."

It was actually a good deal worse than that. On the first night, at 2 a.m. the enemy guns began to "search" for a cunningly hidden British artillery battery close behind where the 9th Norfolks were entrenched: "The shell fire," he told a friend, "became so hot upon our left forward trench (of the village defences) that I started to get the men out of it and across the machine-gun swept street, to the less dangerous right half of the 'keep,' and this was ticklish, as the men, some of whom had never been under fire before, were roused from sleep and had to run the gauntlet across the high and exposed street. I stood in the middle . . . and tried to look unconcerned, but was really afraid, especially as I had a bullet through my cap; also the stretcher-bearers were afraid to take their wounded half a mile down to the dressing station, so I had to find up a useful Lance-Corporal to send, as we had by now wounded coming up the communication trench from the firing line." At dawn the enemy ceased fire.

He learned of his father's death while he was still in the line, on 26 October. "I thought of myself," he told his mother a year later, on the anniversary, "reading one of your letters saying how near the end was – & then the splash-splash of the sergeant coming to say that the Boche had knocked in another part of the trench – & how I went & disentangled the half-buried men & sent the wounded to the dressing station & two days later I got another letter to say he was gone."

He confided to Madge that he had not been sorry to have missed the funeral – "I had got so out of touch with him – still it is sad, but not a bitter [sic] sadder than the deaths of men I see being killed around me all day."

The 9th Norfolks handed over their trenches to the 8th Bedfords on 28 October. They moved to trenches near Ypres and subsequently went into billets nearby on 1 November. Next day they went back into the Ypres trenches, along the line "Forward Cottage" – "Mark Lane" –

"Lavender Hill" – "Euston Road." They were there for five days in very wet weather. Up till 15 November, Ralph was in and out of the line in that sector.

He told his mother: "You cannot imagine a greater test of a new battalion like this with about two per cent regular soldiers than to stand in water all day & all night and rarely fire a shot – I have only used my revolver twice, at a quite doubtful target . . . . The Germans have had to abandon part of their lines here, but keep going with plentiful machine guns & flare lights & concrete forts – we can't attack them through this miles-wide puddle, nor they us, so we just sit and gibber at each other."

"It *was* a show!" he told a friend later: "all I could find was a ditch full of water with some rotten sandbags in front and some broken revetment frames behind. We took over and made the best of it; but it was simply a matter of piling up the black slime in front of you to protect your head; listening posts, dug-outs . . . latrines, everything had caved in, and the sodden earth becoming liquid, what had been excellent in July were now useless in November." The next day, he added, "the men were beginning to feel the 12 hours immersion in water and the lack of sleep. One man, against orders, climbed out on a collapsed dug-out to mend it, and was at once hit between the eyes; it was hard to reach him where he lay, and I would not allow men to expose themselves, so he was very stiff by the time we got him down, this rendering the job of collecting his effects very awkward."

It was quite clear to him that no advance could be made in this sector of the line despite the British having achieved a temporary superiority. By 8 November, the men, the battalion diary recorded, were very exhausted. But in four days they were back in the trenches at St. Jean, in the same area, conditions as wet and stormy as ever. Mottram, who had borne a heavy responsibility during the last few days, began to feel ill, but because he believed that there might be a chance of a successful attack he hung on for two days more. Finally, on 15 November he was admitted sick to 17th Field Ambulance. Later he was transferred to a hospital in Boulogne with the inevitable "Pyrexia of Unknown Origin." From there he was sent to convalesce at Nice in the south of France. It was clear to his commanding officer that he had exerted himself to the limit and both needed, and deserved, a rest.

The month he had spent under heavy fire had drained him psychologically as well as physically, as it would have done most men who had flung themselves so wholeheartedly into such a dispiriting exercise. Before he was withdrawn from the line, he had written to Madge, imploring her to visit him on his next leave, whatever her duties to her school, "because I've seen so many men suddenly killed & others reduced to mere caricatures of themselves lately & I must have you once again entirely to myself because I run that risk."

Out of danger and no longer having to brace himself to combat fear, he had become very depressed; but by the end of December his spirits recovered. He rejoined his battalion in January 1916. It was now part of the 6th Division, and was still in the Ypres sector. Although the trenches were as waterlogged as ever, the fighting was less intense, the casualties were relatively light, and the battalion had managed to adapt to conditions: for instance, they had learned to allow for the loss of vital stores while "staggering about in the open above the muddy drains called 'Communication Trenches'" by helping themselves to rather more than their allowance. Rations and ammunition and post were now better organised. Waders, waterproof capes and goatskin coats were issued to all and tin hats to most. The possibility of being "sniped" had been reduced from a real danger to an occasional nuisance, most casualties from this quarter being random or avoidable. The rifle, he reported, was effectively obsolete. The enemy had become, it appeared, "reliably inaccurate" (he did not add that this was clearly deliberate, although he did describe how "The Bosch is sometimes quite sporting, and will signal in the approved Bisley [Army rifle range] style, when our snipers miss a head shown above their parapet"). He noticed that many of the boys in the battalion, being from Norfolk country villages and used to poaching, had become clever at finding their way about in the dark – valuable in seeing off German patrols or carrying out rewiring at night. He also observed how youth and inexperience could be an asset. The old, regular sergeants, who had been with the battalion from the beginning, were less resilient under prolonged shell fire.

To a friend, he described one night of excitement. He had been conducting a large working party of around 100 men heavily laden with hurdles to mend a communication trench. Their route took them along a riverbank, through a shattered town, and past rows of new war graves, some of them disturbed by shells. "I had just reached a dirty ditch full of water, which in the better weather is one of the main thoroughfares to the firing line, when I heard an awful clatter behind – Number ten of the first group got a stray bullet in his back & had blundered down on the remains of a metalled road, with enough noise to wake dead Germans, let alone live ones listening. You can imagine what ensued – organising the carrying off of the casualty to the dressing station, shepherding of the scared ones (because when one chap is hit by a 'stray' none feels safe) then, the standing on an exposed parapet to give them confidence, waiting every moment for a shower of shrapnel which the Bosch gunners, if they could locate the noise, would be sure to treat us to."

Ralph's view of things reflected that of others in his battalion. He was still cheerful and ever curious – "There are most glorious moments out here. I wouldn't miss it for anything" – but more cautious, certain now that only a slow hard battle of attrition would bring about the collapse of the Germans; aware too of his own and his fellow infantrymen's limitations when it came to fighting the sort of war in which the military leadership was now locked: "We all welcomed General French's retirement. First because no super-man could possibly stand more than about 12 months of this game. I shall probably be looking for an instructors job in England if the war is still on in September." His sympathies were constantly troubled by the anxiety that he knew Madge and his mother felt all the time about him.

Although at one level he was more desensitised, at another the ugliness and wanton destruction were beginning to prey on his nerves: "I am thankful that your home & mine have not shared the fate of so many houses here," he told a friend. "It is awful to see lovely gilt mirrors – old furniture – children's toys – books – all charred & smashed & dabbled with blood and excreta."

He took leave on 8 February 1916, rejoining the Battalion at St. Jean on 19 February, riding up with the transport through rain and shells. When he arrived something happened that changed – and probably saved – his life. There was a call for officers who could speak French. His name went forward and the same day he was ordered to report to Divisional Headquarters. He seized a lift on an artillery limber and the next morning started a job on the British "Claims Commission" in which the French language and a business training were crucial.

"Please don't imagine I'm a 'staff officer,'" he told his mother, "but I live with them, under a real roof & shine my buttons & wash my hands – I [was] walking round to see the company this morning . . . and was greeted with a mixture of envy and admiration." He recognised the importance of what had happened: "So you see, Darling," he told his mother, "after all these years, the loving care and forethought you expended in sending me to Lausanne may bear a little fruit. It does not do to be too certain at present, one never knows what cross-currents or accidents may send me back to my regiment or to any other imaginable sort of job. . . ."

His new work was as a kind of military diplomat. He had to handle claims made by the French and Belgian civilian populations. Under the French billeting law of 3 July 1877, civilians were entitled to compensation if their crops had been destroyed by soldiers marching through them and for breakages if buildings occupied by troops had been damaged. Mottram's job varied from assessing the value of shattered windowpanes to negotiating with refugees from bombarded towns who wanted to turn soldiers out of their billets.

The Commission could not have chosen a more suitable man: his love of France made him a particularly sympathetic negotiator, and it gave him satisfaction to feel that he was able to do something to remedy its desecration: "I hate to see women running with children in their arms," he wrote to Madge, "& falling down in a dead faint screaming . . . I got chilled to the heart, so even my breakfast couldn't stop inside me – & every night we got bombed and shelled & 6 men were killed & 20 wounded about 50 yards from where I sit – only don't tell Fanny. . . ." The only way he could regain peace of body and mind, he told Madge, was to crawl into his blankets as soon as it grew dark and imagine himself in her warming embrace.

Knowing France well, he understood better than most British officers what its people were suffering – not only the horror of bombing and the violation of their property, but also the strain on their soldiers, many of whom had been away from their homes for fifteen months without a day of leave: "You have no idea how little England has suffered – & how much France and Germany have," he told his mother.

He found he got on better with the French and English officers with whom he now worked than with most of those (especially regulars) he had known previously in his division. He liked the padre, too, Neville Talbot, a courageous and capable man, later Chaplain-General of the forces, and even found himself attending the Anglican services. Best of all he was beginning to make friends with the Belgian and French civilians with whom he had dealings in his rides behind the lines.

After what had been one of the coldest winters on record in Belgium, the weather began to grow mild, the blossom came out, and, as spring moved into summer, he was filled with optimism, despite the horrific sights he continued to witness. He began to make more definite plans to marry, and urged Madge to take a teaching job near Norwich to be near his mother. He remained highly apprehensive, however, that his luck might turn, and that he might lose the job that he found "heaven on earth." His fears were almost self-fulfilling, for he suffered for a while from what he recognised as a psychosomatic stomach disorder so acute that there was a danger he would end up in hospital and emerge to find he had been replaced, and would have to return to the line. He asked the doctor to pass him fit whatever happened and thereafter depended on self-medication.

In September, as a "district superintendent," he joined his fellow-officers on the Claims Commission in a house in the middle of a forest near Boulogne. He worked a nine-hour day, dined well, and played golf and tennis in his spare moments or walked on the beach. Best of all, he had a bed, with sheets. All he and his colleagues lacked, he told Madge, were women – the most frequent subject of conversation: "They tell me stories about wives & sweethearts & mistresses – sad or commonplace or only vulgar, with a few fine ones – but all the photos and all the stories are not so truly lovely as the one of you in my heart & the thought of our love . . . ."

No. 2 District Claims Commission moved quarters fairly frequently. In October they moved close to the area where they had first been in battle. The group consisted of the Assistant District Officer (Mottram), the Adjutant, the Commanding Officer (a former Deputy Clerk of Liverpool Council), the Branch District Officer, Captain Cowan, a Liverpool merchant in peacetime, an engineer ("a jolly Scotch boy"), responsible for road damage claims, and three Rent Officers who dealt with claims over the occupation of land. Of the latter, one, Pickmere, also from Liverpool, became a particular friend of Ralph's.

A typical day's work would be "splashing round the skeletons of farm buildings literally kicked to bits having 40 horses stalled where there was, I suppose, before the war, 1 donkey and a sack of potatoes. The wear and tear of this enormous army is extraordinary."

In addition to his investigation he was in charge of organising the office, the feeding, housing, rations, and clothing, as well as the horses and three cars. At Hazebrouck where they finally became established in mid-November, he reported:

"I have a hard job to get away from their continual 'by the way Sir!' and 'did you notice this, Sir?' but eventually about 10.0 I do get off in a big car . . . passing down a paved road, generally lined with trees behind which are marshes, fat grazing cattle . . . and arable and woods – and one or two big houses of local gentry behind fine stables and avenues.

"Then one gets to one's centre for the day, a wealthy comfortable Flemish town, more or less scarred by bombardment, & always containing more troops than inhabitants. First I go to the old town the Spaniards built, where the *Mairie* [town hall] is, & hear what the comic old man who is doing *Maire's* secretary *('pour mon fils, qui est mobilisé, oui, mon bon Msieu, il est dans la Somme')*. I hear what he has got to say about various contentious matters in hand. Then I go off to the various farms, dwelling houses, schools, or convents in which we are billeted & see to all sorts of people, old & young, stupid & clever, grasping or fair. At lunch in the officially sanctioned 'officer's restaurant' I meet men like myself or engineers; or others with odd jobs not directly concerned with the trenches.

"In the afternoons more visits – home if possible by dark – tea in the office . . . & the reports until 7.0 or 7.30 then a run home to dress & work – dinner is not until 9.30, perhaps a game of Bridge & so to bed sleepy."

He found time to confide in his mother by letter about his relationship with Madge and the effect the war might be having on it. For an Englishman of his background he was remarkably open with her on such matters – more so, perhaps, than most sons with their mothers, even today. One letter, where he almost welcomed the way the war seemed to be overturning old-fashioned prudery, contrasts, in its optimism, with his deep feelings about the war's destructive effects on the fabric of civilisation. "I hope I am not very much changed," he wrote, "I know you said last time that I wasn't coarsened – & I find I can still appreciate good music – but the change in me will be a sort of philosophical toleration of rules being broken – I mean, after seeing all the men I have seen, blown to bits at a moment's notice, I can't be expected to take the sort of conventions which obtain on Newmarket Road or Thorpe Village – too seriously – I never did really, did I – Nor you!"

He and Madge took a similarly robust view about the petty anxieties that separation caused. "I won't boast for the future," he added, "but at present we are not jealous of one another." They both understood only too well what the war might bring, and had no wish to dissipate their feeling for each other in groundless and demoralising suspicions. Despite the strain of long absences, their devotion, based on such realism, proved the foundation of a partnership for life.

Ralph moved frequently over the next few months. Mid-March 1917 found him more permanently settled, in the fine, if dilapidated house of a Belgian Count and his wife. Ralph and the Rent Officer, Pickmere, befriended them and frequently dined with them off silver plate. The warmth of their welcome did much to keep up his spirits. The old couple delighted in his company and in Pickmere's violin, and the Countess in turn played Mendelssohn, beautifully, on the piano. Their friendship was one of the happiest results of Ralph's war service.

Otherwise there was little escape from the litany of carnage and waste. By June 1917, indeed, practically all those he had enlisted with, travelled with, commanded or served with, had lost their lives. Although saddened he was philosophical. He told his mother: "These things don't of course have the effect they would have in the ordinary way – one is so accustomed to it all and to the fact that places are soon filled – I have seen so many stretchers with a union jack thrown over them – & quite a number with that formality omitted . . . . I can't think that any of us of my generation will ever have much feeling of the permanence of anything very definite. . . ." Nonetheless he dreaded the prospect of seeing bereaved parents, to whom he had written condolences, on his next leave: "Once I have said or written something to them there does not seem to be anything else to do & I feel as if my comparative immunity were rather superfluous."

The work was hard, and, in its way, a strain. One officer was sent home with a complete breakdown, and his duties had to be spread for a while between his colleagues. Ralph's worst anxiety, however, was over his mother. Her younger son Hugh might at any time be conscripted. Ralph's letters to her became yet more affectionate and reassuring. He had been very distressed by their farewell at the end of his January 1917 leave: "She cried dreadfully and made me most unhappy."

He got leave again at the end of 1917, the fourth Christmas of the war. He and Madge were married on New Year's Day, 1918. Saying goodbye to her became harder than ever. During the great German onslaught of March 1918, so successful in driving back the Allies, the Claims Commission was obliged to move, in a great hurry, back to countryside unscarred by fighting. No personnel were lost nor any essential kit. The battle stopped short of the Count and Countess's home, but in April Ralph went back to persuade them to leave when a new German offensive threatened to engulf the area. The Countess left only under protest, the Count obstinately staying put. Miraculously the chateau was again spared.

The weather by late April was fine and warm. Had it not been for the constant danger from the German attacks, the scene from Ralph's new base, a moated farm with willows and apple trees, ducks and ancient barns, would have been idyllic. His boon companion Pickmere left for home duty, and Ralph himself had leave again in July, when the war was on the point of going in the Allies' favour. He returned to Flanders to find a new arrival in the mess, an American, symbolising, with his open-hearted optimism, competence, and energy, the final, inevitable victory. Being close to Ypres they were still within range of the enemy guns and their work was as intensive as ever. For long periods, Ralph, now living in a pretty eighteenth-century chateau near his earlier lodgings, was working only with his senior officer Sutcliffe. His industry was finally recognised by his promotion from 2nd to full lieutenant. More important was the news, in September, that Madge was pregnant.

As the fighting drew to its hard-won close, the 2nd District Claims Commission moved house again. Ralph made a trip into the area at last liberated from German occupation – a fearful spectacle of devastation. The first effect of the Armistice, he noticed, was the complete dislocation of most of the usual services: letters seemed to be held up for days.

The second was that he felt himself suddenly incapable of doing his work. There were no physical symptoms of this apathy – he slept and ate as well as ever – but could not bring himself to work, as though something overstretched in his mind had suddenly slackened. Sutcliffe kindly gave him a week's holiday and he went to join another member of the Commission, Captain Heyer, in one of the liberated towns; Heyer, in civilian life an organiser of charity matinees, took him off to "a real civilised theatre," which amazingly had been resurrected there.

Late in November Sutcliffe transferred to another district at Malo-les-Bains, east of Dunkirk. Although the fighting had ceased, their work continued unabated. There was a huge backlog of claims to handle and, as Ralph anticipated, it was another six months before he could free himself from the army. During that time he returned weekly to the Hazebrouck area to finish paying off the claims that had been settled there, and took the chance, with Sutcliffe's permission, of going shooting with his friend the Count. Despite his frustration at his plight, he attempted to cheer up his mother: "try and derive some comfort that I am coming home permanently between now & June & that 750,000 fellows are not coming home at all." She was indeed comforted; both of her sons had come through unscathed, and they were reunited at Christmas 1918.

Classed as "indispensable," Ralph stuck it out, often shouldering the whole burden when Sutcliffe was away, and only cheered by the fact that owing to his early enlistment he would not have to join the army of occupation in Germany. The next six months were testing for him and for Madge. The baby, Ralph, was born in April. Madge suffered from a brief postnatal depression while Ralph's war fatigue was beginning to come out like a bruise. Incidents preyed on his mind – in particular the suicide of Harold Burton, a daredevil sergeant in the dragoons whom he had known from his Norwich childhood days. Burton had been one of his father's "wards" and had been almost as close to him as a brother. He had cut his own throat, as a result, it was said, of war strain, though Ralph suspected, perhaps knew, something more and was anxious to protect the family. He went to find out what the military law was in such cases and discovered that if Burton's wife applied for a pension she would be told that she would not qualify as this was a "self-inflicted wound." "This is their idea of sparing people's feelings," wrote Mottram, "and I leave it at that."

The devastation haunted him: "I was lunching today with the *maire* of Bailleul," he recorded, "& heard something of the problems of rebuilding a town something like Thetford say – an old Spanish fortified village round which a modern 'agglomeration' of small factories and railway yards had grown, & which is now unrecognisable. I don't suppose there is a wall six foot high left. The drainage, the roads, the limits of properties & the prevention of unemployment were what they talked of, but I thought of the Spanish belfry, & all the comfortable old Flemish houses & cellars full of wine." It was symbolic for him of the laying waste of all that was fine and wholesome in European civilisation.

He was finally demobilised on 26 June 1919. He had arranged to have a quiet holiday with Madge in Scotland, where he arrived with ragged nerves. Madge, understating his distress and her own, wrote to his mother: "He was, I think, more tired and disgusted with things than I have yet seen him, but we spent a beautiful day – and I think the rest is doing him good already." Her optimism proved well-founded.

Unlike many other soldiers, including some described in this volume, he was going back to a job and to the comfort of a strong, uncomplicated love. Whatever grim visions his sensitive soul had absorbed, and though he did not much relish a return to banking, he faced the future with a sense of increased independence and responsibility – as his wartime letters chart. Furthermore, the Claims Commission work, closer to life in "civvy street" than service in the trenches had been, eased his adjustment to the postwar world, and he escaped the intense feelings of dislocation that affected so many exsoldiers. One great task now lay ahead of him: to write about his war experiences.

He and Madge and their baby moved immediately into "The Birches," his mother's comfortable double-fronted villa in Norwich, and, later, to a smaller place of their own. By 1920 he had started to write his fictional life of a provincial businessman, *Our Mr. Dormer*. He also began a story about his character, Skene, a kind of "everyman" middle-class officer. From this his ideas for *The Spanish Farm Trilogy* were to develop. It was not until 1922, however, when he was staying with the Galsworthys in Devon, that this more ambitious scheme was born: it was not to be a thinly-veiled personal memoir but a book taking a broader view of the war from the point of view of a civilian in arms, with a civilian outlook such as he had always retained himself. He did not believe that the experience of a nonprofessional soldier in wartime could be isolated from his home background. Galsworthy kindly read through his drafts. He counselled massive alterations: the most important was the introduction of the character of Madeleine Vanderlynden, the French farmer's daughter who became the central focus of the book, and supplied the love interest in it. On a practical level, Galsworthy's tactful advice decided Ralph against taking a job with Barclay's Bank in London; Galsworthy felt that as an aspiring author, Ralph would find his deepest inspiration in his native Norfolk where his roots were, thereby avoiding, too, the distractions and expense of living in the capital.

Thanks to Galsworthy's literary influence, Ralph focused upon a theme of the social fabric under strain and of the volcanic impulses that lay beneath the surface of ordered society and that war, like marital turmoil, could cause to erupt. Secondly (for Galsworthy's writings embodied what has been unkindly called "a pot of message") *The Spanish Farm Trilogy* carried a moral. It was not just a case of studying the great forces in society but of making an ethical judgment, albeit from a liberal, tolerant standpoint. Ralph already had this tendency, learned from his mother; with such a mentor as Galsworthy its expression was inevitable.

Thirdly, Galsworthy's dislike of the fantastical and overimaginative, and his own sober style, were reflected in Mottram's writings. This was a less happy influence. What Mottram needed, and lacked, were more hills and valleys in his prose. Although he had continued to write a little poetry, he had decided, early on in the war, that it was not the medium for him. This was a loss, perhaps most of all to his prose, which was often too plain. When a poetical passage found its way into the *Spanish Farm*, it stood out, as good in its way as the generally more highly flavoured war prose of H. M. Tomlinson or Henry Williamson. There was his description of Flanders in spring, for example:

> It came shyly, a northern spring. The sodden greyness of the marshland winter on flat hedgeless fields gave way to cold and fitful sunshine that shone on rich young green everywhere, while the black dripping leaves of the elms in the dank pastures seemed blurred in vapour, that, upon examination, proved to be but a profusion of tiny light-coloured buds.

But most of Ralph's descriptions were explanatory, not aesthetic. It is a frequent criticism that his great war book is a little flat in tone. Gentlemanly reticence is undoubtedly compatible with the deepest feelings but is not always adequate for literature demanding more vivid emotional expression. Here too, his mother's influence played a part: for though as responsive to the beauty and drama of life as he, she taught him that in art fidelity was more important than brilliance – a view that, however true, can easily be a discouragement to poetical writing.

Despite Galsworthy's recommendation, *The Story of a Spanish Farm* was rejected several times before Chatto and Windus took it. Ralph later maintained that this was because the public in 1922-4 were anxious to forget the war and publishers were reluctant to accept any war books, other than Montague's *Disenchantment*, which did sell well in those years. He was not wholly right about this: Ford Madox Ford's "Tietjens tetralogy" and Patrick Miller's prize-winning *The Natural Man* date from this "dead" period, as does Philip Gibbs' highly successful *The Middle of the Road* (1923) and if the theme of returning soldiers were to be included, so do Peter Deane's *The Victors* and Warwick Deeping's million-selling *Sorrell and Son*.

The truth is that *The Spanish Farm* was a very unusual book (as Ford's and Miller's books were unusual). It was contemplative, not about fighting. It posed a great many awkward questions; and it was thoroughly disenchanted. The war was described as "cosmic murder" and "this great stupidity." The boredom of military service was constantly emphasised. Much was made, in satirical fashion, of war profiteering, and in particular of the corruption that accompanied the prospect of German reparations payments after the war – thousands in the ruined areas competing unscrupulously for a slice of "*La Galette.*"

The great heroic campaigns hailed in wartime propaganda were more explicitly dismissed in the trilogy than anywhere in Montague's *Disenchantment*. Ralph spoke of "the long sordid epic of Verdun" and of the battle of the Somme he wrote: "The English Offensive on the Somme, heralded as a great victory, had in reality made infinitesimal gains at the cost of enormous loss. The British Great Head-quarters, then still functioning in complete disunity with Great Head-quarters of France, and often in good-humoured disregard of the advice given it, went on butting, like an obstinate ram, at the same place. This, though it surprised the Germans more than the most subtle strategy would have done, cost the lives of many a thousand English soldiers."

Those very soldiers, the heroes of every patriotic wartime English book, were cut down to size too, not as individuals – helpless and insignificant as they were – but as a glorious army. Their presence in France may have been necessary, but it was not desirable. In one of the closing passages of his second volume, Ralph described Madeleine's final parting from Skene:

> She did not want him, had never wanted him, nor any Englishman, nor anything English. He was just one of the things the War, the cursed War, had brought on her, and now it, and they, were going. Good riddance. Nor was her feeling unreasonable. The only thing she and Skene had in common was the War. The War removed, they had absolutely no means of contact. Their case was not isolated. It was national.

Such hard sayings were not to every publisher's taste; but Chatto and Windus saw the potential success of this book. They were right. In a few months the first volume had sold two thousand copies and won the Hawthornden Prize. In its 1927 edition, bound up with the next volumes, *Sixty-Four! Ninety-Four!* (based on a diary he had kept since he had been in hospital in 1915) and *The Crime at Vanderlynden's* and three short stories, its sales rapidly reached 100,000.

So large is the scope of the trilogy that it almost defies description. Essentially it is a study of what war does to civilised people. Ralph deliberately concentrated on life *behind the lines* and left out any episode based on his direct experience of fighting. Artistically the book is accomplished. It is at times moving in the extreme, and throughout there is finely-turned wit, as: "In its dying stages, those who ran the war were at last learning to put men to the job they could do best," and: "There sprang up between them one of those quick intimacies of the early days, before everyone became bored and bewildered."

Saving Henry Williamson's war volumes of his *Chronicle of Ancient Sunlight*, there is in fact no better account of the Western Front – a rich and detailed picture of the minutiae of people's lives in the context of the vast campaigns that were taking place. The book has the faults of its virtues. It is the product of a mature outlook (Mottram was over forty by the time it appeared) and has none of the still adolescent ardours of Wilfrid Ewart's *Way of Revelation* or Richard Aldington's *Death of a Hero*. The above passages, for example, though sensitive and realistic, lack vibrancy. The Hawthornden Prize (for verse, plays, and fiction) was usually awarded to books of a traditional form, though that did not mean conventional in content (another recipient was Siegfried Sassoon, for his *Memoirs of a Fox Hunting Man*). There was nothing modernistic about *The Story of a Spanish Farm*.

After *Our Mr. Dormer* was published in 1927, Ralph finally left Barclay's Bank. The decision was a risky one. By 1930 he had three children; but Madge, who had helped him with *The Spanish Farm*, as with all his other works, was equally in favour of the change and had confidence in his power to support them. Subsequently she bought a typewriter and taught herself how to type out his manuscripts whenever needed. With such encouragement, he rose to the challenge. Between 1927 and the end of his life no less than sixty-seven books by him were published, not including reissued works under new titles. He drew on all his experience, even banking, as material. Above all, he devoted himself to fictional and factual accounts of life in Norwich, becoming preeminently the chronicler of Norfolk's cathedral city. As an old man, he was indeed sometimes referred to as "Mr. Norwich."

He hoped and expected that the war, by ending certain hidebound prewar attitudes, would lead to much greater social reform, and that the individualism of the Edwardians was now giving way to a more communal spirit. He was never, however, drawn deeply into political life, though active as a magistrate and on committees concerned with the history and preservation of the city. In 1953 he became its Lord Mayor. His views remained liberal and progressive.

Throughout the thirties he was a well-known literary figure, going as British Representative for the annual PEN Club Conference in Buenos Aires in 1936. He was a member of the exclusive authors' dining club, the Omar Khayyam, and a Fellow of the Royal Society of Literature. After the Second World War, in 1966, he was given an Honorary Doctorate of Letters at his local university, East Anglia, which he greatly prized. Apart from Galsworthy, he made many friends among writers. These included several war veterans such as the influential Professor

Bonamy Dobrée, and H. M. Tomlinson, the literary editor of the *Nation*, who had been a war correspondent and both influenced and was influenced by Ralph's writing, his own war novel *All Our Yesterdays* being another (and less successful) attempt to draw a picture of the way the war cut across British life in the early twentieth century.

The Spanish Farm Trilogy was not Mottram's only account of the war. There was a collection of short stories, *Ten Years Ago* (1928); "A Personal Record," in *Three Personal Records*, edited by Eric Partridge, in 1930, an account of Ralph's time in the trenches with the 9th Norfolks; *Journey to the Western Front* appeared in 1936. *Europa's Beast* (1930) described the exofficer Skene's unsettled feelings about returning to his prewar job as an architect, and the seedy and shiftless existence that some exsoldiers were compelled to lead. It embodied a love story in which Skene was cast in the role of a sort of Lawrentian bull-man, taking the heroine by storm. This contrasted oddly with the delicacy of Skene's lovemaking in the trilogy. It may nonetheless have been faithful to some aspects of Ralph's own feelings after the war, expressing his impatience to take on life and fulfil his ambitions.

His volume *Poems New and Old* (1930) included the haunting "Flower of Battle," which had been printed in the *London Mercury* in 1926. That verse caught the eye of Edmund Blunden, by now influential as a war poet and literary critic, and himself destined never to come out from under the shade of the "flower of battle." Blunden was fiercely critical of many of the war writings of his contemporaries, not least Graves' *Goodbye to All That*. Ralph's poem and his "highly humanised history" passed muster with him, however. He wrote to congratulate Ralph as well and received a grateful reply: "I am so pleased to have your letter about my stuff. I have been writing verse for twenty-six years and except for a few individuals it has fallen unnoticed . . . I have always been one of your readers. It is so amusing now to hear people envy me the very moderate popularity of the *Spanish Farm*. They know nothing of what it feels like to be steadily ignored for a quarter of a century. Nor do you, but you can imagine."

Like Blunden, Ralph had emerged from the war with an overwhelming sense of the comradeship of suffering and a conviction that the Germans had not been Britain's enemies: the real enemy, for every nation, had been the war itself. If the Germans were to blame at all it was for their tactless prewar diplomacy and their too-well-organised preparations for a conflict; but as he had told his mother in November 1917: "I begin to think that the great lesson of the war is the uselessness and danger of making people believe what they don't feel — as for example — German militarism. The average German being far less bellicose than you or I." He had moved right away from the simple patriotism he had shown in 1915. His only reason for wishing, later in the war, for the enemy to be overwhelmingly defeated was so that such a war could never happen again. He emerged from the war convinced that it would not.

He kept up with his French friends, but he also made contact with the Germans, travelling there in 1930. In translation, his *Spanish Farm Trilogy* had been well received, and he was invited on a lecture tour to the universities of Berlin, Leipzig, and Cologne to promote Anglo-German understanding. He was so taken with the idea that he also financed this part of the trip himself. Like many of his contemporaries he put his hopes in the League of Nations and in the reluctance of Europeans ever to countenance the insanity of 1914-18 again. When Europe careened into war for the second time, his confidence was shattered. Both his sons were in uniform, Ralph in the R.A.F., winning the Distinguished Flying Cross and Bar, Jack in the Royal Navy. Ralph Senior served in the Home Guard. His sons survived, but it was a time of intense worry. It was as if the full weight of the horrors, all those years before, had been checked by a supporting structure that had worn thinner than he realised, and now came crashing down on him. Acute stress, even over many years, is cumulative in its effect.

Nonetheless he kept going, working also as a forces lecturer, and sharply observant as ever about both the minutiae and the larger implications of the world war. With its end, and after grandchildren began to be born, he recovered. He remained a courteous, dignified figure and active physically, swimming regularly at eighty. He started writing poetry again and was always ready for energetic discussion on favourite topics and still full of aesthetic response to music, architecture, and poetry. He enjoyed, too, the civic ceremonies in Norwich, when he would appear in frock coat and top hat, his war medals gleaming on his chest.

In his later years, slowed down by loss of hearing, he came to rely more and more on his wife in finishing his work. She died in 1970. After her death he went to live with his daughter at King's Lynn, the fine ancient town in the west of Norfolk. "His sad, lonely, gaunt, deaf figure," is remembered, which, "striding determinedly against East Anglian winds in all weathers, still outpaced those half his age." He died on 15 April 1971.

The Spanish Farm Trilogy has stood the test of time better than many war books of the same period. It was reprinted in the 1980s. Having made a successful film, *Roses of Picardy*, in 1930, the book was adapted for television in 1968. There is a case for saying that of all the interwar British novels of the 1914-18 conflict it gave the best *historical* record. Two comparable works have been mentioned briefly in an early chapter, Ford Madox Ford's "Tietjens tetralogy" and Henry Williamson's *A Chronicle of Ancient Sunlight*. All three attempted a massive vision of the war. Ford's was the most idiosyncratic and in many ways the most original perception, but, if his imaginative understanding and sensitivity exceeded Mottram's, and if his characters were altogether more alive, he had less day-to-day experience of the war itself, in and out of the line, and for these purposes, *The Spanish Farm Trilogy* was the more reliable account. Mottram fired no random shots, whereas Ford, never renowned for his veracity, launched into bolder generalisations.

Williamson's book has a greater richness of texture than either of the other two. He was the least intellectual of the three, his views being simple and obsessive – and frequently wrong-headed. Yet the gift of poetical expression, which the other two also possessed, shows more strongly in his writing. Ralph Mottram painted in muted and subtle colours. Williamson's prose has a kingfisher's iridescence. He never grew out of an adolescent rebelliousness of spirit, but this very immaturity gave his work a far greater intensity than *The Spanish Farm Trilogy*. In one sense, too, Williamson's account was more balanced. Writing well after the *Second* World War, he could see the mistakes made by the generals in better proportion than was possible for those who, like Ralph, looked at the war only a few years afterwards. The generals, as Williamson pointed out, had problems to contend with quite as difficult in their way as those of the troops at the sharp end. In other respects, however, Ralph's analysis and his profound reflections on the nature of the war stand up the best of the three.

His own particular war, a combination of brief and terrifying trench experience and a long, relatively calm spell of administrative work with civilians behind the lines, gave him a comprehensive understanding of what was happening, in a manner not vouchsafed to the infantryman in the trenches, whose vision was always limited to the narrow hell that was his part of the line. The picture of war that Ralph drew was of a disastrous assault on ordered society, the undermining of morality in decent people, and above all the senseless destruction of the fabric of French and Belgian lives in the war zone. Only courage and companionship alleviated this a little. All was laid out quietly, even, at times, detachedly, for the reader to absorb. No English author explored with more honesty and plain intelligence the tragedy of the Great War.

PART TWO

❧

WAR REDEEMED

No I see, either the world is mechanic force
and this the last tragic act, portending
endless hate and blind reversion
back to the tents and healthy lusts
of animal men: or we act
God's purpose in an obscure way.
Evil can only to the Reason stand
in scheme and scope beyond the human mind.
God seeks the perfect man, planned
to love him as a friend: our savage fate
a fire to burn our dross
to temper us to finer stock
man emerging in some inconceived span
as something more than remnant of a dream.

—from Herbert Read, *The End of a War* (1933).

6

❧❦❧

Noblesse Oblige
Wilfrid Ewart
1892 – 1922

Mexico City, 1 January 1923. For the second time that day, Angelina, a maid at the Hotel Isabel in the Avenue Republic of San Salvador, knocked on the door of room 53. It was now afternoon, and the young foreigner who occupied it still did not answer, though his light had showed under the door all morning. This time she entered. There was no sign of him, and nobody seemed to have slept in the bed. Then she caught a glimpse of a long pyjama-clad figure stretched out on the balcony. Looking closer she saw that the man had been dead for some time, and was lying in a pool of blood. One of his spectacle lenses was shattered. The police moved in and sealed off the hotel.

The next day the press announced the mysterious death of an English businessman, a Mr. Gore. A photograph of the corpse accompanied one report. When this was posted in the English Club, an acquaintance there quickly corrected the account: the dead man was no less than Wilfrid Herbert Gore Ewart, one of Britain's most promising young writers, the author of the best-selling war novel, *Way of Revelation*.

Shortly after this, his friend, the author Stephen Graham, arrived at the squalid Juarez hospital, which reeked of blood and decay, to identify him. Graham, who had been in the Scots Guards with him during the war, told the police that he and his wife had been travelling with Ewart, but had stayed in a different hotel. The three had spent the evening together on New Year's Eve. Ewart was waiting for his baggage, which was to be sent down from New Orleans. He had been on a voyage to the

New World to recuperate from a severe nervous breakdown. Four years of war, personal disappointments, overwork, and sudden success had doubtless contributed to Ewart's mental illness. In any case, he had always been delicately balanced psychologically.

Way of Revelation had appeared in 1921. It had been an instant success, and within a few months had sold 30,000 copies. By the middle 1930s this total rose to around 50,000. Fifty years later, however, when it was reprinted as a paperback, it made little impact. The book had dated and did not justify the extravagant claims made for it at the time as "the English *War and Peace.*" Henry Williamson, putting it among the two or three greatest works about the First World War in the English language, gave it too high a place. It is long, ambitious, and its message was one in which Ewart genuinely believed, but the very qualities that ensured its success at the time were also the ones that made it ephemeral.

Its story is of a young baronet of moderate means, Sir Adrian Knoyle, and his close friend Eric Sinclair. Both enjoy London society though Adrian is fundamentally serious and has resisted amorous entanglements. Now he falls in love with the enchanting Lady Rosemary Meynell, and he and Rosemary plight their troth in an idyllic river scene reminiscent of George Meredith's *Ordeal of Richard Feverel.* Then comes the war. The young men join up, Eric is killed, and Adrian emerges from the war saddened and haunted.

Yet the war has not been wholly a disaster, indeed by putting good men and women — like Eric's fiancée, Faith — to the test, it has brought out the finest qualities in them. But it has also — and this is Adrian's tragedy — exposed the baseness of trivial and selfish people. Rosemary is seduced by Harry Upton, a rich, arty young man, with an affected manner and pallid countenance, who avoids military service by doing government work of "national importance"; encouraged by Rosemary's mother, he sees her as a useful social connection.

Upton's manipulative bohemian mistress, Gina Maryon, catches him in the end, but only after she has helped him to wreck the love between Adrian and Rosemary. Rosemary herself is destroyed by her vanity and self-will. She lets herself be flattered by Upton and his fashionable circle, "the Clan Maryon," and becomes not only his fiancée but also a cocaine addict. On leave, Adrian discovers her infidelity and returns in despair to the front where he contemplates suicide by exposing himself to gunfire, like the protagonists of Richard Aldington's *Death of a Hero* and Ronald Gurner's *Pass Guard at Ypres* (q.v.). He is saved by his sense of duty to his regiment, by the example of Eric, and, after his friend's death, by the generous letters of Eric's fiancée, Faith, who devotes herself to keeping up his spirits.

Adrian comes back from the war and becomes engaged to Faith. Then he goes to the Victory Ball, the tasteless *beau monde* fancy-dress spree that followed the November 1918 Armistice. In that tawdry gathering he beholds Rosemary, who has renounced Upton, and is clad in sackcloth. His feelings for Rosemary resurgent, he approaches her and they embrace. It is too late, however. Rosemary has wrecked her health with cocaine. She dies in his arms while the band plays the national anthem, and Adrian intones the Lord's Prayer.

Five years pass. Faith and Adrian, happily married, stand one evening on a hill (on the North Wiltshire Downs), surrounded by a vista of natural beauty, the keen air cleansing and revivifying their spirits. In this uplifted frame of mind, they contemplate the enduring place of the dead in their hearts, and the knowledge that Rosemary and Eric are at peace.

This is all melodrama, and not very original melodrama at that. The Society scenes, which occupy a large part of the book, have some accurate observation, but the characters are mere types and caricatures. Even the battle scenes are marred by the author's lack of skill in handling personalities. The finest sketches at the front are the nonhuman ones: the spectacle of flares lighting up no-man's-land by night, or the lush loveliness of the summer countryside behind the lines, in contrast with the bleak desolation of the trenches. Ewart is adept at evoking the joy of creation – the small flowers and the fossils in the stones underfoot, the larks soaring above, the warm summer air, and the silent fall of lime leaves upon the dark waters of a stream. An accomplished prose-poet, as a novelist he was second-rate.

Yet clichés, lack of subtlety, tumultuous scenes of passion and agony – all written with conviction – were the stuff of successful middlebrow fiction. Moreover, though his picture of the war was sombre and tragic, it was also uplifting and optimistic. The sacrifice of good men and women had not been in vain, however hard their lot had been. This was a message that people wanted to hear just after the war: it was comforting, but did not trivialise the calamity. What kind of experience had led Ewart to this conclusion? It might seem easy now to discount his book as a piece of patriotic sentimentality. In fact it reflected his unusual character, and also the nature of his war service, which was both horrendous and inspiring.

Wilfrid Ewart was the son of Herbert Brisbane Ewart and Lady Molly Ewart of 8 West Eaton Place, Belgravia, a large stuccoed house in this most select district of London. His father, who came of a prominent military family, was an upright, old-fashioned gentleman, a High Anglican, proud of his position in society. Without being actually poor, he was far from rich. He worked as secretary, with the pompous title of "comptroller" to the Princess Dolgorouki, the expatriate widow of a Russian nobleman. The princess lived in woodland near Taplow, Windsor, at "Nashdom" (Russian for "Our home"), a massive white neoclassical building by Lutyens, modelled, to her requirements, on the style of country houses favoured by the nineteenth-century Russian aristocracy. The job occupied only a few days of Mr. Ewart's week, but it took him, and sometimes Wilfrid, out of town and into a world away from their disturbed home life.

Lady Mary Ewart, Wilfrid's mother, came from the heart of the British ruling class. She was the youngest daughter of the fourth Earl of Arran. Her sister Caroline was married to the 8th Lord Ruthven. Her eldest brother, Arthur, became fifth Earl of Arran in 1884. One of his daughters married the heir of the Marquis of Salisbury, another married Viscount Hambleden, and a third, the Earl of Airlie. Madness ran in the Arran family of that period. Mary ("Molly") Ewart herself was badly unbalanced.

A highly nervous young woman before marriage, as her diary reveals, Wilfrid's mother was already suffering from psychosomatic illness and would weep for hours on end. She had led the outwardly agreeable but suffocating life of a high-born unmarried girl of her day, kept continually on leading strings – many walks, rides, and tea parties, but little intellectual stimulation.

The Ewarts had three children. Wilfrid, the eldest, was born on 19 May 1892, followed by two sisters, Angela and Betty. Fond and supportive though Herbert Ewart turned out to be as a husband and father, it was not an easy family atmosphere. "Molly" Ewart was unpredictable. Her peculiar behaviour often had a strange logic, which led her cousin

Esther Hambleden to remark, "Molly, with all her oddities, has much more common sense than the whole of her family, husband and children, put together." On one occasion, Lady Mary received her guest seated on the carpet: "Oh, how nice, my dear Mabel! Forgive my sitting on the floor. I always do it now," she explained, "I find it less far to fall." Her insaner moods, however, were alarming. Once when Esther and her husband, a deeply respectable couple, called, just after their marriage, "Molly" glared coldly at them, and after a painful silence rang the bell and said to the butler, "Take this couple away. They are living in open sin." More seriously, she frequently flew into violent rages and from time to time attacked her husband. As the children grew older, it was felt better that they should spend as much time away from home as possible. As a result they were often sent to stay with the Hambledens at their house at Greenlands in Buckinghamshire. Angela, whose cousin Alice Salisbury was also her godmother, was regularly invited to Lord Salisbury's seat at Hatfield House.

Wilfrid treasured his frequent childhood visits to the home of his elderly cousin, Miss Margaret Ewart, near the ancient town of Devizes, on the edge of the North Wiltshire Downs. Broadleas Manor, a house of warm yellow-grey stone built at the turn of the eighteenth century, was like its owner, unpretentious, constrained, and mid-Victorian in atmosphere. At the same time there was an extraordinary sweetness about the grounds and house and a seclusion that made it at times seem more like a home for the birds that sang in the garden trees than for human beings. In the near distance cattle grazed in the fertile Avon valley where Broadleas stood. To the south lay Salisbury Plain, golden-red with ripe grain at harvesttime. For Wilfrid it came to be the most quintessentially English stretch of country he knew. That vision, and the calm presence of his robust elderly cousin, symbolised all that he valued most.

Of the three Ewart children, Angela seems to have been the most resilient. Betty, her sister, later took to drink and drugs and made an "unsuitable" marriage to a chauffeur. Wilfrid was handicapped on two counts. He was blind in one eye, and very shortsighted in the other. He also had more than his share of the Arran disorders: violent angers, depressions, blackouts, psychosomatic illness. This emerged particularly after he was sent at the age of nine to a boarding school, St. Aubyn's in Rottingdean, Sussex, a time for him "of emptiness, chilliness, desolation, of distempered walls and long draughty dormitories, of bare classrooms, cold baths, and rather depressing games on bitter winter afternoons." It was an education, he recollected, supposed to assist in the making of a stout and hearty English boy; but that was something he never became. Probably because of the shadow over his home life, and the separation from his warmhearted father while at school, he retreated into himself, grew egotistic, introverted, and hypersensitive, resenting all criticism.

From early on, Herbert Ewart found his highly-strung son difficult to influence, though Wilfrid was fond of him and they travelled happily abroad together. Mr. Ewart's fervent High-Church and ritualistic religion made little impact on his son, but, as a youth, Wilfrid consented, out of a vestigial respect for tradition, to attend Church at St. Mary's Graham Street, near Sloane Square, where his father was a churchwarden. Wilfrid was not a believer. In so far as he had a faith, it was pantheistic, like that of many of his contemporaries, and bound up with the beauties of the English natural landscape.

His parents had intended him to go to Eton, but by the time he was twelve they doubted whether he would be able to cope. Instead they sent him away to a private tutor in Bournemouth. When he was fourteen he went to work on a farm at Bottisham in the Cambridge Fens, to learn about agriculture.

It was here that his imagination and ambition began to mature. He was fascinated by English rural life and crafts, from poaching to chairmaking. For the writing of Thomas Hardy he developed an intense passion. From this, other literary influences followed, such as the naturewriters Richard Jefferies and G. A. B. Dewar, editor of the influential *Nineteenth Century*, but the Dorset poet and novelist was the foundation of his education. Ewart began to write about what he saw. At fourteen he was already penning articles of a striking precocity – about the fading year, the marshes in winter, and the frozen enchantment of fir woods and snowfields. He also studied the varieties of poultry with diligence, discovering a feeling of affinity with them, and at sixteen began to contribute to *Farm Life*, *Feathered World*, and various other poultry journals. Thereafter he collaborated on a book published in 1908: *Practical Poultry-Keeping for Small-holders*. Other articles appeared on such topics as "The Fowl Races of Central Europe" and "Fattening Chickens on a

Farm." His fondness for hens and fundamental kindness were revealed in his charming, if whimsical, piece, "The Life History of a Black Wyandotte," as told by the chicken itself. In it he spoke feelingly of "our . . . small silent tragedies pitiable enough in any other plane of life, in our own only despicable, uninteresting, to be laughed at."

He was reckoned, at eighteen, to be one of Britain's leading experts on hens; but writing had by now become Wilfrid's greatest passion and between the ages of sixteen and nineteen he made as much as a hundred pounds a year from articles for different journals. In them, he returned time and again to his favourite countryside, the chalklands of Wiltshire and Dorset. His poetical descriptions and his observant accounts of changes in village life and rural occupations remained his forte throughout his life. Less distinguished were the chatty pieces he began to write as he returned periodically to London and, for the first time, to a busy social life - ironical and unoriginal comments on the absurd pretensions of English society, typical of a popular genre in that period.

They demonstrate one side of Wilfrid's makeup. He was extremely fastidious about social matters, and observant of small lapses in diction and dress. His criteria, however, were unsubtle and seem odd in a character fundamentally unconventional. Clearly he needed, as he grew up, to feel that he "belonged" with fellow members of his caste. Yet at the same time the satirical edge to his critique indicates how much he despised about the *beau monde* he inhabited. Hardy and Richard Jefferies pulled him another way.

From the age of nineteen he moved between the two worlds, of social pleasure and of nature and the imagination. The English countryside always had the greater claim on him, whether it was the North Wiltshire Downs above the Vale of Pewsey, the wooded Thames Valley landscape near his father's workplace at "Nashdom," or the "Flats," the coastal mudflats on the Wash, north of Bottisham, where he took a cottage. He loved an outdoor life, exhilarated by stormy weather as much as fine: "What a day it is!" he proclaimed; "What a day for lovers of life and the freedom of living! The Nor'-Easter is blowing from land over the sea, blowing in fierce gusts that make a man bow or shiver."

Yet London Society had also a powerful allure – the spectacle of a midnight ball in a great Hotel; the tall mirrors, the shaded lights, the satin gowns, the gaiety. He enjoyed the music wafting up the staircases and out into the lamplit silence of Green Park – and even the irony, he felt, that everyone there, whom the world outside believed to be carefree, was forced to play a role, to fascinate, to deceive others and themselves. The bittersweet always appealed to him: regrets at dawn, forgotten by morning, over a convivial breakfast in Covent Garden, still in white tie and tails.

In London he lived at home, at West Eaton Place, where he worked hard, writing in a firm, ungraceful hand, the letters large and somewhat florid, but tightly executed. His numerous corrections to his manuscripts indicate his determination to capture the *mot juste*. His evenings were filled with the diversions of the London Season. He was particularly drawn to bohemia, to the circles of the fashionable artists and writers.

Ewart was tall and dignified-looking, very dark, with a clear complexion and high colouring. Despite his bad health, he looked manly and athletic; but his manner was inhibited. He had a curious, heavy, limp handshake as if his forearm had gone to sleep. He was easily repelled by any overfamiliarity, or hints of "caddishness." Among friends however, and over a glass of wine, he was relaxed and cheerful.

One of his closest friends at this time was George Wyndham, grandson of the Hon. Percy Wyndham, who lived at Clouds, the large, late-Victorian house he had built near East Knoyle, to the west of Salisbury Plain. Clouds, with its William Morris furnishings, was a centre of political power in that last age of aristocracy. Percy Wyndham's brilliant eldest son, also called George, had been Conservative Chief Secretary for Ireland. It had been there, in the East Room, that he and Arthur Balfour, the Prime Minister, and Lord Lansdowne, the Foreign Secretary, had signed the 1904 Anglo-French Entente, of fatal significance for the young men of Wilfrid's generation who took their places alongside the French armies ten years later.

Wilfrid's infatuation with Clouds and its surroundings centred round the young George Wyndham rather than on the glittering elder generation who gathered there, including Lady Desborough, Arthur Balfour, George Curzon, and Harry Cust – the famous group known as the "Souls." George had been a close companion of Wilfrid since schooldays at St. Aubyns. He was a dashing figure, clever, handsome, impetuous.

Temperamentally he was the opposite of the painstaking, introspective Wilfrid, and imparted a kind of "patrician oxygen" to his spirits. They walked and cycled together over the downs and later, when Wilfrid was twenty, made a trip to Paris. As in London, Ewart romanticised his experience, revelling in the glittering lights and the bonhomie of the Parisian world after dark. Yet he seems always to have been an observer, making notes and quizzing new acquaintances.

The impression is that despite his fine looks and gentle charm, he was inexperienced in love. Like many another Englishman of his class, and with the added weight of his family problems, he tended to worship from afar and his attitude to women was tentative and immature. It was a theme reflected in his later writing, notably *Way of Revelation*.

Whether or not (as happened to his protagonist in *Love and Strife*) any bruised romantic feelings played a part in his decision to join up when war was declared, his motive, first and foremost, appears to have been simple patriotism. He had watched the international scene, as he watched all political questions, with the greatest interest, debating the issues vigorously with his father.

Although he regarded himself then as something of a radical, his position on the European situation was that of the majority of the Conservative party: he regarded the expanding German navy as a threat to Britain. He thought Sir Edward Grey, the Liberal Foreign Secretary, had been quite right to strengthen his country's links with France and Russia, but wrong not to warn Germany explicitly that Britain would back up her two friends in the crisis of July 1914, for that would have scared the Germans into sense.

When Armageddon came, his friends and relations hurried to enlist. Britain's hereditary ruling class, the aristocracy, their constitutional power only recently shaken by the Parliament Act of 1911, were impelled by the strongest incentives of caste pride and *noblesse oblige* to show an example of courage and leadership. "What surprised me," wrote a former private in the Guards many years afterwards, "was that no physical standards appeared to be necessary to qualify for a commission in the Guards. The main qualifications seemed to be wealth and social position." Wilfrid's case bears this out. His poor health and atrocious eyesight should have disbarred him. However, he encountered no problem. His first cousin, the Master of Ruthven, who commanded the First Battalion, the Scots Guards, suggested that he should join his regiment, and the doctor examining him passed him fit for service, as requested.

That his semiblindness was likely to be, at the least, inconvenient, was soon demonstrated. During a few days given him to clear up his personal affairs, he took off on a bicycle for a last communion with the Wiltshire Downs, crashed into an undetected obstacle and spent the next six weeks resting a badly injured knee.

Finally, he arrived at Caterham Barracks, where Guards officers and men were battered into fighting shape by a notoriously brutal regime designed to produce perfect obedience and fitness. It achieved both, though whether the cruelty shown by some of the sergeants was justified, or the endless pettiness, or the bad habits contracted in order to survive, was queried by many who passed through the ranks. After the war, Stephen Graham wrote *A Private in the Guards*, an account of his service in the same battalion as Wilfrid's, the 2nd Scots Guards. It gives an astonishing picture of contrasts: vicious humiliation of good men; unattainable standards of perfection; general mindlessness; and at the same time an inspiring *esprit de corps*, unselfishness, and displays of disciplined courage in the face of terrifying odds.

Later, in the line, Ewart, like others, would often grumble about the duties heaped on them. In January 1916, for example, he and other men from his battalion were required to train some Kitchener Army battalions; "the extra work they make is a bit of nuisance," he remarked. This complaint was not a sign of idleness, though it does demonstrate the contempt – sometimes excessive – that the Guards felt for "the Amateur Army." The fact was that there was almost no rest for them even out of the line. To a degree that other regiments were spared, the Guards were expected to maintain their strict training, drilling, and standards of turnout. At war, there were very few empty spaces in a Guardsman's day.

Graham's accusations about the Caterham training were controversial. Yet in the main they were acknowledged as correct by Lord Ruthven and they are confirmed in a much later account of service in the Guards, by Norman Cliff. The last-named reinforced another criticism of Graham's that disturbed Ruthven much more: both maintained that during the war the gulf separating the officer from the private soldier was so deep that the officers seldom understood what was going on in their men's minds. Ruthven admitted that he had hardly realised this until he read Graham's book, but rationalised it, perhaps predictably, by saying that many of the wartime officers were of inferior quality. Moreover he believed that often a good company officer knew more about his men than they themselves realised. The fact was however that the class divide was greater in the Guards than any other foot regiment. Middle-class privates like Graham and Cliff were a comparative rarity in those ranks; and few infantry regiments can have had as many noblemen among the officers.

Although the officers' training was also rigorous, there was a sense in which they were spared the worst suffering. Once commissioned, they enjoyed the privileges common to all officers: regular leave; relatively comfortable conditions; less equipment to carry and exemption from manual labour, in ordinary circumstances. In addition, Guards officers' select background gave them some psychological immunity from the grinding-down process of the military machine. On the whole, these young men came from the pinnacle of society. They spent their leave in country houses or drinking champagne in Paris; their fathers kept company with generals – indeed, often *were* generals – and had no desire to "know Lloyd George," Britain's humbly born Prime Minister and the legendary passage to exemption from undesired military duties. Where a middle-class officer from a public school such as Richard Aldington could still feel overwhelmed and helpless in the face of a relentless military system – and even more so a lower-middle-class officer from a day-school like Henry Williamson – most of the Guards Officers had the illusion, at least, that the system belonged to them, rather than they to it. This confidence reinforced their training and was of great value in combating fear. Besides, the majority had been encouraged for most of their lives to show form in the hunting field and in other sports, to keep up with their peers (who often *were* Peers, in the constitutional sense), and to demonstrate their "natural" leadership. Undoubtedly the *esprit de corps* inculcated into Guardsmen made their performance as soldiers outstanding, from rankers like Private Michael O'Leary V.C. to Lord Gort M.C., D.S.O. (and 2 bars) and V.C. But the officers' belief in themselves as a social elite also made many apparently unpromising "Piccadilly Percy" figures, who neither commanded nor deserved much respect from their men out of the line, rise to unimagined displays of courage. The young

Prince of Wales, who was a subaltern in the Grenadiers (Wilfrid Ewart was briefly put in charge of him early in 1916), later wrote: "The Guards Division was a great club; and if tinged with snobbishness, it was the snobbishness of tradition, discipline, perfection and sacrifice."

After passing out from Caterham, Ewart went to Wellington Barracks in London and was detailed for guard at Buckingham Palace. He proved an effective officer on parade, if effectiveness is measured by the ability to spot small imperfections in the state of the men's equipment. Always dapper, he was punctilious, as was required by the regiment's exacting discipline; moreover he was out to prove that his eyesight was well up to standard. He was far from disliked in the officers' mess, but as he was quiet and fastidious and neither swore, gambled, nor chased women, he did not fit in particularly well. Both at home and at the front he performed his work efficiently and bravely, yet the fact that his promotion to captain was a long time in coming suggests that he was somebody who tended to be passed over, his indifferent health being an additional reason.

On 22 February 1915, after several false starts, he finally joined his battalion in French Flanders with a draft consisting of 208 other ranks, 2nd Lieut L. A. Jarvis, and himself. The 2nd Scots Guards were in the Fromelles-Sailly sector, on the right bank of the River Lys, two miles northeast of Estaires. They, like the 1st Scots Guards, had suffered very badly in the First Battle of Ypres, which raged for over a month from 18 October to 22 November 1914. As part of the 7th Division the 2nd Scots Guards and other battalions had held the line against an enemy force that for several days was six times larger than themselves and nearly broke through to overwhelm the British Expeditionary Force and reach the sea ports. In heroic fighting at Kruisecke on the night of 25–26 October, and in a horrible incident near Gheluveldt a few nights later when they ran into fire from their own side, the 2nd Scots Guards' strength was badly eroded, and only partially made up by drafts arriving in mid-November. By the end of the battle the 7th Division had been more or less annihilated, though down in Sailly the 2nd Scots Guards had been away from Ypres for some time.

Their sector was far from being quiet, however. An attack on the German trenches on 18 December resulted in some 180 Scots Guards casualties, about half of those engaged. Throughout the whole of January

and February they were in and out of the line at Sailly. It was a particularly uncomfortable time, the trenches knee-deep in water during wet
weather. On 24 and 25 February there were snowstorms, and for the rest
of the month it remained acutely cold, sometimes foggy. The battalion
was occupied in revetting the sides of the trenches and the parapets and
paradoes that had collapsed in the rain – dispiriting work. Wilfrid was at
least pleased with his fellow-officers' company – particularly Jarvis,
Warner (his company commander), and Sir Edward "Teddy" Hulse, who
had come out a little before him. They made an agreeable contrast to the
"proper collection of bounders" he had encountered at the officers' mess
at Honfleur camp on his arrival in France.

He went into the line on 25 February, when his battalion relieved the
1st Grenadiers. It was a depressing initiation. Sitting down behind the
machine-gun emplacement on a small rise, he surveyed the scene from a
safe vantage-point: "I see a wide and shadowy country. The moon is rising out of the calm night. A little wind whines and whispers among the
sandbags. I see dimly a land of poplars and small trees (dwarf oaks), or-
chards, and plentiful willows. I see flat fields and ditches and plentiful
water, and red farms whose roofs are gone, stark skeletons in the moonlight. I see broad flat spaces and then a ridge – the ridge of Aubers. Only
the German lines are hidden from sight.

"No sign of life. Silence and desolation reign. But here and there the
faint glimmer of a fire indicates the presence of the enemy. Afar off,
rockets, red and green and white, shoot up to the sky; star shells bursting
above the trenches cast their baleful light around. Strange twisted figures
of trees stand out against the horizon . . . ."

Ewart's dugout, which he shared with a fellow officer (other ranks did
not have this luxury) was clammy and messy, but breakfasts of porridge,
bread and marmalade, bacon and eggs, cooked by his servant, made life
bearable. Wilfrid was kept well provided with cake, boiled chicken, and
port, not to mention gumboots and periscopes, his parents being anxious
he should not fare worse than his richer fellow officers.

But if the Guards officers had in general an easier time than the men,
Wilfrid, like many, was irked by the minor monotonies and aggravations
of war. "My servant is an absolute fool," he grumbled to his parents. The
local Northern French population got on his nerves; they were "miserable" people, "Something like Cambridge or Essex but infinitely worse."

He was assailed by toothache – no joke in an Expeditionary Force where most dentistry was carried out by unqualified Medical Officers. He maintained a cheerful front, but, he admitted to his mother, "I wonder how much longer this war is going to last. Everyone who has been out here above a week or two is sick to death of it, & praying for the end, and I am not surprised." "I am quite happy here," he assured both parents a day or two later, "but all the same I shall not be sorry to resume my quiet fancies & I trust that before long we shall happily meet together at home."

By now the battalion were practising at Estaires for a major attack, fixed for 10 March 1915. This was to be a large-scale assault against German positions at Neuve Chapelle and to the north and south of it. It was to test out both the strength of the enemy and the effectiveness of the combined artillery and mass infantry tactics that Sir John French, the B.E.F. commander-in-chief, intended to use on a far larger scale that summer. The 7th Division, of which 2nd Scots Guards in the 20th Infantry Brigade formed part, were to act in support of the 8th Division on the left.

At five o'clock that wintry morning, they marched out of Estaires alongside the other regiments in the Brigade, the 1st Grenadiers, the 2nd Gordon Highlanders, and the 2nd Border Regiment. During the course of the long day that followed Wilfrid met one of his greatest friends, Maurice Darby, who was with the Grenadiers, a welcome contact with a world left behind, for men who had been subjected for hours to the awe-inspiring bellow of British gunfire close at hand. It was the British Army's first major set-piece offensive, but was, as it turned out, both patchy and ill-prepared. The battalion waited all day, gazing out of dugouts at Cameron Lane near Pont du Hem, watching files of German prisoners coming to the rear after the taking of Neuve Chapelle by the 8th Division: "fine great men of the Prussian Guard, very stolid and expressionless (though a few looked scared), with coarse, typically teuton faces. There are smaller fry, too, Saxons and Alsatians, rather untidy and unsoldierlike, and looking with no great favour upon their comrades, the Prussians," wrote Wilfrid. He witnessed too the distressing spectacle of a British plane being accidentally shot down by their own side, the two aviators killed.

The artillery had destroyed the German front line – hence the relative ease with which Neuve Chapelle was captured. But, in a way that was to become all too familiar, the bombardment quite failed to reach German strongpoints further back. So the hope that the infantry and cavalry could now make a serious inroad into the German lines, even as far as Lille, depended on a second attack being pushed through, and this time without the massive artillery bombardment that had preceded the first. It was into a hell of muddy fields and German shell and machine-gun fire that Wilfrid was now to be flung.

At 4 a.m. on 11 March the battalion moved, under orders, to breast-works on the Pont Logy-Fauquissart Road to attack in support of the 1st Grenadiers in the direction of the Moulin du Piètre. Dawn broke as they picked their way silently along a narrow track between fields of liquid mud. As the light grew stronger, so did enemy gunfire. They reached a heavily defended breastwork in which there was little room for the whole battalion to take cover. There followed a weary and dangerous hour of waiting, occupied by eating rations and smoking. Ewart listened, intrigued, to the intermingling of English dialects in this odd place at this odd hour: "Glasgow and Manchester, the burr of Devon, and the cockney Territorials' nasal twang." Then as German shellfire intensified and splinters and shrapnel began to kill or mutilate the closely packed men waiting tensely for the attack, the command came: "'Fix bayonets!' A cold, rasping sound, and six hundred blades flash in the morning sun-light." They had to find their way through a a maze of trenches, knee-deep in water.

At seven the officers' whistles signalled zero hour: the whole front line swarmed through the sandbag breastwork and rushed pell-mell across a hundred yards of open ground, pitted with shell-holes and obstructed by loose strands of barbed wire. Reaching the old German trenches, they found no shelter, for they were broken and overcrowded. Wilfrid saw men fall to left and right of him: "The lad next to me, virile and strong a moment ago, now lies feebly moaning, shot through the body." Advanc-ing in short rushes they hurried on, while the air whistled and tingled with bullets. They took refuge in more abandoned breastworks where British shells had flung far and wide the corpses and equipment of the enemy. Then, after darting along a ridge, they staggered up to their chins in the foul, greenish water of a large ditch that crossed their path, and jog-trotted with their burdensome equipment across an open stretch of ploughed field, heavy with recent rain. Finally, at the far side, and with the enemy not more than a hundred and fifty yards away, they lay down in the only available cover, a long irregular line in a shallow depression. Facing them was a red brick building with a tall chimney that dominated the surrounding country: the Moulin du Piètre, a sinister and invincible obstacle bristling with the enemy's rifles and machine-guns. Shrapnel bursts came as regularly as clockwork within thirty or forty yards. For three hours the 2nd Scots Guards were pinned down there unable to move, their faces in the mud.

Imperfectly sheltered, this crack battalion presented an easy target, and two platoons were eventually ordered to join the 1st Grenadiers in a temporary position further ahead. Ewart rose to his feet with his men, and, as he jumped a ditch, was hit in the left leg and flung down the bank. The pain was such that he could not move for two hours – nor did he dare to do so. As hard to bear was the sound of the German guns close at hand which roared forth in unison every three minutes: "they threatened to burst the brain, they caused a racking headache, these terrible tornadoes of sound. The machine-gun and the rifle fire were as nothing after these." The groans and crying of the wounded were quite as terrible to hear.

Ewart set out to crawl back, but was forced to stop repeatedly as the intensity of the battle grew and receded. Once, he lay for half an hour in a shell-hole with a dead man, thinking the end had come. As the gunfire died down at last, he struggled finally to a welcome line of sandbags, slid precariously past a corpse along a narrow plank straddling a ditch, and made for the dressing station, across a peaceful orchard, full of the dead. He got a ride on a stretcher for the last quarter-mile. From there he was taken in stages by motor ambulance to Number Two Red Cross Hospital, Rouen. To his relief, the medical authorities decided that though his leg bone was not injured, his wound was a "blighty" and in two weeks he went back to England.

As was to be expected, the 20th Brigade had suffered badly at Neuve Chapelle. Maurice Darby lost his life in the same battle where Wilfrid was wounded, while Teddy Hulse died in a renewed and unsuccessful attack the next day. Not long after, the news came that George Wyndham had been killed on 24 March. Ewart did not return to France for six months. Slight though his physical injury had been, the ordeal and the sense of loss undermined his health. After a spell at Princess Beatrice's hospital in Hill Street, London, he convalesced for a long while at his spiritual haven at Broadleas and began to record his war memories in articles that appeared under different pseudonyms. These were among his best writings. They also formed the basis of his descriptions of battle in *Way of Revelation*. After a spell of light duty he returned to the front in October 1915 having missed the battle of Festubert in May, in which his friend Jarvis was killed, and the major offensive at Loos in September.

Since August 1915, all the Guards regiments had been re-formed into a single "Guards Division." The 2nd Scots Guards formed part of the 3rd Guards Brigade. The change was achieved by increasing the number of Guards battalions, but there was little diminution in quality, because the hard training of Caterham was maintained, and because the Division's homogeneity compared favourably with most other wartime divisions: no less than eight of its twelve battalions had existed before the war, and all were from Guards regiments. There was a built-in *esprit de corps* in a division composed of "Jocks," Coalies, "Micks," "Taffys," and "Bill Browns." By contrast, in divisions made up of a congeries of units with different traditions and training, greater efforts were needed to forge a divisional spirit, often successfully, as in the 18th and 19th Divisions, sometimes less so. Though an èlite division, that did not mean the Guards Division was spared any "routine" fighting that was expected of the line regiments; and there were times when they were expected to carry the brunt of the battle.

Wilfrid rejoined his battalion at Cantrainne on 31 October, with a draft of 62 other ranks. He liked his new Company Commander, Captain Arkwright, who unfortunately soon afterwards collapsed with a nervous breakdown, to be succeeded by Captain J. A. Stirling, an ebullient figure with a strong interest in literature who was eventually to be a great ally of Ewart's though Ewart first thought him "an awful gas-bag." During early December there was a twelve-day spell in the trenches at "Winchester House" near La Flinque. These were heavily waterlogged, and full of rats. Out of consideration for the health of the men, it was army policy to keep as small a garrison as was safe during the wetter months in the front lines. This was achieved by a system of lines of posts and strongpoints, rather than continuous trenches. Wilfrid spent much of his time by himself at a god-forsaken spot known as Lonely Post with a depressing view of the line close to the Neuve Chapelle battlefield, of evil memory: "Some of the dead men of the Rifle Brigade still lay out in front, while behind, to cheer me up, there was a perfect forest of little mud graves and crosses, mostly very rough, and marked, 'In memory of a British Soldier, R.I.P.'" Small raids to harass the enemy and secure information were frequent.

His most extraordinary experience of the war came on Christmas Day 1915. For the second time during the war, the battalion was involved in an unofficial truce between fighting men on each side. "Both sides have played the game," Captain G. H. Loder had reported the previous year in the battalion diary, "and I know that this [German] Regiment anyhow has learnt to trust an Englishman's word."

This was easier said than done, however, particularly as the war went on. Neither the British nor the German High Command liked truces. As Stephen Graham later commented: "The regimental tone always forbade admiration of anything in connection with Germans. "Killing Huns" was our cheerful task, as one of our leaders once told us. The idea of taking prisoners had become very unpopular among the men." The truce of the sort that Wilfrid witnessed in 1915, between the 2nd Scots Guards and the 95th Bavarian Reserve Infantry Regiment, was not repeated in identical form, although many truces, in varied guises, were to continue throughout the war. The battalion was in trenches east of Laventie. "So soon as it grows light, we start peeping at each other over the top of the parapet . . . calling to each other. And presently, at about 7.50, a German stands up openly on the parapet and waves his arms. He is followed by two in field-grey overcoats and pill-box caps. Then they come out all down the line, stand up on the parapet, wave, shout, and finally swarm forth from their trenches on either side."

At this point occurred a real moment of tragedy, though it was immediately brushed aside in that strange ecstatic moment: Sergeant Oliver, a fine, popular man, was shot dead almost at once as he stood on the parapet. His body, covered with a blanket, lay there all day: "But it makes no difference," wrote Ewart. "It must be an accident. The supreme craving of humanity, the irresistible, spontaneous impulse born of a common faith and a common fear fully triumph."

The officers, including Ewart, stayed back in the trenches with a few N.C.O.s and sentries. They could see the others meeting at the willow-lined stream in the middle, laughing, gesticulating, shaking hands. They traded bully-beef, cigarettes, ration biscuits, and tobacco for sausage, sauerkraut, concentrated coffee, and cigars. There were exchanges in broken English:

"'What sort of trenches have you?'

'Rotten! Knee deep in mud and water. Not fit for pigs.'

'Aren't you sick of the war? We are!'

'Not a bit.'"

For ten minutes there was peace and goodwill, then two German officers in shiny field boots came out, asking to take photographs of the "Tommies," a request that was refused. Shortly after they warned the British to get back into their trenches before the German artillery opened fire in five minutes. A few Guardsmen were wounded as they returned to their side; but from neither trenches were any shots fired for the next twenty-four hours. As Ewart later recorded: "A common brotherhood of suffering – or is it an act of God, or just human curiosity? – has united Englishman and Bavarian in fraternity this grey Christmas morning which no one on either side who has taken part in this quaint scene will ever forget." This time however the battalion diary avoided saying too much about it: "All very quiet in the morning though there had been a good deal of shouting accross [sic] from one trench to another during the night."

Following a brief period of leave, and a safer spell in February with what he called in a letter, perhaps by way of disinformation, the "Seventh Guards (Entrenching) battalion" down on the Somme, Ewart was recalled to the 2nd Scots Guards, who were moving up to Ypres. He missed the first few unpleasant weeks through illness and another leave. On 19 May he went with the battalion into the Ypres Salient for a week's work on the defences.

It was, as he feared, "unholy Hell." Snipers made it impossible to do anything by day, but at night, in the brief four summer hours between

dawn and dusk, they hurried through their duties, patrolling, engineering, carrying, ration-bearing, and digging new trenches in the spongy,
waterlogged ground full of rotting corpses and rusty war *matériel*. From
time to time the colossal explosions of *Minenwerfer* bombs bursting, and
the terrifying rush of bullets as the enemy machine-guns swept round,
sent the men flat on their stomachs. The barking of German messenger
dogs, the vivid flashes from the British artillery, the stertorous breathing
of the diggers at work, the dark, hardly identifiable figures prowling
about, and the screams of the wounded – it was a scene to haunt the
imagination.

When they were out of the line, Wilfrid plucked up courage to apply
to his Commanding Officer, Col. Roger Tempest, to be allowed to go
back to England on medical grounds to take up a staff appointment. The
regimental medical officer had recommended this because of Wilfrid's
acute indigestion. Tempest was unsympathetic, telling him that he would
not let him go unless he was constitutionally unfit and that he ought to
do very well. "I could say no more," Wilfrid confided to his father,
"though I felt quite justified in making the application especially as I am
afraid I am losing my nerve under fire. I found it an awful strain up in
the salient last week – much more so than before – and if it came to a
fight I think that would finish me off. However I don't like to put it on
those grounds as Roger's remedy for it is to send a bloke out on night
patrol the first opportunity!"

He continued to hope for a chance of leaving the battalion. Roger
Tempest was a notoriously hard taskmaster, though fair-minded. Moving
into rest billets, for part of the time, meant no rest for the battalion who
were trained and drilled incessantly. Wilfrid awaited eagerly the outcome
of his father's approaches to his kinsman, Lieut-Gen. Sir John Spencer
Ewart, about finding him staff work. Meanwhile, he acquitted himself
well, taking temporary charge of his company for a while in July. All the
time, it was as he put it, "pretty lively" for the battalion in the Salient, and
particularly after they moved up, in late June, into the front line, where
the trenches were in an appalling state from enemy shelling and heavy
rainfall. The sense of barrenness and desolation was overwhelming: "with
night in the Salient," he wrote, "there comes a sense of loneliness and
neighbouring death."

Early in July, the battalion had a further spell of duty at the sector of the Salient known as Canal Bank. Their new position had a weird beauty. Ewart recalled the spectacle of the great Yser Canal by night: "this waterway with its countless little lights blinking against high, mysterious banks and its sullen, stagnant, lapping water which reflects the lights, the stars, and, sailing above, the cold moon . . . It looks seductive, exotic, populous, compared to the bleak perilous world outside . . . The Canal is the clear-cut borderline between humanity and the shadowy nether-world of Ypres."

Finally, in late July came the order for the Guards Division to move south to join in the Battle of the Somme, which had been raging since the beginning of the month. No matter what waited for them at the other end, the relief at leaving the accursed Salient, to be marching long distances through the summer countryside, was truly a deliverance. Ewart himself was ecstatic, revelling in the great heat, the shady oakwoods, the flocks of finches, the night skies bejewelled with stars, the laughing schoolboy-like columns of young soldiers, the skirl of the regimental bagpipes. This was the breath of Peace – and Life! Eventually, by 1 August, they were in camp at Bus les Artois. For nearly a fortnight it was for Ewart a time of unsullied enjoyment – despite endless drill and parades and practice attacks – in glorious sunshine. The landscape, rolling chalkland, was after his own heart, with its small villages and scattered woods. When finally, on 12 August, the battalion made their way up into reserve, the trenches themselves were deep and dry.

Ewart's cheerfulness did not last. Although the conditions were far better, the ferocity of the fighting was quite as intense as round Ypres. He also received bad news. His sister Angela's husband, Jack Farmer, an officer in the 60th Rifles (King's Royal Rifle Corps), was killed in the fighting round Delville Wood, only two months after the birth of the baby daughter he had never seen. Greatly upset, Wilfrid searched for Jack's grave, in vain. Then, in September, while on a Lewis gun course at Le Touquet he contracted severe gastroenteritis. It persisted and he was sent home, this time for a long period.

However distressing they had been, he looked back on the past weeks with some pride. Once again he had been acting company commander for a period. The dictatorial Tempest, indeed, went so far as to congratulate him: "Ewart . . . I hear that you are doing very well indeed, I notice you are getting much more self-confidence." All the same it was galling not to receive a company of his own, and his illness postponed any such promotion.

He was away for eleven months, recuperating in Derbyshire and then on Home duty at Wellington Barracks in London. As before he enjoyed *beau monde* life and revels made all the more hectic for the journey to the front that awaited most of the men. "What is the meaning and purpose of it all? And the sparkling eyes, the feverish excited faces, the animated gestures? . . . Night after night it has gone on; and even in the afternoon . . . And on the river and in quiet gardens at weekends and at the tennis parties . . . The pulse beats quickly, the blood races, perhaps it is the champagne coursing through the veins? Not a boy or a girl there but has had a 'flutter,' some trifling *affaire de coeur*, but cherishes some little one to whom the heart (for a while) returns."

Wilfrid's heart was no exception. Dollie Rawson was the granddaughter of the 2nd Earl of Lichfield, and sister-in-law of Lord Leconfield, cousin of George Wyndham, Wilfrid's friend. She lived with her widowed mother in Cadogan Square, near the Ewarts' home, and in the country at Gravenhurst in Essex. She was eighteen years old and strikingly beautiful in a romantic untidy style, with a clear complexion, regular English features, and a cascade of bright brown hair, which she normally wore up, in the fashion of the period. She was bold and vivacious. She throve on parties and gossip. Their romance, as far as it went, lasted no more than a few months.

After Wilfrid returned to the front he realised, like Sir Adrian Knoyle in *Way of Revelation*, though probably less brutally, that Dollie was no longer interested in him. She was too attractive and too young to have stayed faithful, and in any case they were not well matched. Moreover the wartime mood and the abandonment of Victorian ideals encouraged an "easy come, easy go" attitude to which Wilfrid was ill-suited. The war was so awful to contemplate, and so unimaginable to those who stayed at home, that many young women like Dollie slipped readily into a superficial and frivolous attitude towards it. "They recoiled from it," Ewart wrote later, "they could not face it, they could not pause to think things out. It were as though they rushed hence to the bosom of satiety, there to lose themselves, there by all means to forget the shadowy spectre."

The mood among young people at home had changed, he noticed, from a "sombre hush" in the first year of the war, to an increasing spirit of recklessness and a craving for amusement to which women in his world (what he called "Sloane Street") yielded even more than men. The atmosphere at the London parties he went to was strongly sexual, and girls were lucky if they did not lose their sense of decency.

He did not find it a happy mood, though it might seem so: "Gaiety was a tonic. But one may doubt whether this was gaiety in its later phases, whether it was not rather a furious *danse macabre* . . . It was indeed difficult to see spontaneous enjoyment, let alone romance, at a time when tragedy in many forms was being forced home to the hilt day after day. Certain it is . . . that an intense electric current pervaded the world of women, more especially the London world . . . . Nobody can even estimate the burden of surcharged emotion carried in those days; it could never be told."

Ewart was certainly quoting Dollie, among others, when he added that during the war: "The commonest phrase to be heard was 'What's the matter with one? One can't sit still.'" Nobody wanted any entertainment except light comedy and musicals; nor conversation except the purely flippant. "It was modish to minimise," commented Stephen Graham. "Thousands of women sent their men to the trenches with a "Toodle-oo, old thing!" and flirted light-heartedly in their absence."

Wilfrid's was by no means the last heart Dollie broke, and within four years she was married to another Guards officer, with a title and a Military Cross; but Wilfrid took a long time to forget her, and there is little doubt that his unhappiness in the last year of the war came largely from this disappointment. He cast her as "Lady Rosemary Meynell" in his novel, and allowed himself the revenge of consigning her to death by drugs. But the real Dollie was made of tougher stuff, even if he was correct in believing that the war did have a lasting, and disastrous, effect on her behaviour. (Thirty-five years on, and divorced, she was still going to parties, out in Kenya, driving long distances across country alone, despite bandits and terrorists, a gun beside her in her Land Rover.)

Wilfrid took his leave of her at a party at the end of July 1917, walking back home through the rain at dawn, heavy at heart, to bathe, pack his haversack, eat breakfast, and get to the station. It took thirty-six hours to reach his battalion in Flanders, in company with a fellow officer,

Lieut. Hamilton, and a draft of a hundred other ranks, the images of his last evening in England still in his mind – the girls in satin and chiffon gowns, the men resplendent in dark blue and scarlet mess uniform, the black musicians playing ragtime frenziedly, the chatter on the stairs, the excited whispering in parlours and bedrooms thrown open for the revels.

The scene that confronted him on arrival at the bivouac in Deconck, the day after the opening attack of the Third Battle of Ypres, was almost unbearable: "There are a few stunted wind-blown trees, a few husks of buildings scattered about, a landscape that is intersected by ditches, mud-tracks, pools of stagnant water; in the foreground the ghost of a great church tower set amid wind-riven poplars; for the rest, a mere waste of nondescript weed-grown fields, grey and colourless as the sky – and mud, mud everywhere."

On 4 August 1917 his battalion was back in the battle line. They were bombarded all day by the enemy and frequently by their own side. Wilfrid's company commander was Esmond Elliot, the twenty-one-year-old younger son of the Earl of Minto who had been Viceroy of India before the war. Esmond was the model for "Eric" in *Way of Revelation*. Wilfrid has left a description of him that day, as they huddled in what passed for a trench: "The youth in the corner you cannot but admire. He has no fear in the sense that is compatible with one's own safety. To have no fear is to court death, and the reckless ones always pay the penalty in war. But here you have the direct product of our much abused public school system, of that class in England which is said to be effete and worn-out. It is true that physically he is of fragile and delicate build; that he looks as much like a girl as a boy. Nevertheless the small frame is wiry and the heart vigorous and great. Nor is a quick intelligence lacking in one whose patronymic is coupled with an Empire statesmanship."

The two men discussed the future eagerly together and Wilfrid fed his friend with the London gossip until they were interrupted by the roar and hiss of shells as the British artillery bombarded Langemarck, and great columns of smoke, brick dust, and pulverised masonry, copper-red, sulphur-yellow, grey-white, rose sixty feet into the air from the shattered village. At nightfall, the company hastened to strengthen the line, digging down deeper. Then, at about one in the morning, the Germans launched an attack. Esmond Elliot was hit in the back and arm. He was in great pain, and plainly doomed: "Give me morphia and put an M on my forehead," he repeated, and again and again.

Wilfrid took over the company. After the attack had been beaten off they did what they could for Elliot. There was no morphia, only brandy. Now failing and still in agony, he was lifted out of a trench on a stretcher, taking leave of the company with a faint "Goodbye!" – the last word Wilfrid heard from his friend.

There were other deaths in the battalion, and dispiritingly little ground gained. Wilfrid was already yearning for the six months' light duty to which he would be entitled by next April. He also tried to pull strings to get his uncle "Sandie" Ruthven to offer him a staff job. Despite the horrors of returning to Ypres, however, Wilfrid found some mitigating factors. The excellent new Commanding Officer, Lieut-Col. Norman Orr-Ewing, was a good deal more popular than Roger Tempest and Wilfrid liked the officers who were out there with him. Again he had temporary charge of a company, and began once more to hope that he would at least earn recognition in the form of a captaincy. A further compensation was leave in Paris with friends, lunching in the Bois de Boulogne and dining at Ciro's and Maxim's.

By mid-September however he was generally disconsolate. It was quite clear, he told his father, that the Third Battle of Ypres had been a failure so far, and since there was little more than a month of the "biffing" season left, the prospects of a victory here were very slim, since the Germans seemed quite equal to the task of blocking the British. What with the disorder in Russia and the superiority of Germany in the air, he could see the war going on for another two years. He was at pains to point out how much the English press had misled the public on the military situation.

At the end of September, he was sent to the Fifth Army Infantry School for a five-week Company Commanders' Course well away from Ypres, near Amiens. He took the opportunity to go up to the Somme battlefield, twelve miles away; once again he tried to search for his brother-in-law Jack Farmer's grave. Every landmark – roads, houses, and villages – had been blotted out and he only reached the right area, by map and compass, when it was too dark to read inscriptions.

He spent three weeks leave at home in London, perhaps the time when he learned that Dollie was no longer interested in him. If after that he flirted, like Richard Aldington and Adrian Knoyle in his own novel, with the idea of deliberately letting himself be killed, then fate on his return to the front was astonishingly perverse.

The ghastly Third Battle of Ypres was over, leaving the British army exhausted. Before the year's end, however, one more great effort was asked of it, and of the Guards Division in particular. Secret plans had been made for an advance on Cambrai, using tanks in large numbers to force the abandonment of the German "Hindenburg" line. The initial attack, launched on 20 November, was highly successful; but the tanks were unable to cross the Scheldt river and the two crucial points, Flesquières ridge and Bourlon Wood, remained untaken. The 40th Division succeeded in penetrating the wood and were just hanging on after three days when a further German counterattack on 24 November pushed the British into retreat in a state by some described as close to panic.

Meanwhile, the Guards Division had been sent to retrieve the situation. The 2nd Scots Guards entered the wood just after nine o'clock on 24 November. Wilfrid wrote to his parents, when the attack was over: "Bourlon Wood was a nightmare sort of place – pitch dark and no one knew its tortuous ways or quite where the Germans were. It is a big wood divided up by rides and summer roads. After going halfway through it, very heavy rifle and machine-gun fire broke out in front on the farther edge of the wood, lights going up all round. Several men got hit, and down the ride came a surging mob of cavalrymen, infantry, and engineers absolutely out of control, shouting and yelling that the Germans had broken in and were coming through the wood. It was a fine example of New Army discipline." Later he was more charitable, talking of "shattered, nerveless men whose human nature had been tried past endurance." At any rate it proved a false alarm, though the battalion waited with fixed bayonets for some time in an agony of suspense.

Then they advanced slowly in the eerie darkness, hearing only the drip, drip, drip of rain from the trees – no sound of wild creatures: all had fled. The next day there was the same silence. Eventually they encountered the enemy: two battalions of the Prussian Guards were there in force with several machine-guns and were too strong for them; but orders came to clear the wood at all costs.

Reinforced by the three battalions composing the 1st Guards Brigade, the 2nd Scots Guards attacked at 2.0 p.m, lined up along a summer ride and going over at the tail end of a sleet storm. Too late, Command realised the attack was hopeless, and tried to stop it. Wilfrid was with F Company under Lieut. A. R. W. Menzies. They rapidly ran into the main German force. Menzies and Sergeant Maclean were killed with all the leading men when they tried to rush the German machine-guns, which then slewed round on to Wilfrid and those with him, including the heroic Sergeant Fotheringham D.C.M. and a man named Grant. They flung themselves down: "for the next twenty minutes there was nothing but a young oak tree between us three and eternity. The machine-gun fired absolutely point blank, but could not quite reach us on account of the tree. Most of the platoon got down in a depression about twenty-five yards behind, but about eight men, including two Lewis Gunners, were almost up with us. These kept on firing for all they were worth, and the Lewis Gunners working their guns in the open until they were killed. Every man was killed one after the other, and Grant is the only man left alive besides myself."

While Wilfrid was taking cover, he witnessed by far the nastiest sight he had seen in the whole war: the Germans burning up the British dead and wounded with phosphorus bombs. The three remained trapped behind the tree for some twenty minutes. As the firing slackened they tried to make a dash for it: first Grant, then Fotheringham, who was mortally wounded trying to rescue one of the Lewis guns, and finally Wilfrid: "I waited about five minutes then did a lightning sprint on my stomach, and by all natural laws ought to have been hit – the bullets were knocking stones up into my face. However, I got back in the end. It is an experience I shall never wish to repeat, and it is no compensation for the loss of people like Menzies, and Sergeants Fotheringham and Maclean to know that what they were asked to do was absolutely impossible. It is little consolation even to know that the Corps General has been sent home." (Lieut-Gen. Sir C. Woolcombe was still commanding IV Corps on 1 December, but Haig, unhappy about his performance, had asked Gen. Byng, commanding 3rd Army, to take personal control of IV Corps on 25 November, and Woolcombe was eventually replaced by Gen. Harper.)

Ewart was transferred to take command of F Company, and the next day the company marched back six miles and had a day's rest. They were expecting that they would then go out of the line for a month, when the Germans staged a tremendous counterattack, with *Stosstruppen*, èlite shock troops, to the fore. Before this onslaught, the British army in the salient around Cambrai reeled and broke. "The whole of at least one Division were running for their lives," recalled Wilfrid. The 3rd Guards Brigade, including the 2nd Scots Guards, were ordered to advance and engage the enemy. In fact the other two Guards Brigades, advancing coolly in diamond formation, had already cleared the ridge and retaken Gouzeaucourt in the valley beyond. It was one of the Guards Division's greatest triumphs: "if they had not been on the spot it is difficult to estimate where the enemy would have been checked," the Commander-in-Chief of the British Expeditionary Force, General Haig, wrote in his diary. Although the 3rd Brigade and Wilfrid's unit, F Company 2nd Scots Guards, had contributed relatively little to this or to the British counterattack that followed, he shared in the pride felt by the whole Division.

Despite his ordeal, Ewart was for a while buoyed up by the experience. He actually seems to have enjoyed Christmas and the battalion dinner and a still more riotous sergeants' concert, "a fearsome orgy," a day or two later: "They all got blind to a man, and everybody's health had to be drunk in whiskey punch. One blighter kept shouting out: 'Good old Mr. Ewitt! Good old Mr. Ewitt! he led me over the top,' but personally I could not remember the occasion."

The inevitable reaction came, and Wilfrid was not alone in feeling dejected and nervously exhausted in that grim New Year of 1918. After a brief respite on a wireless telegraphy course, he returned to the trenches in the Gavrelle-Roeux sector, east of Arras. Hard frosts of 20 to 30 degrees followed by violent thaws had caused the trenches to collapse on the entire front of 500 yards. Neither the Germans nor the British could use them and both sides took to walking about in full view of one another, without shooting.

Despite the warm praise of his commanding officer, Norman Orr-Ewing, Wilfrid, still unpromoted and racked with neuralgia, was thoroughly depressed. His February leave had been cancelled. He tantalised himself with the possibility of six months light duty in England, to which all officers were entitled after two years actual field service; but he knew he had not yet clocked up this amount, even though he had done longer service than any other subaltern and had been over the top three times. "Often I feel extraordinarily weary," he wrote, "and that they have had the best out of me. I cannot look forward with confidence to any more battles." Once again he asked his father to approach "Sandie" Ruthven about a staff job for him.

Eventually, in March, his leave came through and spared him the ordeal that he and his battalion had been dreading for weeks: the great German attack, long in preparation, which burst on them on 21 March. He missed the Fourth Battle of Arras in which the German attack was finally contained, after they had pushed the Third Army back almost to that city. When he rejoined them, the 2nd Scots Guards had retreated to positions in the Bucquoy-Ayette system of trenches, southwest of Arras, along with the rest of the Guards Division. Despite the continued German efforts to break through, he and his battalion were not involved in any of the heaviest fighting faced by the British during April and early May. His luck was beginning to turn a little: he at last achieved his captaincy and in June he was appointed General Staff Officer 3rd Grade to a Division with the 36th French Army Corps (liaison), a possibility that had been tantalisingly held out to him for most of the previous month. His only disappointment at this time was that nothing came of his citation for an M.C. for his part in the Bourlon Wood attack.

In June, he had another leave in Paris, this time in a morbid, *danse macabre* frame of mind, repelled by the world of vice but also fascinated by it as an observer, finding in it a sexual expression of his feelings of horror and desolation and a kind of vicious antidote to the London Society life, which he felt had betrayed him. It did little for his stability.

A more down-to-earth sickness caught him when he returned to his duties, designated, as usual, P.U.O. – the latest version of trench fever. It put him in hospital for three weeks, which was just as well, for his liaison job had been postponed. The best aspect of his present existence was that Private Stephen Graham had now joined the battalion. A well-known prewar journalist and author, Graham was an expert on Russian life and politics, had travelled widely in Eastern Europe, and was a fervent Christian. Major Stirling, who had succeeded Orr-Ewing as Commanding Officer, introduced the two men. They were drawn to one another:

"there seems to be a breadth, strength, and humanity about him which I have never known approached in our limited intensely mediocre circle," Wilfrid told his sister Angela. "I can't imagine him going down at say, 7 Knightsbridge or 8 West Eaton Place. But does it matter? I have an idea that I shall like to accompany him on one of his wanderings after the war."

Graham was nearly ten years older, and there were the constraints of the military system between them. Yet as Graham said, "our true calling was evidently greater than the call of arms." They spent hours when they could talking about life and literature, the only kindred literary spirits in a unit that counted talent for writing a defect rather than a distinction. "It is difficult to write much and be a soldier too," Wilfrid confided to Graham. "It's not liked. You see, in all these things you have read, I never use my own name or refer to the regiment." Graham later claimed that it was he who put the idea of *Way of Revelation* into Wilfrid's head, with the suggestion that he write up all this wartime experience as a novel, using his London life as a background for it. "You can then say what you like, and you can write it over your own name. And if it succeeds it will be far more effective than any volume of essays and sketches could possibly be in England."

Graham was his orderly when Wilfrid returned to the front in the fourth week of August and became Battalion Transport Officer, taking up ammunition and rations to the battalion every night. The Third Army was now involved in a major push against the enemy as the war began at last to go in the Allies' favour. On the second day of their attack the Third Army captured St. Lèger, to the east of their position near Arras. The fighting was extremely fierce, though during the next few days the 2nd Scots Guards did not sustain the worst casualties, and Wilfrid himself, on his long night rides to and from the advancing battle front, was unscathed. Nonetheless he still hoped to escape by means of the ever-elusive staff appointment that he craved. The war was as dangerous as ever, for all that the Germans were losing it; and it was ugly: "The Battalion killed a lot of Bosches," he told his parents on 1 September, "the order being "No prisoners," so they did in everybody, including the blokes who put up their hands." Finally, a riding accident delivered him. He was thrown while galloping along a track near Berles au Bois, and knocked unconscious for two hours. It was the end of the war for him.

Wilfred stayed in the army until 1919. He did not rejoin his battalion for its triumphal march through Belgium into occupied Germany, but remained on home duty as the demobilisation officer. He felt only a great weariness after the Armistice and, like Richard Aldington, was suffering from a delayed reaction to the horrors of the past four years. The scandalous aftermath of the Victory Ball in November 1918 intensified his depression: the popular young actress, Billie Carleton, who had been at the party, had died the next day from an overdose of cocaine, and as a result the fashionable couturier, Reggie de Veulle, and other more disreputable figures, were imprisoned for drug-dealing.

Wilfred resumed his journalism. He took digs in Drayton Gardens, near his father's London home, and led a spartan existence, turning out articles on his war experiences, on changes in English society, and on country life. Periodically he tried to heal his unhappy spirit by seeking rural solitude. In the winter of 1919-20 on the North Norfolk coast he watched the wild geese coming to land. After four years at sea during the war, one Norfolk longshoreman told him; "the first thing I heard was the ould grey-legs calling, and then I sez to m'self, 'Oh well,' I sez, 'now I'm really home at last.'"

Striving for that kind of reassurance, Wilfrid also rode out on his motorcycle to Dorset, where in secluded villages he found "aloofness from the world . . . and from the distortions of men and from the very spirit of the times in which we live." He paid a pilgrimage to Thomas Hardy. Both men were tongue-tied on meeting, but a sort of silent good feeling was established.

His chief escape from the restless modern world became closed to him in March 1922 when his cousin Margaret Ewart died, Broadleas passed to his cousins and her abiding spirit, the mainstay of his existence for so many years, was now withdrawn from it. He commemorated her and the house in one of his best pieces, "The Passing of a Victorian."

There was another obligation to his family that he had fulfilled in October 1919, travelling with his sister Angela to try, for a last time, to find the grave of her husband Jack Farmer, at Longueval, near Delville Wood. Orchard Trench, the object of the attack of 18 August 1916, was still full of helmets, muddy boots, and shaving tackle – the debris of war. The crosses marking the resting places of British soldiers were forest-thick nearby, but the light failed before the two pilgrims could find what they sought. In the end Angela laid the laurel cross she had brought at an apple tree's foot close to the place of Jack's death.

"The rain," wrote Wilfrid, "began to sweep up in gusts and a grey drab light to blend with the sombre landscape that now became a monochrome in grey. Grey-green the slopes of the valley, grey-green the soil at our feet, greyish-white the stumps of the shattered trees, grey the German crosses, and the crosses of the unknown British soldiers, grey the ruins of the chateau and village, grey the sky above."

For much of the time, he devoted himself in earnest to the war novel that he and Graham had discussed. A first effort, "Love and Strife," did not satisfy him, and remained unfinished, though it was probably quite as true a statement of his feelings and experiences as the far more ambitious project into which he now plunged. Angela, just remarried, though still mourning her first husband, helped her brother by reading his proofs and looking after him while he worked on *Way of Revelation*. Stephen Graham and his wife loaned the use of their cottage at Faygate, near Horsham in Sussex, where he wrote for many weeks, outdoors, at a table under the trees.

Of all the publishers approached, Putnam's were the only firm not to be daunted by the book's gigantic scale. They imposed cuts. Otherwise there is some confusion about the degree of their intervention. During the 1920s, Henry Williamson came to feel a strong affinity with Wilfrid after reading his book and claimed in an essay he wrote several years later that Wilfrid was so upset by the alterations forced on him by Constant Huntington at Putnam's that he had a stroke and a nervous breakdown and that the Victory Ball chapter was completely rewritten, against his will, by Mrs. Huntington.

This was mostly nonsense. In the summer of 1921, after the book was finished and Wilfrid was waiting for it to be published, he was commissioned by *The Times* to write a series of articles on the "troubles" in Ireland. He did this efficiently, the result being later anthologised as a book. During his investigations he was often in danger and showed considerable *sang-froid* – impossible for a man on the verge of collapse.

As to the actual changes to the manuscript, it is clear that Huntington was worried about how the public would respond to Lady Rosemary's moral decline and wanted Wilfrid to cut out any hint of depravity in the description of her at the climax; there is only the scantiest evidence, however, that Wilfrid took any notice of what Huntington wanted, or that the decision to make her a drug addict was any other than his own, though a letter from the publisher suggests that in one version, which has not survived, Rosemary may have been depicted as pregnant with a love-child. Williamson himself later admitted that he had probably been misled; for he subsequently learned that a close relation of Wilfrid's (who can only be Angela) vigorously denied that the author of *Way of Revelation* had suffered a nervous collapse while writing it.

What is certain is that Putnam's insisted on extensive cuts, so that the book, though massive, is not impossibly long. In other respects, too, they were helpful: they paid a good advance, met all his typing expenses, and let him run up large printing bills for corrections at the galley-proof stage. The book came out in late autumn after an energetic publicity campaign and was an immediate success. Wilfrid revelled in his triumph and threw himself into the London literary world, grateful for admiration at last.

It was too much for him. It was now, in April 1922, and not the year before, that he broke down. The loss of Broadleas exacerbated this. He could not write. His fingers seemed paralysed. He rambled inconsequentially. He was close to tears. He lost weight. He was forced to abandon his literary undertakings and, so Stephen Graham claimed, his hopes of marriage to a woman he loved. As he calmed down, he accepted Graham's invitation to stay with him and recover in Santa Fe, New Mexico.

He crossed to America in September, carrying with him a metal box containing notes for a history of the Scots Guards in the war. In the dry New Mexico climate, he recovered the use of his fingers and was soon writing two thousand words a day. He developed new enthusiasms, particularly for watching the ritual dances of the Indian tribes, which he described with considerable poetic power.

He was still not back to normal, however, when he learned that the Grahams, on whom he was very dependent, had decided to go to Mexico for a winter holiday. They felt that he should stay and finish his book now that he was properly settled, or he would risk another breakdown. He protested that he felt bitterly cold, so they compromised on a plan for him to spend Christmas in New Orleans. His baggage was despatched in advance.

On his way to Louisiana, he changed his mind and decided to travel via Mexico City, a detour of a mere four thousand miles. When he arrived in the Mexican capital, he was delighted by the parks and the climate, and, ignoring the city's dubious political reputation and violence, resolved to send to New Orleans for his tin box of papers and his clothes and finish the Guards book in some pretty village outside the city.

The Grahams had heard of his wanderings, so they were not surprised when they came upon him, an eccentric Englishman in jodhpurs and puttees, standing on a street corner gazing myopically into the sky. There was a happy reunion, and a delightful trip to San Angel outside the city, where they devoured strawberries and gazed from the terraces down at the plain below and the great mountain masses of Popocatapetl and Ixtaccihuatl. After a revue at a theatre in town, and a late dinner, they parted on the last night of the Old Year, 1922, with Wilfrid resolving to join the Grahams at their hotel the next day. He seemed full of life and plans for the future. On the streets the merrymakers were sounding the horns of their cars and firing their guns into the air.

Back in his hotel room, Wilfrid could hear the revels reaching a crescendo as midnight struck and went out to the balcony to gaze at the street scene four floors below. It was then that a bullet, fired at random by a reveller, caught him in the eye – his blind eye – and killed him immediately. The bullet must have been almost spent, for though it entered his brain, it did not make an exit hole.

It was a freak accident, but not a strange one for Mexico City. The same evening an English journalist had been knocked down and killed by a carload of drunken men in carnival mood, and in that week an English businessman had been shot in the crossfire between two duelling army officers.

Wilfrid was buried in the English cemetery on 3 January at a funeral attended by 24 members of the British colony. In London, his father learnt the heartbreaking news in the cruellest way, by receiving calls from the press. After all the anxiety over his son during the past nine years – the war, Ireland, the breakdown – it was bitter now that he should lose him through this unlikely, almost absurd, mishap. Wilfrid's family held a requiem mass for him at St. Mary's Bourne Street, and subsequently put up an altar incorporating a memorial to him, designed by Goodhart-Rendel, a fine example of "Gothic revival revival."

A year later Stephen Graham also commemorated him in a volume: *The Life and Last Words of Wilfrid Ewart*. Based on reminiscences of Ewart's family and friends, as well as on many of his articles, it is a valuable memoir, if a little cloying and with a tendency to exaggerate – the Ewarts' poverty for example. It contains a reproduction of a fine portrait of Wilfrid by Norah Cundall, showing a grave, contemplative seated figure, impeccably dressed and looking closer to forty than thirty.

In 1925, *The Scots Guards in the Great War* appeared, containing Wilfrid's opening chapters. These were slightly criticised by fellow guardsmen for relying too heavily on the diaries of an officer, Jamie Balfour, who does not seem to have been popular, but they were otherwise well received.

These two volumes were not, however, destined to be Wilfrid's last words. Eight years later, new books by him began to appear. The first, *When Armageddon Came: Studies in Peace and War*, came out in 1933. The introduction, signed "G," described Ewart as a great writer who had "immortalised a generation" in *Way of Revelation*. It would ultimately rank, "G" proclaimed confidently, with the best of Gorki, Balzac, and Zola. The new book was a rather loosely assembled collection of articles Ewart had written long before, but was justified by some excellent wartime recollections, "At Neuve Chapelle" and "Memory of Bourlon Wood," describing climactic moments in the fighting.

It was followed a year later by *Scots Guard*, an autobiographical account of Wilfrid's war service, his postwar pilgrimage with Angela to the Somme battlefield, memories of the English countryside, and impressions of North America and Mexico just before his death. It is laid out as a diary, compiled from Ewart's letters. It is actually Ewart's best book, his letters having a spontaneity and power lacking in his novel.

In 1936, Ewart's abandoned novel, *Love and Strife*, was published by Richards. It tells the story of Michael Urquhart, who goes to the war after a crisis in his emotional life, and is left wounded and stranded, at odds with his times. After the war ends he searches for a world he had lost and finds inner peace finally in an old hill-fort, Stane Hill, gazing over Salisbury Plain, convinced that this view of the England to which he has been born will outlast all wars and turmoil. Soon afterwards he dies of consumption.

For all its patchiness, *Love and Strife* is an interesting work and has more distinction and individuality than most war books of its period. The passages on the English countryside are particularly fine and, save for a contrived end, it is altogether less theatrical than *Way of Revelation*.

It was the rural scene, again, that was the subject of the dead Ewart's last book, *Aspects of England* (1937). Although it was made up of articles he had written many years before, it was a book well suited to the ribbon-developed England of the thirties when nostalgia about a disappearing country way of life was the vogue.

"G," the individual who brought about this momentary resurrection of Ewart's reputation as a writer, was no less than the egregious "John Gawsworth" (Terence Fitton Armstrong), a good traditional minor poet in the Georgian vein, and a man of wide erudition and sensibilities. Gawsworth's unusual literary palette, and eye for forgotten authors of talent, made him an indefatigable reviver of reputations. Wilfrid appealed to him as a tragic and romantic figure, a nature mystic in revolt against the *beau monde* from which he came.

Wilfrid's father was delighted when Gawsworth began to take an interest, thanking him warmly for *Strange Assembly*, a book of poems dedicated to Wilfrid's memory. He provided Gawsworth with copies of letters and articles and the manuscript of *Love and Strife,* which he unearthed when he sold his house and moved to a grander one, having come into money. He exercised very little control over what Gawsworth printed, only asking that some personal details, such as Wilfrid's string-pulling to get away from the front, be left out of *Scots Guard.*

There was a nice irony in the whole story. Wilfrid Ewart had been the most correct of men, his manner, despite his passionate nature, restrained and diffident. Gawsworth, the new channel through which his posthumous work flowed, was fantastical and un-self-conscious; not a poseur, nor without distinction, but undignified and clownlike – an inspired, enterprising drunk. His glowing face with its bold, jutting nose, gave him the appearance of a hilarious and slightly diabolical Falstaff. He described himself as a "dung beetle," a collector of the literary debris of writers he admired. In his lifetime he acquired two fine libraries and a barnful of literary manuscript material – and sold them for drink. He was also the self-styled "King of Redonda," in the Caribbean, and a freeman of the City of London, who, after being rescued from sleeping on park benches, lived almost to the end of his days, bibulously, in Fiesole, Italy, never having gained the Civil List pension that Richard Aldington and other supporters strongly felt he deserved. Such was the leading champion of *Way of Revelation*. Neither his nor Henry Williamson's plaudits, however, have persuaded a later age to rank it with the works of Sassoon, Manning, or Aldington. Nonetheless to dismiss it as a fourth-rate work is to miss the point of its interest, which is that it reminds us of how differently a great many people at that time saw the war.

Both Ewart's inhibited nature — showing in his overformal manner an uneasy relations with women — and the reticence cultivated at that time by his class in particular, prevented him from handling his subject with the emotional force required of it. It seems as if to his parents alone he could voice his fears and imaginings freely. His accounts of battle to them are far better than anything in *Way of Revelation*. Yet if that work falls short of its author's ambitious aims and his depth of feeling, that novel is nonetheless eloquent of the combined effects of regimental pride and a spirit of *noblesse oblige*. In terms of what he was required to do in battle and in training, Wilfrid's ordeal was much worse than that of A. D. Gristwood. He shared with that luckless individual a delicately balanced nervous system. He longed to get away from the front. He was as sensitive to ugliness and squalor as Richard Aldington and if less sophisticated intellectually, quite as elevated in his artistic ideals. His health was far worse, however, and he was more of a "loner."

Yet unlike the war novels of Gristwood and Aldington, his own was unqualifiedly patriotic in its message and, in its unhappy way, it was actually optimistic. Coming as he did from a family that accepted without question its elevated position and its duties, and serving as he did in an elite division that considered itself, with reason, the best in any army, he could not write off his suffering and service as wasted. *Way of Revelation*, with its reassuring conclusion, its romance, and its melodrama, may have suited the public mood of the time, but its success rested on its real strength: Wilfrid Ewart's absolute faith in the convictions he expressed.

7

A Parson's Life Laid Bare
Robert Keable
1887 - 1927

"When I was a child," wrote Robert Keable's niece Doris, "Uncle Bob was surrounded by an aura of taboo and labelled a cad, the black sheep of the family and never mentioned. At fourteen I was caught reading *Simon Called Peter*. Instantly all his books were removed from the house – lost for ever, all those first editions."

Today, however, though out of print for years, *Simon Called Peter* is easy to buy secondhand; for by the time of his death its sales had topped the 300,000 mark and close on a million copies of all his books had reached the shops. *Simon Called Peter* was Keable's only novel to describe his First World War experiences. It was a largely autobiographical account of a young padre, Peter Graham, disenchanted with the Anglican church while serving at the front, who, after release from its constraints by a passionate affair with a nurse, was spiritually reawakened.

The novel was widely attacked in the religious press, and was even pronounced obscene by the magistrates of Cambridge, Massachusetts. It featured, too, in a New Brunswick murder case, where an adulterous clergyman and his paramour were found with their love letters, containing a reference to Keable's works, lying between their corpses.

It was often compared to Mrs. Humphry Ward's famous novel, *Robert Elsmere*, which, half a century before, had so disturbed the great liberal statesman, William Ewart Gladstone, that he summoned its author to debate the religious issues. Nevertheless, *Simon Called Peter* went beyond theological questions to challenge conventional sexual morality. "The Grand Old Man," as the Christian moral voice of his age, would have been quite as outraged by the more amorous passages as by the religious implications of the book – take, for example, the scene between the padre and his mistress in their hotel bathroom:

> She jumped up and stretched her arms. "Am I not good-looking Peter? Why isn't there a good mirror in this horrid old bathroom? It's more necessary in a bathroom than anywhere, I think."
>
> "Well I can see you without it," said Peter. "And I quite agree, Julie, you're divine. You are like Aphrodite sprung from the foam."
>
> She laughed: "Well spring from the foam yourself, old dear, and come and dress. I'm getting cold. I'm going to put on the most thrilling set of undies this morning that you ever saw."

Nonetheless, it is hard to imagine the Robert Keable of his novels as the reprobate that his family maintained he was. His fluent, sincere books – novels, essays, poetry, travelogues – were devoted to spiritual crises, the corrupting effects of Western civilisation, the meaning of Christ, and the healing power of sexual love. Nor did his appearance, in his thirties, at the height of his success, suggest a feckless debauchee – rather a very clerical excleric: a slender man, of middle height, with a long, plain, bespectacled face and reddish hair. Only his gait, quick and uneven, and "his bright whimsical sidelong glance," betrayed something mercurial in his temperament.

Although it was slow to find a publisher, the book took him a mere twenty days of writing time, two chapters a day, in the later months of 1919. It was, he said, "a tour de force, a vivid, living, passionate thing which I couldn't help writing ... it may owe some of the six editions [it made many more after this 1921 letter] to the fact that I laid a parson's life bare and didn't care a damn."

Simon Called Peter is set, mainly during 1917-18, amid the well-evoked squalors of dockside Le Havre and the calm beauty of the wide Seine valley with its ancient Norman towns and castles – Caudebec, Rouen, Jumièges, Duclair, Tancarville. There Peter Graham, a newly arrived army chaplain, trying to organise religious life behind the lines, realises, to his consternation, that nobody is greatly interested in it. The soldiers' blasphemies and still more their loose morals disconcert him; but in time he decides that their cheerfulness and unselfish companionship come closer to true Christianity than conventionally virtuous behaviour. It was not the first time this had been said in a popular form. The point had been made in Donald Hankey's highly successful *A Student in Arms* in 1917. What was new was the frank manner in which Keable described how Peter Graham coped with this discovery.

Desperate to be accepted, and for the Church to count for something in the soldiers' eyes, Graham gladly takes over the tedious chores of mess secretary, and drinks – sometimes heavily – with them. He even makes friends with a French prostitute, and his notions of morality are further shaken by finding that she does not regard her way of life as incompatible with her love for Jesus Christ.

Still more disturbing to his life and religion is his affair with Julie, a high-spirited nurse, and, by the time of the voluptuous climax in the closing chapters, he is ready to put Christianity on one side. However, during an interval in their lovemaking, he has a direct experience of Christ while watching a celebration of the Roman Catholic Mass. Julie realises that she will always take second place to his religion and that her passionate feelings cannot be allowed to interfere with his spiritual destiny. She therefore renounces him: "thus did Julie, who knew no God, Julie of the brave, clean, steadfast heart, give Peter back to Him." Peter, devastated by the price of loving God, travels back to the front.

What made the book so popular? First, it was vividly written and fast-moving. Secondly, albeit moral in its own way, it took a tilt at Victorian sexual hypocrisy and conventional English religion, both contemporary targets for attack; but it also stressed hope and self-realisation, and so cannot be compared with the later, classic type of "disenchanted" war novel. For this reason it met the English public's wish at that time to believe that though the war had been terrible, it had been worth fighting. Thirdly, despite Keable's carelessness about the historical order of wartime events, it was nevertheless an absolutely authentic account of a padre's experience, as is confirmed in many other writings by his clerical contemporaries. Fourthly, many pious readers were lulled by the religious title into buying it on the assumption that it would be an improving book of a traditional sort, while others who knew better were drawn by its controversial reputation. Besides, it was sentimental, romantic, and titillating and the message was a reassuring one: that breaking the sexual rules, far from cutting Christians off from God, could even be instrumental in leading them back to Him.

It was this message that enraged the organ of Anglicanism, the *Church Times*: God was not to be found through unfaithfulness but through repentance, its reviewer declared reproachfully. Keable, replying, maintained that his readers were welcome to draw whatever conclusion they chose; and it is true that when he had written the book he himself had been far from certain how his war experiences, including a "Julie" in his life, had affected his spiritual future. Because of Keable's uncertainties, the close of his book now seems unconvincing, despite his obvious sincerity. Yet at the time, this final chapter, which was both erotic and uplifting, inspired tens of thousands of admirers.

Religion was still a very popular subject for fiction, as can be seen from the case of another clergyman, Ernest Raymond, also a war novelist, whose romantic, idealised work, *Tell England,* was destined to be read well into the 1950s. His sentimental tale of lissom ex-public schoolboys dying for their country in Gallipoli had a religious message entwined with its patriotic one: "England's past is holy; her future is unwritten. But idealism is mightily abroad among those who shall make the England that is to be. And all that remains for the preacher to say is that nothing but Christianity will ever gather in that harvest of spiritual ideals which alone will make good our prodigal outlay." The illegitimate son of a retired Major-General and a woman he was brought up to believe was his aunt, Raymond was first a teacher, then a priest, going out to Gallipoli with the Army Chaplains' Service in 1915. He served also in Sinai from 1916 to 1917, was briefly at the Third Battle of Ypres, and ended the war in South Russia with "Dunsterforce," the army led by Rudyard Kipling's old school companion, General Dunsterville. By a curious irony, when his book was published in 1922, Raymond had temporarily lost his faith and withdrawn formally from the church. He married, twice, wrote several other books about the war, and achieved a well-merited success as the author of darkly dramatic popular fiction.

Robert Keable's origins were more conventional. He was the son of a pious evangelical businessman, formerly a nonconformist, who, in 1904, when Robert was seventeen, became an Anglican priest. Until 1907, Mr. Keable was curate at St. Matthew's Church, Croydon, the prosperous town to the south of the capital only recently swallowed up into Greater London. Robert recalled "miles of trim villas ascending to avenues of detached houses; churches . . . swept and garnished, or empty with an Evangelical Christian emptiness; Municipal buildings, dignified, sufficient, new and clean . . . in short, an air . . . almost wholly neatly and simply Conservative."

Robert was a popular and successful pupil at Whitgift, the illustrious local school that dated from the sixteenth century. "Kibbles" was much praised for his fluent and facetious contributions to the *Whitgiftian* magazine and gained an exhibition to Magdalene College, Cambridge, in 1905, going on to achieve a First Class Honours degree in history.

The Whitgift evidence is important. For apart from the testimony of a woman who adored him, and a certain mischievousness in his letters, there is little elsewhere to suggest he was other than an exceedingly solemn man. His own writings are not humorous, or only mildly so, though they do convey a strong appetite for life. "At school," remarked his obituarist in the *Whitgiftian*, "Robert Keable was well loved; he was altogether companionable . . . To himself he was perhaps too conscionable [*sic*] and this at times led to moments of austerity." Ardent, quick-tempered, friendly, affectionate – these are the adjectives that came to his schoolfellows' minds when they thought of him. Because of the serious message of his books, it is easy to be misled into seeing him only as "tragic," "shipwrecked," "self-centred," and "tormented," all adjectives applied to him later. In truth he was all these things, but he was also vital and responsive – which made it hard for him to settle for the comfortable but narrow certainties with which he was encompassed when a boy, and which was why, later in his career, he earned the affection of high-spirited, pleasure-loving people.

At home, his life centred round his father's church. The faith in which he was brought up was austerely Protestant. His family abhorred alcohol, card-playing, and the theatre, and looked on Roman Catholicism as diabolical. By his later teens Keable, who was a devoted son, was an active lay preacher. Although he outgrew the mildly-voiced but implacable bigotry of his early years, his upbringing left its mark. First, in his driving belief that he must use his talents to the full, which made him prodigiously industrious. Secondly, he could never do without some kind of religion, even when, for a time, he shrugged off Christianity; thirdly, in all his writings there was more than a trace of the preacher, and, like a greater author who passed through the evangelical mill a hundred years earlier, Thomas Babington Macaulay, Robert was clear and vivid, but never subtle. Fortunately, subtlety is not a prerequisite for success as a writer.

At Cambridge, his life was permanently changed. The neat, efficient schoolboy with a scientific interest in nature began to respond to its beauty. Under the influence of his tutor, A. C. Benson, and – even more – of the latter's brother, Mgr. Hugh Benson, he became an asthete and a ritualist; he dropped his Protestant hostility to religious ceremonial and came also to enjoy embellishing his surroundings – which was to be a lifelong pleasure to him.

How did this change come about? On the surface, there could have been no greater contrast to the earnest and unsophisticated Robert Keable, whose social life as a freshman revolved round the college eight and student bible meetings, than the two cultivated, cosmopolitan Benson brothers, sons of a late-nineteenth-century archbishop of Canterbury and a remarkable, lesbian mother. Part of their attraction for Robert was that the two men were the most intelligent he had ever met: the elder, Arthur, was a distinguished man of letters; chastely homoerotic, he was observant and witty, sometimes overfastidious in his judgments, a sensitive soul who took endless pains with his pupils – even those, like Robert, who did not attract him romantically, whilst he appreciated his sensitivity and fire. Arthur's brother Hugh, small, fantastical, and stammering, was a more brilliant creature, with a burning energy that wore out his slight frame before he was fifty. He was forever working on his powerful sermons, on his novels, on schemes for beautifying his "sweet and secret place" at Hare Street in Hertfordshire, where he settled after leaving Cambridge, and above all on the instruction of undergraduates who came to the Catholic Rectory seeking conversion to Rome. There were many stories about his eccentric ways: his rage at a laundrywoman for starching the lace on his cotta; his stormy friendship with the notorious Baron Corvo; his habit of caterwauling in the shrubbery to annoy the convent dog. These humanise his memory, but should not be allowed to obscure his genuine spirituality.

The imaginative side of Robert, which had been stifled by his up-bringing, responded to Hugh Benson's love of beauty. He admired his prolific fictional writing and the priest influenced his own prose style. More importantly, he became dissatisfied with the explanations of life's mysteries that he had learned at home – particularly where they seemed to dismiss so much of the richness of creation. This shook him and he longed for the certainties of the all-embracing faith to which Hugh Benson adhered – the certainties he desired increasingly as he lost re-spect for the whole intellectual basis of evangelical Protestantism, its ethos at last fading after its long domination of the nineteenth-century Anglican Church.

For years, however, this conflict between Robert's Protestant back-ground and his inclination to Rome, which greatly distressed his father, remained unsolved. He persisted in following his long-chosen path, the Anglican priesthood. As a curate at Bradford Parish Church in the West Riding of Yorkshire, he was priested at Ripon in 1911. He continued to see Hugh Benson at his home at Hare Street; but finally, wrestling with his doubts in the romantic chapel the priest had created there from an ancient barn, he found no clear sign that he must abandon Anglicanism. Benson was greatly grieved: "I know you are all wrong where you are," he wrote, "and really it is like watching a person freezing to death in a crevasse, when he ought to be walking." Perceptively, he sensed that the decision not to come over to Rome would lead ultimately to an aban-donment of all religion, for there had been intimations of this in Robert's arguments. Hugh Benson's last letter to Robert before he died added: "My dear, you are running away from Christ . . . I have never written such things before to *anyone* . . . Because you are the first I ever met of whom I could say 'I know that he knows Christ, and that he is turning his back on him; and I know he knows it too.'"

To save him from Rome, Westcott House, Robert's former theologi-cal college in Cambridge, specially requested during 1912 that he should be taken on by the University Mission to Central Africa, in Zanzibar. The twenty years before the war had seen a steep rise in European mis-sionary activity in Africa, attracting some of the most dedicated young men in the Anglican Church. Apart from the exotic beauty of the place, Robert was drawn by the opportunities for self-sacrifice. The Bishop of Zanzibar, Frank Weston, did not spare himself or those working under him. "Bishop Frank" was an extreme High Anglican and a convinced socialist, a not uncommon combination at the time. A tall man, with a severe, impressive face, he was capable of walking for as much as seventeen miles in the equatorial heat in the course of his duties; often all the priests at a mission, though light-headed with fever, were expected to keep on working without relief. Such a rigorous regime and, later, gruelling war work in charge of a native carrier corps, were undoubtedly the cause of Weston's death in his early fifties. The life probably undermined Robert's health as well, though his recurrent problem, nephritis, an infection of the kidneys, may well have had an earlier origin.

Keable taught in the badly understaffed missionary school, Kiungani College, a spacious stone Arab building on the island of Zanzibar, overlooking the sea, with palm and mango groves behind it. "We kept him from Rome, as we promised," wrote Bishop Weston; but those two years alienated Robert further from the Anglican Church. He should have established a rapport with the bishop, who, like him, had been brought up an evangelical and had become, doctrinally, almost a Roman Catholic. Besides, Robert was quite able to share Weston's fiercely antiecumenical views, which gained the bishop a reputation for religious intolerance at this time. Yet they failed to be friends. There was wrong on both sides. "The Zanzibarbarian," as Weston was nicknamed, was notoriously authoritarian: "he is simply a Pope," Robert complained, and as one missionary put it, he had "differences more or less serious with nearly everyone in the diocese." They quarrelled over the training of the African priests. Robert thought the bishop turned a blind eye to irregularities in their outlook and religious practice. To him, the bishop was just making up the rules and compromising, as it suited him, in a typically Anglican fashion. Weston was incensed. He was devoted to his black priests – a love that was reciprocated. He regarded colour prejudice as the greatest danger to the spread of Christianity in Africa, and thought he detected it in Robert. He was irritated by the self-confidence that made the younger man so ready to find fault; and he perceived, not unjustly, the influence of the Bensons – Hugh in turning him against the Church, and Arthur in flattering his vanity. He noted also Keable's highly-strung, overemotional nature. Nonetheless, he recognised that he had unusual spiritual qualities. Robert's first book, written in Zanzibar, was a history of the Universities' Mission to Central Africa, *Darkness or Light,* a deftly composed, information-packed volume, which he completed with amazing speed during 1912. His impressions of Zanzibar, *City of the Dawn* (1915), were introduced by Arthur Benson, who praised the book's brilliance and freshness, contrasting it with the dry works the public had come to expect from missionaries. The book showed genuine religious fervour, as well as a characteristic sentimentality. It evoked a frangipani-scented paradise, rock pools full of rainbow-coloured fish, woods bright with scarlet acacia, and the waving green fans of palm leaves – and at night all of this transfigured into an unearthly calm under the light of the crescent moon: "Ah if this be His likeness," Robert wrote, "how shall I be satisfied!"

Several other volumes of his essays and verses on religious topics appeared during the same period and sold well. Returning to England in 1914, he turned down the offer of a living in Sheffield, because, once again, he felt the pull of Rome would compromise his position there; he elected to return to Africa, this time to Basutoland (Lesotho), in Southern Africa, where he became Rector of Leribi in the Diocese of Bloemfontein.

During June 1915 he married, in Durban. Sybil Armitage, whom he had met in Bradford, was admiringly equipped to be the wife of a parish priest: passionately religious, with a strong social conscience and robust health, her exuberance and her cheerful ripples of laughter were said to have a tonic effect, particularly on children. She was a big, handsome (some thought beautiful) woman, with auburn hair. Robert admired her moral strength. The devout, courageous Edith in his novel *Peradventure* is based partly on her, though a rather quieter version of the original.

She was not, unfortunately, an easy person to live with, least of all for Robert. Unlike him she was very certain of herself, and tended to be over liberal with advice, taking offence if this was ignored. Even those, including Robert, who were most fond of her, found her domineering. Emotionally, he and she were out of tune. Sentiment and poetry were a large part of his makeup, while she was down-to-earth. More importantly, it is unlikely that they were sexually compatible. One of Keable's clerical colleagues out in Africa later declared that he had always felt sexual suppression lay at the root of Robert's difficulties. There were no Keable children.

Hugh Benson, who believed that Robert was cut out to be a monk – a Redemptorist – had concluded shrewdly enough that his decision to get engaged at this time was a way of escaping from the dilemma, by making it impossible for himself to take the vows that a Roman Catholic religious life would involve; and even if Benson was clearly wrong in thinking that Robert would be suited to celibacy, he may have put his finger on the reason why the Keables' union was less solidly based than it appeared to be.

It is possible, however, that had their life as missionaries not been interrupted by the war, they might have submerged their tensions successfully in their work. A most successful and zealous priest, under his care the number of communicants in his area tripled, and he led the way in spreading elaborate ceremonial and sacred music in Basutoland. There, as nowhere else, he felt that his call had a meaning, at least in the eyes of his congregation, for whose childlike, wholehearted faith he had a deep affection. In the mission's little stone chapel at Sekubu, they were packed so densely that those at the front were touching him as he conducted the Sunday services. Besides, the dangers of existence in that wild land often brought him and Sybil closely together. Once he nearly lost his life when a mad African shot him in the leg, up in the Berg – the rugged highland country he loved, with its peaks like great round towers or vast altars of orange-russet rock. He later described his ordeal vividly in his novel, *Recompence*. No wheeled vehicle could reach him where he lay, and it took nearly five days to find a doctor. Eventually he was carried by stretcher-bearers over miles of precipitous terrain before he reached a hospital in Natal.

His ties with his work seemed to him, at the time, very strong. He made, he claimed, a particular friend among the priests at the Mission, Francis Thomas Wilfrid, an eccentric, impatient but spiritual man, who found the routine duties of their life arduous, and ran into trouble with the local white settlers for denouncing their bigotry. Wilfrid found it hard to form relationships: those whom he approached were put off by the overeager fashion in which he responded to any show of sympathy. Keable, however, was drawn to the romantic and mystical in him – Wilfrid's thirst for beauty and his belief in another reality behind the harsh existence they led in the mountains, with "their fierce sun, blistering wind and bitter cold in quick succession."

Shortly after recovering from his mountain accident, a new adventure was destined to have a fateful effect on Robert's *modus vivendi* with Sybil and on his whole life. During 1915 and 1916, as Britain's commitment to the war effort intensified, there was a growing demand for labour from all over the Empire to build the railways and unload the ships that served the Western Front. The South African government organised a Native Labour Contingent of some 21,000 men, who went to work in Europe for a wage of £3 a month. These included many Basutos, chiefly illiterate peasants, but also mission-educated men, believing loyally in the benefits of British rule. Robert pressed the Bishop of Bloemfontein to be allowed to accompany them to the front. He was appointed army chaplain on 26 May 1917. He thus became part of the South African or-ganisation and, since all army religious matters came under the Assistant Chaplain-General for the area to which he was sent, he was also ex-pected to be at the disposal of the British and Empire forces generally. Padres were given the equivalent of captains' rank but only received a second-lieutenant's pay.

On his return to Europe, Robert visited his parents. Their second son, Henry, was then serving in the Royal Navy, and died of typhoid the fol-lowing year. For a brief period Robert worked in a fashionable Kensington parish before going out to work on the lines of communica-tion in the Rouen sector. His expectations were evidently high, higher than those of many who were joining the Army Chaplains' Service by 1917. C. E. Montague, in his classic memoir of the war, *Disenchantment* (1922), accused the padres of contributing to the network of illusion that undermined the fighting man's faith in authority. The fact was that C. of E. chaplains themselves underwent a process of disillusionment that was similar to that of many soldiers. The leaders of the Church were swept off their feet as much as anyone else by the mood of 1914. They hoped that dedicated work at the front would yield a huge harvest of souls. There were indeed gains for religious life, insofar as the war deepened the faith of some of those who served as chaplains and severely shook their more self-righteous preconceptions. But these gains did not come about until chaplains realised that their priority was not how they could

1 (*left*)
Richard Aldington as an
officer 9th Royal Sussex
Regt.

2 (*top right*)
Hilda Doolittle (H.D.) in
1913

3 (*lower right*)
Brigit Patmore,
c. 1930

4 (*left*)
V.M. Yeates in R.A.F. uniform

5 (*above*)
Henry Williamson, c. 1923

6 (*below*)
J.A. Gristwood's letter,
about his son's death,
to H.G. Wells

26/4/33.

Amelia
Brockham Lane
Betchworth
Surrey

My dear H.G. I am sure you will be
grieved to learn that my dear boy Donald
passed away yesterday! I felt I must
let you know.

Excuse brevity

Y Sincerely
J.A. Gristwood

7 (*left*)
R.H. Mottram
(standing left)
with Claims
Commission
colleagues

8 (*below*)
R.H. Mottram
(fifth from right,
with eyes right)
Peterborough,
1914

9 (*left*) Wilfrid Ewart, c. 1921

10 (*top right*) Dollie Rawson, c. 1916

11 (*lower right*) Sybil Keable in middle age

12 (*below*) Robert Keable and Jolie Buck, Tahiti, c. 1923

13 (*left*)
Gilbert Frankau,
portrait by Flora
Lion

14 (*lower left*)
Ford Madox Ford as
a soldier

15 (*below*)
C.E. Montague as a
conducting officer,
c. 1917

16 (*left*)
Ronald Gurner as Head
Master of Whitgift,
Armistice Day 1928

17 (*top right*)
Ronald Gurner in uniform
c. 1916

18 (*lower right*)
Rosalie Gurner, Whitgift

19 (*top left*)
Herbert Read in
uniform, c. 1917

20 (*lower left*)
Oliver Onions, c. 1916

21 (*top right*)
Pamela Hinkson, c. 1932

22 (*lower right*)
Jacket of *The Victors*, with
illustration by
Eric Kennington

23 Richard Blaker as an
undergraduate

24 Mamie Blaker

25 Louis Golding, May Owen
and (*centre*) Mamie Blaker at the
launch of *The Needle Watcher*, 1934

26 'Forward Observation Post': sketch at the front by Richard Blaker

about until chaplains realised that their priority was not how they could serve their church by bringing men to it, but what their religion could do for the men.

The majority of the ordinary soldiers derived their notion of a clergyman from the music halls and were almost surprised not to find them wearing white socks and brandishing a bath bun. Some clergy were shocked by bad language, which confirmed this impression. Until 1916 chaplains were unwelcome in the trenches and were expected to stay with the ambulances, in the rear. As a result they were often thought of, quite unfairly, as shirkers. Not a few padres ignored this directive, like the first clerical V.C., the Rev. E. Mellish. From 1916, the military authorities decided they could, after all, do valuable work at the front in maintaining morale and relaxed the rules. Subsequently they proved their worth, by exchanging cheerful gossip with lonely sentries, by writing to the bereaved, by running errands and brewing tea; but best of all, by accompanying the men into battle and helping hard-pressed medical teams to rescue the wounded. There were numerous heroes, like the fabled "Woodbine Willie," the Rev. G. A. Studdert-Kennedy; out of 3,050 who served, three were awarded the V.C. and 205 the M.C. There were casualties too – 170 were wounded, 88 were killed in battle or died of illness contracted on active service through sharing the hardships of men far younger and fitter than themselves. The demands of the job proved a great strain for some who were psychologically ill-suited to be part of a war machine. The sophisticated and self-critical Rev. C. E. Raven, for example, felt at times completely alienated, even in a unit as friendly and well-knit as the 22nd Royal Fusiliers, though faith kept his nerves steady after a bad start. The hapless Padre Warne, who went off his head in C.R. Benstead's nightmare novel, *Retreat*, was an example of one of those for whom the war proved too much: "Warne's sort are too civilised," remarked one officer, "they can't accommodate themselves to this unrestrained indulgence in a primitive lust." Warne, like many real-life clergymen, continually felt the contrast between his beloved parish at home and the brutal order of things at the front. Others were all too aware that they never fully shared the experience of the soldiers: "I was and still am shamefully conscious that we did not go right into the depths," wrote one infantry chaplain, the Rev. Geoffrey Gordon. This lack of direct experience was one reason why few clergy wrote books denouncing either the purposes or the conduct of war. They did not feel it was their place to do so. Robert was no exception. The Rev. Ernest Raymond's *Tell England*, with its sentimentally patriotic message, is overtly pro war. The only really critical war novel by a padre is Edward Thompson's *These Men Thy Friends*. Thompson, a Methodist minister, was awarded the M.C. for bravery in Mesopotamia, which put him in a position of equality with the other soldiers.

Even padres who fulfilled all their duties manfully still had to exercise tact. Soldiers resented church parade, with its enforced attendance at morning service, fully turned out, and, in the earlier stage of the war, carrying their rifles. Despite many padres' objections, the military authorities insisted on it as a discipline, and a fine show for any journalists from the Home Front. The troops also took very much amiss any calls for repentance before a battle. In Ernest Raymond's *Tell England*, the padre, "Monty," calls on his young officer friends to go into battle "white" – pure in mind and body. In real life, probably only a few would have appreciated an appeal couched in such terms, though many, undoubtedly, gained strength from taking Holy Communion on the eve of an attack. What most soldiers seemed to expect of their chaplains, however, was an informal version of the kind of service they remembered at home.

As Keable also discovered, the padre's place was not, as so many imagined, at the bedside of the wounded and dying. Whereas many soldiers had moments of "wind-up religion" before an attack, few were interested in a deathbed conversion. In *Simon Called Peter*, Peter Graham is put in his place by a dying officer who nonchalantly refuses the comforts of religion:

> [Peter] choked back panic and knelt down. He had imagined it all before, and yet not quite like this. He knew what he ought to say, but for a minute he could not formulate it.
>
> "Where are you hit, Jenks?" was all he said.
>
> The other turned his head and looked at him.
>
> "Body – lungs, I think," he whispered. "I'm done, padre; I've seen chaps before."
>
> The words trailed off. Peter gripped himself mentally, and

steadied his voice. "Jenks, old man," he said. "Just a minute. Think about God – you are going to Him, you know. Trust Him, will you? 'The blood of Jesus Christ, God's Son, saveth us from all sin.'"

The dying man moved his hand convulsively. "Don't you worry, padre," he said faintly. "I've been – confirmed." The lips tightened a second with pain, and then: "Reckon I won't – shirk. Have you – got – a cigarette?"

Peter felt quickly for his case, fumbled and dropped one, then got another into his fingers. He hesitated a second, and then put it to his own lips, struck a match, and puffed at it. He was in the act of holding it to the other when Langton spoke behind him:

"It's no good now, padre," he said quietly, "it's all over."

And Peter saw that it was.

If badly wounded, soldiers were either in agony, in which case the padre could do nothing, or, knowing that for good or ill they were out of the fight, they needed no message of consolation. The people who welcomed a chaplain were the duty men, exhausted and overwhelmed with the horror, and grateful for a chat and a companionable cigarette.

Even a flock as devout as the Basuto labour contingent presented problems for Keable. He was disappointed by the native priests accompanying them, who seemed to care too much about their own position and not enough about their congregations. He blamed the white South African army authorities for refusing these black clergy any rank higher than lance-corporal, so that they did not even enjoy the limited status and comforts of a sergeants' mess. He also felt that the missionaries had been at fault for raising the African priests' expectations too high. They were reluctant to eat with the African labourers or be medically examined alongside them, which was, he thought, hardly consonant with their Christian calling. In his view, they would only fulfil their duty properly by being proud of being Africans among Africans rather than trying to identify with white men. He cited the fact that they made no effort to adjust their religious services to the novel situation of their congregation, and it had been left to him, a white padre and a ritualist, to devise extempore prayers for them.

These criticisms, aired in *The East and the West* journal in January 1918, drew an angry riposte from the Bishop of Zanzibar, always quick to defend African Christians and his own training methods. How could Keable blame the black priests, he asked, for wishing to escape the humiliations and coarse diet to which the African labourers were subjected by the white military authorities? He still resented Robert's earlier criticisms of the priests' moral failings. It might be true that sometimes they were not morally perfect, in sexual matters, for example, but, he added pointedly, such falls from grace were not unknown among English clergy. It was not for Keable to criticise a band of men some of whom, as Weston knew at first hand, had gone through horrific ordeals in East Africa at the hands of the Germans in the belief that they were spies. "If English priests are to help Africans to the holiness of priesthood they must first learn not to chastise them in public, as Mr. Keable has chastised his two fellow chaplains in France."

At least, however, the Basutos were mostly pious believers and were grateful for the diversion of religious services. The South African authorities confined them to their compounds when off-duty and forbade them contact with the French locals, particularly women. Robert's real difficulty was in providing a Christian message with any relation to the lives of the white combatant soldiers resting from front-line service. It was in this struggle to gain acceptance that he came to realise how absurd the finer points of morality and doctrine seemed to them. They wanted from their padres, he concluded, only what the Y.M.C.A. provided in France: entertainment and a barely spiritual form of practical Christianity. Sectarian differences were thus meaningless.

Interestingly enough for one so idealistic, all this struck him as reasonable. The war had changed his perceptions. The role that the Protestant padre was required to play seemed to him an anomaly retained simply from tradition. In fact, he concluded, it would be better to absorb the whole Protestant chaplaincy into the Y.M.C.A., leaving only the Roman Catholic padres, who were fully accepted by their (chiefly Irish, Scots, and Lancastrian) flock. Predictably, in view of his penchant towards Rome, he was impressed also by the way the Roman Catholic religion had penetrated so deeply into the lives and natural feelings of many of the French soldiers. In this reaction he was not unique, but it was controversial for an Anglican padre to make the point so openly.

He seems to have won his fellow officers over by being "an all-round good sport – his hands full of kindly occupations . . . a smoker, not averse to a glass of whisky and soda." Although *Simon Called Peter* only describes life behind the lines, he certainly did see something of the fighting and could not be accused of shirking: he never lacked courage. Like Peter Graham in his novel, he seems to have been on friendly terms with French prostitutes, as his memoir, *Standing By*, shows. We may take it that the substance of his letters to his wife was the same as that of Peter Graham's letters to his fiancèe, revealing his alienation from conventional Protestantism and his wish to mingle with "publicans and sinners."

The most important relationship he struck up while on the Western Front was with an English girl of 18, Elizabeth "Jolie" Buck. "Jolie," the model for Julie in *Simon Called Peter*, was a tall beauty with fair hair, a wide-cheeked face, and a slender, athletic figure. The daughter of William Tennant Buck, a Major (retired) in the Durham Light Infantry, she had graduated to her arduous duties driving lorries for the Canadian Lumber Corps from ambulances and before that, from conveying Royal Flying Corps/R.A.F. officers to and from their headquarters at the Hotel Cecil in the Strand. Her radiant sex appeal made her an anxiety to her well-connected family, who boasted Beresfords and Manners (a rather wild element) in their ancestry. In those days the sanctions against a young woman for breaking the moral code were ferocious and they led to rebellion in a spirited, pleasure-loving girl like Jolie, though probably only to the extent of kissing and saucy conversation. In conventional society, having a reputation for being fast could in extreme cases lead to the loss of worldly prospects, and signified moral inferiority and an absence of finer feelings.

But Jolie, though resilient, as she had to be, was neither hard nor morally weak. Despite her youth, she survived the punishing ordeal of the Western Front, seeing sights as horrible as had anyone who was there. Like other girls out there, she had to fend off the frequent attentions of young officers whose demands were underscored by the threat of their imminent death. Not that she always rebuffed them. She was flirtatious and tender-hearted. She rebelled against the rules of conventional social behaviour, and she was naively excited by the effect she had on men.

By 1917 all women in the British Expeditionary Force, other than nurses, were generically known as W.A.A.C.s (Women's Auxiliary Army Corps), though, being a driver, Jolie herself had probably first enrolled in the Women's Legion. In any case for social purposes she would have been under the W.A.A.C. discipline, with its rigid rules to preserve the reputation of the new and often criticised organisation. The girls had to keep strict hours. Many areas were out of bounds to them. If they went out with an officer, they had to be accompanied by at least one other couple.

The sexual morals of the W.A.A.C.s were a matter of pride to Dame Helen Gwynne Vaughan, their supremo. Duty came first for these patriotic girls under military authority. Jolie and her fellow W.A.A.C.s worked far too hard to have time for much drinking or flirting. Though, eventually, she was ready to have an affair with Robert, it is clear that she regarded this as the sign of a serious commitment. It was, of course, a bold departure from the moral code governing unmarried girls of her class; but it took place in the completely new social context of the war, albeit well away from the gaze of W.A.A.C. spies on the Western Front.

In fact Jolie personified the spirit of the Western Front, and throve in an atmosphere where the social niceties were set aside. She was a "good sort," a "brick," loyal and courageous. For Robert, her significance was not simply that she stirred him romantically as no other woman had ever done, but that she symbolised a new womanhood, which beckoned to him to free himself from his past. He confessed to finding the W.A.A.C.s uniform "beautiful," adding, with a typically clerical touch, "The swing of their skirts seemed a sacrament of emancipation."

For her part, Jolie had come to need someone who could take her in hand and treat her seriously. She had no desire for marriage with a "suitable" young man of the kind her mother would have chosen; but the fact that she was attracted to a man of great earnestness, unusual talents, and little obvious glamour, shows how deeply she sought, on her own unorthodox terms, the equivalent of a "good marriage." Robert's attractions were completely different from those of the average young officer. He combined experience with a kind of innocence, which made him relish new enjoyments of all sorts. She may well have hoped against hope that he might give up his wife at the end of the war but at that stage it was not to be, and the affair languished.

Keable was far from ready to cut loose at once from his past. He continued to teeter on the brink of the Roman Catholic Church, praising it in a controversial set of essays, *Standing By*, which appeared in 1919; but even now he would not take the plunge, though his wife was sympathetic. There remained his obligation to his Basuto congregation at Leribi. After the war ended, he returned to them and remained until April 1920. Colleagues noticed that he had become more "worldly"; and there were rumors (which may go back to his earlier time in Basutoland) that he had had affairs in the parish – with "a red-head" and with native women – and that it was not safe for women to let him escort them home after an evening at the Rectory.

During that time he poured out his feelings in a novel, "as sincerely and as simply," he wrote, "as ever pen was set to paper." This work, *Simon Called Peter*, was destined, two years later, to make him world-famous. Finally, in great agony of mind, he resigned his living and left the mission.

He had one last debt to pay to Leribi. His old friend, the Rev. Francis Wilfrid, had died while Robert was still with the Mission. Before this, Wilfrid had entrusted him, so Keable claimed, with a packet of "letters" he had written to a female correspondent unknown to any save himself and Keable, pencilled on scraps of paper while he had been on his missionary travels. They consisted of meditations on his work, on the wild country of the Berg, and on his hopes of seeing the face of God. Robert made an edition of these writings, *Pilgrim Papers*, which appeared in 1920. The closeness of Wilfrid's views to his own, on many points, suggests the possibility that Keable may have written the "letters" himself, as a means of conveying some unconventional opinions of his own, and that Wilfrid may have been a literary creation. Whatever the truth, it was not one of his more impressive productions, and perhaps this is hardly surprising considering his confusion of feeling at the time. It was dedicated to "Sybil, a Resolute Pilgrim." In a foreword, he recollected seeing Wilfrid off on a last trip into the mountains: "we were standing in the dying day on the edge of a little acacia spinney where a path ends at a gate so set that a watcher may see afar off the sunset lights on the great Basuto peaks. Wilfrid stood long gazing at them and then turned to me with rather a wistful smile. 'The grand old Berg,' he said, 'has chiefly taught me after all, *how to wait*.'" He was right, Keable added, concluding with a conventional phrase about seeing through a glass darkly until the day broke and the shadows flew away. He hid the extent of his own inner conflicts from his readers. He himself was far from resigned to waiting long years for some divine revelation that would make his path plain; and he was also growing acutely fearful of missing more immediate excitements and satisfactions such as the experience of war had brought him.

His journey back to England was leisurely: a liner to the Canaries, and from there a cargo boat along the Moroccan coast; then he set out on foot through Spain and France, taking stock of his life. Back in England, he settled with his wife in a Tudor cottage at West Wratting, near Cambridge. Both apparently took instruction in the Roman Catholic faith. From then on Sybil became a devout convert. Robert's father, now Vicar of Pavenham, near Bedford, refused to have her in the house and, for a time, Robert would not visit his parents.

All this while, however, he had been avidly reading books on science, psychology, and Darwinism, and metaphysical works like David Lindsay's remarkable *A Voyage to Arcturus*, newly published. Since he had ceased to be a parson his doubts about Christianity – even Roman Catholicism – came to overwhelm his faith. "I think R.C. is beautiful, wonderful, the best form of religion, a glowing vision; but I can't believe what it says about itself. I don't believe it is . . . Christ Incarnate in the world." He concluded gloomily that the human mind, throughout the ages, finding a gulf it could not span, had simply invented God to fill the breach: "I can see creative evolution at work. What is behind it, I don't *know*. But I'm inclined to think that I do not believe it is anything which the old concept of God really covers."

His publishers, Constable, were beginning to realise that *Simon Called Peter*, taken on as a gamble, was likely to be a great success. At their request, he began to write a second novel, *The Mother of All Living*. It was the product of his digging into psychology, anthropology, and the occult. Still influenced by Hugh Benson's ideas, he had an open mind about the real power of black magic, which contrasted with his rationalist approach to Christianity. An intense love-drama set in South Africa, the novel showed that he had at this time begun to substitute a Bergsonian "life force" interpretation of existence for his discarded Christian beliefs.

To keep going financially, he took a temporary job as a schoolmaster at a leading public school, Dulwich College, and later at Dunstable Grammar School. He discovered a talent for teaching, but now that he felt released from Christian morality and thus bereft of his main emotional focus, he was restless for more intense experience. He felt, he told a friend, "an absolutely passionate desire for *life*. All I felt in poetry, all that I felt in faith, I feel a thousandfold."

Simon Called Peter appeared in April 1921. It had an immediate success. Robert was fêted, interviewed, and offered the prospect of stage and film versions of his book. He began to make new friends. One was his publisher, Michael Sadleir, of Constable, the writer and bibliophile, who shared Keable's interest in social commentary and historical change and was delighted with the second novel he began that year, *Peradventure*, charting the course of a young man's spiritual journey from his evangelical childhood to his vision of "a new Heaven and a new earth" in the arms of a girl on a Zanzibar beach. It included vivid portraits of Mgr. Hugh Benson ("Father Vassall") and Frank Weston ("the Bishop of Mocambique").

Robert's abandonment of Christianity was not only a result of his spiritual wrestling. Jolie was in his life again. Their common experience of the war, as with other veterans, was an enormously strong bond, and the more he became alienated from Sybil, the more he needed Jolie's love. By early 1922 he was with her constantly, though they could not go about openly as a couple. Instant fame as an author meant that he was in the public eye, and there was bound to be a keen interest in his private life, given the subject of his best-selling book, which was dedicated, in veiled form, to Jolie. Outside the most bohemian circles, "living in sin" was punished by social ostracism. They had to consider the feelings of his wife and Jolie's family, who were distressed at the relationship.

They met where it was safe to do so, in particular at an exotic household at No.1 Ralston Street, close to his Chelsea lodgings: Gwen Otter's well-known salon had been going since before the war. A fantastic little figure in gold turban, Chinese coat, and chandelier earrings, she held her artistic and literary soirées in rooms hung with Beardsley drawings and strewn with huge brocade cushions. Robert, still short of money, was delighted to be lionised by his hospitable neighbour and took Jolie along with him. It was through this connection, though probably not in the sometimes louche company that made up the parties at Gwen's house, that he encountered a young doctor, Jack Elliott, who was treating Gwen's alcoholic brother. Jack Elliott's wife Rita, though far from bohemian herself, was uncensorious and took a liking to Robert and Jolie. Success and love had released in a rush Robert's huge enjoyment of life. Jolie, or "Betty" as she was now more often called, was becoming, in her twenties, the poised young woman described by Keable in the character of "Lady Ann Carew," the heroine of *Lighten Our Darkness*: "She had fair bobbed hair under a simple little hat with a scrap of pheasant's wing in it. She had large Irish eyes. She had firm full lips and clear healthy skin. Her ungloved hands were finely modelled, well-proportioned and clasped about her knees as she sat."

Though she had calmed down somewhat, away from the hypercharged atmosphere of the front, Jolie retained her *joie de vivre*, and their liaison was still intensely passionate. The possibility that he might lose her seems to have been often on Robert's mind. One scene in *Lighten Our Darkness* shows that his jealousy was even mingled with an element of excitement at the possibility of her betraying him, though there is nothing to suggest that she ever did. At any rate he convinced himself that she had a right to go with other men. If she wished to do so, it would only be because it was part of her natural, generous character. When he later dedicated his book *Numerous Treasure* to her memory he added the words of Christ, in Luke VII, blessing the prostitute who anointed him: *Quia multum amavit* ["Her sins, which are many, are forgiven, *because she loved much*"]. As he said elsewhere: "What does this mean but that a loving heart towards men, even in harlotry, was enough to occasion her forgiveness?" He had come to persuade himself that a warm and spontaneous sexual nature, far from being in conflict with Christian love, was in fact a manifestation of it. He had become at least a theoretical believer in an "open relationship." There is indeed some vague evidence to suggest that he was himself unfaithful to her on one or more of his trips to the U.S.A. during subsequent years.

Although love had driven Robert and Betty to make a break with conventional morals, neither were intolerantly anticonventional in their tastes or outlook. So their friendship with the Elliotts, with their solid, commonsense values, was a natural one. They went to stay with them, frequently, at their country home near High Wycombe, an hour from London by train, and for a while Betty went to live with Dr. Elliott's mother. Neither couple can have guessed, however, how closely their lives were to be intertwined.

Robert's rift with his wife deepened. She not only detested his books, but could hardly ignore his renewed contact with Betty. She found his soul-searching and growing loss of religion incomprehensible. The war, which had brought such a change to his life, cast its shadow between them. Apart from her conversion to Rome, she remained true to the conventional English life in which she had been reared and which had continued regardless of the great conflict on the Continent. She was embarrassed by his views and by his trying habit of chucking social engagements, on one occasion forgetting to be present when they were entertaining. Nonetheless, she remained devoted to him, and as a Roman Catholic she believed that their marriage could never be ended. This left Robert and Betty unable to marry and at odds with the English society he had come to hate.

His literary success offered him an escape. By July 1921 he had already realised that he would soon be rich enough from *Simon Called Peter* to uproot himself from England and go wherever he wished. Arthur Grimble, an old Cambridge friend on leave from a Colonial Office job in the Gilbert Islands, had just approached him for literary advice. Grimble was a humorous and imaginative raconteur, as shown in the best-selling account of his career, *A Pattern of Islands*, which he wrote many years later; his stories of "emerald lagoons and an ocean of petunia and cobalt" fired Robert's wanderlust.

The isles of the South Sea, though ravaged by disease and with their aboriginal cultures undermined by Western commerce and missionaries, had become fashionable with adventurous visitors in the years just before and after the war. Modern luxury travel had put them within reach. Waltzes, plangently rendered on the Hawaiian guitar, songs, and ragtime melodies about Polynesian enchantresses, such as "Ukulele Lady" and "Chili Bean," were very popular by the 1920s. From the beginning of the century artists and writers, drawn by the tales of Loti, Gauguin, and Stevenson, travelled there from Europe and the United States: Jack London, Robert Gibbings, Zane Grey, Jack Hastings, Eric Muspratt, Rupert Brooke, George Calderon, Cecil Lewis. It was Gauguin above all who fascinated Robert Keable: the painter who in middle life had left wife, family, and a comfortable job to pursue his art, dwelling as a primitive among the natives.

Keable told Grimble how much he wanted to be alone "or the next thing to it." He was still, even then, writing of his wife joining him out in the Pacific; but, he confessed to Grimble, "she might be rather glad to see me go for a bit. I expect I'm a beast to live with, especially now."

In the end, however, he was legally separated from her in 1922 and it was Betty who accompanied him to the South Seas, meeting him in Australia, where he had arranged a much publicised literary tour. Her voyage was characteristically full of amorous episodes: "Two proposals! One from a sweet boy from Hailerbury [sic] 2 years younger than me. His people would faint if they knew." It was diverting for her, but by now she did not need to seek out such predictable shipboard encounters. She was deeply in love with "Bill," as she called Robert.

Meanwhile Robert, pipe in hand, applied himself with missionary zeal to preaching his newly discovered sexual ethics to the Australians. If an unmarried couple felt that they could "swing together," he informed his audience at the Protestant Hall in Sydney, that constituted a true marriage; but if a married pair ceased to love each other, but continued to live together for mere respectability's sake, then that was the grossest immorality. To emphasise his credentials he told a gathering of advertising men that the modern novelist had now become confessor, priest, and teacher for the public. These pronouncements had a mixed reception: "Mr. Keable's views," wrote one correspondent to the *Sydney Telegraph*, "represent the prevalent canker of the present day, namely selfishness." It was a reaction to be expected from some quarters, but the writer failed to perceive that there was nothing hypocritical or cynical about Robert's high-minded stance. Robert was convinced that Christian and erotic love could be reconciled, though he could not manage, as his contemporary Eric Gill apparently did, to flout sexual taboos under a Roman Catholic banner.

The Bishop of Zanzibar understood Robert's spiritual difficulties better, though he was wholly opposed to the course he had taken. He received, at this time, an enquiry from an anxious cleric, alarmed that Robert might have corrupted some young Australian novices with whom he had travelled. Weston was reassuring: "It is not a bad thing for theological students to meet a shipwrecked priest: it may help them to avoid his perils." After a brief escape into the mountains together, Robert and Betty set sail for Tahiti on 9 November.

Tahiti, "the Queen of the South," then, as now, was a colony of France, a mountainous island the size of London. It was no longer the unspoiled paradise where Fletcher Christian had been tempted into deserting from the *Bounty*. Putting in at Papeete, the principal port of the island, Robert and Betty saw a forest of masts and sails at the quay, and beyond, the rectangular stores roofed with corrugated iron, the villas and the jerry-built little churches. The appurtenances of modern life – curio shops, telegraph poles, tourist hotels, and cinemas – were there in all their banality. It was a disappointment for the man who had told Arthur Grimble: "I hate civilisation, a half-Xtian, compromising, conventional civilisation and I love, I worship, the sunshine, the wind, the sea – freedom, colour, life. You know Richard Jefferies? He came closest to putting it into words."

Further down the coast, to the south, he and Betty found their first home: Ventura at Punaavia, the former dwelling place of Paul Gauguin during his final years in Tahiti between 1895 and 1901, following the second failure to gain recognition for his art in France. The situation was spectacular with its view, across the bay, of the fabulous island of Moorea; and all the while the murmur of the sea upon the broken reef, and, when the southeast trade winds blew, the thunder of mighty breakers on the open ocean beach. Pacing up and down that stretch of shore, Keable frequently brooded on Gauguin's gesture against spiritual suffocation, which he himself strove to imitate.

Not that Betty or Robert, now living as "Mr. and Mrs. Keable," opted for the primitive existence that for Gauguin had constituted "union with the soul of Polynesia." Betty threw herself with characteristic verve into rearranging the artist's bungalow. She made a drawingroom with "a topping little cosy corner." Although there was no electric light, only oil lamps with soft green shades, there was at least a bathroom with a proper bath and a shower outside. For Betty, the real advantage over English life lay in the cheap and delicious French wine, a girl to do the washing, another to do the cleaning (who changed the flowers every day), and an excellent Chinese cook and general servant: "Plenty of scope," wrote Betty, "for giving really topping parties and moonlight picnics always being free and unconventional, and not being in terror of your cook because 4 people turn up three days running and stay to lunch and dinner." Ice was sent out from Papeete every day. To complete this agreeable life, Betty reported self-mockingly, "I have a jolly car called a Dodge which Bill got for me knowing my dislike of walking." She could not buy any fashionable clothes, but swirled around in her own loose-fitting creations of *crêpe-de-chine*. What she most welcomed was not having to wear stays. All in all, she told a friend, they got the best of everything for £250 a year.

Later, in 1923, they moved into a fine building, which Robert had constructed in the native style, at Teahuahu, near Papeari, close to the isthmus of Taravao, the narrow join between the two halves of the island. There the countryside was wilder and more unspoiled and the view of the *Presqu'île* of Tautira to the east was the most beautiful of the southeastern Pacific: "the scene below and around utterly fulfils the all but legendary story of the far South Seas . . . Coconut and pandanus crowd down to the still lagoon on the right as solid almost in reflection as in life; and away to the left, across the bay, in a wide majestic sweep, the mountains of Vairao and Teahupoo, with crown of drifting cloud and swift play of sun and shadow, rifted with great valleys and clothed with wealth of fern, give true promise of the magic that is theirs."

Their house, long and low and white, stood high on a slender spur of land with water on three sides. Its large music room had a polished floor, spread with oriental rugs. In the well-stocked library, containing about two thousand books, was a great bay window overlooking the sea, a cushioned seat running round it, and the author's desk across the arc. The building partially enclosed a small lawn, where a fountain played and scented shrubs perfumed the air. A path led down to the boathouse and a small jetty.

In his eyrie, commanding garden, ocean, and mountains, Robert worked obsessively on his novels, his fan mail, and the lectures he gave during periodic promotional trips to the U.S.A. Betty did her best to interest herself in his books and to tease him out of writer's block. The price of such a peaceful life was isolation. They found that the local French population, with conspicuous exceptions, discouraged intimacy, though they were amiable enough. "The Keables" both welcomed any new arrivals, and Betty implored friends, such as the Elliotts, to come out and join them or at least to write: "We only get a mail once in four weeks, and you can't think how I long for letters . . . Bill gets hundreds . . . literally from adoring females and earnest young men every mail."

Even so, amid this nostalgia for old friends and their agreeable enjoyment of whisky and cocktails, the picture she painted was one of great marital happiness: "You would love my dear Bill," she wrote. "He is so clever and knows such a lot. I never realised how appaulingly [sic] ignorant I was before I met him . . . .You can't think how grateful I am to my small amount of common sense that I did not marry the first man who proposed to me, but waited for the right one to come along and I am afraid I should have never settled down and become a dull and dutiful wife."

Photographs of the time show them preparing, with friends, to bathe from the jetty, dressed in their native pareos – swathes of brightly coloured cloth; wandering through dense jungles of fern; wading rivers in broad-brimmed sun hats; setting sail in Tahitian outriggers; or, garlanded, at dinner with native islanders. How long such an arcadian existence could have continued, given Robert's capacity for inner torment and Betty's amorous, sociable nature, it is impossible to say.

In 1924, she became pregnant. Having children around does not seem to have fitted into Keable's scheme of things. When *Recompence*, his successful sequel to *Simon Called Peter*, appeared that year, it contained scenes and characters suggesting that he regarded childbirth with horror. His views cannot have failed to influence Betty, who only a few months before had told a friend: "I certainly do not want to start having babies for at least four years." For medical reasons, chiefly, they decided the birth must take place in England. Betty's mother, Mrs. Buck, rose to the occasion and welcomed her daughter with affection, though the illicit relationship upset her. She seems to have been temporarily reconciled to Robert, too, writing to him and sending affectionate messages through her daughter. Betty went ahead of him to organise a new home for them – Harman's Corner, in a village on the Kent-Sussex border: "I hope to have everything comfy for when you arrive. Have your hair cut and trim yourself nicely, my cabbage," she wrote. So the year passed, the two of them as close and affectionate as ever.

In August Betty was helping Robert with a new novel – one on the discovery of Tahiti – and he was also exploring the theme of the impact of Europe on the island in more recent years, which bore fruit in his bittersweet tale of the South Seas, *Numerous Treasure*. During this time they saw many old friends, including Fr. Dowling, a Catholic priest who had been a padre out in France and who was clearly unaware that they were not legally married. Remembering Betty in wartime, he remarked on the change in her: her spirit, he told Robert, had "come into the sunlight ... She never had a chance until you gave it to her." He was impressed by the strength of their relationship and the disappearance of her rebelliousness. Like H. G. Wells's feminist heroine, *Anne Veronica* (1909) having chosen her man in defiance of convention, she seemed content to surrender authority to him. Independence, after all, was an exhausting burden then for a woman of orthodox background to carry for long, even in the liberated 1920s: "Paddy, you know all my thoughts are my husband's," she told the priest.

Her devotion to Robert may have been all the stronger because of her fears about childbirth. One day she asked Rita Elliott if she and Jack would look after the baby should anything happen to her. Keable, she felt, would not be able to look after a small child on his own. Mrs. Elliott was surprised, as the doctors did not foresee complications; but they agreed. In November 1924, the baby, Anthony, was born. His mother, however, died shortly afterwards, on 14 November, in a nursing home at 7 Mandeville Place, Marylebone, London. Her heart, her sister was later to claim, had been fatally weakened by the strenuous work she had done on the Western Front, though the immediate cause was given as influenza and blood poisoning. The real reason was excess of chloroform, which she had fervently demanded against the pain. Its use in childbirth cases was still experimental, and the anaesthetist miscalculated the amount.

After her death, Robert's frail health, further weakened, began to collapse. Grief-stricken, he accepted doctors' advice to return to the kindlier climate of Tahiti. In the New Year, he drew up a will, leaving his son all his property on the island, including money, on his attaining the age of twenty-four. The income from a war loan was to pay for Anthony's education until his twenty-first birthday. Thereafter, this fund, some £2,500, was to go to found a scholarship for Old Whitgiftians to Magdalene College, Cambridge. Sybil Keable, his legal wife, was to receive an income of £400 annually for life, and his parents an income from the residue during their lifetime, which was thereafter to pass to Magdalene College.

The little boy had been born prematurely and was too weak to travel with his father. He was left, therefore, with Jack and Rita Elliott while Robert thought over what should be done. In his parlous state of health and without a wife he knew he could not cope responsibly with a child.

Thereafter, things were allowed to drift, and when Rita Elliott told them they were prepared to look after Anthony, Robert accepted, reiterating his confidence in them, while admitting to a "haunting and occasional sense of obligation."

Though Betty's family had been kind and helpful – particularly Betty's sister Kathleen – his relations with them after the tragedy had been uneasy. Like so many of those bereaved during and after the Great War, Mrs. Buck and her daughter took comfort in spiritualism.

They claimed to be in contact with Betty's spirit, though the messages that came from beyond the grave were, as usual in these cases, mere banalities that neither convinced Robert nor comforted him.

"I was a lonely man until I met Betty," he wrote, "and I am doomed to be a lonely man now till it is over . . . one does things and laughs and eats and sleeps and plans, but what does it matter?" His health was deteriorating; he was only 38 but his arteries were like pipestems, one doctor said; and in the spring of 1926 he reported a recurrence of disturbing maladies arising from his kidney trouble – boils, fever, high blood pressure; he was diabetic and he was becoming painfully thin. From time to time he made the expensive trip to see a specialist in San Francisco, who put him on a butter-and-cream, low-protein diet, which brought about a temporary improvement.

Overwork has been blamed for his decline. More likely, his defiant determination to keep going prolonged his life where men of lesser willpower would have given up the struggle. His novel, *Numerous Treasure*, appeared in 1925, with its poignant end, written in the intensity of his own tragic loss. After a slow start, the book sold well, despite his fears that he was losing his touch. As a picture of Tahiti at the beginning of the twentieth century it has an historic value, as does his gracefully written travel book, *Tahiti, Isle of Dreams*, which was published in the same year.

He began to use a secretary to relieve him of some of the labour. No book, however, appeared in 1926. His social life remained active. He was a generous host to streams of guests, and some of these, such as the Swedish artist Paul Engdahl and his wife Ilonha (Lily), made themselves indispensable. Lily, an aristocratic Hungarian, who had starved in Vienna during the war, could have served as a model for Richard Aldington's Katia, the heroine of his novel *All Men Are Enemies*, a story often dismissed as improbable. For a few months she acted as Robert's house-keeper, making his home comfortable. The boost this gave to his spirits enabled him to continue writing.

In fact, his life on Tahiti never seems to have been short of amuse-ments. There was the trip to the island of Rarotonga in the Cook archipelago, to visit its king, Tiniaru, in the company of three princesses of the old royal house of Tahiti (Pomare). On Rarotonga, a British colony, alcohol was forbidden. The result was incessant smuggling and illegal brewing and parties that were orgies of overindulgence: "If after a month on this I am still alive, I think you will admit I can't be in ex-tremis," Robert joked. Confident once more, he took the steamer to San Francisco and thence to visit the Elliotts and tour Europe with his par-ents.

His partial resurgence was helped by his relationship with Ina Salmon, a Tahitian of mixed race (no pure-blooded natives remained), partly French, elegant, somewhere in her early thirties. She had two or three children by a previous relationship and in February 1927 she became pregnant with Robert's child. Her letters reveal her as shrewd, highly-educated, and affectionate. Robert was devoted to her, but his feelings never matched the intensity of his love for Betty. He found her some-times passionate, at other times disconcertingly detached, like a child. She gave him romance, comfort, and good cooking in his declining months, and the arrangement, though somewhat pragmatically con-ceived on both their parts, was a happy one.

He celebrated his return from Europe in 1927 with a large party at the Diadem Hotel in Papeete. The writer Alec Waugh was a guest. Among other books, it was Keable's *Numerous Treasure* that had led him to Tahiti. The next day, Robert drove him out, in his Buick, to Papeari. Waugh later recalled how astonished Keable's prewar English congregation would have been, could they have seen him "reclined among cushions, clad only in a pareo, while his Tahitian princess, bare-shouldered and bare-footed, her black hair falling to her waist and a white flower behind her ear, glided negligently about the house," but it gave Waugh a certain pleasure to add that when Keable said, "And now how about some tea?" his voice "had the parsonical intonation with which fifteen years earlier had summoned the parish children to a Sunday school treat." Waugh later told a friend, "I am sure he will die a monk," echoing Hugh Benson's estimate of Robert fourteen years before.

Despite continued protestations that he was unlikely ever to become a Catholic, Keable's mind had never ceased to dwell on the faith of his old mentor. Hugh Benson's tale of a Roman Catholic priest, *Richard Raynal*, was his favourite novel, Keable told readers of the lively literary journal *T.P.'s Weekly* in July 1927. It was "a literary gem, human to tears, all spirit . . . I do not know a beautiful modern book of fiction to equal this." Meanwhile the Bible remained dearest to him of all: "I think I could be happy endlessly trying to put the Minor Prophets into English verse and rereading the most beautiful historical fiction this world has ever produced."

Keable's last important novel, *Lighten Our Darkness*, had recently appeared. The dust cover showed a naked girl walking out of a cave, and stretching her arms up to the light. The theme was an apostate Roman Catholic priest's discovery of a new kind of religious belief through the beauty of a woman's love. It was Robert's final tribute to Betty and for a while, at least, he found he was actually able to live by this faith. Though the new novel was not his best work and fell short of his ambitious message, it contained touching glimpses of his devotion to his dear lost companion and of the torment he had gone through earlier when he left the priesthood. By comparison with previous works it was poorly reviewed. At the time, Alec Waugh was sceptical about its ideas, while listening sympathetically to Robert as he confided his grief. Later, following a passionate love affair of his own, Waugh admitted that he had been surprised to find himself undergoing the same kind of transcendent experience that Robert had described to him.

The fatal kidney disease was progressively weakening Robert. Further disagreeable symptoms notwithstanding, he finished writing a novel begun while Betty was still alive, *The Madness of Monty*, which was to come out in 1928. It was a plea for everyone to seek out some extraordinary experience once in their career, but also to put up with a humdrum existence in the long term. Was he confessing that he had expected too much from life? A kindly, innocuous comedy, it lacked the intensity that gave even his weaker works their power; but it was all he could rise to at this time. He continued to struggle, unsuccessfully, with his historical novel, also planned earlier, about a very early European encounter with the Tahitians.

As always however, he was boyishly optimistic. Indeed there was something a little hectic about his schemes for the future. He planned to revisit England, to enlarge his home with a picture gallery, and to build a chapel, complete with altar, dedicated to Christ, Buddha, the Virgin Mary, and "some few philosophers." He went on making new friendships. One was with Zane Grey, whom he joined on a fishing trip, watching, as, strapped to a swivel chair, the thriller-writer fought with a 540-lb. swordfish. Another was with two fans from America, a mother and daughter. He claimed to find the girl disappointingly overweight when he took her bathing and, to his amusement, her pareo fell off in the water. He was still, astonishingly, fit enough to dive down to look for it, while she waited, "in the costume of Eve, literally."

The last great friend he made was James Norman Hall, also from the U.S.A., and later coauthor of the best-selling *Mutiny on the Bounty* (1932). During the Great War, Jimmy Hall had fought with distinction in the British and American Expeditionary Forces and as a flier with the French Escadrille Lafayette. Learning that Keable's eyes were failing and that he desperately needed to earn more money, he generously helped him to finish his work in progress. The book, *The Great Galilean*, was a curiosity. In it Keable tried to reconcile his love of Jesus with his failure to believe in him as a God. He argued for the historical existence of a nondivine Christ, a great sage who believed in free love, but was two thousand years ahead of his time. At the same time he acknowledged a divinity with whom the historic Christ was in harmony – the spirit of all life – and whom Keable celebrated in a lyrical closing passage, describing sunrise over Tahiti (and Ina greeting it) on Easter Day. The book eventually appeared in 1929.

In November 1927 he began to institute divorce proceedings against his wife Sybil, in order to legitimise his baby son, Henry Reheatoa (Glorious Warrior). There had been no repetition of the tragedy that had accompanied his first son's birth. Ina was hard at work in the garden a few hours before he was born, and four days later was cooking the dinner. Robert was delighted with his new love child. He felt that the birth was a last fling at morality and conventional society. He told Rita Elliott that it gave him an heir to his various properties and a stake in Tahiti, "which, blind and poor, I may need." With these words, he effectively cut his elder son off from any inheritance in the "Isle of Dreams."

The following month he made plans for a Christmas party for the children of the Papeari district where he lived; he was expecting a box of toys and Christmas-tree ornaments ordered from Australia. He was planning to make a start on the fourth chapter of his new novel, with the aid of Jimmy Hall. Ten days before Christmas, however, he felt ill with an intensified infection of the kidneys. Despite the constant attentions of two doctors, his condition, unknown to Keable, was worsening. He remained optimistic, telling Hall, "Jimmy, from what I've seen of knocked-out men I think I've turned the corner." It was not to be. He suffered no pain, but his system became entirely intoxicated. When awake his mind was clear sometimes, and at others would wander to long-ago scenes of his past. On the evening of 22 December he died. He was forty.

At some stage, shortly before the end, it is firmly asserted that he had been formally received into the Roman Catholic Church or at least accepted Catholic rites. If this is true, what prompted this, after his pagan sentiments about his new son, so recently expressed? Late repentance, like Manfred or Casella in Dante's *Purgatorio*? A wish to please his legal wife Sybil? Or the knowledge that the time for this pursuit of enticing unorthodoxies was over and the feeling that it was better to die in an ancient faith – true or not – than in none at all? Most likely, he found himself able finally to reconcile his two ideals, romantic-erotic and religious, and could die peacefully accepting the rituals he loved. He was apparently buried, however, with Protestant ceremonies in the Papeete cemetery. There is no evidence to suggest the reason for this, but it may be that it was done for the sake of his parents, at his own request.

Thus the island idyll ended, five years after it began. It was decided by the lawyers that since satisfactory provision had been made in Robert's will for Anthony, Betty's son, and since there were obvious difficulties of administration, all the Tahitian properties that Robert owned should be allowed to pass to Ina and her son Henry – the big house at Teahuahu, with its library and pictures, papers and car, and another little place in the beautiful Vairao valley. Ina firmly indicated that the Engdahls would have to quit the hut at Hitiaa where Robert had allowed them to live. She talked vaguely of bringing his two sons together, of arranging some joint education when they were older, of sharing the 2,000 books; and of giving Anthony Betty's portrait and mementos of her "Bobby" when she paid a visit to Europe. But such plans were the very stuff of Tahiti: evanescent, full of well-meaning, on-the-instant warmth, they faded, cooled, were forgotten.

Anthony was left with his devoted foster parents and a small income to cover his education. He grew up wishing to follow Jack Elliott's career as a doctor. Unfortunately, a doctor's training goes on well beyond the age of twenty-one, so that he could not support himself by that age, as his father had assumed. It required great sacrifices by the Elliotts for him to gain his medical qualifications. He repaid their care, rising to the top of his profession, but for years remained mystified and saddened at the strange hand of cards he had been dealt.

Sybil Keable lived on, her religion increasingly important to her. She stayed at first at her brother's house, but kind and tolerant though he was, he found her personality too strong at close quarters and had to ask her to leave. Thereafter she lodged in Catholic convents, until she died, in 1970, at St. Mary's Abbey, Mill Hill.

Being at the Front had brought hope to Robert Keable and had led him, in the end, to break away from a set of religious values with which he had been brought up and which, like many contemporaries who also went through the war, he had come to find oppressive. He enjoyed the temporary release that army service gave him from a frustrated marriage and he saw relatively little of the worst horrors and dangers. Above all, he fell ecstatically in love. So his war novel, though full of angst, was optimistic in tone. Rightly so, in one sense, as it turned out, for during the years that followed he fulfilled his deep desire for adventure, romance, and companionship.

Christian commentators have called his life tragic, and the war, by implication, a destructive influence in it. According to his own unorthodox
standards, however, the only true tragedy was the loss of Betty – not the
abandonment of Sybil, nor his break with the Anglican Church. Despite
the pain these decisions cost him, he enjoyed, partly because of them, a
richness of experience that is given to few. Moreover, from early in his
career, he had used his talents to the full and seized life with both hands.
His works, though seldom read now, were no mean achievement, intellectually or artistically, even if their high quality was rarely sustained
throughout a whole book.

His three best novels, *Simon Called Peter*, *Peradventure*, and *Numerous
Treasure*, and his accounts of Africa and Tahiti can still be read with real
pleasure and interest. In many respects they have, however, dated, as have
many great popular successes. What was shocking and new in *Simon
Called Peter* is no longer so, and that book – particularly the dialogue – is
full of extinct expressions fascinating to the social historian, but setting a
distance between those days and our own. There are few moments either
when the overwhelming fact of the war, with all its horror, comes fully
across to the reader. This is not least because, for all his frankness and adventurous spirit, there is something inhibited and self-conscious about
the book, which was precisely the fault that he desired to shed. Even so,
the novel deserves respect, because it was so close to its author's experience. Although it is not a work of great subtlety, the difficulties of a padre
on the Western Front are treated in *Simon Called Peter* with sensitivity
and courage and there is no better account of them.

More than that, Keable's war novel is a vivid illustration of the inner
confusion and conflict that are so much a part of the modern Western
consciousness. Even though Jolie had such a releasing effect, there was
still, eight years after the war, when Alec Waugh met Robert, something
indelibly parsonical about him. He was quintessentially the divided
twentieth-century man, yearning for self-realisation and for a faith, and
full of guilt and self-hatred. Yet as we have seen, *Simon Called Peter* is not
an unhappy book, in the way that Gristwood's *Somme* or Aldington's
Death of a Hero are. Robert Keable did not feel cheated as did those two
writers: quite the reverse. He was fortunate. To him, as for Wilfrid Ewart,

though Robert's experience of war was decidedly less harrowing and their moral conclusions differed, the war seemed to reveal the nature of real goodness, loyalty, and love.

❦

8

The Patriotic Identity
Gilbert Frankau
1884 - 1952

A ll his life, Gilbert Frankau, author of the best-selling *Peter Jackson, Cigar Merchant*, was an ardent patriot. His politics were conservative, his style of life opulent. He was, as his grandson recalled affectionately, "a cracking snob." Well into his middle age, assisted by Savile Row tailoring, he kept his Edwardian matinée-idol looks. He was broad-shouldered, on the stocky side, but with fine aquiline features, a thin, pencil-line of a moustache, and dark curly hair, impeccably barbered. His small, neat feet were shod by Peel's; platinum and gold glinted in his flawless cuffs: in his wardrobe he had forty white ties and kept a plentiful supply of these on his person so that throughout a long evening he was never seen without a clean one.

Energetic and athletic, Frankau (pronounced "Franko") kept fit with fencing and tennis, though a lifetime of smoking in the end affected his heart, his "ticker" as he called it. His demeanour was suave and controlled, but he was highly-strung, despite the persona he cultivated of a sophisticated, insouciant man-about-town, fashionable writer, and *homme d'affaires*.

He strove hard to achieve this effect and to attain the success he knew his parents, particularly his mother, expected. His capable intelligence showed in his prize-winning achievements at school, in his linguistic skill in the foreign side of the family business, and in his rapid grasp of the technicalities of gunnery when an artilleryman, although he despised mathematics as "ungentlemanly." Equally important was his iron determination to prove himself, to show himself no man's fool, to be "on form" always, with military and business associates or with women. He prided himself, like Peter Jackson, the hero of his war novel, on his "adequacy" and liked to believe "that what he went for, he got." In part this came from a disinterested desire to do a job well; in part from plain egoism. Until his fifties this held good: he was attractive, companionable (though not easy to live with), affectionate, and talented – and on the make.

Gilbert was born on 21 April 1884, the son of Arthur Frankau, a cigar merchant with a successful London business, and Julia Davis Frankau, the novelist. Julia Frankau wrote under the *nom-de-plume* of "Frank Danby" and was one of the founders of the famous Independent Theatre of London club, which staged advanced drama of a high standard at the end of the century. His youngest brother Ronald, born ten years later, became a successful comedian. The family lived, during Gilbert's childhood, in the West End of London, near Portland Place.

Gilbert's grandfather, Joseph Frankau, came from a Jewish clan long resident, with many of their coreligionists, in the Bavarian village of Dispeck. The slow pace of emancipation and fresh outbreaks of anti-Semitism seem to have been the forces that drove Joseph Frankau eventually to London, where he set up his cigar-importing firm in 1837. He himself had received a solidly Jewish religious upbringing in Germany, but the Jewish education he arranged for his son Arthur in Frankfurt was without a pronouncedly orthodox colour, a shift away from the earlier piety of the family in the direction of assimilation.

When Arthur himself married it was at the Reform Synagogue in Upper Berkeley Street, near Marble Arch. After the wedding, he and his wife withdrew still further from Judaism. Julia, Gilbert's mother, probably the moving spirit in this, was in revolt against her own Orthodox background, as shown by her account of English Jewish life in Maida Vale, North London. The first of her sharply satirical "Frank Danby" novels, *Dr. Phillips: A Maida Vale Idyll*, attacked the narrowness, the obsession with money, and the lack of culture in the circle she had known as a girl. Her devastating portrait may be accurate up to a point, but is unduly harsh when one bears in mind that Maida Vale and neighbouring South Hampstead were also the home of such eminent Jewish intellectuals as Israel Zangwill and Nahum Sokolow. The tormented figure of Dr. Phillips is the best thing about the book: ambitious, competent, amorous, kind-hearted, yet with a callous streak, the Jewish doctor seems like a portrait – perhaps of a close relative. His makeup indeed has something in common with that of her own son Gilbert as he grew up to be.

Effectively Julia Frankau and her husband turned their back on the Jewish way of life they had known, its culture and social exclusivity as well as its religion. Many of their friends were Jewish but this was in a largely assimilated and cosmopolitan world of literature, theatre, politics, and big business: they included Rufus Isaacs, later Lord Reading, the Attorney-General; Sir Charles Higham; Lord Melchett; Solly Joel; Phillips Oppenheim; Jack Grein; and Ada Leverson. Neither Julia nor her husband carried their refutation of their background to the point of changing their family name to an English one. Equally, however, they did nothing to transmit a sense of a Jewish religious and cultural heritage to Gilbert, Ronnie, or their other children, Jack and Joan. Gilbert was sent to a private boarding school, Hawtrey's, a stepping-stone to Eton, where he went in due course, having successfully taken the scholarship examinations. His housemaster was the eminent Hugh MacNaughten. At Eton he gained award after award, a network of useful contacts, a suave manner that failed quite to conceal his thrusting ambition, and some fairly lowly "colours" for rowing and Eton football, the path to acceptance in that boy's world.

Unlike his brother Ronnie, who in reaction became a communist during later life, Gilbert undoubtedly loved Eton, though he grew out of it before he was eighteen. It was there that his literary career began, not only with his prize-winning efforts, but also in the shape of a school magazine he started in 1901: "X – a magazine (edited by Xman) for E's, O.E's & everybody else's ease." Those who have heard any of Ronald Frankau's comedy records of the thirties (he sold over 100,000) will recognise here the Frankau brothers' brand of humour: witty, flash, casual, in the Etonian style, though Ronnie's more risqué jokes – for which he became famous in such shows as "Sauce Piquante" – were an embarrassment to Gilbert, who liked his sauce a little less piquante. After his brother's show "The Intimate Revue" in 1946, he would not go backstage to see him. The two were never close.

Intimately bound up with Britain's imperial status and sense of superiority was a mystique that Eton, like all the great English public schools, then had, and that now, a century later, it has lost, despite

continuing to attract the rich. At that time the school was an all-absorb-
ing microcosm from which many never entirely emerged. It set its stamp
on both Gilbert and Ronnie, which their parents welcomed, as it contributed to the obliteration of any residual sense of Jewish identity in
them. When Gilbert met Guards officers at Loos during the war, he
found it reassuring to mix once again with Old Etonians, particularly in
such dangerous circumstances, because, as he said, Old Etonians always
did their best to appear unruffled by disagreeable facts and as though the
job in hand, however vital, really did not matter too much. He himself
shared the curious brand of philistinism, conceit, and self-deprecation so
characteristic of the public schools of his day: "Luckily," he observed in
Peter Jackson, "there is no 'education' at English public-schools. They
merely train boys to be men."

It is noticeable that in *Peter Jackson*, the leading characters, Peter himself and Francis Gordon, though they are distinguished from specifically
Jewish characters like "Pretty" Bramson, are described as having "an ad-
mixture [with early 'yeoman' stock] of "exotic Hebraic blood" through
their grandmother. That seems as far as Gilbert wished to go then in
hinting publicly at his Jewish origins. In the novel, moreover, Bramson,
unlike the honourable and gentlemanly Peter and Francis, is held up as
an unreliable business partner because he is not only incompetent, but
also too close to a Jewish cousin in a rival firm – a stock anti-Semitic accusation in business circles.

Gilbert later described himself as being brought up in the Church of
England and as remaining in complete ignorance of his Jewish ancestry
until he was over sixteen. He had been baptised at Holy Trinity, Albany
Street, in August 1897 at an age when his parents deemed that he could
understand what the Christian religion was about. He does not seem to
have been offered the chance of becoming Jewish. He remained a pious,
if not a virtuous, Anglican until the middle of the Great War – when
many young men lost their faiths. What he claimed to have put him off,
however, was not the all-too-frequent feeling that the existence of a be-
nign God was inconsistent with a horrific war, but an "official prayer"
that he had heard at church parade, "that our enemies may be healed of
their bodily hurts." War was war, he had decided, and loving thy enemy
neighbour had no part in it.

His bombastic war poetry, some of it a pastiche of the "Viking" stanzas of Chesterton's *Ballad of the White Horse,* had a blatantly pagan ring:

> We scorned the Galilaean,
> We mocked at Kingdom-Come:
> The old gods knew our paean-
> Our dawn-loud engine-hum:
> The old red gods of slaughter,
> The gods before the Jew!
> We heard their cruel laughter,
> Shrill round us, as we flew:

Throughout much of his life Gilbert remained an alienated personality, without a central focus, and this was essentially because of his lack of a fully Jewish identity. In many ways his mother had given him a very Jewish upbringing, with emphasis on cleanliness, hard work, excellence, ambition, and the enjoyment of the good things of life combined with a certain puritanism: for all his love of pleasure Gilbert was a highly disciplined man. He seldom drank to excess. He was never idle and worked round the clock at his business. Later on, as a writer, he kept unfailingly to a schedule, rising early and labouring six or seven hours at a stretch until lunchtime. Yet for all these high standards that he had learnt from his parents, he lacked the vital sense of race and culture that should have lain at the centre of his existence.

Gilbert's deep-seated desire to establish a marked identity to compensate for this led him, from the war years to the midthirties, into an extreme patriotism. He reached such a pitch of right-wing fervour that the journalist Hannen Swaffer, a former ally, referred to him as a "Jewish fascist," for which he sued Swaffer, successfully. Gilbert was always litigious. In the very last years of his life he became a convert to Roman Catholicism, a faith that demanded complete and absolute commitment in contrast with the undefined boundaries of modern Anglicanism. It also appealed – as with so many English converts such as Evelyn Waugh – to the romantic in him. It was necessary, given his upbringing, to find something spiritually as strong as the birthright he had lost. It would have been open to him to make the return to Judaism, but his mother, his most formative influence, must have always stood in his subconscious mind blocking the path back.

She died in 1916. He had been much closer to her than to his father, whom he loved as an unselfish and loyal parent more than he admired him, reckoning him at once too cautious and too emotionally vulnerable. Gilbert's account of his mother in his *Self-Portrait*, however, though meant as his special tribute to her, gave an unintended impression of hardness: a brave, tough, not easily rattled woman, sharp, witty, and good-looking, with that attribute so important for Edwardian ladies – "fine shoulders." *Dr. Phillips* was a bold book for her to have written in the 1880s, not just because of the offence it must have given to the formidable society into which she had been born, but because of its strong - and quite shocking – undercurrent of sex.

According to Gilbert, Julia Frankau never cried – he saw her with her eyes slightly moist at their last parting during the war – but that was the only time when she came near to tears. He described her as registering no grief at his father's death, keeping her feelings entirely to herself. The English "stiff upper-lip" was at its most fashionable in that era and Gilbert followed her assiduously in cultivating this. Hence he was bitterly ashamed of the nerve storms he suffered during the war as the result of shell shock.

He was Julia's favourite, and undoubtedly she did much to inflate his considerable self-esteem. It was partly to impress her that he affected a shallow cynicism and worldiness, which was the best that a young man with a strong romantic streak could manage in the way of realism. Much later, long after her death, he seemed able finally to absorb her down-to-earth view of existence constructively, as a help in seeing his life in its true perspective; but in the shorter run, his desire to please her seems to have encouraged him to suppress the gentler side of his character.

Not that he always followed her wishes. Despite his academic attainments at Eton, he elected in 1901 not to go to Oxford, but to enter the family business. This went against the grain of his intellectual development, and disappointed Julia, who, he recalled, had wished him another Disraeli. However, he now desired to prove himself as a man among men, to show he could be rich and glamorous. After spending two years learning about the trade on the continent he started at J. Frankau & Co.'s offices in the City. He worked very hard and in close association with his father. After Arthur Frankau died in 1904, Gilbert bought out one of the partners and became director of the now re-formed company. He was capable of being astute and was always thorough. Unfortunately however he also had a reckless, gambling side and made errors of judgment. In the later part of the war the firm, which had expanded into two companies, collapsed, and though Frankau's survived as a business for years under different ownership, it ceased to be run by him.

Long before this had happened Gilbert entered another important commitment. He married, far too young, a dashing red-headed girl a year or two older than himself, Dorothea – Dolly – Drummond-Black, from a Roman Catholic background. She was a journalist, lively, intelligent, much-loved, and wildly extravagant – a challenge, in short, to a man ambitious to make his financial and social mark. He was only twenty-two, but had played the field precociously for a while and felt he should now settle down. Marriage seemed a hallmark of being the head of a firm, and a grown-up figure to be taken seriously. His mother did not object, though she and Dolly did not take to each other. There was a fashionable wedding at St. Margaret's Westminster.

They had two daughters, too rapidly for Gilbert's liking. He would have much preferred a son, and took little interest in them, plunging himself obsessively into the business. He strove for commercial success so as to be able to maintain his image as head of the family and to afford a luxurious style of life for his wife, whom at first, certainly, he loved passionately. Yet deep down, it seems, he never cared about the business and came to dislike the role of paterfamilias and faithful husband. It was with a saddened honesty that he years later admitted: "my main love, my overwhelming passion, must have been for myself." In 1912 he took a long trip abroad to drum up custom for his already ailing company and seems to have enjoyed a far from celibate existence on his travels over the globe. This voyage was to provide the material for his first novel, completed during the war, *The Woman of the Horizon*.

Even before this year abroad his interest in writing had begun to revive. In his autobiography he suggested that there was always the pull of literary endeavour lurking underneath, though he seldom put creative pen to paper between leaving school and around 1910. His earliest published work had been a volume of verse, *Eton Echoes*, which came out in 1901.

In 1912, his first notable book, *One of Us,* appeared, a Byronic picaresque verse epic encompassing Eton, Business, Society, and Love. It was a *succès d'estime*, but he dismissed his excellent reviews with the words: "*This* isn't what I want. I'm going to write a book that sells a hundred thousand copies." His ironic-romantic verse story, *Tid'apa* (What *does* it matter?) was also well received in 1914, but it was not until *Peter Jackson* that he achieved his ambition. His evident role model in all this was his successful novelist mother, not his conscientious entrepreneur father. Realising that his interests were shifting, his wife Dolly commented on his attitude towards the family business and his home: "You are like a man keeping up a golf course who doesn't play."

Soon after the war broke out and at the age of thirty, he enlisted in the 9th East Surrey Regiment, "the Gallants." For him, like his public-school contemporaries, it was a case, he said, of: "My dear fellow, I was at Eton (or Winchester, or Haileybury, or Harrow, or Radley, or a hundred other of those foundations that pacific intellectuals affect to despise) and *one does, don't you know, one just does*."

His need to establish his identity made him more fervently patriotic than most. He had also two particular reasons for joining the army. Having a German name was a potential embarrassment and it was important to prove that his credentials as an Englishman were impeccable. In wartime, when the British press reached a scandalously low moral level, demagogues such as Horatio Bottomley, the dissipated editor of *John Bull*, were whipping up hatred against English people with Germanic-sounding surnames. Even the Admiral of the Fleet, Prince Louis of Battenberg, lost his job as a result of these raucous denunciations. The writer Dorota Flatau, whose promising journalist brother had been killed as a British soldier during the Somme battle, still felt it necessary to show herself more English than anyone with an English name, by penning a popular spy novel, *Yellow English*, about how German plans to destroy England went back decades before the war.

Gilbert's own virulently anti-German feeling derived also from his cigar-dealing experience. Thanks to a particular act of treachery by business associates in Germany, well before the war, his father had lost very heavily. Early on, therefore, Gilbert had acquired the conviction that the Germans were ruthless and could not be trusted to behave like gentlemen. He frequently referred to German atrocities in his war novel and in his memoirs.

Commissioned in October 1914, he flung himself enthusiastically into his training. However, during his first few months as a junior officer with the battalion in England, he and others who had joined up with equal fervour found themselves being manipulated by a scheming and incompetent adjutant. When Gilbert later published a frank and easily recognisable portrait of this man in *Peter Jackson*, the officer in question took steps towards a libel action but, to Gilbert's regret, died before the case could go to court.

In March 1915, because he could stand this no longer, Gilbert transferred out of the battalion to the 107th Brigade, the Royal Field Artillery. Although his brigade was in the thick of combat at the battle of Loos (September 1915) and the Somme (July 1916), Gilbert reckoned that the transfer saved his life. Had he stayed with the 9th East Surreys, he would almost certainly have been one of a majority of officers who were killed or badly wounded when they were first thrown into action. The artillery generally had an easier time than the infantry, as a fellow-author, "Patrick Miller," himself an artilleryman, admitted in his novel *The Natural Man*: "Never till that moment," wrote Miller, describing an attack in Picardy, "had he realised how utterly damnable the infantry job was." A preponderance of war novels by gunner officers – Archibald Ingram, Herbert "Beb" Asquith, Mark Severn, Patrick Miller, and Frankau himself – were optimistic in their message.

Another reason for Gilbert's positive tone about his own army service was that the morale of his new unit was excellent, led as it was by his admirable and adored commanding officer, Lieut-Col. D. R. ("Sleepy") Coates, a red-haired Ulsterman who once spent part of his precious leave visiting Gilbert's dying mother to bring her the news of her son. Such consideration demonstrated a strong brigade spirit. Gilbert was always immensely proud of it and of his own part in its achievements. In January 1935, given a sight of the original brigade diary, he signed, with a flourish, a page that he himself had written in January 1916, next to Coates' signature as Commanding Officer.

The 107th Artillery Brigade, like the 9th East Surreys, Gilbert's for-mer regiment, was part of the 24th Division, which left from army camps in the Aldershot area of Hampshire for the continent on 29 Au-gust 1915. To read both units' war diaries however is to get a very different picture as to the preparedness and professionalism of the two. There was a general air of muddle, fuss, and jumpiness among the East Surreys in the weeks that preceded their fateful first day in action. Some of it reflected, of course, the tension in the High Command and the ex-peditionary force as a whole before a battle that, it was hoped, might win the war for the Allies. To avoid pictures falling into the wrong hands, all officers, on pain of arrest, were ordered to send their cameras home. The authorities were clearly afraid, too, that disease might decimate the men's ranks in advance of "the Great Push," and, over in France, an outbreak of spotted fever, causing meningitis, led to orders for other ranks who had gone outside their assigned areas to be quarantined before returning to their billets.

Much of the inexperience among the soldiers of what the author Patrick MacGill called "The Amateur Army" of Kitchener volunteers, could have been remedied by a gradual breaking-in process in a quieter sector of the line. Unfortunately the 9th East Surreys were given no such chance. Judging by their later courage in battle, the battalion were deter-mined to do their best and their nerves were as yet intact. However they were still not a fully-trained body. In France there were frequent indica-tions of minor incompetence – the adjutant temporarily suspended for confusing instructions; the company quartermaster sergeant court-martialled for neglect of duty; a regimental draught horse dying because someone overfed it. The commanding officer was agitated about men wasting supplies or rendering their equipment unserviceable through neglect. He also had to order them not to smoke in barns where they were billeted for fear of causing fires and excessive claims from the locals. Evidently their relations with the French, many of whom he suspected of being spies, were not good. The local wine presented a further prob-lem: one inebriated East Surrey private was remanded for striking an N.C.O.; a sergeant was reported drunk, while another was beaten up by troops from another regiment after he tried to stop them drinking.

The tragedy that followed cannot however be laid at the feet of these spirited amateurs. Through a disastrous decision by the Commander-in-

Chief, Sir John French, the infantry brigades in the 21st, 24th, and Guards Divisions were kept in reserve a long way back from the sector intended for the autumn "Great Push," near the mining district round Loos. It was not until 22 September, three days before the battle began, that the infantry of the 21st and 24th Divisions were hurried up to the front in a series of forced marches along cobbled roads with full pack, covering something like 20 miles a night. By the time they reached Bethune, 5 miles from the line, at 2.30 a.m. on 25 September, they were utterly exhausted and had not been fed for two days. A few hours later, they struggled seven miles south to the village of Vermelles through a chaos of transport and ammunition wagons and ambulances full of the wounded. It took them all day. As they passed, Gilbert recognised his old battalion and spoke to some of them. Though ravenous and tired, even then they did not seem dispirited. That night they were billeted at a place called "Suicide Corner," which the Germans were shelling. They slept little. In this condition they, as the eagerly expected reserves, were ordered to follow up such gains as had been made on the first day of the battle. These were limited, for many attacks had been made in places where the German wire had not been cut successfully by the British artillery. In cases where this had happened the infantry had lost so many men and were so tired from digging themselves in that there was little that they could contribute to the fight into which the reserves were now flung. In other parts of the line, where the attacks had succeeded, the effect of surprise had long gone by the time that belated reserves went into action. Poor communications, however, left the High Command still optimistic about what had been achieved.

In contrast, though the 107th Artillery Brigade was subjected to great difficulties by the confusion near the front, its diaries present a more orderly picture. Many of their entries were in the neat hand of Gilbert himself, who had been appointed brigade adjutant. They reveal that his fictional account of the operations of Peter Jackson's brigade before and during the battle of Loos was absolutely authentic, and very close in detail to what actually happened.

The brigade, horses and men, travelled from French ports by train to the valley of the Canche. At Marenla, where they arrived on 1 September, they took part in a massive and pointless military exercise around the Ancien Moulin de Sempy, watched over by the XI Corps commander,

Major-General Haking. On 12 September they went on to Annequin, near Bethune, arriving in the evening and occupying prepared gunpits there. On 21 September and for the next three nights the batteries began firing on the crossroads to the rear of the enemy entrenchments and bombarded the German front lines on the morning of the 24th, the day before the Battle of Loos was to begin. At a quarter to six the next morning (25 September) the brigade was involved, with other artillery, in an intense bombardment of the German front, just before the British attack was launched. Later in the day, they fired at Cité St. Elie to repel an enemy counterattack.

At 6.0. p.m. on 25 September, Colonel Coates received orders to move the 107th Brigade to Le Rutoire farm, closer to the front line and further south, to support an attack by the 71st Infantry Brigade. However when Coates arrived at Le Rutoire at 9 p.m. to make arrangements, he could find no trace of the 71st Infantry Brigade or its commander. The whole artillery brigade – six hundred men, five hundred horse, guns, limbers, ammunition, and supply wagons – nonetheless began to move to Le Rutoire, but conditions made progress almost impossible. It was a pitch-black night, the rain was pouring down; the roads and fields were packed with cavalry, infantry, ammunition carts, and heavy equipment such as pontoons, travelling to and from the front. Shellfire was incessant, the terrain unfamiliar, and most of the officers had never been in action before. Coates' ability to hold the brigade together that night was clear evidence of his exceptional organising skill and power of command. At 1 a.m., there being still no sign of the 71st Brigade, after having struggled along for several hours with Gilbert riding close behind, Coates, like "Weasel" Stark, the artillery brigade commander in *Peter Jackson,* made the decision, based on his accurate estimate of enemy gun positions, to dig in where he was. There was no possibility of reconnoitring any alternative before dawn. At 4.30 that morning he was ordered again to report personally to Le Rutoire farm, this time to be under 21st Division artillery, whose commander approved Coates' positioning of his guns, confirmation of the colonel's excellent judgment in the most difficult circumstances.

At 11.45 a.m. the same day, Coates received a verbal order to reconnoitre a new forward position in view of the expected advances by the infantry reserves. Gilbert was sent into the battle zone with the brigade orderly officer to do this. Pressing ahead regardless of the danger, he reached the spot on the ridge known as Lone Tree, where an officer from the 107th Brigade on observation duty gave him the grim news that the infantry attack, by the 72nd Brigade – the 9th E. Surreys and the 8th Royal West Kents – had failed. They had reached the enemy trenches, but had been unable, despite repeated efforts, to get through the wire. Casualties were devastating: the East Surreys lost 14 officers and 430 men, wounded or killed. Subsequently Brigadier General Mitford, commanding the 72nd Brigade, visited their battalion and expressed his "pleasure" to the remaining officers and men "for the way in which the attack had been carried out." Of the men's courage, in their first fight and last time of simple optimism, there could be no doubt, but they should never have been ordered to carry out such an impossible operation. Gilbert, through his fortunate transfer to the artillery, had escaped their fate. In *Peter Jackson* he paid them his respects by telling their story.

Not that the artillery were especially secure during that battle. When the 107th Brigade were later ordered (with the usual muddle of a missed rendezvous) to come under the Guards divisional artillery command, to support the Guards Division's attacks on 27 and 28 September, they were battered by heavy enemy shellfire directed by observers from Fosse 8, a high point the Germans had captured at St. Elie. Two officers and two other ranks were wounded and Coates' charger and several other horses were killed. His stalwart leadership earned him a personal visit from the young Prince of Wales who was with the Guards at the time. Subsequently, a corporal and a sergeant were both decorated with the D.C.M. for gallant conduct, and two officers – the commander of "A" battery and the orderly officers – were invalided home, the result of battle stress. Of the brigade's sixteen guns – twelve eighteen-pounder Mark I quick-firing field guns, and four 4.5-in. howitzers – only one, a brand-new replacement, was sound; the rest had to be sent for repair, with faulty recuperator springs, the result of cheap, rushed manufacture, as well as of a design fault revealed by constant usage.

This brought the gunners a well-earned rest. After being relieved in the line they moved to Noeux-les-Mines then on to Sercus and subsequently into Belgium. In January 1916 they were in the Ypres Salient. The poet and war veteran Edmund Blunden once observed that "soldiers always retained very clearly in mind the places at which their unit had been, and their pleasant or unpleasant associations." It was even so with Gilbert Frankau. Years afterwards he recollected almost affection-ately – as did so many veterans whom the experience set apart from other people – the devastated Flanders landscape that he had known:

> Wipers! Does the mere name conjure up its pictures for you? Can you still see, in your mind's eye, that long, long turnpike – slimy pavé between shell-torn poplars – leading out from "Pop" [Poperinghe], by the red ruins you knew as Vlamert-inghe, to a skeleton of a city with its broken dog's teeth of shattered spires?
>
> Thousands living can still recall that picture, and so many more – a bed bulging three-legged through the upper win-dow of some ruined home – a dug-out in the canal-bank where the rats pattered over the faces of men sleeping – the Square with those blocks of crumbled masonry piled high against the bent iron lamp-posts – the stone Convent – or Vauban's red-brick Ramparts – or that Gate (only there was no gate) wherethrough the hoofs of the mules clattered o'night-time, left and north-east to Potise, straight on past the Schools to Hellfire Corner where the twisted rails spanned the last pot-holes of the Menin road.

The 107th Artillery Brigade stayed at Ypres until March 1916. Late that month, they were rested at Eecke, then moved to Neuve Eglise in France. There they were engaged in covering raids and frequent artillery duels, with some casualties from gas and heavy shellfire. Further medals were handed out to them on the King's birthday, 3 June, with Coates getting a mention in despatches.

The Battle of the Somme, which began in July 1916, was the Brigade's next great ordeal. Gilbert up till then had led a relatively dan-ger-free existence, as adjutant with Brigade Headquarters. Now he was moved to an artillery battery, B 107, on 24 July. The field artillery brigade moved to the Daours sector, and subsequently Longueval, where the artillery activity on both sides reached a great intensity from 16 August onwards. For nineteen days the brigade was under constant fire, losing four or five killed and about eighteen wounded. Of this, his only prolonged stay in the line, when his nerves began to be severely frayed, Gilbert later wrote a highly-coloured account in *Peter Jackson*.

During the spell, he went up as forward observation officer to assess the effect of his battery's fire and was nearly killed when he was bowled over by a shell. An infantryman at his side was decapitated. The brigade was relieved on 5 and 6 September. Shortly after, during the rest in billets between 7 and 10 September, Gilbert returned to England and to new war work.

All this time, army life had not stopped him from writing: a novel, *The Woman of the Horizon*, and regular contributions in verse to the famous trench journals, the *Wipers Times* and the *Somme Times*. He was also beginning to make a name back at home as a war versifier. His poems were published in Hilaire Belloc's wartime weekly, *Land and Water*, and three collections appeared – *The Guns* (1916), *The City of Fear* (1917), and *The Judgement of Valhalla* (1918). Their tone was savage and theatrical. His bloodthirsty evocations of infantry or Flying Corps attacks were not written from experience. Many were heavily influenced by Kipling, in style if not in quality:

> "We are the Guns, and your masters! Saw ye our flashes?
> Heard ye the scream of our shells in the night,
>   and the shuddering crashes?
> Saw ye our work by the roadside, the shrouded things lying,
> Moaning to God that He made them – the maimed and the dying?
>   Husbands or sons,
> Fathers or lovers, we break them. We are the guns!"

Later, doubtless after hearing his former comrades' were unimpressed by his poems, he wrote in a style closer to the ironic Sassoon vein, disclaiming his gung-ho effusions, and giving the ordinary artilleryman's more realistic perspective on the war:

> ... I see you now,
> Staggering into "mess" – a broken trench,
> Two chalk-walls roofed with corrugated iron,

And, round the traverse, Driver Noakes's stove,
Stinking and smoking while we ate our grub.
Your face was blue-white, streaked with dirt; your eyes
Had shrunk into your head, as though afraid
To watch more horrors; you were sodden-wet
With greasy coal-black mud – and other things.
Sweating and shivering, speechless, there you stood.
I gave you whisky, made you talk. You said:
    "Major, another signaller's been killed."
    "Who?"
    "Gunner Andrews, blast them. O my Christ!
His head – split open – when his brains oozed out,
They looked like bloody sweetbreads, in the muck."

And you're the chap who writes this clap-trap verse!

This did not however stop him from publishing the "clap-trap verse" in the same volume as the one in which this disclaimer appeared.

Rudyard Kipling, who inspired so much of his verse, was, of all writers, Gilbert's greatest hero. Many of Gilbert's later novels had in their lightweight fashion a Kiplingesque flavour – tales of strong men, from military or public-service backgrounds having manly talk together, part of an elite of patriots and men of action. In his imagination, Kipling, whom he met very seldom, became almost a father figure to him. It was the romantic patriot, and something of the outsider, in Kipling that appealed to him, as well as the famous writer's combination of forcefulness and gentleness of manner, and even his dapper dressing.

For H. G. Wells, Kipling's illustrious contemporary, Gilbert had, in contrast, a deep contempt. He has described how he met the eminent author at a party in Fitzroy Square: Wells, faced with the impeccable Old Etonian young officer, clearly decided to tease him. He had never been an admirer of army or the public schools, and though he wrote propaganda for the government, was increasingly disillusioned about the war.

"I see," he piped in his shrill falsetto, "that you're wearing spurs. Why are you wearing spurs? Are they necessary in the trenches?"

"One rides occasionally," said I, pitying his ignorance. He'd never kicked an unclipped hairy over a wet ditch under shell-fire...

"How are you chaps getting along with this war?" he continued. "Do you think you're going to win it?"

I believe he added, "Wearing your spurs," but of this I am not quite certain. All I know is that I was not liking him. One did at least expect some decency, some understanding from a civilian.

"You can be certain of one thing," I said, "We shan't stop till we've smashed the German empire."

"That'll be all right," he piped, [in a sentence that condemned him forever in Gilbert's estimation] "as long as you smash the British empire at the same time."

Towards the end of 1916, Gilbert moved, at his own wish, to a staff job with Captain's rank and was given a special and thankless propaganda post in Italy, persuading the none-too-enthusiastic Italian people that the war was worth fighting and that their allies were making major efforts to help them – which the Italians did not believe. During the course of his duties, which he performed with some success, he began to have a nervous breakdown. He lost weight, going from 149 lbs. to 90 lbs. in a few months. He shook uncontrollably, and his temper deteriorated. He was impudent to high-ranking officers, raged and fumed over petty and important matters alike, and generally made, as he admitted, something of a fool of himself.

Finally it was realised that he was suffering from shell-shock. He was invalided out of the army in 1918 with a temporarily awarded 80% disability pension – which he was not allowed to keep, once he had recovered. His condition was caused by the prolonged strain of battle and the traumatic jolt his nervous system had received from the shell-blast on the Somme and the sight of the man next to him horribly mangled. His business and marriage problems exacerbated his condition, by preventing him from resting, and there were the added tragedies of his mother dying of cancer in 1916 and his brother Jack, a 2nd Lieutenant in the 1/8th Scottish Rifles, being killed in November 1917. Gilbert had suppressed his grief while serving at the front but inevitably this came out like a bruise after he left the army. Like many officers he regarded his shell-shock symptoms as weakness and refused to discuss them with the medical authorities. This hindered his recovery.

He had reached a crisis, too, in his private life. He felt trapped in his marriage. Even before the war Dolly had become virtually a widow to his obsession with the family business, and Gilbert had already begun to confide his dissatisfaction with matrimony to a former lady friend. His obvious preference for his mother's company and his neglect of his children deepened his wife's unhappiness. The war, by separating them for long periods and causing his nervous difficulties, increasing the misunderstanding between them. Since 1916, too, he had become closely involved with a new friend, the actress Aimée de Burgh, to whom he wrote several love poems, included in his third collection of war verse, *The Judgement of Valhalla*.

Finally, in 1919 he walked out on his family. He obtained a divorce and, in 1922, married Aimée. These actions left a legacy of bitterness that lasted for years. When he first worked on *Peter Jackson* in the late summer of 1917, he may still, despite Aimée, have hoped that his marital situation could be retrieved, and possibly the happy ending he planned for the novel reflected this. Even after his hopes died, worldly motives made him stick to the same plot. Happy endings, he knew, were good for sales.

It was natural enough that he should have had the market so firmly in mind at the time. His business had failed. He had turned to writing, his first love; but he had to be sure that his novels would do well. He had grown used to being rich. "Making do" financially would have been a disaster. It would have cut him off from from the smart social life that he and his mother had always enjoyed. As for Dolly and his two daughters, he intended to support them, but no alimony, in the end, was paid them. Dolly had to work – in the fashion business – for the rest of her life, while Pamela and Ursula went into jobs, advertising and antiques, giving up hope of attending university.

Peter Jackson, Cigar Merchant was sketched out during 1917, then rewritten. In 1919, it was serialised in *Land and Water* and appeared in book form the next year.

The story closely follows Gilbert's military experience. The hero, Peter Jackson, cigar merchant and unsatisfactorily married, with two daughters, joins up in 1914, torn between his obligations to his family and business on the one hand, and his patriotic duty to fight "the Beast in Grey" on the other. Briefly in an infantry battalion, Jackson transfers to the Royal Field Artillery, where he proves brave and competent. His commanding officer is "Weasel" Stark, based partly on Gilbert's former commanding officer, Colonel Coates, the epitome of the military ideal to which Peter (like Gilbert) aspires, even down to his physical appearance, which the author gives in some detail:

> . . . flat auburn moustache over firm lips. The tight long-skirted tunic . . . fitted like a skin over the muscled shoulders, the in-curved back: his slacks fell straightly creased to shining brown shoes. His hands — clean, capable hands — shewed a hint of freckling, the suspicion of auburn fluff. The domed forehead betrayed intelligence. A brand-new D.S.O. ribbon completed the picture.

Jackson takes part in the battles of Loos and the Somme. Eventually he suffers from shell-shock, the result of fatigue and being nearly killed by a shell (the infantryman standing beside him is pulped by the same explosion). Jackson, like Gilbert, cannot reconcile a nervous affliction of this kind with the robust character he aspires to be. It takes months for him to recover and face what has happened to him — a common enough fate among tough and sensitive soldiers alike who passed through the ordeal of the war.

The author evokes the fighting in vivid if somewhat melodramatic language, like his highly-colored war verse. Aware as he is, for example, of the failure of the High Command to bring up reserves in time, bitterness creeps into his description of the battle of Loos as he draws on his own memories of that fateful first day of the attack:

> Light grew and grew. Fitful gleams of sunshine danced across the plain. More cavalry came, squadron after squadron, wheeling into line on the fields just below. But they made no movement forward, those wheeling squadrons. Peter saw them through his glasses – dismounting, loosening girths, fume of their cigarettes blue in the air.
>
> Came *one* English aeroplane, drifting aimlessly across the sky.
>
> Walking wounded came, trudging painfully across the fields, singly and two by two, arms dangling, heads bandaged. (There were no steel helmets in those early days.)
>
> Came a gray company of prisoners, capless, weaponless; fell out; squatted on their hunkers among the root-fields. Came a dozen peasant-children, sprung somehow to life; wrenched up roots from the field; pelted the captives as they squatted. The company fell in again; trudged off towards Bethune, followed by the spitting, cursing children. (And there were many "gentlemen" in England still abed that morning!)
>
> Came, towards noon, down the road from Sailly, long brown columns of infantry, guns and horses, marching towards Noyelles. The Northdown Division! gun-range away behind the grimy remnants who were even then bombing out the cellars in Loos village beyond the skyline ... But from Beuvry to Annequin the roads were bare. And on the left of the attack, round the Hohenzollern Redoubt, in the Chalk Quarries, at the foot of Fosse Eight, men fought unsupported, died cursing the chance that was never taken, the help that never came.

Even more strikingly, Frankau's description of the condition of shell-shock illuminates what so many soldiers endured. At the time it appeared, thousands of men were returning home to wives and mothers, or to a life alone, in a state ranging from total nervous collapse to insomnia, lack of emotional balance, listlessness, and mental paralysis. For them, and for those close to them, the book brought consolation.

For its message was optimistic. Gilbert had long contemplated writing a romance of the world he knew – of rich, well-connected young people, enterpreneurs, men-about-town, fashionable ladies. He had decided on Peter Jackson's character and that of Peter's cousin, Francis Gordon, as early as 1912. The two cousins represented what Frankau saw as his own two sides: Jackson, hard-headed, reliable, obsessed with his business at the expense of his marriage; and Gordon, the romantic socialite and writer. The one is described as "too self-concentrated," the other "too flamboyant" for easy relationships. In his first novel, *Woman of the Horizon* (1917) Frankau had introduced the reader to his Francis Gordon-ego, poet and sensualist, travelling the world in search of the perfect love companion; but it was Gilbert's intention to tell a single story encapsulating the two men and their views of life. *Peter Jackson* was the result: side by side with his frank account of the realities of war he constructed a double romantic tale of love.

In it, Francis Gordon becomes a spy for the British, and, after passing through numerous dangers in Germany, resumes his normal military duties and is wounded on the Western Front. A cripple, he now feels it would be dishonourable to marry Beatrice, the American girl who has long been his ideal. Without telling her of his wound, he breaks off his correspondence with her. He goes into an elegant decline and is on the point of suicide. However, his cousin Peter's wife alerts Beatrice, who hastens across the U-boat-infested Atlantic and throws herself into his arms just in time.

The novel's other romance concerns Peter Jackson and his wife. Neither have ever felt passionately about one another. They are a worldly modern couple who consider that emotion interferes with their smart, comfortable way of life. Against her inclination, however, Patricia Jackson, who is intended to "typify all that is best in the 'maternal' woman," finds herself falling in love with her husband when he stops thinking about his business and joins the army to defend his country. It is not until she tends him as an invalid that she reveals her changed feelings for the first time. At first he is too ashamed of his shattered nerves to respond. In a passionate scene, she storms his defences:

He shook under her hands as a ship shakes when she heaves propeller free . . .

"What are you frightened of, boy? Tell me what you're frightened of. I'm your wife, boy. I won't hurt you."

. . . Clinging to her, straining her to him, he spoke; fiercely, as men speak in fight:

"You mustn't love a coward. Do you know what that means? . . . I'll tell you . . . Everything frightens me . . . I am afraid to go out alone . . . I am afraid for the children, for you, for myself . . . I am afraid of life . . . I am afraid to go on living . . . And I haven't got the pluck to kill myself . . ."

Clinging to her, straining her to him, he began to cry – cruel, dry sobs, deep down in the throat. She could not move: she could not see him. Her breasts were two burning torments . . .

Moved by Patricia's newly kindled ardour, Peter finally falls in love with her. They have an idyllic "honeymoon" punting on the Thames, and in a tent at Godstow, near Oxford, pass an ecstatic night of love. Next morning she rises, "like a nymph in the dawn," and wanders in her shift through the dewy meadow. In due course she bears her husband the son for whom he longs. Settled in the country, he decides to farm the land for which he has made his sacrifice.

The book's message is that men such as Jackson deserve the nation's thanks for their steadfast courage in arms; and secondly that to suffer from shell-shock, which is just as fearful to endure as any laceration of flesh and bone, is an honourable sacrifice for a soldier to make. The war has been a "great cleansing storm" bringing brave men to true love after their trials; and it has been the agency in lifting Peter's character "up from the pursuit of money in business, to the creative and natural pleasures of country life."

The book was written in a light, jaunty style, popular at the time. Apart from the love stories in the book, which were the stuff of daydreams, it was completely authentic in detail, as ex-gunners afterwards attested, though the war atmosphere was somewhat flatly evoked in comparison with the work of such as Yeates or Aldington. For the student of war, *Peter Jackson* was particularly interesting: despite its ultrapatriotic message, it was unillusioned in its treatment of army life. Some of its criticisms anticipated C. E. Montague's famous *Disenchantment* by three years, and can be compared with a contemporary work, C. E. Jacomb's eccentric personal reminiscence *Torment* (1919), which combined a white-hot jingoism with a bitter resentment of army bureaucracy.

Peter Jackson was intended as a portrait of the Kitchener volunteer army in training and in combat, like Ian Hay's best-selling wartime propaganda novel, *The First Hundred Thousand*. Unlike Hay however, Gilbert did not present a broadly happy, if tough, picture of the British Tommy's first experiences, but a harsh one of army life "in all its naked & beastly disorganisation, jealousy & general lack of efficiency." It spelt out for the first time how thousands of loyal citizen soldiers had to contend with small-minded selfishness and slackness from those in authority. Gilbert balanced this with a picture of the profiteering on the Home Front that was so much despised by serving soldiers.

The book gave an unfamiliar and very frank account of the fiasco of Loos in 1915, a striking footnote to the military history of the war. Until then the public's most vivid account of the same battle came from Patrick MacGill's *The Great Push* (1916), powerful for its time and full of picturesque and pathetic detail about soldiers of the Irish Rifles cheerfully dribbling a football across no-man's-land. It had been MacGill's "official line" on the war in such recollections that had aroused Richard Aldington's resentment (q.v.). After his harrowing experiences as a stretcher-bearer at Loos, MacGill had been put to more widely useful work producing accounts of the war and giving public recitals of his writing, heralded by pipers of the London Irish regiment, to tug the heartstrings of his audiences. Now that the war was over and there was no need to hide the facts, Gilbert Frankau offered readers what he felt to be a more accurate (and ironic) gloss on earlier writers' heroics.

Similarly he drew what were, in 1919, shocking pictures of the war-weariness of troops in the Ypres sector and the almost impossible conditions of fighting during the battle of the Somme. This, for many readers, was the real thing for the first time – even closer, it seemed, to actual experience than the tough war stories of "Sapper" or soldiers' personal accounts in journals such as *Blackwood's Magazine*. Censorship at the front had meant that the front-line reports that had appeared in the newspapers consisted very largely of the anodyne or castrated despatches of accredited war correspondents such as William Beach-Thomas and Philip Gibbs.

At the same time, while placing great emphasis on truth-telling, Gilbert was careful not to overburden his narrative with military history, and he varied his vignettes of campaign life with those of hectic London in wartime and of the tranquil English countryside to which people escaped.

In singling out the rural scene as a symbol of peace and personal regeneration, Gilbert was exploiting an already very popular vein and one that was destined to be mined energetically for many years to come. Mary Webb's *Precious Bane* and Sheila Kaye-Smith's lyrical evocations of rustic existence had not yet been satirised in Stella Gibbons's *Cold Comfort Farm*; and even after that book silenced the more intense novels of country life, the middlebrow prose bards of the commuting classes continued to conjure up dreams of thatch and cider and Devonshire cream for an insatiable readership. It made no difference that Gilbert Frankau was as urban a human being as it is possible to imagine, a figure more suited to spats than leather gaiters, to dry martinis than tankards of ale. His conception of the countryside – a half-timbered cottage for ten shillings a week, new-laid eggs, apple-cheeked children, a stout stick, and a pig to scratch with it – was a happy fantasy relished throughout citified England. In the worldly-wise spirit of the rest of the book he pointed out that there were bad countrymen, out to trick the innocent townsman; yet the true peasant, he attested, was a natural gentleman, endowed with moral and aesthetic sensitivity of the highest order.

There were many other books that served the public with a similar vision of recovering from the war in a rural elysium. These included two comparable best-selling works, *Seven Men Came Back* (1934) by Warwick Deeping, a wartime medic, and *One Increasing Purpose* (1925) by A. S. M. Hutchinson, an ex-sapper; and in a more sophisticated guise, the fourth volume of Ford Madox Ford's "Tietjens tetralogy," *Last Post*. Gilbert Frankau however seems to have been the first of the well-known British Great War novelists to use this formula.

The period 1919-25 could fairly be called the period of the popular patriotic war novel, with Frankau's *Peter Jackson* beginning the trend. The works of Robert Keable, Ernest Raymond, and Wilfrid Ewart, which come into this category, are discussed elsewhere. A. S. M. Hutchinson's novels, *If Winter Comes* and *One Increasing Purpose*, had more in common with *Peter Jackson* than simply their shared bourgeois dream of the English village. Like Frankau's work, they were about men finding their way to the truth through their war service. *If Winter Comes* (which appeared in 1921 and remained in print into the 1950s) presents the war as part of a purgatorial process that brings the blinded hero eventually to connubial bliss with an aristocratic lady. Though the virtues the book extols are normality, honesty, and modesty, it appeals to none of these qualities in its readers, being masochistic, unreal, and snobbish. In *One Increasing Purpose*, Hutchinson again describes a man who gains from the war, in this case a sense of religious mission, through asking the question: "Why am I spared?" This was not an uncommon reaction and Hutchinson himself seems to have felt something of the kind, which he turned to profit.

Unlike Gilbert's book, however, neither of these two novels has any interest as a testament of war experience, for Hutchinson, a General's son, did not draw on memories of his service with the Royal Engineers or the Canadian Tunnelling Corps, or on 20th Corps Headquarters Staff after the Armistice. In his thirties at the start of the war, he was already an experienced writer and journalist. In common with Frankau he had an eye for what would sell and was militant in defence of the popular novel: and like him too, he was a staunch patriot.

In the same nationalistic or positive genre were Warwick Deeping's *Sorrell and Son*, described elsewhere, and *No Hero – This*, a much later work by him, which, even more than *Peter Jackson*, was an exposé of the petty politics and bureaucracy of army life, combined with a passionate defence of England's cause: "We have managed to save Europe from military damnation," Deeping concluded. Trained as a doctor and already the author of successful historical romances, Deeping served in the R.A.M.C. in Gallipoli, Egypt, and on the Western Front. *No Hero – This* shows him to have been particularly sensitive about slights to his dignity. Forty-one by the end of the war, and already a well-known literary figure, he must have resented being ordered about by "some savage little cad" almost half his age.

The fact that Hutchinson and Deeping so clearly drew inspiration from *Peter Jackson*, or at least from the same wells that it had tapped, testifies to its influence. As late as 1930, Captain Cyril Falls, in his annotated bibliography, *War Books*, picked *Peter Jackson* out as an exceptional war novel. For all the sentimentality of the love interest, it was a soldier's book and too honest to be written off as unthinking jingoism.

The critical reception of *Peter Jackson* was enthusiastic. Its success exceeded even Gilbert's own sanguine expectations. A stream of other novels by him followed over the next thirty years, interspersed with works of autobiography and travel. He enjoyed a readership which relished his fast-moving, dramatic plots, based on careful research. He wrote of businessmen, ex-soldiers, beautiful women: elegant people obliged to choose between love or money or honour. The tone was light, balancing worldly cynicism with a touch of passion – amorous or patriotic. He always made sure that his facts were correct, whether they concerned the effect of League of Nations sanctions on a merchant in silks trading with Mussolini's Italy in 1935, or the possible causes of loss of memory during the First World War. At the same time he was careful, as he explained to one of the distinguished experts he consulted, not to vex his readers with too many technicalities or "gruesome" medical details.

One of Gilbert's most treasured possessions as a young man was his pigskin dressing case, with its silver-topped bottles and ivory brushes, a twenty-first birthday present. His novels had something of the dressing case about them – a man-about-townliness, glitter and sophistication. His twenty-odd novels have dated now. The world they celebrated, of loyal, stylish English gentlemen with a love of tradition and a touch of the bounder about their manner and their way with women, is not one to appeal today. They never caught on in the United States. No tears for their passing, however, need be shed on their author's behalf. He sold over two million copies of his books during his lifetime. Shallow and ephemeral, they were hardly works of art; but they were a credit to his professionalism and craftsmanship.

Gilbert was in fact a lifelong defender of the popular novelist, whose work, he maintained was, through its accessibility, one of the most important educative forces of the day. A Fellow of the Royal Society of Literature, he eventually resigned because the Society would not elect the best-selling writer Denis Wheatley, a friend whose work he admired and who had also served in the Great War.

His high professional standards went with a ruthless work regime. Deprived of a ready outlet in his former business career, or in the army, he played the martinet in his home, imposing, while he worked, a rule of total silence on everyone from his wife to the housemaids.

There was always however another, companionable side to him. He enjoyed life at his club, the Cavalry, was a member of a dining society, "the Honourable Order of Frothblowers," and kept up with his wartime regimental companions. For years he was a member of the committee of the East Surrey Regiment's reunion dinner organisation, together with R. C. Sherriff, author of *Journey's End*, Britain's most famous play about the First World War. Gilbert had several close ex-officer friends. One with whom he often stayed, Edric Weldon, an Eton contemporary and formerly of the 8th Hussars, lived after the war what to Gilbert was the idyllic country gentleman's life, near Honiton in Devon, in a huge, ramshackle house.

After *Peter Jackson*, Gilbert wrote no further novels exclusively about the Great War, though a number of his books such as *Three Englishman*, *Martin Make-Believe*, and *Royal Regiment*, contained war scenes or harked back to the 1914-18 period. On the strength of being a rich and successful author of fiction, he made a fool of himself in the 1930s trying to play the romantic extreme patriot, publicly denouncing political leaders such as Stanley Baldwin for their half-measures and lack of fire. He started a short-lived jingo paper called *Britannia*, launching himself into stormier waters than he could navigate. Mussolini's fascism for a very brief while caught his interest, though the connection with German Nazism soon made him drop that particular fancy.

When the Second World War came, he enlisted once again, this time in the R.A.F. He became a Squadron Leader – on the ground. After the intense work and strain of the Battle of Britain, he collapsed physically and for a second time in his career was invalided out. By then his health was beginning to succumb to a lifetime of heavy smoking.

He had married a third time. His obsession with *Britannia* and his literary work had made him an impossible companion for his second wife. The ill effects of shell-shock on his temper were protracted. It seems however that his third attempt at marital harmony was finally rewarded with happiness, despite great strains on the two of them at this time. There was the war and his breakdown; and their pretty house in London was bombed, though miraculously his latest manuscript survived the disaster.

Yet during and after the war he continued writing as industriously as ever; and there was a change for the better in his life and personality. He was reconciled at last to Pamela, his younger daughter, herself a successful novelist. In her first memoir, *I Find Four People*, written before she was thirty, she had drawn an unattractive portrait of him. She came to regret what she had written, not because he had not deserved it at the time (she remembered him saying, at a party, "I suppose I've got to drag my daughter round the floor," when she had craved a more demonstrative response from her father), but because it added to the many psychological bad debts that had been allowed to stand between them for so long. Besides, she herself had not been a model daughter: she had been wildly extravagant and regularly expected her long-suffering father to pay for her lunches at the Savoy.

In this last phase of his life, however, Gilbert, as she described him in a further reminiscence, *Pen to Paper*, written after his death, emerged in a more sympathetic light, good-hearted, touching, affectionate, the prickly pride and aggression gone. It was an impression confirmed by others who knew him at the time, such as his grandson, Timothy d'Arch Smith, who remembers his kindness to himself and other children, and the "fiver" – no mean sum in the 1940s – that Gilbert used to give him.

The knocks of life, combined with the reassurance of success, had taught him at last to look back on his political and business and marital adventures with a critical and far from complacent eye, and his natural generosity of spirit flowered. His third wife, Susan, who was twenty years younger, suffered from severe depressions. One of his later books, *Michael's Wife*, dealt sympathetically with that problem. After Gilbert's death in 1952, she recalled that though her husband even at the end of his life had still felt compelled to put on some attempt at toughness ("Darling, you're so badly educated I can't think why I married you"), he was in fact "the sweetest, kindest person." He was buried beside his parents and two brothers in the Frankau family mausoleum in Hampstead Cemetery, an elaborate edifice of marble and bronze surmounted by an large winged globe and writhing serpents; "may there be no moaning of the bar," ran the inscription, quoting Tennyson.

There may have been much to forgive Gilbert Frankau during his life, but his posturing and ruthlessness were at least understandable. He was dominated by a desire to live up to his mother's expectations, and that powerful influence lasted long after her death. If during much of his life he was undemonstrative, particularly to his children, this was something that was encouraged widely in the upper echelons of English society in his time and was even deemed a sign of strength. Above all, the severe jolting his nervous system received in the war, so well described in *Peter Jackson*, left him for a long time emotionally disturbed and exacerbated his less agreeable characteristics. He always maintained that he should have received a permanent disability pension, having come to feel passionately that shell-shock should be treated as a proper medical injury and not as a weakness of the character or the nerves. He pursued the matter for years in the courts, until he was successful in 1944.

Though his literary achievement cannot be rated among the highest, *Peter Jackson, Cigar Merchant*, the volume that brought its author his greatest fame, merits a significant place in the history of First World War popular fiction. It was full of clichés, but at the time it told truths that had hardly been uttered to the public before. For all its optimistic, nationalistic tone, it tackled, for the first time in a British novel, many of the less impressive sides of the army at war and much of the horror of battle. That unexpected combination reflected, on the one hand, Gilbert Frankau's service in a high-morale unit, together with his need to find acceptance and a strong patriotic identity, and on the other, his disinclination to suffer fools, especially army incompetents, gladly. A far more highly strung, and vulnerable, personality than he cared to admit, his inner sufferings were worse, probably, than most, despite his relative immunity, for some of the time, from front-line fighting; but his loyalties, values, and drives made him take an ultra patriotic rather than a disenchanted line on the war, however outspoken and angry he might feel about much of its conduct. More than most of the writers in this book he was aware of his audience, and the romantic interest was deliberately shaped to capture a readership. The military section, on the other hand, was faithful to his experience. If it reads less well than the works of Aldington or Yeates, that was partly a matter of talent and of his having accepted a second-rate literary convention, which the other two rejected; but we are also up against the problem, not so much of reticence, as of inhibition; once again we find a writer who, in the same way as Wilfrid Ewart, cannot deliver the full emotional charge to this objective, despite his anger and his desire to unburden himself of his torment about his shell-shock. The stiff upper lip was a useful defence against panic, but it limited the emotional range. In such circumstances, theatricality tends to substitute for the true feeling.

Yet in writing the book, Frankau went beyond either mere commercial ambitions or even the re-creation of his war experience: it was a statement of his whole view of life. Its last lines encapsulated his adoration of country, army, and women, and something of his fundamentally benevolent nature:

> But late that Armistice Day afternoon . . . when the Weasel, speaking solemnly as though he were proposing the King's Health on guest-night, gave them: "Our men, God bless them, our splendid, splendid men!" then Beatrice and Patricia could have sworn that they saw the tears of their own hearts reflected not only in their lovers' eyes, but in the hard blue eyes of Brigadier-General Douglas Stark, Royal Field Artillery.

9

Answering Remarque
Ronald Gurner
1890 – 1939

TO YOUTH

Why should you, living in a world now free,
Read of dead evil things of long ago?
If men fought thus, why, what is it to you?
If from the distance hands are stretched, and low
Faint cries of those that fell and those that slew
Find utterance, because they haunt me so,
Telling of agonies you never knew –
What then, of that? Yet, of your charity,
I ask you, bear with me, for to me
Ypres rises mystic in the sunset glow,
The Menin Road winds where the waters flow,
And those strange ghosts that ever come and go
Speak to me sometimes, when the waves beat slow,
Their voices mingled with a Sussex sea.

The "Sussex sea" whose waves resounded with the voices of strange
ghosts and the thunder of guns is tranquil, almost to the point of desolation: the small resort of Pagham, on the West Sussex coast, boasts no pier,
no esplanade, no man-made features save the blackened wooden groynes
on its long strip of pebble beach and the wreckage of sea walls round the
old harbour. It is a Paul Nash landscape, reminiscent of some quiet sector

of the Western Front. In August 1929, when Ronald Gurner wrote the poem *To Youth*, though Pagham had begun to attract visitors, the holiday chalets that stood back from its shore were still improvised affairs. From one of these, a quadrangle of converted railway carriages, Gurner's wife, Rosalie, and his little adopted son, Lionel, could watch him pacing the foreshore on his daily walks, a shabby trilby hat on his head and a pipe clutched between his teeth. A powerfully built man of 39, with flushed, handsome face, he had been, for the past year, Headmaster of Whitgift School, Croydon, the day school where Robert Keable, now in his grave in Tahiti, had long ago been a star pupil.

Other dead would have been on Ronald Gurner's mind as he wandered along the beach: close companions in his unit who had fallen during the war, and the poet, Charles Sorley, formerly his brilliant pupil at Marlborough; Keith Rae, Ronnie's friend and colleague at the same school and, like him, in the 8th Battalion, the Rifle Brigade, who had perished after the German liquid-fire attack at Hooge on 30 July 1915; Sidney Woodroffe, also of the 8th Rifle Brigade and an ex-head boy of Marlborough, who had won the first Kitchener Army V.C. in the same action and was killed that afternoon in a futile counterattack alongside Billy Grenfell and Gilbert Talbot, Ronnie's famous Oxford contemporaries; and, perhaps most admired of all, the handsome, scholarly Frank Copeland Worster M.C., of the Royal Worcester Regiment, who had died of wounds in May 1918, a fellow athlete and classicist at St. John's College Oxford. Worster was the "Copeland" of Ronnie's war novel *Pass Guard at Ypres*, just nearing completion in that summer of 1929.

Pass Guard, when it appeared, made little money for Gurner – indeed none of his works sold very well, though they received respectful treatment. Even so, his war novel is undoubtedly sincere, and it had not been forgotten at the time of his death. It is a dark, tortured, wistful book, like a sad, shadowy dream, the work of a man who has suffered; its sombre, brooding quality gives it power. Its real interest lies however in its message, which differs from that of any other English war novel – namely that loss of illusions is one of the sacrifices that a soldier must expect to make for his country; that such sacrifices, however hard, were worthwhile in the struggle against Germany; and that the courage, stoical endurance, and devotion to comrades displayed by the soldiers are proof that life really does have a value.

The tale itself is simple enough. Freddy Mann, a young shopkeeper's son, barely out of school, with innocent, childish looks, goes over to France as a 2nd Lieutenant in the Loyal Southshires. He comes up immediately against the physical ugliness of war: the sickening sight of death and decay, the menacing, dangerous country round Ypres, and the gaunt and ghostly ruins of that great town, symbolising the life and death struggle of civilisation against barbaric militarism. Later he encounters moral ugliness, in the shape of the bullying Corporal Sugger, who, though he proves an abysmal coward, escapes punishment; Mann loses close companions in battle. At home, his parents are incapable of understanding what he is enduring. The girl he loves is too unresponsive and respectable to comfort him adequately. He consoles himself with a warm-hearted actress and has to recognise that chastity and moral conventions are a soldier's enemy in wartime. He gets drunk. He is wounded. He loses faith in his country's cause, but carries on, his nerves and temper fraying. He longs for death. His greatest friend is killed. Finally he himself is fatally injured. Thus far, one would say, it is a classic novel of disenchantment, written when such works were at the height of fashion; but at the end – in the last two pages – there is a sudden change of tone and the author's message comes through:

Hear now, Freddy Mann, for the Voices are speaking clearly: lie still upon your stretcher, for you cannot move, and answer as they speak.

"You have returned: has all been taken from you?"

"All."

"Comrades?"

"Yes, comrades."

"And strength?"

"Strength also."

"And the hopes that once burned brightly?"

"They are dead."

"What have you left to dwell with you?"

"But memories."

"And to speak with?"

"Ghosts."

The Voices are louder. They are very clear.

"What do you seek now?"

"Rest."

"You did not know that this would be the end, the day you took the Road?"

"How could I know?"

"You had much to give. Were you ready to give it?"

"Yes, ready."

"And now that you have given all, and for you the fight is ended?"

"I am tired."

"Is pain yet with you?"

"I am past pain. I am tired."

"Is there anything you seek for?"

"Nothing, nothing. I am very tired."

"New life?"

"Not now."

"Or hope, or warmth, or friendship?"

"No, not now."

The Voices are louder: they are clearer yet. It is the Cathedral now that speaks, and the Church of St. Martin, the crucifix of St. Jacques, the Square, the Cloth Hall, the Menin Gate. And, as they speak, their Voices swell suddenly to a mighty flood of sound that fills the midnight, so that at last of their mingling is born the Voice of Ypres.

"Mine are high lessons, soldier: have you learned?"

"What lessons should a soldier learn?"

"Courage."

"I have learned much of courage."

"Faith?"

"Yes, Faith – but I had forgotten."

"Friendship, too, so great that before it death is a little thing?"

"I have known such friendship: Robbie –"

"Sacrifice, also: have you learned to give?"

"I have given all."

"And Pain: is Pain your master?"

"No."

"Or utter Weariness?"

"I have fought Weariness and overcome."

"Death, then. Is death yet fearful?"

"I am prepared to die."

"These are high lessons: have you learned them all?"

"A little: I have tried —"

O mighty Voice of Ypres triumphant, speak!

"PASS ON, THRICE TRIED, TO BE FOR EVER OF THE BROTHERHOOD!"

Somehow there is a false note: the melodramatic language of this climax is incongruous with the understatement in much of the rest of the book, like the swelling music at the climax of a film that overemphasises what we can see with our own eyes. Yet this is the nub of the book.

It demands closer examination in the light of Gurner's own tragic life and reflects feelings he had not only during the war but long after it was over. It was, Ronald Gurner told a colleague, "My answer to Remarque's *All Quiet on the Western Front.*" The message of that book was irredeemably black. The war, according to Remarque, had been a senseless, futile struggle that brought no benefit to anyone, least of all to the soldiers who had believed so fervently in their country's cause when it began. *Pass Guard* acknowledged the disenchantment of many soldiers, but explained that such wounds and destruction of the spirit were comparable to the physical wounds received in battle: they were an inevitable part of winning a great victory and they could not invalidate it. Nor could anyone deny the intrinsic value of the loyalties and self-sacrifice involved. Though this distinguishes it from other British war novels, there are obvious similarities in detail. For example there are other works, such as Ewart's *Way of Revelation*, where the leading figures court suicide by exposing themselves to enemy fire. The end of one German novel, *Fahnenjunker Volkenborn*, by Georg Grabenhorst, bears a striking likeness to that of *Pass Guard*, with heavenly voices whispering patriotic encouragement to the once innocent young *Volkenborn*, disillusioned and going blind after passing through the horrors of the Western Front.

Indeed *Volkenborn,* which was originally published in 1928 (it appeared in translation in 1930), has sufficient overall resemblance to *Pass Guard* to make one wonder whether Gurner (who could read German) took some inspiration from it. Even so, he clearly arrived at his own conclusions about the war, and any influence of *Volkenborn* concerned the form rather than the content.

At the time of *Pass Guard's* publication, Gurner told an interviewer that he could not think of anything in it which did not have a foundation in fact. There are a number of pen-portraits of people he remembered; not all can now be identified, but "General Vicke" is certainly Major-General Victor Couper, commander of the 14th (Light) Division, in which Gurner served. Gurner paid him a soldier's tribute, singling him out ironically from the normal run of military leaders, for his unwillingness to waste lives:

> The worst that could be said against General Vicke as a soldier and a Divisional Commander was that he was too attached to his men. This fault had been the subject of comment at Aldershot and was increasingly in evidence during the operations in Belgium in 1915. Care for one's men is, of course, inculcated as one of his first duties into the mind of every junior officer, and previously in South Africa and India General Vicke had shown that he had learnt his lesson to the full. When, however, one arrives at the rank of Major-General, and finds oneself in command of 12,000 infantrymen and gunners, to say nothing of mounted troops and details, care for the individual must to a certain extent be merged in considerations of strategy and of the unit as a whole. It was by this time sufficiently established that a division in such a sector as Ypres loses 60 per cent of its strength every three months, and entirely changes its personnel, sometimes more than once, in a year.
>
> The wise commander, in view of this, will therefore steel himself against undue interest in the subaltern or private soldier . . . It was a pity that with all his excellent qualities General Vicke never quite appreciated this point. To have done so would have in no way conflicted with his well-estab-

lished habit of slipping off whenever possible to the front-line trenches, and dropping into dug-outs to share a drink from flask or canteen with subalterns or men. He could have done this, and still known every officer and many N.C.O.s by their names, while recognising without mental disturbance the fact that within a few weeks or at most months they were almost bound to part. As it was, as Corps Commanders and high Staff officers would remark, this damned paternal interest was all very well, but there was a war going on, and you can't make omelettes without breaking eggs, and all this worrying about casualties upset corps commanders' equanimity and the peace of Army Conferences.

Ronnie Gurner was born in 1890. He had lived as a child with his family in Charterhouse Square in the City, a big square with a residents' garden in the centre and presided over by a beadle. The Gurners were ambitious for their intelligent children and placed great emphasis on their intellectual achievements. Mrs. Gurner was energetic and pleasure-loving. She ran the house as a hotel, while Mr. Gurner, whose family owned the building, worked in a bank. He was small, lively, and artistic in his tastes. He had produced an unpublished translation of the *Divine Comedy* and turned out stirring and technically inept poetry. He also gambled and mismanaged his money and felt constantly humiliated by his more practical and domineering wife. The climax of humiliation came when Ronnie was twelve years old. Mr. Gurner's father, who greatly preferred his daughter-in-law to his son, died, leaving her all his money. Mr. Gurner retaliated by finding another lady and disappearing altogether. His children paid the price.

Ronnie, his mother's favourite, had been a mischievous boy, caned often at the London school he attended, Merchant Taylors' (he himself became a caning schoolmaster). He was vital, hilarious, at sports "almost electric," and an impetuous tackler in rugby football, but already, before the war, a wounded spirit. Because of his father's desertion, the family were always short of money and lived with daily fears about it. In his late teens, Ronnie stammered. (Later, when a teacher, he was to give sympathetic help to stammering boys in his care. Shouting out orders in the Officer Training Corps, as one of the masters in charge, eventually cured him of this disability.) His school career, however, could be rated a success and he left in 1908 with the prize for being "the boy of best conduct during the year" and a scholarship to St. John's College, Oxford.

At the university he came close to carrying off the chief Latin verse prize, coming second only to Ronald Knox, the future eminent Catholic divine. He gained a first class degree in Honour Moderations. Whether he neglected his formal academic work in the next two years, like his character James Strang in *The Day Boy*, there is no record. He seems to have spent lavishly on drinks and tobacco before the examinations for the second part of his degree, Litterae Humaniores. On the eve of his Finals, he had an acute nervous crisis and went completely off his head for several hours. A friend had discovered him in his room with a note beside him: "Call a doctor; my mind is going." He was awarded an aegrotat degree, but the episode called into question the wisdom, and indeed the possibility, of entering the prestigious Indian Civil Service, to which he had aspired. He took many months to emerge from his terrible depression, though in time he gave every appearance of recovering well from it.

By 4 August 1914, Ronnie Gurner had become a schoolmaster at a leading English public school, Marlborough College, with two years' teaching experience behind him. He had found his vocation, after a brief period of indecision, largely under the influence of his hero, Cyril Norwood, headmaster of Bristol Grammar School. Dr. Norwood, the greatest headmaster of his age, represented the educational idealism of that pre-1914 era – upright, high-minded, anxious to extend educational opportunities to the poorer classes but also a fervent upholder of traditional classical learning and an eager promoter of the Officer Training Corps. In all these respects Gurner, an ex-Merchant Taylors' boy like his mentor, had tried to follow Norwood's example. As one of the masters in the O.T.C. at Marlborough, he was occupied, for the first two months after the war's outbreak, in the patriotic duty of training cadets for their future role as officers fighting for Empire and civilisation.

The school itself had strong links with the army (as well as the church). Among its old boys were Field-Marshal Sir Evelyn Wood and General (later Field-Marshal) Sir Henry Wilson, one of the most assiduously political soldiers of the Great War period. The regime was spartan: boys ran through storm and sleet over the ancient Wiltshire downlands "'neath the big bare sky" and shivered long hours in heatless classrooms.

Even at that moment of the highest patriotic fervour, other duties called the conscientious as strongly as military service, and the older generation were less than convinced that all the best men must flock to the colours. Gurner's friend, the brilliant Frank Worster, had the greatest difficulty in persuading the High Master of St. Paul's to let him leave his post as head classics teacher there. Eventually, before the end of 1914, Gurner and his fellow-teacher Keith Rae (a boy's club leader at Oxford and professing similar ideals) decided that they too must enlist. They were gazetted as officers in the 8th Battalion, The Rifle Brigade, part of the 14th (Light) Division, in the new Kitchener Army ("KI," "The First Hundred Thousand"). After initial training amid the pines and heath of Grayshott, Surrey, Gurner was transferred to the newly formed divisional Cyclists' Company. He claimed in his autobiography that there was no room for him as an officer in his battalion; certainly all the Rifle Brigade battalions were oversubscribed. The Cyclists' Company posting was hardly prestigious; such "funny" units were known to have been something of a dustbin for useless elements and this was no exception. However, it is probably safe to assume that since responsible and self-assertive officers must have been required to control this potentially troublesome crowd, he would have been an obvious choice; he had already some years' experience of authority and had an impressive rugger-player's build. After further training at Brook and Aldershot (at Badajoz barracks) he went overseas with the company on 19 May 1915.

The War Office files at the Public Record Office recount in detail the doings of the 14th Division Cyclists (in May 1916 brigaded with other divisional companies to become the 6th Corps Cyclists Battalion). They confirm Gurner's autobiography: unpleasant and risky work in the line some of the time, on salvage duty or burial duty, building machine-gun emplacements, and digging cable trenches, but no assaults on enemy positions and the dangers usually far less than those that ordinary infantrymen had to face in the trenches. They were not even required to do a great deal of cycling. He would appear to have suffered nothing worse, physically, than a twisted ankle. It was the horrendous spectacle of war, the assault on his beliefs and sensibilities, that was clearly the greatest ordeal. Above all, the shattered ruins of Ypres came to embody that experience. If they now became irrevocably part of his much darkened inner landscape, they also became the central focus of his hopes and loyalties as a fighting man.

Gurner's impressions of Ypres are a major feature of *Pass Guard* and also of his autobiography. The retention of the Ypres Salient was strategically a nonsense. It was vulnerable on three sides to German fire from higher ground. It cost, in April and May 1915 alone, some 60,000 British lives; but as it was in the front line of the last patch of Belgian territory held by the B.E.F., for most British wartime volunteers it was what they had joined up to defend. "Whether we knew it or not," Gurner wrote later, "it was deep spiritual as well as political wisdom that was deciding the awful sacrifice. To me at least, though I loathed every stone in its streets, Ypres was full of meaning that the years have only deepened."

The monotony of Gurner's normal duties was varied by occasional work as Intelligence Officer to various brigades in 14th Division. His first day in action, 10 April 1917, supporting the 6th Bedfords at the outset of the Battle of Arras, proved to be his last. In 1921 he gave a full description of the episode to his elder brother Cyril, a dedicated Indian civil servant, later knighted. Cyril Gurner wrote it down, inaccurately as far as place names were concerned (for which one may partly blame Ronnie's French and perhaps his memory at the time), but this account captured, to a greater degree than Ronnie's subsequent memoirs, the extreme danger to which the troops had been exposed.

On 9 April, a bitterly cold day, the whole British line advanced at the start of one of the largest battles of the war. The attack of Ronnie's unit, following the direction of the road from Arras to Cambrai, was launched along a crest of high ground. According to Ronnie, it was "like a field day" and went on throughout the night. After a brief stop while the British artillery shelled the Germans out of a village, the advance continued. That same day, 10 April, Ronnie and his company, consisting of 70 men, a lieutenant called French, and two Lewis light machine guns, were ordered to take the village of Guémappe ("Grapchy" as Cyril Gurner recorded it) and hold it until relieved the next day. Another company of the Cyclists, with which Ronnie was not in close touch, was on his right flank. To his left was a company of the Royal Warwickshire Regiment, under an officer named, according to Cyril "Grout" (though no Warwickshire Regiment officer of that name is recorded as having been killed in this action, as he seems to have been). The Warwicks, who were heading for the same objective, joined forces that afternoon with Gurner's company. Ronnie found himself acting captain of this mixed force. A blizzard came on, through which they decided to march, using the cover it gave. The snow fell so thickly that each soldier could see no further than the bayonet of the man next to him.

They made swift progress and by two o'clock had outdistanced their own guns, getting no artillery support until about six o'clock when a shell fell short on their left. They continued to advance unopposed through the snowstorm, suspicious of the unnatural and sinister calm, and fearful that the Germans were holding their fire at some point very close at hand. Not long before dusk, the snow stopped. They were close to Guémappe, in front and to their right, and also, on the left, to Monchy-le-Preux (which Cyril Gurner recorded as "Monghy"). At this point, German machine guns and artillery opened up *en masse* from the direction of Guémappe, and from the flanks, the heaviest concentration of firepower Ronnie had ever experienced. Taking cover with their men, Gurner and "Grout" together leapt into a shell-hole about two and a half feet deep, Gurner directing his force to keep up as strong a fire as they could. It was a contingency he had prepared for with his Lewis gunners, including the provision that if one Lewis gun went out of action, the other gun should take over its ammunition. At first this was unnecessary, for neither jammed and one of the guns poured about two thousand rounds into the enemy positions. These were very close – some within fifty yards – so much so that Gurner was able to compute, from direct observation, the whereabouts of several large German guns and send the information back to the British artillery – a display of sang-froid "in the cannon's mouth" that was as much to the credit of his training as of his courage. All this took place in the full knowledge, which the whole company shared, that when the expected enemy counterattack took place, the force commanded by Gurner and "Grout," right at the front of the advance, was almost certainly doomed. All they could hope to do was to hold out that night until reinforcements arrived.

By dusk, it had become a sniping contest between British and Germans, with rifles, Lewis guns, and revolvers. One of Gurner's Lewis gunners was hit by a sniper, who was promptly killed by "Grout." But that luckless officer had not risen from his shell-hole for three seconds before he too was shot in the neck, crying out, as he fell back, that they were trapped. Gurner successfully retaliated with his revolver, hitting the man who had shot "Grout," then, noticing that some of the Warwicks on his left were wavering, tried to reach them, well aware that he, too, might lose his life. At first he hardly noticed when he was hit in the left arm, "hoiked it up as best he could," then hurried to rally the fleeing Warwicks, and survey the higher ground, "with a not unnatural desire to see what was happening." Growing weak, however, he looked at his arm and saw blood spouting from the brachial artery.

His memories thereafter were confused. He remembered his personal servant reaching him in the gathering dusk and, helped by other men, getting him away, but not before, dizzy with loss of blood, Gurner had taken his rescuer for a German and tried to fend him off with his revolver. As they carried their stricken officer, his men met an armoured car and prevailed on the reluctant driver to let them tie the wounded man on to the back. It took him some way, before transferring him to another vehicle going on to the dressing-station at Tilly. Owing to the intense cold, the blood froze where Gurner's artery had been severed and this saved his life. He came to, momentarily, while he was at Tilly and was seized with all the fearful anxiety of an officer exposed to extreme stress, torturing himself that his company had been wiped out owing to his leadership.

He was moved from Tilly to Boulogne where he was operated on and sent back to England. His luck held, for he persuaded the doctor on board the channel boat to leave his dressings alone, following a timely warning in Boulogne that the man in question was incompetent. Subsequently he learned, to his enormous relief, that in the battle Lieut. French had struggled over from the right wing, as the light fell, and had taken command. Gurner's men were hanging on resolutely, but the Warwicks were a different matter: French had to threaten with his revolver any men who left their positions. As a result of his determination, he succeeded in holding on during the night, until the line was consolidated by a relieving force. On their way back to the rear, Ronnie's company were greeted with cheers as the news of their bravery spread throughout the division.

Like French, Gurner was awarded the Military Cross. During the whole brief but momentarily exhilarating nightmare, he had proved equal to the occasion. He had showed initiative, "learned not only during training in France, but also in the old days of the O.T.C." – as he later wrote – and a courageous disregard for his own safety. As a result of the episode, he nearly lost his arm. In the London hospital where he was taken, it was two or three weeks before the doctors could be sure whether it could be saved. He was incapable of using it to full effect, which did not prevent him from continuing, despite his handicap, to be a good fives player. When he bathed, in what was, in the thirties, still a "modern" style of bathing costume, exposing the shoulders, a deep pit could be seen above his left biceps, where the wound had healed. Aside from the pain, which is said to have recurred throughout his life, the time of his treatment was one of extreme depression, the consequence, immediately, of cumulative fatigue and the shock of his injury. On top of already being seriously disillusioned about the war, he saw the worst sides of the military at this time, such as the petty bullying of broken soldiers back at base hospital by sergeant-majors who found an outlet for their sadism. He had four operations, over a period of a year. When he had partially recovered his health, and was sleeping at Mornington Lodge, a convalescent hospital in West Kensington, he was given a job in the intelligence department of the War Office, as officer in charge of censorship and distribution of War Office propaganda, a staff position with considerable responsibility. Here he enjoyed "a spring and summer of unforgettable companionship and interest." In his autobiography, he attributed this happy state of mind to a revival of his religious beliefs. Yet it cannot be unconnected with two events of profound importance in his life that year. The first was his engagement to one of the nurses who had tended him in hospital. Her name and indeed anything about her beyond the fact that she was young is lost to history; but as long as they were together she must have meant comfort and stability.

More momentous was the unexpected reappearance of his father. The story of their encounter is remarkable. When the war came, the elder Mr. Gurner had dyed his hair, for he was well over military age, and joined up as a volunteer. Quite soon it became noticeable that he was too old for front-line activity and he was sent back to do a War Office job in London. He was put in charge of a typing pool in an office near the Embankment. After Ronald Gurner took up his duties as War Office censor, in 1918, his father was told by a secretary that there was a man of the same name working on one of the floors above. Full of curiosity, the Mr.

Gurner decided to investigate. Instead of sending a girl up with the letter tray, he took it up himself and there he found his beribboned son. For some time the Gurner children were able to keep in touch with him, though he did not return to their mother and they did not tell her that they had found him. After a while, however, he once again disappeared and only reappeared a few years later (about the time *Pass Guard* was being written) looking worn and neglected. He died shortly afterwards.

One of the great family fears had been that he had "gone missing" having helped himself to money from the bank where he worked. A thorough investigation, by Cyril Gurner, exonerated him, to the profound relief of all. Although the desertion itself had left unhealed wounds, Ronnie was at last rid of the haunting feeling of disgrace. There is no reason, however, to doubt his claim that his recovery in the summer of 1918 was also in part through religion. His renewed faith was a consequence of his determined struggle to repair his life; it was consciously willed rather than coming as the result of revelation. During the war, as he recalled later, he had relied on a kind of kismet fatalism.

Between March and May 1918 he underwent a kind of conversion; it was to a narrow and evangelical kind of faith, and though he eased up doctrinally in the years that followed, it set standards that he must have found hard to maintain and that left a mark on his mode of expressing his beliefs. The end of *Pass Guard* quoted earlier has a simplistic and bombastic ring, elevating patriotic devotion to a spiritual level, which was already present in his war poetry, but had been reinforced by his efforts to attain a balance in his inner life. He described his conversion in his autobiography.

> My faith was no doubt crude; but it was the sort of faith that a good many soldiers and sailors evolved, and having evolved clung to as their one salvation, and looking back I am not ashamed of it. It was clearcut, and it worked. It brought a solution of the world's problems, and it meant, as I saw it and still see it, the defeat of sorrow, sin and death, the three ultimate forces that stand with their clubs raised as humanity passes uncertainly along the highway . . . I was a soldier, and here, like the centurion of old, I found final authority

and call to duty and service; there was that in me that had led
me, even in my schooldays, to look askance upon pomps,
pageantries, and the established order, and here was rebellion
glorified against those in high places, the complacent, the
tyrannical, the hard, the blind. Here was the Law of Love, and
I had seen enough of hatred. I believed, however vaguely, in
the eternal: now at last my belief had basis and form. Painfully
enough, for after all, unless one is content to be a self-con-
fessed and utter hypocrite, such a revaluation of life is apt
to cause a War Office staff subaltern to change some of his
workday habits and ways of thought, I accustomed myself to
a new outlook and faced its implications.

Gurner had written to his mother throughout the war, but only one
letter is known to have survived, in which he posted to her, as a precious
souvenir, his old makeshift regimental crest which he had kept throughout his first year at the war. It is an indicator of the high value he set on
performing his patriotic duty at the front. On leave, in common with so
many soldiers, he talked little to his relations about it. Sometimes he entertained his brother's fiancée, Phyllis Carver, at lavish lunches while she
was working for the French military attaché. She remembered him as
most at his ease, exuberant and humorous; he saw no reason to dwell on
horrors that were disagreeable to contemplate and incomprehensible to
anyone but another soldier. He seemed cheerful in hospital and made
light of his wound. It had been "quite unnecessary" he told Miss Carver,
and he had got it "in a very stupid way."

War's Echo, a collection of poems that he had been writing since he
had been out in Flanders, was published in 1917. The dominant tone was
one of patriotic defiance towards Germany. He had disliked the prevailing spirit of Imperial Germany ever since a visit there before the war,
though, as he went out of his way to tell readers in his autobiography, he
had been in love with a German girl. Much of the language he used in
his poetry was archaic. Although jingoistic clichés resounded through
the verses, there were some with a weary and disenchanted ring. Conspicuous among these was "The Front Line," dated June 1916:

The wires run stark from star to star,
The stakes are gaunt against the sky,
Half hidden by the racing clouds;
And here and there the corpses lie
With huddled limbs beneath their shrouds;
Here too the muffled groan, the cry
That sinks to choking suddenly.
Ever the shadow passes by,
The hand of death is never far.
These things and these alone we know.
"Fight on," they say; "it had to be;
And you are blessed who play your part
In fighting for the cause."
But we – we only see the red blood start;
We only watch the young life flee,
We seek a goal we cannot see,
With dead to haunt us as we go.

For all his patriotic defiance, Gurner's defences had worn thin in hospital. This made him all the more bitter when he heard the news that an old family friend, Lieutenant Max Plowman of the 10th West Yorkshire Regiment, had resigned his commission, as Siegfried Sassoon had done, in 1918, as a public protest against the war. Plowman made little impression at the time and was saved from punishment by the war's ending. He became a leader in the postwar peace movement and published a celebrated memoir of his service years, *Subaltern on the Somme*, in 1926. He received many letters at the time of his resignation, some hostile. Gurner felt betrayed and told him that he never wished to see him again. Ronald's brother Cyril continued to do so (and was godfather to a Plowman child) but Ronald and Max Plowman were unreconciled.

Gurner remained staunchly patriotic throughout the interwar period. He expressed deep disgust and distress at the appeasement of Hitler, and it has been suggested that the international events of 1938-9 contributed to the onset of his later depression – not uncommon among soldiers who had believed they had fought the war to end wars. The case of R. H. Mottram, discussed elsewhere, is an example.

The Great War overshadowed all the rest of his life. When he came to write his autobiography, *I Chose Teaching*, published in 1937, he devoted two chapters to his years in the army. He actually apologised to his readers for this, since the book was supposed to be the story of a working schoolmaster and his testament of belief. His justification was that "the Himalayan experience of the war" was inextricably bound up with how boys should be led, instructed, and inspired. The lessons of war – loyalty, discipline, comradeship, joint sharing of burdens – were referred to throughout the book. In discussing self-discipline and dedication to work, for example, he recalled being told during his vigorous combat training before the Arras attack that military discipline amounted to "a realisation of the sanctity of one's job." In another passage, which links his autobiography with *Pass Guard*, he describes, with typical melodrama, how the war overturned his immature and conventional ideas of human nature:

> . . . no man, least of all a schoolmaster, could go through the War unchanged. What promising young moralists were some of us before the trial came! What a shipwreck it has made of our certainties, our nostrums, our panaceas, our rectitudes, before we took up cap and gown, and set us to our desks again! Whatever else war brought, to the thinker it brought reversal after reversal of accepted values. The worthless, lazy schoolboy smiling confidently when trapped, together with his men, by a flare in no-man's-land; the roué who died, like Sydney Carton, for his comrade; the crook turned saint; the man of righteousness who cursed God before he died – how all these rise to the memory, as if they were rising from actual graves, to jibber now with laughter at our petty codes!

There was a strong element of autobiography in Gurner's compelling, gloomy novel, *Reconstruction*, which appeared in 1931. This told the story of Roger Carbury, a dedicated schoolteacher and former war hero, who was determined that his pupils should benefit by the lessons of the war and sacrificed his marital happiness and his career in the process. The book, an interesting revelation of his conflicts, was a kind of debate between two sides of himself: the enlightened reformist looking to the future and the embittered defensive disciplinarian for whom the war was still all-important. Although the author was only too aware of the shortcomings of the passionate Carbury, who courted rejection at every level, he made him more vivid than anyone else in the book. As with Hardy's *Mayor of Casterbridge*, Carbury is a tragic figure, whose personality dooms him from the start.

A constant theme of Gurner's speeches on educational reform was how the war had demonstrated that boys from day schools had made quite as effective a contribution in fighting for their country as those from boarding public schools: "They did not fail, those sons of our day schools, sons of little tradesmen or working men who led platoon or company or battalion to victory against the most closely nurtured ruling and officer class that Europe has ever known," he told the British Association Conference in 1926. During his headmastership, he took much interest in the Officer Training Corps, even insisting that in the drill tests the cadets should be judged according to the standards of the regular army (as Carbury had required in *Reconstruction*). When he took over as Headmaster of Whitgift School, Gurner celebrated the tenth anniversary of the Armistice with an impressive parade; a sound recording of the O.T.C. band was made at his request and widely sold; and though he did not ram the war down his boys' throats on every possible occasion, he was one of a large band of headmasters who encouraged the reading of that oddest of war memoirs, *The Seven Pillars of Wisdom*. In his professional connections the war was a bond – as with many veterans. He became a good friend, for instance, of T. F. Coade, who recovered from shell-shock to become Headmaster of Bryanston School, Dorset, where, the boys claimed, he continued to salute imaginary officers as he walked through the grounds.

Gurner had resumed his teaching career in the summer of 1918, when Cyril Norwood, who had become Headmaster of Marlborough, invited him to return to his old job. He was glad to leave the army, but his nerves were still in a delicate state, and tragedy struck at his newfound happiness: his fiancée died in the Asian influenza epidemic that killed so many that autumn. Whether, had she lived, his later fate could have been averted by her emotional support we shall never know. The archivist at Marlborough has described Ronnie at that time, visibly wounded, with rough unruly hair and a wild, wandering look. Others have recalled that look, which persisted in later years. J. L. Fanner, a schoolboy at Whitgift in the 1930s, noticed his strange manner, accentuated by the anxieties of his last months: "In the middle of a conversation his florid face would go blank, his eyes would glaze over and he would appear to be far away." Mrs. Enid Canning, Norwood's daughter, has spoken of his "stare," a direct legacy, she believed, of his ordeal at the front.

His experiences created a gulf between him and his charges. Sidney Sheppard, a schoolboy at Marlborough in Gurner's time, remembers being taught by shell-shocked masters back from France: "We were terrified of them. They did not teach, but imposed ruthless punishment." Another old Marlburian has told a cruel story of boys banging their desks to sound like machine-gun fire when a shell-shocked teacher entered the classroom. Small wonder Gurner wished to move on, sensing, like Vera Brittain in postwar Oxford, indifference to the sacrifice and torment of the previous years. "I could not rid myself of the feeling that the world had changed and that Marlborough . . . was stagnant," he later wrote, so much had war altered his perspectives:

> Those worthy young men, so closely guarded . . . those doggedly conscientious, pleasant-faced, complacent adolescents, whose one aim in life sometimes seemed to be to kick a ball about the countryside, who knew nothing of the working classes, nothing of the true problems and complexities of life, to whom the war itself was presented as a kind of glorified football match in which, if peace did not come, they might yet take their places in the English team – were they all that, in this greatest issue that England had ever known, the public schools were able to produce?

Even Norwood's leadership could not keep him there, and with his assistance he became in 1920 the headmaster of an L.C.C. secondary school, Strand School, Lambeth. He made an immediate impact. One of his former pupils recalled: "For me he was like Julius Caesar and Hadrian rolled into one – one of the Gods of the earth . . . to a certain extent I modelled my life on the kind of man he was." During Gurner's six highly successful years there he made it his mission to help poorer schoolboys and promote the day school: his desire to bring about an understanding between the classes came from fighting alongside working-class soldiers during the war. This was a change of outlook he shared with many other ex-officers from his background – an important revolution in social attitudes, only recently the subject of historical investigation. While in charge of Strand, his message inspired one of his pupils, the future Labour Party municipal leader, Reginald Goodwin, who was to regard him as a lifelong influence. Many of Gurner's colleagues in the profession, including Norwood, were upset by his accompanying attacks on the narrowness of the public schools, though for these institutions he saw a future role: the training of "a new race of Samurai" to lead the nation. He was not the only headmaster to express such hopes, though the extravagance of his language shows that his feet were not always firmly planted on the ground.

His public speeches were delivered in a high, pleasant, well-modulated voice, rather lacking in force compared with his normally incisive style with intimates. They were orotund in style, full of the jargon of the pre-1914 teacher. This was complemented by his sometimes eccentric dress: shabby old serge suits and black boots of antiquated shape. He expressed many of his opinions through his novels. His first, *The Day Boy*, was a naive and heartfelt piece of propaganda.

Although he may have voted Labour for a period, he did not depart much from his Liberal background. His difficulties in the post he next took up did much to dampen his radical ardour: in 1926, he was appointed as head of King Edward VII Sheffield, an outstanding day school. During the snowy winter and bitter spring that followed he was plunged into conflict with Sheffield's Labour-controlled education committee, who abolished the governing body and moved to control the internal decisions of the school. Gurner fought back, as it turned out successfully, with Norwood's aid, but made his escape to Whitgift and left his successor to benefit. What he had resented particularly was the committee's insistence on getting rid of the school O.T.C. because of its alleged "militarist" character.

He was much acclaimed on his arrival at Whitgift. Norwood's testimonial had enthused about his qualities of leadership, his first-class classical learning, his wide experience at war and on the Head Masters' Conference, his impressive physical presence, and his bodily health.

Clearly, whatever ordeals he had been through in France and Flanders, he was restored at least in stamina and outward appearance. His reputation as an improver had gone before him. He emphasised the traditional disciplines, but was also determined to strengthen the study of drama, the arts and music, though no musician himself. Taking over as he did during a time of increasing economic contraction, he nonetheless chose the path of expansion. On arrival at Whitgift he had the immediate prospect of advising on the design of new buildings and of organising the school's transfer to Haling Park, three years later.

Gurner's assertive presence was strongly felt during his eleven-year reign. The school had an excellent record, with an increasing number of boys gaining scholarships at Oxford and Cambridge. He was capable of being a good leader of other masters, decisive, and taking the trouble to thank the most junior ones warmly for good work. As a teacher he was stimulating (though not always accurate) and was particularly good with a certain kind of difficult boy, having an informal confidential manner with them and being able to understand some of their weaknesses – perhaps because he shared some of them, as F. H. G. Percy, now the school Archivist, then a young master, has observed.

As time went on, however, these weaknesses – and others – emerged. He sometimes decided policy too hastily, without consultation, while taking credit for the better judgment of others. Too often he promised, to both boys and masters, more than he could deliver. He would have been less criticised had he possessed greater dignity, though he was a formidable boss. Everyone was kept on their toes, (though the Rev. P.C. Blagdon-Gamlen's account suggests a sometimes chaotic and slack regime), which may have been to the good, but a lot of nervous tension was generated in the process.

Harold Parr, a mathematics master at the time of Gurner's death, has recollected his own impressions of Gurner's leadership:

> Staff meetings under R. G.'s headship were always interesting and sometimes exciting. R. G. opened at the start of a new term with prayers, which impressed H. E. P. [Parr] as a young man. Occasionally during a meeting R. G. would break off the discussion and become a really inspired and inspiring headmaster, concerned with the fundamental ques-

tions and ideals and our duty to those in our care. At the end he would go the rounds of the various departments: "French Jones? Handicraft Robinson? Art all right Potter? History, Woodgate?" Heads of departments shivered in their shoes before their turn came and heaved a sigh of relief when the cross examination passed off without any untoward incident.

Other masters recollected that when, after Gurner's death, the running of the school passed into other hands, there was definitely a feeling that things had become easier for the first time for many years:

> . . . not indeed that R. G. couldn't be pleasant when he so wished; but he was such a man of moods – which became increasingly trying as the years went by – that we felt as though we were housed on the slopes of a volcano which might at any moment burst into eruption.

Like any other institutional head, Gurner was the subject of frequent gossip. The gifted and embittered head of classics, G. E. H. Ellis, was jealous of him and was responsible for some of the most uncharitable tittle-tattle. Ellis, as Deputy Head Master, had to shoulder much of the burden of running the school, for Gurner, when he was not writing books (typed in school time by the school secretary) was off on periodic educational jaunts. On one occasion, for example, he took part in a lecture tour of the Soviet Union in company with such luminaries as Malcolm Muggeridge, who was working as a correspondent in Russia at the time. On another, he went over the Atlantic to North America with his sister Kathleen. Every Easter vacation for several years he was on a "scholars' cruise" round the Baltic on the R.M.S. *Lancastrian* – a subsidised voyage for poorer schoolboys, organised by a body of which he was chairman. He was an indefatigable member of the Head Masters' Conference. Ellis was not slow to harp on Gurner's absences. He found fault with him in most ways, not least because Gurner, who thought highly of him, repeatedly claimed that he had "made Ellis," by showering him with responsibilities. Ellis once accused him of deliberately hitting him in the eye with his mortarboard, but much of his gossip turned on Gurner's marital life.

Ronnie's marriage, contracted when he was an impoverished Marlborough housemaster, was an unsatisfactory one. His wife, Rosalie, was a shrewd, angular lady, the daughter of a Master of Chancery. During the war she had been the warden of a munition girls' hostel in Sheffield, with qualifications in sanitary science. If love was the original reason for the marriage, it did not last long. She possessed a will as strong as her husband's. She and Ronnie had fierce rows, which were clearly audible to their alarmed neighbours. Ronnie also let himself go about her in his letters to his brother Cyril. His sister Kathleen took his part – too loyally, for his judgment was not faultless. He expected a great deal of marriage, as he did of himself and of his colleagues. Disappointed, he looked for compensation in his work; his indefatigable industry at the typewriter in the evenings and during holidays created a vicious circle. His wife's views were often more realistic and practical, but expressed in uncontrolled language; he sadly lacked the confidante and the soothing influence he needed. It was noted that when Rosalie spent her holidays apart from him, she too calmed down and appeared to enjoy herself. As a Headmaster's wife she was conscientious.

The sexual side of the marriage was a source of disappointment. They were unable to have children, and adopted a son. Mrs. Gurner told F. H. G. Percy in 1970 that her husband "was practically incapable of the sexual act, and that this must have preyed on his mind." This was linked, in her opinion, with his war wound. "When we married I did not expect his life to be a very long one, as he had not recovered from his injury of partial shell shock." Medically this is perfectly credible. "Shell-shock" was often the cause of impotence – sometimes for the rest of the sufferer's life. Not all the evidence, however, tallies with this version of the facts. One master at Whitgift, Harold Parr, thought differently: the trouble, Parr believed, lay with Mrs. Gurner – "a more unsexed woman I have never met." All the evidence has to be approached with caution. Gurner was highly susceptible, he had a succession of women friends during and after the war, and fell in love passionately more than once after his marriage, albeit with a certain possessive desperation.

On one occasion, in the thirties, it was with a young actress at the Croydon repertory theatre of which he was a director. On another occasion it was with the widow of his old friend Frank Worster, on whose shoulder he wept (literally) about his marriage. She began to find his self-absorption a burden and ceased, after a while, to see him. He was also deeply involved with a Swedish girl, Astrid, who worked for a while for the family as an *au pair*, and subsequently became an air courier. When she "stopped off" for a few days every month at Croydon aerodrome, she stayed with the Gurners. Early in 1939, to Gurner's distress and indignation, she became pregnant – the result, it was said, of a liaison with an airline employee. Gurner sent an angry letter to her firm remonstrating with them for letting such a thing happen, and according to his account the airline saw that matters were "taken care of," though this seems to have been more the result of the girl's own initiative in confronting her seducer. Gurner was left upset as much by his own jealous feelings as by the episode itself.

Gurner's manifestly strong response to feminine charm, his apparent lack of inhibition, and his virile though increasingly disorderly appearance would seem to conflict with Mrs. Gurner's assertion about his sexual drive. His fearsome burden of debt, on the other hand, was a fact. After his death it was revealed that he had been borrowing money from moneylenders since 1930; he was repaying it, it appeared, at a rate of 48% – a burden that even a headmaster's income of £1800 (before tax) could hardly have carried.

Mrs. Gurner could, or would, offer no explanation for her husband's debts, though looking back, she suggested that they originated early on. Harold Parr has speculated that Gurner had proposed marriage to Rosalie in return for a financial reward, but the money had not been forthcoming. This rests on an unfinished letter by Gurner, probably many years old, found by Parr in his desk and read before being consigned to the flames at the bottom of the Headmaster's garden when Parr was helping Kathleen Gurner to sort her brother's papers after his death. In the letter, Ronnie apparently demanded money from an unknown correspondent that he said had been promised him on a walk in the Savernake Forest (near Marlborough) "if he married Rosalie Romer." But this would seem to be open to quite an innocent interpretation: as a junior housemaster at Marlborough, Ronnie Gurner would have been too poor to have made a comfortable start to his married life. He may have been promised financial aid by a friend who failed, subsequently, to honour the undertaking. This unidentified would-be benefactor may have been Rosalie's wealthy aunt, who was expected to name Rosalie as an heir but in the end failed to do so; or it may have been a Mr. Thom, the lover of Ronald Gurner's mother, whose profitable refrigeration business collapsed in the midtwenties.

Debt seems to have dogged Gurner from that time. His stream of literary productions, which show signs of hasty composition, was partly the consequence of financial urgency. His royalties, small though they were, provided a vital income. On one occasion, Phyllis Gurner remembers, he spied his first publisher, Grant Richards, in a restaurant, dining, as he put it, off the proceeds of *The Day Boy*, when he himself had received not a penny in royalties. "See that swine over there," he said to his companion with a grim smile, "I'll nail him!," and rose from his seat. The publisher – a man with many financial problems himself – abandoned his meal precipitately and left with Ronnie in hot pursuit. He escaped in a taxi. After that Gurner took his books to Dent. His very last book, *We Crucify*, was sold to them for cash – evidence of his increasingly urgent needs.

There is probably no great mystery about the debts. The Gurners lived simply on the whole, but Ronnie may never have settled his early financial problems and had an expansive – and attractive – pleasure-loving streak inherited from his mother, who liked to go to the theatre two or three times a week and ordered champagne regularly from Harrods. He organised frequent holidays abroad and ran an Austin 12, which he drove hard. He could be extravagantly generous (though never, seemingly, to his colleagues). Once, for example, he bought a miniature steam railway for his son on which guests could actually travel round the garden on a narrow-gauge track. He lent his mother money and showered expensive gifts – furniture and, in particular, jewelry – on her and his sisters even at times, such as during the Great War, when he could not afford to do so. He liked to treat them at fashionable restaurants. One of his favourite haunts was a jeweller's in the City. He never felt he was being self-indulgent if he spent his money on others. His spendthrift streak was quite in line with his often quixotic acts of kindness and also with his increasingly hasty methods of doing business in his job: as, for example, in 1938, when he introduced, without adequate consultation, a new school custom requiring the sixth-form boys to wear a strange variety of Homburg hat. He paid for most things on credit, running up huge bills in the neighbourhood, while admonishing boys that they should "always pay cash." This mismanagement was his doing, not his wife's, for after his death, without his salary, she coped admirably.

In the last two years of Gurner's headmastership it became evident to members of staff that something was seriously amiss. His behaviour became increasingly erratic and eccentric. Irregularities in the school accounts had been noticed for some time: he had been borrowing money from various funds for longer or shorter periods and paying one back from another. The governors were sufficiently alarmed to confront him with the matter, give him a chance to repay and even offer to help him do so – and to recommend medical assistance. Gurner denied culpability and refused to take advice. Moreover he became aware that the governors were keeping him under surveillance after that, and this must have contributed to a feeling of persecution. One of his pupils remembers seeing him from a school window in the spring of 1939 pacing up and down in the rain obviously wrestling with some terrible anxiety. His mother, who lunched with him at a restaurant near Victoria Station on 1 May, recorded how very quiet he seemed.

What happened two weeks later is not, and never will be, quite clear. It seems as if on 14 May Ronald tried to explain something of his difficulties to his mother-in-law, Mrs. Romer, with whom he was on good terms and from whom he hoped to borrow money. His wife insisted on hearing the facts from him. "I wanted an explanation and I think that he felt it was too much for him," she later explained. On Tuesday 16 May, it seems that Gurner went in to Whitgift, but slipped away again later, unnoticed, leaving a note for his wife, explaining that he had been in the hands of moneylenders for nine years, that various school accounts had got mixed, and that he had an overdraft of £1400. He had been living on his insurances. "It was impossible to tell you. I struggled to get straight but it is the old story." The best thing, he felt, was for him "to go away for a time." He made no attempt to contact any other member of his family. His mother, all unknowing that his life had reached its crisis, was spending a quiet day returning a copy of *Mein Kampf* to Smith's Library and having her hair curled.

He went to Paddington, where he arranged to rent a service flat at 36 Sussex Gardens for a week. After staying there for several hours, presumably in a turmoil of resentment and misery, he went out at five o'clock.

He posted a letter to the Clerk to the Governors in which he explained the complete extent of his raids on the school funds. It was addressed to Croydon, but his agitated handwriting made the last word on the envelope look like "Ceylon" and it did not reach its intended destination for some weeks. By then the worst had happened. He returned to his flat with a bottle of Lysol, a corrosive disinfectant fluid, sat on the edge of his bed and drank it straight off. His death was caused by shock from the burning action of the Lysol. One needs little imagination to picture the agony of his end – the end of a man, as the coroner put it, "of excellent physique and muscular" – not a body that would succumb quickly to even so frightful a poison. His precipitate flight and his massive debts led Whitgift staff, not least Ellis and the ever-imaginative Parr, to speculate that Gurner killed himself to evade a blackmailer. They resented his action deeply, feeling he had brought disgrace on the school, and were ready to believe the worst. No evidence whatsoever has been found for such a conclusion; nor at this distance is it likely to be. Nothing that Parr saw before he and Kathleen Gurner consigned Ronnie's private papers to the flames indicated any guilty secret behind his financial trouble, though the fact that Gurner had evidently been drawing large cash sums regularly over a long period led both of them to discuss this possibility at the time. However Kathleen Gurner, partly, perhaps, to spare her mother and sister the painful details of his financial muddles, eventually expressed the firm opinion that his death was due to delayed war strain.

This conclusion, from a close relative, is crucial in an examination of a war writer and his experience. Did the long hand of the war reach out to Gurner in the end? There is plenty of evidence that it did. Moreover we must remember that suicides are rarely uncomplicated in their origins. The psychologist Karl Menninger has pointed this out in his work on suicide, *Man Against Himself*:

> A wealthy man is one day announced as having killed himself. It is discovered that his investments have failed, but that his death provided bountiful insurance for his otherwise destitute family. The problem and its solution, then, seem simple and obvious enough. A man has bravely faced ruin in a way that benefits his dependants. But why should we begin our interpretations only at this late point in such a man's life, the

point at which he loses his wealth? Shall we not seek to discover how it came about that he lost it? And even more
pertinently, shall we not enquire how he made it, why he was
so driven to amass money and what means he used to gratify
his compulsion, what unconscious and perhaps also conscious
guilt feelings were associated with it and with the sacrifices
and penalties its acquisition cost him and his family?

It is unlikely that either Ronnie's immediate worries – the borrowing
from school funds and the distressing episode in March 1939 over the
Gurners' former *au pair* girl – or even the debt or his marriage problems,
lay at the deepest root of a decision to kill himself. One must look
further back to see why Gurner got into such a state and indeed to understand why he had a predisposition to take his own life rather than
seek some other way out of his difficulties.

It seems probable that an event as overwhelming as the war would
have played a more decisive part in undermining Gurner's apparent
ebullience and strength of personality and have been responsible for his
eventual disintegration. When he killed himself, at least one newspaper
pointed out that there was an analogy between Freddy Mann's craving
for death and the case of Gurner himself: "HEADMASTER'S MYS-
TERY FATE. SIMILAR TO HERO OF HIS WAR BOOK" was the
headline in the *Daily Telegraph*. Two passages from *Pass Guard* may be
quoted here:

> You have lost so much and you are so very tired. Those that
> were with you at Hooge and Bellewarde have left you. A
> hope that was dead and had begun to struggle to life again
> has died its second death: a city that you half hated, half cared
> for has forgotten you, for it has had many to care for it and
> hate it, and you are far away. Why grope further like an ani-
> mal, or wander through the filth of daylight any more? There
> is a Being here that will hold you, and never let you go. Its
> embrace is soft, and already as you sink within it the pain that
> made you breathe in spasms is lessened. You have had no
> respite and here at last is rest. The face of day is hideous, and
> the sun but shines to breed a greater foulness. Here, in your

hiding place, you will lie sleeping, for the Being that has found you and taken you to itself will keep you, and will see to it that you do not start at any sound or open your eyes again to the corruption overhead.

It had got most of the others, had death: it would get him soon enough. Why not – he laughed and raised himself a little higher on the parapet – why not save it trouble? He didn't want to die in agony, his guts dropping out and his blood pouring out of a hole the size of a pudding plate like Martin's. He didn't want to crack, like Bill had cracked. He'd just had enough, and he wanted to slip away. It was so easy, too – just a walk along the canal bank past Essex Farm and Hull Farm towards Boesinghe, where the German lines drew to the canal, on and on, with the light breaking, till it came; or a walk from Foch Farm, out towards the Pilkem Ridge – there wouldn't be more than five yards there to go; or in daylight, over Hilltop Farm, or past Forward Cottage over the ridge towards the line; or simpler still, just over and through the wire, and then on through the marshes till you came to the High Command Redoubt; or, without bothering to walk at all, this pistol – all those fellows out there were peaceful enough, and they didn't care now whether they stank or not. Why go on, when all you had to live for was to crawl like a hunted rabbit through mud, and see bloody fools who came to you from time to time and told you you were saving Ypres? Why, come to that – he laughed aloud, and looked behind him. Ypres was dead.

We have looked earlier at the manner in which he regained his religious faith, and with it, the will to fight his despair. But beneath that faith are indications of doubt. His efforts to keep a hold on some kind of religion were very determined. His views were unorthodox and centred largely in doing good in this world, though he encouraged his son to pray and attend church regularly in Croydon, if only to satisfy the expectations of that conventional and inward-looking community. He had several close friends among the clergy, such as the Bishop of Lichfield.

He saw a great deal, in the years that followed the war, of his old school and St. John's College friend, the Rev. Cuthbert Layland Parker. Parker, a university oarsman of picturesquely rugged appearance, had served briefly as a padre in 1915 but had been invalided out because of a typhoid injection that went wrong. He was an inspired, born-again pentecostalist who managed just to remain within the Anglican Church despite causing a split in the congregation of his church, St. James, Clerkenwell, in the 1940s. Ronald Gurner sought his constant spiritual help – so much so that as she later confessed, Parker's wife began to resent his demands on her husband's time. On one occasion, impatient of their long conversation out on the street after Ronnie Gurner had left the house, she opened the window and emptied the dregs of a jug on their heads.

Deep down, it seems as if Ronald Gurner could still feel the despair that had afflicted him in the later part of the war; but he fought it and his other severe anxieties successfully for a while with religion, with friendship, with patriotism, with the pursuit of personal ambition, with devotion to work, with whisky. By 1939 he seems to have been virtually an alcoholic though it is clear that his colleagues were not fully aware of this. Phyllis Gurner remembers meeting him accidentally one evening near Oxted, some miles south of Croydon, pub-crawling in an area where he hoped not to be seen by anyone he knew. Drink may have been good in the short run for taking the sting out of his problems, but a prolonged regime of hangovers left even as strong a man as Gurner more exposed physically. It made him more unreliable too, more forgetful of undertakings, and largely explains some of the erratic behaviour of which he was accused. He had been a fairly heavy drinker at Oxford and the trenches must have reinforced the habit. Paul Crowson, one of the Whitgift pupils most enthusiastic about his teaching and leadership, commented with understanding: "Ronald Gurner . . . was a severely wounded war casualty, always in pain, who kept going on increasing doses of whisky. This was better, more gallant, than giving up and dying in 1919."

It is probable he frequently felt after the war that his whole life was unreal. In his autobiography he admitted that he had often wished that he had died on the battlefield with his friends. His colleague, F. H. G.

Percy, who has studied his Whitgift life closely, feels that in his profes-sional career, at least, he presented the world with a façade. The real Gurner, whoever he was, was not like Norwood, with a powerful and simple moral outlook and a clear grasp of realities; the claims Gurner made for Whitgift were sometimes the product of wishful thinking, as though he had decided in advance how things were to be. One cannot help thinking that there is also something *voulu* about the end of *Pass Guard*, something he tried to tell himself that, in his heart of hearts, could not console him. That is certainly the impression that the book gives.

We cannot leave it at this, however. The trouble must have gone deeper than war-weariness and disillusion, for other soldiers felt this and did not try to do away with themselves during or after the war. We know for certain, however, that even on the Western Front Gurner lived with the idea of suicide. There is a highly significant passage in Cyril Gurner's lengthy account, cited earlier, of how his brother won the M.C. The in-cident occurred just after Ronnie had been wounded. Here Cyril recorded that his brother's last conscious act had been to find the *two grains of arsenic which he carried on his person*, so that he could swallow them rather than be taken prisoner. It is quite certain that there were not many officers who carried arsenic into battle with them, and it implies a readi-ness to seek out death deliberately, as well as a strange ignorance of how long a time was needed for a poison like arsenic to take effect.

The existence of a deep-seated instability in Gurner's makeup was confirmed at the inquest. His great friend, the Rev. Cuthbert Parker, was a key witness. He testified that Gurner had suffered repeatedly from mental illness. He recalled how he had broken down at Oxford, while the "shell-shock" after his wound in 1917 had brought on another series of such attacks over a period of years. Parker regarded the suicide as be-ing wholly attributable to nervous depression. Though saddened and shocked by the incident, therefore, he had not been in the most pro-found sense distressed by the suicide, for he had seen it as purely a medical crisis and not the result of moral failure. He himself had been laid low with acute depressive attacks over the years, as a result of delving into spiritual matters with an intense concentration. He believed he could recognise the symptoms of depressive illness clearly. Gurner had many of the characteristics of the manic-depressive type in his personality and these may have been inherited traits. It is possible, but clearly his father's desertion must have been a root cause of his depressions and instability.

Irreparable damage had been done psychologically. It had been a cruel blow to Ronnie in particular, not least because his mother took up for a time with a new man, the engineer Thom, whose generosity to the family has been mentioned earlier. Divorce at that time was out of the question and she and her lover moved discreetly into a flat in New Oxford Street. Ronnie deeply resented Thom's open displays of affection towards her and despised his heartiness and lack of culture. Though too young to be so directly affected, Ronnie's beautiful younger sister Enid plainly also felt the reverberations of the disappearance. Insecure and disappointed in love in her late teens, she withdrew into eccentric spinsterhood, rearing goats and horses and swimming all year round until the end of her long life. She also mismanaged her financial affairs, putting her slender resources into a pig-farming project, which collapsed. (Before then, unfortunately, she was photographed by the press sitting beside one of her pigs; this fetching picture reached the Indian syndicated newspapers, to the embarrassment of Cyril Gurner, who had to explain away his sister's behaviour to horrified Indian colleagues.)

A betrayal and a loss of the kind that the Gurner children experienced can have many effects. It is not far-fetched to see Ronnie's wish to excel as a teacher as an effort to become the father-figure his father had failed to be. Much of his early indebtedness may have been the result of trying to replace his father as provider of luxuries for his mother, in rivalry to Mr. Thom. The suicide was a disappearance in its most absolute and terrifying form, betraying his own family as he himself had been betrayed. Even if the decision to kill himself came very much at the last minute, a wish to abandon both job and family, at least for a while, had been on his mind for several years. A surviving letter from his mother in 1926 suggests that he contemplated leaving them and setting up house with her at that time. The thought must have recurred. A few months before the tragedy he wrote to Cyril in Calcutta saying that he was desperately unhappy and that he was going to throw up his job – that he was likely to be thrown out anyway. Cyril replied inviting him to work in India and sending him a draft for a ticket to the P & O Office in India, a sensible solution that might have saved his life. Ronald Gurner never acknowledged the letter; possibly his wife suppressed it; more likely he could see little future for himself in India and procrastinated about taking up the offer.

Besides this, Gurner always felt he had let down his friends by not joining them in death during the Great War. He may have felt, too, that they had betrayed *him* by walking out of his life. Given the palimpsest of elusive evidence going endlessly back into the obscurities of his childhood, it is too late to unearth completely the mystery of his suicide. What is certain is that his attitude to the war cannot be explained solely by his direct experiences in it. On the surface Gurner believed what he wrote in *Pass Guard at Ypres*: that a man's happiness and his dearest held convictions were not too high a price to pay in his country's cause and that this knowledge in itself should console any soldier who has despaired. His life story suggests, however, that this almost mystic patriotism and devotion to the hallowed ground of Ypres could not give him real comfort, because it had not been the war as much as his father's disappearance that had undermined his confidence in life. It was part of a determined effort by an admirable, gifted, and courageous man to shore up a psychological house of cards that for a long time he had felt might collapse at any moment. As a result of his childhood experiences he was much more vulnerable than his robust outward appearance and ebullient personality suggested; and although he was only in one serious military action, three years of war and personal loss had damaged his fragile inner stability.

> Let now the buried past remain
> Grey walls with you: I shall not come again,

he had written in February 1916 at Ypres; but he could not escape his past. It rose up and stalked him down the long years.

"Damned Proud of It We Are"
Herbert Read
1893 - 1968

In my case, I was to discover, with a sense of self-confidence
wholly new to me, that I could endure the experience of war,
even at its worst. This is far from claiming I was fearless: the
first days in the trenches, the first bombardment or attack, was
a draining sickness of the spirit. But I presently recovered, as
from a plunge into a cold sea.

Among English prose works on the Great War, Herbert Read's
writings convey, uniquely, a quiet, detached sense of personal
destiny. He emerged from the war hoping for a world in which
both individual self-realisation and a cooperative, unselfish society would
be possible. On his experience of the fighting, he was resolved:

to tell the truth without rhetoric
the truth about war and about men
involved in the indignities of war.

In fact Read, "the best mind in Britain," who was to have a central influence in promoting the Modern Movement in Britain during the
interwar period, wrote relatively briefly on the subject of his career as a
soldier. There is no great novel of the kind one might have expected
from so capable and imaginative a mind. What he left, however, over a
lifetime, was a body of poetry – of which the best-known volumes are

Naked Warriors (1919), written while on active service, his meditations on war in *The End of a War* (1932) and *A World Within a War* (1944); there were also – and very importantly – short stories, such as his fictionalised memoir of a crucial episode in his life, "The Raid," which incorporates thoughts central to his attitude toward the war; there were also personal memories and "a war diary" – extracted from his wartime letters to his future wife – which appeared, among other places, in his various autobiographies. The war was never far from his thoughts, and pervaded his strange surreal novel, *The Green Child*.

Read's contribution to the literature of the Great War is of particular interest, not only because of his intense vision and philosophical turn of mind, but also because his heroism was matched by only a few other writers, such as Siegfried Sassoon in England and Ernst Jünger in Germany. This gives a different perspective from the many memorable but unheroic angles on the war offered by such authors as Richard Aldington. Much of the interest of Read's writing lies in the calm intellectual authority with which he was able, later, to describe battle – very unlike, indeed, the urgent tone of his wartime poems, *The Happy Warrior*, for instance:

> His wild heart beats with painful sobs,
> His strained hands clench an ice-cold rifle,
> His aching jaws grip a hot parched tongue,
> And his wide eyes search unconsciously.
>
> He cannot shriek.
> Bloody saliva
> Dribbles down his shapeless jacket.
>
> I saw him stab
> And stab again
> A well-killed Boche.
>
> This is the happy warrior,
> This is he...

Read had a complex personality. His reactions were refreshingly un-predictable. His political and intellectual viewpoints were not those usually encountered in a warrior, happy or otherwise. He was a theoreti-cal pacifist before the war, a socialist and an admirer of Georges Sorel and the Syndicalist movement. He was an aesthete, and even in wartime a contributor to radical cultural journals, usually on subjects far removed from the conflict itself. He could absorb himself, just after a punishing ordeal in battle, with Thoreau's *Walden* and claim that Henry James's works kept him going during those dangerous years. In later life he was well-known for his anarchist views.

Yet he was outstanding as a soldier. His nature and inheritance con-tributed to his ability to survive and excel in the trenches. His nervous vitality showed in his large brilliant eyes. Slight, of shortish stature, with sloping shoulders, he was tougher than he looked. Already at twenty-four, when he was photographed as a subaltern in the army, his face showed tenacity and distinction. His lower jaw was small; yet this was no sign of weakness, as conventionally believed. Indeed his character was exceptionally strong. In self-reliance and intellect he was mature beyond his years.

Though he had lost his father when he was eight and his mother at twenty-one, the essential years before his father's death, when his family lived on the farm, Muscoates Grange, near Kirbymoorside, North York-shire, gave him a rock-solid rootedness, which all the turmoil of the years that followed could not shake. Coming from the yeoman class, he had a deep sense of belonging to his country and people, which did much to insulate him against the snobbery of the young public-school officers with whom he first trained at Wareham Camp. The large place that he gave to his early, rural years in his memories and in the haunting first section of *The Green Child*, set in the Yorkshire countryside, shows how dominant that childhood paradise remained in his vision of the world: the red-tiled farmhouse in the Vale of Pickering – "a basin, wide and shallow like the milk pans in the dairy"; the orchard of ancient moss-en-crusted apple trees; the Foldgarth, where the cows were milked in "the glow and atmosphere of the Nativity"; and the magical shrine of the blacksmith's shop, where the bellows roared and the "clang, clang, clang on the anvil, the heavenly shower of ruby and golden sparks."

From that Garden of Eden, after his father's death from pneumonia, the family were expelled, Herbert going to a bleak orphan academy. In Leeds, "a wilderness of stone and brick," as he later described it, the family endured years of financial insecurity. Intellectually restless in a monotonous job as a clerk at the Skyrac and Morley Savings Bank, he took out his frustrations on his mother, who had grown more domineering in temper as the anxieties of widowed parenthood weighed her down. Their unresolved quarrels made Mrs. Read's death, in December 1914, all the more more painful for her son. Subconsciously for a while, when he was serving at the front, he refused to accept that she had died.

Yet given his precocity and his already affirmed independence, manifest in the flowering of his intellectual life even before he went to Leeds University in 1912, the loss of his parents did free him from family ties in a way that made him a more effective soldier. In "The Raid," he described "P—," a fellow-officer who had become a coward. Read wrote:

> He had a mother and a sweetheart, and he spent a lot of time writing letters. He never got free from his home thoughts; he was still bound in some sort of personal dependence to these ties. His mind, at any rate, was not free to lead its own existence. I think that is why he was a coward.

Read – and most others – had enough vestigial "home thoughts" in their minds to recognise the dangers of being too much fixed on them. He corresponded throughout the war with his future wife, Evelyn Roff, the pale, petite, scholarly daughter of a "drysalter," making patent medicines, from Bradford. He and she had met while they were at Leeds University. However, whilst he derived confidence from the relationship and whilst it afforded him a romantic "dream of home," he was not really dependent on her in a way that might have undermined his will to endure – though because Read drastically edited his letters for publication, and the originals were destroyed, it is hard to be absolutely sure on this point. He was probably too young emotionally to be really attached and his supposed feelings for her were exaggerated in his mind by unfulfilled sexual longings. He had dropped Christianity in his teens and was keen to throw over the conventions, while she still stuck to the respectable morals of her artisan background and resisted the idea of their sleeping together until they could be married.

Religion, though he did not despise it, played no part, indeed, in sustaining his morale, despite his use of its images to describe the suffering and endurance of his men. During those years he brooded on the philosopher Nietzsche, regarding him as "my real teacher" throughout the university and army period. This did not directly affect his conduct during the war, but played a part in how he came to see himself. He seems to have felt that his war career was an indication that he had been selected for greater things – was almost, in a sense, a kind of superman.

In August 1914, Read was a member of the Leeds University Officer Training Corps – surprising for one whose views were becoming radical and pacifist, but among many Edwardians such paradoxical behaviour was far from uncommon. The various available paramilitary activities, such as the O.T.C. and the Boy Scouts, offered outdoor adventure in direct reaction to the hideosities and pollution of Victorian city life. Henry Woodd Nevinson, the war correspondent who gained fame through his best-selling account of being besieged in Ladysmith during the Boer War, was a radical with strongly antiwar feelings; yet for years as a young man he had drilled cadets in the East End of London, because he believed in the social benefits of discipline and fitness. R. H. Mottram, as we have seen, once took an equitation course in the local barracks to find out how the "other half" lived. What membership of the O.T.C. signified, in short, for Read, was not a latent militarism, but idealism and a longing for outdoor life.

When war broke out he felt no upsurge of patriotic emotion. Both sides seemed to him inspired by commerce and imperialism. He was sorry – even surprised – that the war had not been stopped by an international workers' strike in every country. However, his pacifism was theoretical and easily put aside. Possibly a residue of the loyal rural Toryism he had grown up with still influenced him more than he realised. Most Edwardians and late Victorians romanticised war. It promised chivalry and emancipation from a tedious and complex existence.

"To this romantic illusion must be added in my own case," he wrote, "a state of uncertainty about the future. Though I was ambitious and full of determination, I had no precise career marked out: I was to be a free-lance of some sort, and a free-lance finds a very appropriate place in an army. The war meant a decision: a crystallisation of vague projects: an immediate acceptance of the challenge of life. I did not hesitate."

In January 1915 he was commissioned in the Yorkshire Regiment, familiarly known as "the Green Howards," proceeding for training to Wareham Camp in Dorset. Eventually he went out that November with his battalion, the 7th Green Howards, to the area between Ypres and Hooge. It was a tolerably quiet month for the battalion, but the mud, rain, and frosts were very demanding on the physical endurance and determination of the troops. Read, with B company at Sanctuary Wood, soon became aware of the price the army paid for hanging on to the Ypres Salient, the cherished symbol of resistance to the German invasion: "To maintain this thrust in the enemy's side was the insane will of the whole army. It was not justified in a strategic sense. It was a blind impulse, to which hundreds of thousands of lives were sacrificed." It was, as he later recorded, "nervy business for a raw subaltern. The first time he goes out in daylight a shot from the front cracks like a whip in his ear. He draws in his breath and the blood deserts his face. Immediately the air cracks behind him and a bullet ricochets from the bank he faces. Terror melts his limbs. He falls to the ground and grasps the rungs of the duckboard."

Any idea of war as physically and aesthetically exhilarating soon evaporated. He never became used to the sight of corpses and blood, nor was he prepared for the long, tedious periods of inaction. The ugliness of the broken landscape haunted him. The work at the front was exhausting and repetitive – wiring parties, night patrols, and supervising the revetting of trenches in that noisome morass of a battlefield. Christmas was spent in the battered shell that was Ypres, and they were back in a heavily bombarded line by the New Year. Early in January however they went for a month's rest at Polincove, a village between St. Omer and Calais. Then, once again, they were in heavy fighting against German attacks near St. Eloi, for several weeks. In March 1916, Read was accidentally injured and returned to England.

It had been an ordeal, but "the unscaled peak of experience" that he and his fellow-soldiers were required to surmount was proving less hard for him than it was for some of those who had looked down their noses at him in Wareham Camp days: "In England we had unconsciously accepted the habit of command and the air of superiority that environment and education had conferred on the sons of the elite. Now we discovered that something else mattered more: that irreducible element of personality which is the raw material of education and the principle of growth persisting through every environment. It is my conviction that education and environment cannot change this innate spirit of an individual . . . [War], which is so often made the melodramatic agent of changes in character, does not affect the inherent quality of the person."

Whether it was at this stage or later, he came to envision a picture, which he usually found consoling, of all humanity springing continually from a tree of life, which lived on, while individual lives were like leaves that died when they had had their time and were shed. It made his own life seem less precious to himself, and sometimes the lives of others, though it did not always insulate him from the deepest grief. When his brother was killed, towards the end of the war, in October 1918, he was overwhelmed with sorrow. As he wandered, forlorn, through a park near his army camp at Middlesbrough, he found in the sight of the leaves strewn in his path a metaphor that was heartrending:

> The fallen leaves were an augury
> And seemed to intend
> As they yellowly drooped in the languid air
> That life was a fragile mood and death
> A tremendous despair.

Back in England in 1916, after convalescence, Read was sent in June to train recruits with the 11th Green Howards, at Rugeley Park in Staffordshire. It was a "dreadful place" according to him, where the authorities' idea of "light duty" was twelve hours of yelling at recruits on the parade ground. He made it bearable by keeping up his literary and artistic interests, drawing and contributing to cultural and political journals like *The New Age*. The aesthete in him found a diversion in embellishing his "studio" (a room 15 ft. by 12 ft.): "with a series of Japanese prints, three charcoal sketches of Watteau's, two of Whistler's, three or four of my own productions . . . a shelf of books, an oak table, a writing table and a few photographs of friends. Add to this a tapestried dado of discarded coats (etc.) drooping in languorous attitudes around the room and you get *a tout ensemble* that makes an illness Elysium!"

When eventually he returned to the front in April 1917, his long period away from the war, when he had developed so much in very different, artistic, directions, had not, seemingly, destroyed any inclination he had for further fighting, as it would have done in many other soldiers. He felt calm and happy, he told Evelyn, although two years of war had not made him a whit more keen on "King and Country" as a cause. Nor did he hate "the hun" any more than he hated many of his own compatriots! Yet even now, the mood of Rupert Brooke possessed him – the desire, at least, he said, "to turn, as swimmers into cleanness leaping." For he continued to see the war as being the ultimate test, the purging of the soul through courage and duty properly performed.

In the months that followed this was borne out by his conduct in battle. He had been transferred to the 10th Green Howards, now forming part of the 21st Division, on 27 April 1917. The Battle of Arras, Britain's contribution to the big French offensive led by General Nivelle, had been raging for over a fortnight, and was petering out. For Read, the renewed experience of war in an isolated outpost at Boiry-Becquerelle, under continuous bombardment, was an unpleasant rebaptism of fire, as was a night patrol, walking and crawling 500 yards towards the German line in bright moonlight, to examine the state of the enemy's wire. After a few such "quiet" days, the battalion moved back to Hendecourt for training. Early in June, it returned to heavy shelling at the front, while keeping up training for a projected raid of considerable importance. This was to have a central place in Read's military experience.

The raid was launched just north of Fontaine-les-Croisilles, to the south of the Arras-Cambrai road. Two officers of proven courage were needed to lead it. Read was selected, together with Lieut. J.L. Smith M.C. In his later, fictionalised account of the incident, Read suggested that Smith was only chosen after "P—" the first choice, revealed himself to be a coward, and Read felt himself obliged to warn the Commanding Officer, for fear P— would jeopardise the raid:

he was a coward, in the only concise sense that can be given to that word. A coward is not merely a man who feels fear. We all experience fear; it is a physical reaction to the unknown extent of danger. But it is only cowardice when it becomes a mental reaction – when the mind, reacting to the flesh, submits to the instincts of the flesh.

Yet however vividly he conveyed the impression that he had really known the person he described in this passage, his character P— would seem to have been introduced here for literary effect, even, it has been suggested, to personify Read's own secret fear of losing his nerve. It seems unlikely that Read, a junior subaltern, would have been sent on a raid of this type with another relatively inexperienced officer, and the choice of Smith in the first instance, with his record of courage, seems far more likely.

"I am very glad," wrote Read to Evelyn, just after being chosen, "glad in the first place because it gives me the first chance I've had of doing something – glad in the second place because it means that others recognise that I'm of the clan who don't give a damn for anything." However, as with other "fire-eaters," there was nothing suicidal in his attitude – rather a burning desire to win through to fight another day.

The "stunt," as he called it, took place on a "dark and dirty night." The battalion diary reported: "A most successful raid was carried out by a party from the battalion at 2 a.m. on night 30/31 [July]. A very important identification was obtained and the only casualties sustained were one NCO missing and one man slightly wounded, the latter not belonging to the raiding party.

"The party was formed by C. company . . . and great courage was shown by all concerned in sharp fighting at close quarters with the enemy."

The objective had been to kill as many Germans as possible and bring back a prisoner to identify the German division they were facing. Forty-seven men volunteered out of a possible sixty – a measure of the willingness to serve. The emphasis was on stealth and surprise, and the company went out with blackened faces and with daggers as well as firearms and bombs. Read, Smith, and their men had about 550 yards of no-man's-land to cross, crawling the last half at a yard a minute. They encountered a German wiring party, strongly protected by other soldiers. Read and the other raiders had to decide immediately on a change of tactic and go on the defensive. However, as the Germans were coming very close to where Read lay, he realised he must attack first. He leapt to his feet and ordered them to put up their hands. Instead, they fired on him and his sergeant: both returned the fire, hitting one German and taking the other prisoner. For five minutes there was an inferno of rifle shots, in which the guns on both sides, now alerted, joined. The enemy sustained about twenty casualties. Covered by Lieut. Smith and others, Read was able to hurry back with his prize, a German officer who, it turned out, had been decorated for capturing 85 prisoners at Verdun. He was taken down to Brigade. Read claimed to Evelyn that he and his prisoner, a cultivated man, formed a close, on-the-spot friendship; though he afterwards remembered the incident more ironically in his poem, "Liedholz":

> Going to the Brigade with my prisoner at dawn,
> The early sun made the land delightful,
> And larks rose singing from the plain.
>
> In broken French we discussed
> Beethoven, Nietzche and the International.
>
> He was a professor
> Living at Spandau;
> And not too intelligible.
>
> But my black face and nigger's teeth
> Amused him.

It was a reminder that for all the common ground that might have existed between combatants on both sides, it was easy to sentimentalise the notion of the "international brotherhood of the trenches." On the other hand there is no doubt that the companionship that Read knew in the Green Howards left a profound impression on him. The mechanism that squeezed out the cowardly P—, in his story, from the group, for fear he should endanger them, was the same that drew the others together, as though by a powerful magnet, members incorporate of the same body, more willing to risk death together than surrender separately. Read's protagonist Kneeshaw, in his poem "Kneeshaw Goes to War," returns home without a leg, on crutches, haunted by his experiences and his failure of nerve. The lost leg – symbolic of the soldier torn away by death from his companions – and the lost nerve – the betrayal of comrades through an involuntary spiritual desertion – these were central to his outlook on the war.

It was not that he could not sympathise deeply with the man who allowed terror to dominate his spirit: "What wrong have I done," he makes another protagonist, Cornelius Vane, say, in a further poem ("The Execution of Cornelius Vane") "that I should leave these:/ The bright sun rising/ And the birds that sing?" All the same Read seems to have feared giving way to cowardice above all else, and was obsessively determined not to betray his own men. He observed how the gift of physical fearlessness could be destroyed by shock, though it could often carry a man on to great feats of courage; he put his faith in his will to fight through a sanely balanced outlook on life and death, backing up his own natural allowance of physical bravery. Cowards had not the strength of will or "decency of thought," as he put it, to make themselves overcome fear.

All goes well
So long as you tune the instrument
To simulate composure.

(So you will become
A gallant gentleman.)

But when the strings are broken...
Then you will grovel on the earth
And your rabbit eyes
Will fill with the fragments of your shattered soul.

The battalion were duly thanked, in August 1917, by the commander of the VIIth Corps to which they belonged, for their work during and after the battle of Arras, and on 18 August the Commander-in-Chief,

Field Marshal Haig, awarded a bar to Lieut. Smith's M.C. and the Military Cross to Herbert Read. Subsequently Read was promoted full lieutenant and received medal ribbons from the General commanding the 21st Division. He went on leave in late September.

Thus he had encountered his first great test and won. He had clearly feared that it would go otherwise. Experience, he had told Evelyn in June, had taught him how much more valuable a "simple soul" and a stout heart were than "bombast" or intellect, which were so useful in civilian life. At the time he did not confess to her how afraid he had been, in case it might unman him to do so, and because it would have upset her as well. Much later, he admitted that all men shared these fears.

By going on leave he missed some of the horror of the 3rd Ypres campaign, which his battalion went through in the autumn of 1917. In the muddy battle of the Broodseinde Ridge, lasting 3½ days, the Commanding Officer was badly shaken, one officer and 74 other ranks were killed, and nine officers and 249 other ranks wounded or missing: "I feel a little ashamed at having escaped it all," Read told Evelyn. "There is always a regret in not having shared dangers with friends. Perhaps one is jealous of their experiences." Meeting comrades afterwards at their billets at Sercus, he wrote: "They have gone through what was probably the most intense shell fire since the war began ... One or two of my special pals among the men have disappeared, especially a jolly little Irish boy who was worth a thousand for his cheerfulness."

It was not long, however, before he himself was in that hellish struggle, for five days in the line near Zillebeke Lake. He was now commander of his company, "C," holding the right support position. For 24 October, the third day, the battalion diary reported: "Enemy artillery active throughout the day. The condition of the trenches was extremely bad, there being several heavy downpours of rain; as the subsoil was sandy the water drained away fairly well, but the slightest concussion shook down the sides of the trenches."

Immediately afterwards, Read wrote to Evelyn: "We have had a terrible time, the worst I have ever experienced (and I'm getting quite an old soldier now). Life has never seemed quite so cheap nor nature so mutilated." He recalled the horror of it, in "Kneeshaw goes to War":

A man who was marching at Kneeshaw's side
Hesitated in the middle of the mud,
And slowly sank, weighted down by equipment and arms.
He cried for help;
Rifles were stretched to him;
He clutched and they tugged,
But slowly he sank.
His terror grew –
Grew visibly when the viscous ooze
Reached his neck.
And there he seemed to stick,
Sinking no more.
They could not dig him out –
The oozing mud would flow back again.
The dawn was very near.

An officer shot him through the head;
Not a neat job – the revolver
Was too close.

There was a bitterness, reminiscent of Siegfried Sassoon, in Read's reflections; the absurd overreaction at home to a few paltry air raids on the capital showed how little most people understood what the fighting was really like: "They raise a sentimental scream about one or two babies killed when every day out here hundreds of the very finest manhood 'go west.'" He wondered, indeed, if he should not tell the full horror of it to the world, so that in a mood of revulsion it would call an end to the war.

Yet, amazingly, he still derived satisfaction from what he was doing – his power over his men as company commander, punishing, promoting, redressing grievances, exacting obedience, keeping up their spirits: "I got four military medals today out of seven for the Battalion ... And damned proud of it we are," he wrote to Evelyn.

The comradeship, as he had told Evelyn earlier, would he thought overcome any horror or hardship. "It is this comradeship which alone makes the Army tolerable to me. To create a bond between yourself and a body of men and a bond that will hold at the critical moment, that is work worthy of any man and when done an achievement to be proud of."

For the men in his charge, Read's feelings acquired an intensity, familiar to soldiers, which a later age, enslaved to crude psychological categorisation, labels homoerotic – as if all physical manifestations of love and companionship, for mother, brother, son, daughter, or dying friend must indicate a concealed lust. He wrote of that most heartrending ordeal for most soldiers – to see a comrade die and decay on the wire, because it was too dangerous to bring him in and offer a last tribute of devotion:

> A man of mine
>   lies on the wire;
> And he will rot
> And first his lips
> The worms will eat.
>
> It is not thus I would have him kissed,
> But with the warm passionate lips
> Of his comrade here.

The process whereby an officer became one with the men he commanded took time. When was it that this occurred? Read reflected in a poem:

> Perhaps when one summer night
> We halted on the roadside
> In the starlight only,
> And you sang your sad home-songs,
> Dirges which I standing outside your soul
> Coldly condemned.
>
> Perhaps one night, descending cold,
> When rum was mighty acceptable,
> And my doling gave birth to sensual gratitude.
> And then our fights: we've fought together

Compact, unanimous;
And I have felt the pride of leadership.

What the companionship gave Read was a deep conviction of human goodness and love, and that these were possible only in small units. This belief lay at the root of his anarchism, and this was why, though he rejected the army as a way of life, he set immense store by his experience at that time.

They only had a week more in the Ypres battle, heavily shelled in their trenches as the British army made its final push to take the Passchendaele ridge. They rested for over a week then moved south, reaching the Cambrai battle area on 1 December 1917. They remained in the same sector till the end of January, doing, as was usual, four days in the front line, four in support, and four in reserve, a weary, dispiriting time, though not the most dangerous. In February, the 10th Battalion, like many others whose strength had been depleted in the previous months, was finally disbanded. Read moved to the 2nd Battalion. He was suffering severely from war-weariness. In January he had sent an article to the *New Age*, giving what he regarded as the soldier's point of view – that the game was no longer worth the candle: "there has been," he told Evelyn, "an immense growth of pacifist opinion." Dreary winter weather, monotony, and high casualties earlier, leading to the breakup of battalions with their sense of identity, contributed to this widespread mood.

The following month, March, however, was to show that the army's spirit was far from broken, when they faced their greatest test, and Read himself displayed a sustained courage that finally justified, for him, his decision to go to war. He wrote a detailed account of that time, *In Retreat*, a few months afterwards. On 21 March the German Army, strengthened by divisions released from their Eastern Front by the defeat of Russia, attacked the thinly manned Allied lines along a forty-mile front. Read, whose battalion was a component of the 30th Division, in Sir Hubert Gough's Fifth Army, was part of a force rushed forward to man a redoubt in the 3rd line of defence, at Roupy. There, they were besieged by a determined enemy over a period of two days. In the middle of the second day the enemy reached the inner ring of the redoubt. "We fired like maniacs," Read wrote. "Every round of ammunition had been distributed. The Lewis guns jammed; rifle bolts grew stiff and unworkable with the expansion of heat."

Determined not to be trapped in their dugout, Read and the Colonel commanding left it and established headquarters at an old gun pit 25 yards back. There they came under "friendly fire" from British gunners who believed, mistakenly, that Roupy had been evacuated. Soon after, the Colonel, "Nutty" Edwards, bleeding dangerously from a wound in the arm, was forced to go to a dressing station. Read, now the senior officer, extricated the survivors and led them back to eventual safety in a withdrawal that took six days and six nights, without sleep and often without eating, as the Germans, surging forward, harried the Fifth Army. Time and again he and his men took up a defensive position, only to be almost surrounded and compelled to break out. It was a brilliant feat on Read's part. He revealed himself as a resourceful tactician as well as heroically brave. He was greatly helped by the determination of his men, at the limit of their powers, not to let themselves be forced into surrender, preferring to fight their way out at great risk of their lives.

As a result Read was later awarded the D.S.O., a medal not often given to junior officers in that war, unless they had just missed a V.C. He was also promoted to Captain.

The situation was far too critical for him to enjoy a long period of rest and he was involved in further hard fighting in April and early May, the scene of operations moving up to the defence of Ypres at the Dickebusch Lake. There the 2nd Green Howards came under exceptionally heavy bombardments first from gas, then from high-explosive shells. There were many casualties and their trenches were almost obliterated. A ferocious enemy attack on the morning of 8 May penetrated a part of the line they were holding. Captain Colin Davidson, Read's particular friend, was taken prisoner.

For the rest of the month and into June, the 2nd Green Howards held trenches around Mazingarbe, Hulluch, and St. Elie. At this point, on 16 June, Read left the battalion for England to undergo a medical examination for entry into the R.A.F. Missing Davidson, he was exhausted and sick of the war, and increasingly horrified by the wanton slaughter, the death, "in inconceivable torment," of German and English young men – "beautiful fresh children," whose values were love, joy, and hope – exploited by states and politicians whose values were power, vanity, and commercial expansion. Again one can see, in his revulsion against the all-powerful nation-state, one of the roots of his anarchism.

He was rejected by the R.A.F. He was lucky. Far from being an escape from strain, air combat in 1918 was very dangerous, as the story of V. M. Yeates has shown. To Read, however, the idea had seemed attractive – that of stepping, as it were, heavenward. It conformed with his Niet-zschean notions of the Superman. Pilots at the time regarded themselves as an élite.

Read did not return to France. As the war drew to a close he played for a while with the idea of remaining in the peacetime army. The long periods of idleness might be devoted to his literary career from which he hoped ultimately to earn a living. He had liked the manliness of the army, the courage it demanded, and the companionship. However, its re-lentless, machine-like side repelled him; and he soon abandoned the idea. In the years that followed he watched with sadness the spectacle of the dissolution of the bonds that had joined him and his companions as each one went their separate, unidealistic ways. Like C. E. Montague, Oliver Onions, and others, he had imagined the massed battalions of the war survivors, with their marvellous spirit, sweeping away the old hypocrisies and betrayals and founding a new, fair, and creative social or-der. However, he admitted that even he, with his great hopes for himself and for the future of British culture, finally took the bourgeois path of marriage and a salaried job in the Civil Service though he devoted his spare time to literary and cultural criticism, and as far as possible, to cre-ative writing.

For three years after he was demobilised in 1919 he was employed at the Ministry of Labour and the Treasury. Then in 1922 he secured a transfer to the Victoria and Albert Museum, where he worked in the De-partment of Ceramics. After a time he became Personal Assistant to the Museum's Director, Eric Maclagan, who soon began to envisage the brilliant and efficient young man as his successor. The post greatly ex-panded Read's knowledge and understanding of the arts and enabled him to become the most influential English art critic of the century.

The war was to remain a dominant element in his thought through-out his life. In common with many idealists who had taken an active part in it, he found it unbearable to think of that tragic past, unless, through understanding of it, the world could be reshaped. There were some whom such a view took on the path of the Peace Movement or the League of Nations, such as Vera Brittain, the Rev. Dick Sheppard, Max Plowman, and Lord Robert Cecil. Read was among those who wanted a new order of society to emerge with new moral values expressed through the arts.

He shared, however, with many others, the pernicious exhaustion of spirit that afflicted former servicemen. As a result his natural Yorkshire reticence was intensified by the emotional numbness that the war experiences had left. Some of the friendships he had clung to at the tail-end of the war – with Richard Aldington, Wyndham Lewis, Ford Madox Ford, Osbert Sitwell, F. S. Flint, and others – had been sought largely because he and they could not let the war go; and for a time their fellow-feeling concealed differences that were only to emerge sharply later.

Aldington, for example, was a firm ally for a while, who believed in Read's writing and encouraged him generously. Read warmed, on first meeting, to his "jolly open-faced . . . quite boyish" new friend. It was thanks to Aldington that *The Green Child* found a publisher. Both men felt at odds with postwar bourgeois England, yet in the end their paths diverged. Aldington was not truly part of the Modern Movement that Read came so passionately to champion, and he felt that as Read became more famous he let their relationship lapse. On his part Read felt less close to Aldington when the latter changed, in the thirties, from struggling poet-critic to successful novelist.

Even before these rifts opened between the two men, it early dawned on Read that few of Britain's war veterans were going to be the creative force of the future – they were exhausted and could not generate the kind of new culture that Eliot and Joyce were offering the world.

Yet that strong spirit of his that had to face these conclusions did not lose hope. It had been too tough to break in 1918 and it was still too strong in 1930. His war heroism, reinforcing the heritage of his background, had conferred great inner confidence on him and the belief that he had power to educate and influence. He was indeed one of the only members of the war servicemen's generation who by the mid-1930s had taken a central position in the cultural leadership of the nation. Few such stars rose quickly from the furnace of war.

Read married Evelyn Roff in 1919. Though there was an intellectual affinity, even a similarity in their inhibited temperaments, strains between them began soon to show. Read had lost much of his initial ardour, which had been artificially heightened by the emotional intensity of the war years. Evelyn, rather than he, was doomed to be the casualty of Armageddon.

He was closely involved in the literary world. For much of the twenties, he attempted to deny his deep-rooted vein of romanticism, settling for the bleak austerities of T. S. Eliot's critical outlook, and though he never felt easy with Eliot or his ideas, he admired him greatly and tried to explore his own feelings about the arts – and his own development – in the pages of Eliot's *Criterion*. He became affected by Eliot's poetry; as Richard Aldington put it, he now renounced his Imagist past with its concentration on beauty, instinct, and sudden impulse and came to look at beauty "as a phenomenon, not a passion," to analyse love, not to overflow with it. In the end, however, much of his verse remained Imagist in form and objectives, though expressed more plainly than before. This was a worthwhile process, however painful. By the time he wrote the poems published as *A World Within a War*, in 1944, Read had developed into a far better poet than Aldington.

By the later twenties, Aldington had some success in weaning Read away from Eliot, particularly after that influential figure turned to the Anglican Church. He also urged Read to abandon "the sordid sterility of criticism." Ford Madox Ford had said much the same thing earlier: "I don't believe you are the chilly intellectual ... that you think yourself," he told Read, "you are a temporarily unthawed emotionalist."

Although Read ultimately rejected Eliot's icily classical approach, and returned to passion, Yorkshire roots, and humane anarchist theories, he did not take to the path Aldington advised by cutting criticism out of his life and concentrating all his efforts on creative writing. However, on Eliot's advice Read was chosen to give the Clark literary lectures at Cambridge in 1930, an exceptional honour. Through Eliot's help too, he secured the post of Professor of Art History at Edinburgh, which, Read hoped, would give him financial security and more time for writing than when trying to combine it with the work at the Victoria and Albert Museum.

Such prestigious appointments and his much-admired and lucid work on the visual arts were to gain him an international reputation particularly as the promoter of the British Modern Movement – represented, notably, by Ben Nicholson, Barbara Hepworth, and Henry Moore, all close friends. After the Second World War he was one of the founders of the Institute of Contemporary Arts. He was also an effective and responsive "ambassador for English arts" in the same era, still alive to new developments the other side of the Atlantic and delivering the Mellon Lectures in 1954. In the field of cultural education, his influence was revolutionary. Eventually he was awarded a knighthood for his scholarship and services to art. His acceptance seemed curious for a self-acclaimed anarchist, but not to those who knew his feeling for the artistic achievements of the past and that in the field of battle he had come closer to the genuine article than such Falstaffian literary knights as Sir Jack Squire.

It was at Edinburgh, in the early thirties, that his marriage, long under strain, came apart. Ambitious and emotionally aloof, though kind-hearted, Read cannot have been an easy companion in the decade after the war when he was in his "temporarily unthawed" state. Evelyn felt increasingly isolated. She yearned for the north of England. At first they lived near Regent's Park in the heart of London, but Purley, the genteel Surrey suburb where they settled subsequently, was miles from the centre and their eventual home at Seer Green, in the Buckinghamshire countryside, even more remote from friends. Nervously troubled, she clung ever more desperately to her husband, who felt trapped. In Edinburgh he fell in love with a young violinist, Margaret Ludwig, with romantic raven-haired looks and a passionate, determined nature. He was then over forty, but youthful and distinguished in appearance, dapperly dressed, his hair still thick, his figure lean. His wife by contrast seemed dowdy, and her face, through an affliction of the thyroid gland, had grown puffy. When the marriage ended, her mental health deteriorated, particularly when their son John, who continued to live with her, left to serve as a soldier in the Second World War. Passing her later days in mental institutions, she outlived Read, who died of cancer in 1968.

From 1931, with a sense of freedom accompanying this breach with his past, and his later resignation from his Edinburgh chair, Read plunged into creative work. One of his finest poems, *The End of a War,* appeared in 1932. It was based on an actual event involving, it seems, his own battalion, the 2nd Green Howards, since it is dedicated to Captain Lancelot Smith, a friend in the battalion who may have told him the story, Read having returned to England four months earlier.

In a preface to the poem, Read recounts how, at the very end of the war, a British force was about to attack a French town, supposedly still occupied by the retreating enemy. However, a dying German officer told them that his regiment had just evacuated it. It was a trap; the British troops entered the town, were ambushed, and a hundred of their men and five officers were killed. After they cleared the place, a corporal and an officer returned to bayonet the German who had deceived them. Later a dismembered French girl's corpse was found in one of the houses. She had probably been killed for spying for the Allied forces.

The 2nd Green Howards were involved in precisely this sort of fighting in October and November, near and beyond Valenciennes, a place mentioned in the poem. However the battalion diary does not correspond in detail with Read's story. Their worst casualties were in the relief of a village called Epinay, but this was on 27 September, and the number of those killed in the battalion in November was only 8, with 48 wounded and five missing, three of the total being officers. At the very end of the war, the 2nd Green Howards had in fact gone over the border into Belgium, and their casualties in the relief of the last villages from which they drove the fleeing enemy, Meaurain and Gussigny, were relatively slight.

Read's poem meditates on war in general; the narrowness and cruelty of dedicated patriotism; disillusion, nihilism, and despair; the joy of mere unheroic survival; the callousness of the soul towards the innocent body. Yet it also almost certainly expressed the pain he felt about the end of his marriage and of a relationship that had been inseparable from the war. The three protagonists in the poem – the hard, heroic German officer, treacherous in the hour of his death; the less heroic English officer, glad to be alive and inherit the world; and the body and soul of the girl broken on the wheel of the war – these stood in some measure for two sides of Read, and for the woman whose life with him, begun in the shadow of the war, had now to end.

Read kept up his output of war writing over the interwar years. The short stories published in a collection, *Ambush*, in 1930, had mostly been written some time before. Fascinating in their variety, they included "The Raid," described earlier; "Killed in Action," in the brutalistic Wyndham Lewis vein, and uncharacteristically immature, which had first appeared at the end of *Naked Warriors*; "First Blood," recalling the horrors of initiation into warfare at Ypres; "Man, Melodion and Snowflakes," a vivid moment on a winter march in wartime; "Cloud Form," in the Lawrentian vein, about a young schoolteacher, disturbed by news from the front, whose turmoil finds release in an orgasm, as she lies gazing at a cloud; and "Cupid's Everlasting Honeymoon," a dreamlike fantasy of a glamorous hotel during a war, peopled with soldiers and classical gods. There is great richness in this collection; and visually the stories are very strong. Not unexpectedly from such a pen, they evoke for the reader all kinds of images in (mostly modern) western art: such as those from the vorticists and C.R.W. Nevinson; from Brueghel, Delvaux, Gertler, John and Paul Nash. Here is the war depicted at the sharper end. With all its horror and fear, and with its lyrical side too; its testing of courage; the anxiety, sexual tension, and tender feeling engendered by it; and a detached view of it, as both a crazy dream and also a part of history, as both in frenetic motion and fixed in time like a statue. Although Read wrote no sustained war novel, these short works say a great deal of what he felt.

Dominant in much of Read's writing was the theme of self-understanding in battle and the power this confers. "The Raid," in particular, focuses on the mastery of fear. In *The Green Child* the schoolteacher Oliver leaves Yorkshire after his faith in the innocence of his pupils is ruined by a malicious act of destruction perpetrated by the uncouth schoolboy Kneeshaw. Oliver seeks out adventure, longing, as he puts it, "for external circumstances to force action on me" – in just the same spirit as Read himself had gone to war. His boldness and intelligence lead Oliver during his thirty years of exile to become president of the republic of Roncador. Finally, after many years of responsibility and domination, he arranges his own faked assassination, and returns to his home village in Yorkshire. There he encounters Siloen, the Green Child, the strange visitant whose discovery, with her brother, near the village, had caused a sensation just before he had originally left it. Rescuing her by force from her harsh protector, the miller Kneeshaw, who as a boy had caused the young Oliver to leave the village, Oliver follows the mill-stream, which is flowing backward to its source. Reaching this, he and Siloen plunge in and sink down to her native country, a limbo-like underground world full of pale green, translucent people like Siloen herself, where Oliver passes the rest of his days. Whatever the overall significance of this strange tale, it is clear that the book reflects symbolically, and perhaps unconsciously, Read's sense of the dramatic break with his past that the war caused. The book's second half is evidently about the testing of the spirit in a dangerous real world, akin to the war. Through his adventures, the young schoolmaster, too ineffective at first to defend his ideals, acquires power, in the end, to wrest the delicately beautiful Green Child, embodying an aesthetic ideal, from the hands of the coarse and ignorant Kneeshaw and pursue the pure path of beauty discovered through entry into her world.

After his war experience, Read had the same sense of destiny and power as Oliver. While he remained convinced of the utter evil of war, his description of his adventures in *Retreat* and "The Raid" are dispassionate and calmly analytical and they convey, in a self-effacing manner, the fact that he was very proud of what he had achieved – proud of having come through without cracking, or coarsening and with exceptional distinction.

This makes his war writing very different from that of most other English authors on the same subject, and gives him some affinities with the German man of letters, Ernst Jünger, author of *Storm of Steel*, who fought as one of the elite *Stosstruppen,* the German army's crack troops responsible for penetrating the enemy defences in the vanguard of a major offensive. Jünger had earned the highest decoration for bravery, the *Pour le Mérite*, and saw the war as an ennobling test of the soul, raising a man to a higher plane if he acquitted himself well. As young officers, Read and Jünger shared also a certain cultural dandyism. Jünger's protagonist in one of his novels, *Sturm*, has a dugout adorned with frescoes, including one of a primitive "Willendorf Venus," a reproduction of a Hobbema in a rosewood frame, an engraved wineglass, hand-grenades elegantly arranged on lines, and a collection of eighteenth-century leatherbound books on cookery and classical erotica. All this recalls Read's "studio" in Rugeley Camp.

Though Jünger had not a trace of Read's pacifism – "What can be holier than the fighting man?" he asked – he was far too sophisticated to be an unthinking jingo, and like Read his interest in war lay in the way it tested the qualities of the individual. Read thought well of his work, though less so than of that of Jünger's brother Georg, who later gained underground fame with his anti-Nazi poem, "The Poppy."

From one angle, though no other, one can even see resemblances between Read's view of the war and that of Adolf Hitler (himself an admirer of Jünger) who wrote in *Mein Kampf:* "At last my will was my undisputed master. If in the first days I went over the top with rejoicing and laughter, I was now calm and determined. And this was enduring. Now fate could bring on the ultimate tests without my nerves shattering or my reason failing."

Read's dignified and subtle war works had nothing, however, in common with the German book he praised unreservedly, Remarque's *All Quiet on the Western Front.* "This is the greatest of all war books," he wrote in the *Nation:* "It is the first completely satisfactory exposition in literature of the greatest event of our time." He agreed eagerly with Remarque that the war had "withered something in the war generation that should have come to full growth." Read extracted his own truth from the book – "a greater truth than even this book expresses: that although modern war is totally devoid of glory, the glory of the human spirit is indestructible, and nowhere was this more evident than in the brutal and degrading experiences of those four terrible years." In fact, the absence of any such message in *All Quiet* was one of its chief defects. For though he lamented his lost companions, Remarque vulgarised their memory by his self-pitying tone and concentrated much more on the cynical and depraved actions of the soldiers than on their steadfast devotion to each other. It is far from clear too whether Remarque wrote much of his book from direct experience; his detail is sensational and sometimes downright inaccurate.

Although Read's tone in "The Raid" was more disenchanted than in his earlier descriptions of the same incident, in his correspondence and poetry, it is still a long way from the "embittered" school of British war writing, for he was not himself "embittered." As he said in one poem, he had "no visible wounds to lick." He could not summon up much enthusiasm for Aldington's *Death of a Hero,* though it contains far better evocations of battle than Remarque's book. He disliked its (to his mind) heavy-handed hilarity at the expense of Ford and Eliot, while sharing some of Aldington's views on those two writers. Nor did he have anything in common with more "optimistic" interpretations of the war as an agent for good. The only British book of real merit that came near Read's view of the experience was *The Natural Man*, a prize-winning work by "Patrick Miller," the *nom-de-plume* of George Gordon MacFarlane M. C. He was the brother of the author Catherine Carswell, D. H. Lawrence's biographer. Trained as an architect, he was a gentle, romantic, and eccentric man, talented as a writer and illustrator, whose adventurous career (including getting into Devil's Island as a journalist), came, in the end, to little. It is clear that soldiering fulfilled him. Severely wounded, and later gassed, and his courage recognised, MacFarlane emerged from the war with a sense of being, at last, his own man. His book ended with a statement of belief:

> He no longer expected life to raise him and bear him gloriously forward on a wave-crest. Whatever the force that buoyed him up might be, he must strike out across it. Whatever life might be, his life was in himself, and he must be the guide of it.

This is as close as any other British writer comes to Read's own view of the experience of war; but there is still a wide difference. The tone of MacFarlane's book is less restrained, more neurotic. The protagonist's obsession with the need to prove himself, seemingly without regard for anyone else, makes an egoistic impression absent in Read's book, though this stemmed from a disarming frankness on MacFarlane's part, inseparable from an unworldly, generous nature.

In forming a final estimate of Read's outlook on the war, his own regiment, the Green Howards, cannot be left out of consideration. It is quite evident both from his accounts and from battalion diaries that the battle spirit of both the 2nd and 10th Battalions was outstanding. Though there were Durham miners, Welsh, Irish, and West Countrymen among the officers or other ranks, a significant proportion were rural Yorkshiremen with a strong sense of collective identity. It was small wonder, then, that Read came to elevate such cooperative human endeavour in small units to so high a plane. His regard for courage was not simply a matter of wishing to display that virtue himself, but as being a quality essential to the survival and success of the whole group. Many British war writers – Edmund Blunden M.C., Robert Briffault M.C. and Bar, Edward Thompson M.C., Siegfried Sassoon M.C. – were men of outstanding courage. Yet none was so assuredly a soldier as Herbert Read, the pacifist and syndicalist, the admirer of Sorel and Kropotkin, the poet and artist, and enthusiast of one of the enemy's best-known modern philosophers, Nietzsche. This curious combination of intellect, idealism, confidence, and efficiency give his postwar war prose writings a quiet air of controlled power, unique among his English literary contemporaries. "*In Retreat* is so moving," Richard Aldington told him in 1961, "that it will surely outlive the more ambitious things. Henry Williamson might have done well, but I think he will drown himself in that *roman fleuve*." Read's war short stories, too, have the same lasting quality. This is because they share *In Retreat*'s brevity and concentrated strength – qualities that people of future ages, to whom the extraneous detail of this early twentieth-century war will have come to mean little, are sure to value as leading them quickly to its heart.

PART THREE

AFTERMATH:

"THE GENERATION OF THE BROKENHEARTED"

When men are old, and their friends die,
They are not so sad,
Because their love is running slow,
And cannot spring from the wound with so sharp a pain;
And they are happy with many memories,
And only a little while to be alone.

But we are young and our friends are dead
Suddenly, and our quick love is torn in two
So our memories are only hopes that came to nothing.
We are left alone like old men; we should be dead
But there are years and years in which we shall
    still be young.

—Margaret Postgate, "Praematuri."

11

꾸꾸꾸

The Bridge Builder
Oliver Onions
1873 – 1961

By the early 1920s, after the neglect of the war years, Bailey's Hotel, a handsome late-Victorian building in South Kensington, had become a little shabby. It was still a "gentleman's hotel" and some of its past splendour endured in the pillared entrance hall with its elaborately moulded ceiling, but very few of its inhabitants looked as prosperous as its pre-1914 clientèle would have done.

Every evening, at opening time, its smoke-wreathed bar, adjoining the diningroom and billiardroom, became the haunt of a crowd of young ex-officers whose chief link was their First World War service and their present lack of secure employment.

As they sipped their "gin-and-Its" and discussed the racing form or their endless plans to start a nightclub or a casino, they exuded an air both dashing and threadbare, nonchalant and strained. "Their ties, no longer regimental, were perfectly knotted and their spats perfectly brushed for one and the same reason . . . Their faces . . . were capable of a brightness that positively startled one, so instantaneously could it be assumed." They were the honourable, supernumerary flotsam of the war, ex-servicemen who had joined "another army, that of the unemployed" in the postwar depression. Untrained save for giving and taking orders, killing and being killed, they were now, five years into the peace, an embarrassment that most people preferred to forget.

Among these wary-eyed, loudly laughing blades there was one figure different from the rest who joined them, on most evenings at 5:30, in the same crowded spot. This was the author, Oliver Onions, who before the war had made a name for himself as the writer of powerful, sinister fiction. At fifty in 1923, he was twice the age of many of his drinking companions. Short, spare, strong-looking, with stick and pipe, he had something of the air of a retired boxer. In repose, his face was serious and concentrated, his eyes close together and deeply set, his chin firmly moulded; his hair, once tawny, now greying, was cut close to the head. He spoke quickly and quietly and must have been hard to hear in that noisy company. His purpose however was more to listen and to look than to be heard.

What they talked about added up to one thing: their desperation to earn their living as honestly as they were allowed. There was, as he observed, a certain sameness in their ambitions – to own a poultry farm, to breed dogs, to run a dancing school, and, "had all the golf club secretaryships existed for which they sighed, England would have been one vast links."

Oliver Onions heard too about those who could no longer afford the companionship of the bar, who were sleeping rough on the Embankment, or had even killed themselves out of a sense of worthlessness. He met men also who had preferred to degrade themselves a little to spare themselves the worse degradation of extreme poverty, becoming the lovers of older, *nouveaux-riche* ladies, escorting them, driving their limousines, and teaching them how to get on in smart society. A few turned to more dubious activities. A Captain Phillips ran a speakeasy serving drinks at illegal hours and got into trouble over the management of his gaming club; others had a line in smuggling currency and jewellery.

Onions admired the courage with which these men coped, for year after year, with a seedy and shiftless existence. He was a kind man, belying a certain hardness in his demeanour, and as his books show, was always sympathetic to young people trying to survive in a tough world.

He was living at the time with his wife, the novelist Berta Ruck, and their two young sons in Queen's Gate Gardens, a white-porticoed Kensington street, two minutes' walk from Bailey's Hotel. When he and his family moved out of London, to the riverside town of Henley-on-Thames, he kept up with his ex-officer friends. He paid one of them, Dick Buttery M.C., a huge red-haired man, to take his children rowing. Buttery was probably a lost cause (even his M.C. may have been bogus); it is easy at any rate to see why he was out of work and how it had become a habit with him. He would row the boys as far as a pub that over-looked the water, and, disembarking, invite them to take the oars and amuse themselves as they wished, while he disappeared inside to drink. They liked him very much.

Onions was all too aware that what he could offer, in the way of small jobs for his jaunty, unwanted young friends, could make no difference to a national problem of massive proportions. The most useful thing he felt he could do was to write about them, and this, in 1923, he did. He dedicated his book, *Peace in Our Time*, to "the lads of the village" – where were they now? No longer, as in the popular song, on the "continong," save for some smuggling trip, or showing tourists round the battlefields, but back in "Blighty" hawking insurance if they were lucky, or, if less so, down by the Thames, on a bench. He wrote the entire book from his own experience: "There is not a passage," he said, "which has not been checked with actual observation of incidents and events."

Peace in Our Time is not the best-known work, nor even an outstanding one, by an author who, at his finest, touched genius. Its knowing, jocular irony is often irritating, as are its deliberate obscurities, mannerisms present even in his better writings. Such tricks of style were not unique to him; they were indeed fashionable among eminent authors writing before the First World War: for example, C. E. Montague, theatre critic, novelist, and later, the author of *Disenchantment* (1922) and *Rough Justice* (1926), two highly successful war books. Rudyard Kipling also used such devices, especially in his later work. It was a literary tradition going back at least as far as the mid-Victorian author so many looked up to in the pre-1914 era – George Meredith, master of the arch allusion, the teasing obfuscation, the sly jest between writer and reader. All of which is to say that, tiresome as this trait was, it was by no means incompatible with genius, or poetical imagination. In *Peace in Our Time*, where the setting is prosaic, the intellectual calibre and rigorous honesty of the writer and the occasional vivid physical description of a room interior or a man's appearance single this story out from the commonplace.

Oliver Onions was born in 1873, in the city of Bradford, Yorkshire. The hardship of his poverty-stricken background, on the edge of working-class life, bred in him a determined toughness and a typical northern bluntness of speech. His writings vividly reproduce the rougher sides of life which he saw outside his home. "Mish" Murgatroyd in Onions' novel *Back o' the Moon,* with his "brute of a brindled dog" and oiled calf-licks of hair, is a figure straight off the Bradford streets, although the book's setting is an eighteenth-century market town. Onions' mother, widowed young, was an earthy little Yorkshirewoman full of no-nonsense West Riding wisdom, who, when she could afford it, liked to add a slug of whisky to her tea. Yet this was not an uneducated family: his father studied Hebrew, and though their morality was a rugged one, it was neither heartless nor uncivilised. The self-discipline and regard for truth that Onions adhered to in his writing career had been drilled into him at home. He gained a scholarship to Bradford Grammar School, one of the leading academies in the country, and from there, in 1895, a National Scholarship to the National Art Training School (subsequently the Royal College of Art). At this time he had no literary ambitions. An able draughtsman and mathematician, he seemed cut out for engineering, but his dearest ambition was to emulate the feats of the *Illustrated London News* artist Richard Caton-Woodville, who had visited colonial battle-fronts for years to compose such masterpieces of patriotic art as "The Guards at Tel-El-Kebir."

After leaving art school, he touted for work in Fleet Street and the Strand as a press illustrator. The coming of the South African War in 1899 seemed to offer him at last the hope of regular full-time work. Unfortunately this did not consist of direct war reportage in the manner of Caton-Woodville, but endless artists' impressions. Sooner than expected, however, cheap photographic reproduction put the newspaper illustrator out of business. "Seven of us hit the pavement one week," Onions remembered. For him, however, the landing was softer than for most. He had already begun to write. His first novel, *The Compleat Bachelor,* a humorous work, appeared in 1900. It was completely atypical of what he was later to do best, but the flippant, almost gossipy note that characterises his two "war" novels, *Peace in Our Time* and *Cut Flowers,* had its first airing in this early and successful volume.

His ghost stories made a stronger impact. The three decades before the First World War saw a fine flowering of British imaginative writing and Onions was a master of the genre. The best of his prewar eerie tales was "The Beckoning Fair One" set in a decaying eighteenth-century square in Hampstead, and describing the moral and physical disintegration of a promising writer under the spell of a ghostly seductress. The tension in the tale is between the excessively imaginative writer and his affectionate, practical female literary agent who is trying to get him to work.

It reflected a tension within Onions himself, but it seems as if his morbid and dreamily imaginative side found release only on paper. He kept himself well under control. As Herbert Read, his fellow-Yorkshireman, observed of people from their county, "their most extraordinary characteristic . . . is their capacity for masking their emotions. It is not a question of suppression, nor of atrophy; the normal feelings of the human being are present in more than their normal force, but banked up against this impenetrable reserve."

Onions was also busy writing in an opposite literary genre – the careful observation of daily existence, pointing a moral about society. *Little Devil Doubt* (1909) was a vivid satirical picture of life in a printing works at Bradford and of the early Harmsworth Press. In writing this type of book he was following a contemporary trend that ranged from the novels of Arnold Bennett to the social reports of Seebohm Rowntree and Mrs. Pember Reeves. During the 1890s he dabbled in socialism, and never wholly relinquished a sense of "fair dos," though his more idealistic political thinking was tempered by a strong sense of the past and the traditional values learned from his parents.

Most impressive of his literary achievements in this period were his historical stories, set chiefly in Yorkshire, and based on legal records and local archives. Onions seemed to understand the stark life of the mid-eighteenth-century Yorkshire uplands as well as if he had lived in that far-off time himself. *Tales of a Far Riding* (1902) was so grim that as a sister-in-law remarked, "I'm glad it is 'far.'" *Back o' the Moon* (1906) and *Pedlar's Pack* (1908) tapped the same rich sources.

He was prolific: between 1900 and 1914, he wrote some eighteen volumes of fiction. As an author, his way of life resembled his earlier experience as an illustrator, when his livelihood was least secure. As before, he found that he had to hawk his work around from one paper to another and from publisher to publisher, to the extent that he feared making himself unpopular with editor friends, who often regarded his unorthodox works as the last thing likely to appeal to readers. Nor did they pay on the nail, but only, with luck, on publication. The one time he was able to persuade an editor to advance him money was when he told them he was getting married.

Onions became engaged to Roberta Amy Ruck in 1909. Five years younger than him, and several inches taller, she was a woman of singular vitality. The Rucks were Welsh gentry from Merionethshire. Both her parents were of Indian army background and Berta had been born in the Punjab in 1878. When she first met Onions she was an art student at the Slade. She was not conventionally pretty. Her features, particularly her chin, were pronounced, but she had a graceful athletic beauty, with fine hands and shoulders. A tomboy in childhood, she remained vigorous into extreme old age.

Temperamentally Berta was very different from her husband. The speed with which she dashed off her novels – adding up, over the hundred years of her life, to over a hundred and fifty – made her industrious husband seem plodding. She chose a theme, plunged immediately into the dialogue between her characters and hardly gave the plot a thought. Inconsistencies were left for Oliver Onions to sort out, as her devoted editor. The end-products were love stories, relentlessly bright in tone, and their endings were always happy. Her writing was compulsive. It never worried her that it was superficial, for her formula worked; her books were best-sellers.

Although Onions had received many good reviews, they began their married life without money, and with only the hopes of future success. At first they occupied a flat in New End Square, Hampstead, an old house "of bloomy old red brick," the setting for his story, "The Beckoning Fair One." Berta's first novel, *His Official Fiancée*, appeared in the spring of 1914 and from that date the family fortunes had a chance of improvement. The coming of war gave her copious new material. For example, she made friends with the wife of the author Maurice Hewlett, a successful though less impressive rival to Onions in writing historical fiction. Mrs. Hewlett, at that time one of the only women pilots in England, had become head of an aircraft factory producing war planes, and Berta, after visiting it in the autumn of 1914, based her third book, *The Lad with Wings*, on her impressions. Later in the war she joined the Women's Land Army. This bore fictional fruit in *The Land Girl's Love Story* (1919), full of ferocious hun-hating sentiment, of which she later repented, admitting that the German prisoners she had met on English farms had been decent and industrious.

Meanwhile Onions decided he must enlist. At forty-one in 1914, he was officially too old to fight. His fellow-author, C. E. Montague of the *Manchester Guardian*, who was even older, had not been deterred, but had dyed his grey hair and volunteered. The popular writer, W. B. Maxwell, managed, at nearly fifty, to become an officer in the 10th Royal Fusiliers and served 2½ years at the front. Onions' skill as a draughtsman and his mathematical ability made him an obvious candidate for an engineering job. He succeeded, through joining a uniformed volunteer body known unofficially as "The Old Boys' Corps" (Non-Combatant Corps), in serving at home in the commissariat department with additional duties as a sapper (military engineer).

At this time the army were technologically ill-equipped to construct bridges to carry heavy guns and lorries in regions of Belgium and Northern France criss-crossed with drainage ditches and massive canal works, stretching for hundreds of miles. What were required were new designs for bridges and transportable sections to be mass-produced and shipped across the Channel, and also training schools for the engineers involved. Onions was posted to Brightlingsea on the Essex coast, where he took charge of stores and was made responsible for the design and construction of a bridge intended as a prototype for new models to be deployed on the continent. It was a solidly-built job, and stands to this day, a monument to his skill.

Berta visited him there and the low-lying, featureless country of mud flats and inlets provided a setting for her fourth novel, *The Girls at His Billet*. It was dedicated to him, though this was one book of hers on which she did not take his advice. Nor did she announce to him the subject of her next work, *The Bridge of Kisses*, the story of a romance between a young girl and an officer in charge of constructing a bridge (the character based not on Onions himself but on a younger Welsh colleague). "I can almost see the narrowed look on O. O.'s face when he realised what she had been up to," their son, George Arthur Oliver, later wrote. The reader of *The Bridge of Kisses* will look in vain, however, for anything shedding light on Onions' way of life in the army. Nor do official records help. Indeed, though his older son has recalled him in sappers' uniform, Onions does not appear in the Army List under his own surname or that of Oliver, which the family had begun to call themselves. It is likely at any rate that he was not engaged in engineering throughout the war, and possible, as family legend suggests, that he was subsequently occupied in decoding work. This may have been for the navy. Its secret intelligence headquarters at "Room 40 OB" (Admiralty Old Buildings) employed many men of high intellectual calibre from the world of the arts; and he was acquainted with Admiral "Blinker" Hall, its chief, enough for that dignitary to invite Onions and Berta to join him at an Admiralty window to watch the Victory Parade in 1919. However the only Onions to be listed in the intelligence unit was C. T. (later Professor) Onions, the lexicographer, with whom Oliver Onions was often confused, even receiving some of the professor's intimate personal correspondence.

The closest Onions himself came to describing the nature of his wartime activities appeared in *The New Moon. A Romance of Reconstruction*, a remarkable novel published in April 1918. This was a speculative fantasy about what Britain would be like a few years after the war was over. It was interspersed with extracts from Thomas More's *Utopia*. The book, though critical of socialism, and in favour of competition and a free market, was by way of being a practical man's non-Marxist *News from Nowhere*, William Morris's celebrated dream of a communist future. Onions' Britain of the postwar era was organised, and cooperative, while retaining strong supporting pillars of capitalist enterprise. Pollution was being tackled, clean air acts passed, buildings cleaned of their grime. The problems of demobilisation had been solved. Full employment was maintained through keeping many men in the army to carry out constructional and supply work. The hero of the book, Dick Helme, was a fair-haired, decent young army engineer, and the girl he married a lissom country lass of good birth. They went on an idyllic honeymoon in a caravan and bathed naked in a woodland glade. During their wanderings, the state of the country was examined. It was one of Onions' less successful novels, but, like everything he set his hand to, it was thought-provoking, with moments of vivid description.

Biographically, the book gives an idea of the kind of ramshackle and improvised conditions under which he worked as a engineer: for Helme and his colleagues, living quarters were found on disused four-ton barges towed back from Imperial service in Egypt and the Persian Gulf; the stores officer's workplace was a former yacht house close to the water-side, with a boat-repairing shed at ground level and his own office in a long narrow loft employed for stacking spars, and reached by a precari-ous ladder.

Most interesting was what the book revealed of Onions' reaction to the war: his animus against profiteering and political chicanery in con-trast to manufacturing and public service of a truly patriotic nature; his concern for the soldiers on the fighting front who, in his view, must be the moral arbiters of the new order and would expect a fair deal. Most of all, unlike many in ruling circles after the war, he understood, as he showed by a score of accurate prophecies, how irrevocably England had been changed:

> As one thing was certain, namely, that the England they re-turned to would never be the same England they had left; it might as well be a better as a worse one.
>
> Whichever way it went, no different England of any kind whatever should be contrived behind their [the soldiers'] backs. They were millions strong, the best heart and will that England had to show, and those at home had better take note of the fact.

The closing words of C. E. Montague's widely-read *Disenchantment,* which appeared four years later, were strikingly similar: "There is only one thing for it. There must be five or six million ex-soldiers. They are the most determined peace party that ever existed in Britain . . . The fu-ture is said to be only the past entered by another door. We must beware in good time of those boys, and fiery elderly men, piping in Thessaly." In *The New Moon,* Onions held out to his readers the prospect of a better land after the war; but he, another "fiery elderly man" like Montague, could see how easily things could fall back into the hands of the liars and self-seekers.

In the end, he, far more than Berta, lost out through the changed face of England. The best of what he had to offer, those painstaking, old-fash-ioned, passionately felt dramas of England's past, were going out of favour. The romantic movement, from which they drew their energy and their popularity, was dead. Lesser lights like Warwick Deeping, who had made their name with imitation Maurice Hewlett medieval romances before the war, now turned, with great success, to realistic fiction.

In that bleaker postwar world, there were new, exciting artistic opportunities, but Onions was already too old, too rooted in the past, to turn himself into a "modern." His postwar "war books" – *Peace in Our Time* and *Cut Flowers* (1927) – represented his effort to come up to date, to get away from gaslight and gibbets and repeat, in a contemporary context, the modest successes he had enjoyed with satires like *Little Devil Doubt*.

It goes without saying that he would not have written *Peace in Our Time* or his later novel about former "women at war," *Cut Flowers*, if he had not been interested in the questions of the day. But there was more in it than that. Onions was intensely curious, always, about the lives of young people, men and women alike. To say he idealised youth is the wrong way to describe the outlook of so hard-headed a man. Yet as he grew older, he looked back with regrets to the time of life when his dreams, passions, and imaginings had been at their most intense. He was drawn to the young ex-officers at Bailey's Hotel by their *élan vital* and envied them an irresponsibility that he, with his grim, psychic explorer's heart, had not felt for thirty years. Intensely private in his social tastes, he sought out their company in preference to the salons and literary parties where his reputation guaranteed him an entrée.

There was a further reason that made him take up the cause of these ex-service castaways: his guilt at having stayed away from the fighting. Had he been frustrated, too, at being unable to put himself to the test alongside others, to release the violence that in his imagination was so strong? Had he felt like the vengeful innkeeper Thorgumbald, his creation in *Pedlar's Pack*: "Trouble had now no dread for him; he only dreaded lest it should not come in its perfection" (perfection, in this case, taking the form of carving the "blood eagle" on an enemy's back)?

But Onions' rational side, at least, told him that whatever might now happen to him, he, unlike the war veterans half his age, could look back on a prewar life when he had learnt his trade and find some fulfilment. Should he die in 1923, he would have achieved more than they ever had. He realised that the great tragedy for so many of these young people was that war experience was all they had and for them its unhappy consequences were still not over. The theme of "Overhead Charge," a short story he wrote later, was a wounded veteran's desperate desire to serve again – even to the extent of wishing for another war to make it possible. In *Peace in Our Time* the dashing twenty-six-year-old Kenneth Chacey M.C., D.S.O. faces an unbridgeable gap between himself and the idealised younger girl with whom he has been in love because he, unlike her, is still caught up in the war. Luckily, in her stead he finds a Frenchwoman of his own age who has shared the same experience of dislocation. Similarly, in Onions' novel *Cut Flowers*, about girls trying to keep up wartime comradeship after the war, the society beauty "Frills" is left with nothing at all after she has given up her efforts to hold her old companions together; and her friend Joan, having lost her only love in the war, abandons all expectation of future romance.

Other fiction on the same theme appeared in that decade: apart from Onions' works, *The Victors*, by "Peter Deane" (q.v.), is the most effective novel on the subject. In contrast, William Mackay's *Ex-Soldier We Are Dead* (1930) is a self-dramatising wail about officer unemployment. MacKay takes his readers on a tour of Rowton House and the vaults of St. Martin-in-the-Fields and other charitable institutions, to show the degradation into which ex-soldiers had been forced. Unfortunately whatever sympathy he might have aroused is dispelled by his meretricious and misogynistic tone. Warwick Deeping's much more famous *Sorrell and Son* is a snobbish work about the struggles of a well-born ex-officer, Captain Sorrell M.C., to survive unemployment. The author's sentimental reverence for the gentry was evidently shared by his thousands of readers at the time and is of historical interest, though it does not contribute to its literary merit. *Seven Men Came Back* (1934), by the same author, is only slightly better, in that it presents a greater variety of ex-army types. Compared with *Peace in Our Time*, however, it lacks subtlety or depth.

At the end of *Peace in Our Time*, Kenneth Chacey starts a nightclub in the London house where earlier in the book his uncle Rex and his mother have tried to preserve the semblance of their vanished pre-1914 existence. On the opening night, Rex, middle-aged and reluctantly accepting the change, prays by himself, "with bowed thinning head and his travelling-cap in his hands" among the hats and coats. He prays, not only for the new generation "in whose unknowing hearts lay all the hopes to come" and for the war generation, "those luckless ones, contemporaries with none but themselves, who were being pressed out from life and its joy between two generations," but also for the prewar age group like himself, "and for the strength which he so sorely needed." In the years that followed, Onions himself was to need that strength. He went on working steadily, and was treated with respect; but apart from his ghost stories, which were always well-received, he found there was little interest in his most original work – the combination of historical realism, fantasy, and poetry – and he restricted himself, for long periods to more prosaic themes, diffident about his achievement and tempted to give up writing altogether. He spent longer at favourite drinking haunts such as The Eight Bells in Chelsea. His satire in these years was distinctly bitter.

For Berta, by contrast, the interwar period was one of intoxicating success. She wrote several books a year, dictating to a secretary and correcting the typed manuscripts before hurrying them off to the publishers. She relished her increasing fan club, and the numerous literary friends and acquaintances, such as Alec Waugh, Rebecca West, H. G. Wells, A. P. Herbert, Charles Morgan, and Gilbert Frankau, that she made in the salons of Gwen Otter and others. She was constantly on the move, travelling to New York and taking to flying – as a passenger – with a passion.

Their marriage, however, was at a low ebb. Her husband never found writing easy. Her social life and speed mania disturbed the contemplative atmosphere in which he preferred to work, and for long periods she devoted no time to their children or to looking after the household. It was not much to his liking, either, that the family, at her demand, had changed their surname to "Oliver" because "Onions" caused her embarrassment. Her romantic interests had chiefly transferred to her attractive blonde female secretary who was usually inseparable from her on her travels. In fact, however, he and Berta valued each other too much to split altogether and though they lived apart, they had a civilised arrangement of meeting often for tea.

The coming of the Second World War brought them together again. Both their sons joined the armed forces (and survived). Berta returned to her roots at Aberdovey, overlooking Cardigan Bay. Although he did not much like Wales, Onions went with her. Elderly and with his health failing, he became increasingly dependent on her. There is much to be said for the company of someone who, even if at times overwhelming, relishes life. She remained as strong as ever. She bathed daily in the sea, summer and winter. Her hair was still brown (as it remained in her 101st year). This was thanks, she claimed, to an indescribable concoction with which she insisted on washing her own and her husband's hair. The formula was secret but a key ingredient was "Spanish fly," more normally used as a violent aphrodisiac.

In the country, Onions began to tap again the deep levels of his imagination. The result was an astonishing, bewitched tale incubating there for forty years, based on a true story from seventeenth-century Yorkshire about a boy under a curse. *The Story of Ragged Robyn* appeared in 1945, when he was seventy-two. It was his masterpiece and one of the major imaginative works of this century. With the exception of J. R. R. Tolkien's *Lord of the Rings*, it is the outstanding example of the pre-1914 sensibility surviving with all its force despite two world wars.

Other historical works followed in this last, golden period of creativity: *Poor Man's Tapestry* won him the coveted James Tait Black Memorial Award, though the prestige, unfortunately, was greater than the prize money, which, faced with doctors' bills, he badly needed. *Arras of Youth* followed and was well received, for all that it did not match the power of *Ragged Robyn*.

The last years of Onions' life, until he became blind, were productive and happy. He and Berta continued to see much of their friends and visitors found him, contrary to their expectations, not forbidding, but courteous and pungently humorous in his conversation. A small, slight figure, he could be seen amusing himself and his family over the latest absurdities in the newspapers, a "Passing Cloud" cigarette between his fingers; or after his day's work, sitting and gazing out over the estuary of the Dovey river towards the sandhills on the far side. He died in April 1961, aged eighty-seven. Berta, still working four hours a day at the age of eighty-two, outlived her husband by seventeen years.

The First World War had cut across Onions' life, invalidating, it seemed, what he had done before. Seeking a direction, he identified for a while with others, younger than himself, whose lives, at an earlier stage of development than his own, had been broken apart by the same force. Yet he was fortunate. His creative spirit revived at an age when many artists can expect to have left their best work behind. In the middle of a second world war, Oliver Onions, the brooding force of his imagination undiminished, found, at last, peace in his time. It was not for him to share the elderly anger of that stock character of English humour, the opinionated, bibulous ex-officer, reminiscing about the trenches, a figure whose testiness must often in reality have sprung, not from the authoritarian habits of military life, but from a bitterness that, after his terrible ordeal, there seemed to be little use for him and so many of his sort.

❦

12

The Broken Bridge
"Peter Deane"
1900 – 1982

Ten years after, one had a clear perspective certainly," wrote Peter Deane in 1930. "But something was lost . . . That something lost is like a road suddenly broken in two. There should be a bridge, but the bridge is broken (Blown sky high in that show last week by a heavy shell. You can see the dim shape of a wrecked lorry, a dead horse on the road beyond)."

There are few writings by Peter Deane – only a collection of short stories, an article or two, and one tragic novel, entitled, with deliberate irony, *The Victors*. It is the tale of a young officer in the same situation as Oliver Onions' character in *Peace in Our Time*. After the war he finds that society cares nothing for those who have served their country. For years he fails to get any work, save the occasional soulless job as a clerk, or brief seasons as a battlefield tour guide in France. Finally he cannot stand the feeling of being isolated from the working world and those too young or too old to have fought. All sense of his own value gone, he gasses himself in his bed-sitting room.

The Victors has close parallels, too, with other novels of the time, most of all with A. P. Herbert's *The Secret Battle*, which tells of an officer shot for cowardice as a result of one momentary loss of nerve after a long period on the battlefield. That book demonstrates the callousness with which many such cases were handled by the British authorities. Like Onions, the authors of both these tragic stories wrote them to rally public opinion, though the experience that inspired them was widely different. A. P. Herbert had served on courts martial during the war, when he was with the 3rd (Royal Naval) Division. *The Secret Battle* was based largely on the painful case of Temporary Sub-Lieut. Edwin Dyett, of 189th Brigade, who was shot for desertion on the evidence of a man with a grudge against him and another who had done badly in a previous campaign. Herbert's book, the work of a trained advocate who later made a name for himself as an M.P. and writer championing public causes, was highly influential. In the preface to the second edition Winston Churchill, the former Secretary of State for War, described it as "a soldier's tale to melt all hearts" and eventually a more merciful approach towards nervous cases was adopted.

The effect of works such as *The Victors, Peace in Our Time* and Warwick Deeping's *Sorrell and Son* also contributed to a change of attitudes. After the Second World War, most of those returning found some job – in contrast with the miseries that accompanied the postwar depression of the early 1920s.

Whereas Warwick Deeping was a well-known popular writer who had served in the Royal Army Medical Corps, and Oliver Onions had a considerable reputation, Peter Deane, whose writing career apparently ended a few years after the publication of *The Victors*, was an unknown figure to readers. Yet the inference one might draw – that the author must have committed suicide like the hero of that book, and like Donald Gristwood, after a brief and unsuccessful effort to become an author – would be incorrect.

The author, "Peter Deane," had never served as an officer in the British army during the war, being below military age, had no direct experience of unemployment after it, and was in fact female.

Pamela Hinkson was the talented daughter of the Irish poet Katherine Tynan, and her literary career under her own name continued for another thirty years after "Peter Deane" ceased to write. Her pseudonym may have been taken from the name of a serving officer.

Pamela had a passionate, masterful temperament. Her outlook on life was intensely romantic. Her nature showed in her appearance. She had old-fashioned, Victorian looks – spiritual, a little like a Brontë; fine, strong features; a demure mouth; from a high straight forehead her dark brown hair swept back in wings to her shoulders. Tall, strong, and, until her midthirties, slender, she loved the Irish country life and was never happier than when walking her dogs over the hills, rowing on a lough, or riding with the hunt – though she adored animals and hated the moment of killing the fox. Her mother confessed that one of her own favourite occupations was talking to a good listener. Pamela, too, was an indefatigable and earnest conversationalist.

The novels Pamela wrote in her own name were solemn and poetical. The tragedy of the war and Ireland's troubles entered her life early and coloured most of her writing. Her relationship with Ireland was ambivalent. Its beauty was her inspiration; but she loathed the later politics of independence and was passionately devoted to the English connection, despite the past cruelties of Britain's colonial rule. She wrote with sensitivity and refinement – sometimes to excess – rarely with humour. At times the solemn incantatory rhythm of her prose slowed the action. At best however – as in her most important literary achievement, *The Ladies' Road* – the beauty and poignancy of her style perfectly matched the theme she had chosen.

She was born of Irish parents, in Ealing, on the outskirts of London, on 19 November 1900. She had two elder brothers, Theobald ("Toby") and Giles Aylmer ("Pat"). Her father, the minor novelist Henry Albert Hinkson (1865-1919) was a member of the Irish Bar and a Fellow of Trinity College Dublin. He married her mother, Katherine Tynan, in 1893. Miss Tynan had been writing poetry since she was seventeen and by the time of her death, at the age of seventy, had penned over a hundred novels. The public liked her sometimes dreamy, sometimes jaunty, verse. Through her father, she had known Charles Stewart Parnell. Her greatest claim to fame was that she was, for a while, a close companion of the youthful W. B. Yeats – a friendship that did not last, though in her memoirs, where his and other famous names drop as thickly as leaves in Vallombrosa, she claimed to have been a formative influence.

Katherine Tynan was warm-hearted, vital, and socially ambitious. She was a pious Catholic and a devoted mother to Pamela and her brothers. All her life she was periodically blinded by excruciating headaches; but she was courageous and cheerful. With her thick spectacles, gaudy clothes, and tubby figure, her appearance was oddly at variance with her romantic outpourings. She was not oversensitive. There were times when her uninhibited opinions ruffled susceptibilities. On the whole, however,

Mrs. Hinkson's blatant approach reaped dividends for herself and her children and during her spirited battle through life she made and kept many faithful intimates.

Her husband, Henry Hinkson, earned his living partly as a classics tutor, but most of the money that came in was the fruit of his wife's journalism; in consequence, she set the tone of family life. The children grew up admiring the luminaries of her artistic and *beau monde* circles. Like many in her milieu, she expected a great deal of her progeny, fostering their efforts at writing. In Pamela's case too, she encouraged an intense, overromantic view of the world. In their politics, the Hinksons worshipped Parnell, and lamented the oppressions of the English; but they had no wish to see Ireland become independent, though that was logically the destination to which Parnell's policy of Home Rule must lead. Until the First World War such a viewpoint was a fairly comfortable one for a family outside the political world. In England Katherine Tynan played the professional Irishwoman and encouraged her children to take a pride in the history and culture of their country. Pamela, who did not visit Ireland till she was eleven, viewed it as an Earthly Paradise.

Great as was her mother's influence, Pamela had a little of her father's temperament – an uprightness and rigidity in the performance of duty – which showed as she grew older. However, she was never very fond of him. A weak stomach and heavy drinking made him irritable. His snobbishness, too, was less amiable than his wife's and derived from an overinflated view of his status as a gentleman, rather than from an admirer's worship of culture and high society. Pamela came to despise him, and by extension, men in general.

Though her elder brother Toby was a brave, adventurous boy, he was the least literary-minded of his family, and Pamela had a decided preference for her younger brother, Pat, to whom she was closer in age. As small children they were devoted companions, and as they grew older they rode, fished, and wrote together. A passage in *The Ladies' Road* about the brother and sister, David and Stella, suggests the quality of their relationship, as important to Pamela as Vera Brittain's was with her brother Edward, or Margery Perham's with Edgar Perham (see Chapter 13): "he had not laughed when they were small children alone in the nursery before Nanny came upstairs and Stella had seen horrid faces when she closed her eyes and had called out to him, 'David I'm frightened,' and he had come awake, struggling with sleep to comfort her. He had never failed her."

For a while after her birth, Pamela's parents continued to live in "green, sweet lovely Ealing." It was still the old semirural Middlesex beloved of Lamb and Keats, with winding lanes and rose-wreathed cottages. There, the Hinksons entertained friends such as Alice Meynell, the poet, who shared Mrs. Hinkson's romantic outlook. Pamela's mother was always restless, however, and whisked her husband and children off to Notting Hill, in London, to be closer to the influential Mrs. Meynell and her circle, which included many Roman Catholics.

Among the numerous acquaintances Mrs. Hinkson laid claim to at this time were the novelists Mrs. Belloc Lowndes and May Sinclair, the playwright J. M. Barrie, the poet-critic W.E. Henley, and Harry Cust, the glittering editor of the *Pall Mall Gazette*, to which she contributed. At Henley's house, she first met one of the great idols in her pantheon – George Wyndham (the uncle of Wilfrid Ewart's friend of the same name). An enlightened Secretary of State for Ireland, close, like Harry Cust, to the Edwardian ideal of male beauty, good for a sonnet at any time and, whether drunk or sober, charming to all, Wyndham – whose much admired son Percy was later killed in the First World War – became an honorary member of the "Lost Generation" in the eyes of Mrs. Hinkson, though it was bottle not battle that ended his life.

Later they moved north of London, to a village they loved, Chipperfield, on the edge of the Chiltern Hills, and, in 1910, to Southborough near Tunbridge Wells, where they allegedly found themselves victims of anti-Catholic bigotry and class resentment. Pamela had to be escorted to school to protect her against the hostility of the board-school children, and next year her mother decided they must go back to Ireland, ponies, children, and all, for good.

The first winter they spent at Dalkey overlooking Killiney Bay, near Dublin. The coast, with its caves and rocks, was a child's paradise, Pamela remembered. She and her brother had one great adventure there, saving up one shilling and sixpence to pay a boatman to take them to Dalkey island. Dalkey itself was "a toy town, full of the small delicious, one-storied houses they have built about South County Dublin with the added fascination of many sailors' marks and devices – models of ships above the low doors, and in the windswept gardens smelling of the sea." Best of all were the little harbours with the fishermen's boats and nets. It was, as Pamela said, "as foreign to small London children as anything to be found in France."

Eventually they moved to a big surburban house close by, in Shankill. As the two boys were away for long periods of the year at boarding schools, Mrs. Hinkson's attention was concentrated on "my Pamela," who was educated locally. She took her for long walks in the surrounding countryside and showed her off to the neighbours.

She also revived old friendships. One was with the mystic poet, painter, and utopian reformer George William "A. E." Russell. The massive, gentle Russell welcomed her back and came several times to dinner at Shankill. Pamela liked to talk to him about her dog, the pomeranian "Fritz." "You know the secrets of animals," she asked: "What does he think of us?" "He thinks we are his gigantic slaves," replied Russell. Her mother's reunion with Yeats was less satisfactory and he did not feature in the salons that the Hinksons held at Shankill, though other well-known writers of the Irish renaissance, such as James Stephens and Padraic Colum, were regular attenders.

Great as was Mrs. Hinkson's delight in Dublin's literary life, she was keener to involve her family in Dublin Castle society. They rapidly became friendly with the Earl of Aberdeen, the Viceroy, now responsible for implementing the Home Rule policy that the British Liberal Government were struggling to enact. The levées, the balls, the enthralling encounters with high-born eminences almost as noble and selfless as the Viceroy and his consort, occupied the forefront of Mrs. Hinkson's imagination, for all that Lord Aberdeen's social regime was widely regarded as far from glamorous. As confirmed "Castle Catholics," Katherine Hinkson and her husband were distressed, however, to find a quite different political atmosphere from when she had last been in Dublin and the talk had only been of Home Rule. Revolution, socialism, and republicanism were in the air. Whatever compassion the Hinksons might have felt for the miseries of the Dublin poor, they did not relish the prospect of Sinn Fein and the likes of the labour leader Jim Larkin taking over the country.

By 1914, there was little discussion about anything save the impending civil war that would be fought between the Protestant Ulster

Volunteers and the Catholic Irish Volunteers in the South, over the introduction of Home Rule. This threat, however, was soon eclipsed by the vast storm that was gathering on the continent. For the Irish the two dramas – the world war and the fight for liberation – were to be fatefully intertwined.

Ultimately the combined impact of these two great historical forces was to have a traumatic effect on Pamela. Before the war, however, buoyed up by the optimism of childhood and by having but lately entered the long-promised "Earthly Paradise," she cheerfully brushed aside the prophecies of doom. The writer H. G. Wells, whom the Hinksons met at Lord Dunsany's home in Meath in 1913, was impressed by her confident air of understanding. He immortalised their conversation in his novel of the war, *Mr. Britling Sees It Through* (1916):

> "My one consolation" [Mr. Britling said] "in this storm is a talk I had with a young Irishwoman in Meath. She was a young person of twelve, and she took a fancy to me – I think because I went with her in an alleged dangerous canoe she was forbidden to navigate alone. All day the eternal Irish Question had banged over her observant head. When we were out on the water she suddenly decided to set me right upon a disregarded essential. 'You English,' she said, 'are just a bit disposed to take all this trouble seriously. Don't you fret yourself about it . . . Half the time we're just laffing at you. You'd best leave us all alone. . . .'"

The outbreak of the First World War at first pushed local issues into the background. Dublin Castle society life changed. Adjutants disappeared with their regiments to the continent. Lord and Lady Aberdeen were distraught. The Hinksons were warned that they must be prepared to evacuate their home on the coast at any moment if the Germans landed. News of the death of "Perf" Wyndham, George's son, came through in September. Pamela rapidly became aware of being enfolded in a great disaster affecting them all.

Her mother reacted by launching into the composition of patriotic poems. Her first, "Flower of Youth," was used by Arthur Winnington-

Ingram, Bishop of London, in some of his renowned recruiting speeches, which sent thousands of young men to join up with her memorable lines ringing in their ears:

> Lest Heaven be throned with greybeards hoary,
> God, who made boys for his delight,
> Stoops in a day of grief and glory
> And calls them in, in from the night.
> When they come trooping from the war
> Our skies have many a new young star ...

Evidently people found her poems consoling, and throughout the war she became what would now be called "a grief counsellor" for countless correspondents. Pamela, hearing so much of these painful cases and her mother's talk of "the glorious fallen" she had known, such as the poet Francis Ledwidge and the peerless Lord Elcho, was profoundly affected.

Towards the end of 1914, thanks to their friendship with the Aberdeens, Pamela's father at last had a chance to prove himself his own man. As a staunch Home Ruler, loyal to the British government, he was thought a good choice as one of the Resident Magistrates for North Mayo, in Connaught, to the far west of Ireland. The post of Irish R.M. was eagerly sought after, but it was not an unmixed blessing; it was poorly paid and the expenses were high. It involved much travel and, as the number of R.M.s had been cut, a great deal of work. Because of war economies there was no pension for his family, should the magistrate die, as the family found to their cost.

To make matters worse, though Mayo was far from being a hotbed of rebellious activity, it was not a friendly county and a stranger there could easily feel isolated, as the Hinksons were to do. In the stormy weather, Claremorris, where they were based, looked bleak. The local "quality" spurned Henry Hinkson for supplanting a predecessor they liked better. Carradoyne, the first house they took, was a forlorn Georgian building with "a feeling of loneliness and darkness in winter."

In her spirited way, Mrs. Hinkson made the best of it. The chief compensation for her – and most importantly, for the children, now in their teens – was the haunting beauty of the countryside, especially in the northwest, when they could get away to it: the delphinium blue of the lakes, and the great mountain mass of the Nephin Beg, dark purple and black against the watery sky.

When the weather was too bad for expeditions, Pamela and her brother Pat amused themselves by helping their mother with her reviews for the *Bookman*, he taking the military subjects and his sister the schoolgirl stories. This was no indication that Pamela was less absorbed by the subject of war. With her, it was becoming an obsession. On a train journey to Dublin in September 1915 she whiled away the journey by repeating poetry, including, again and again, Julian Grenfell's "Into Battle." Earl Grey, a family friend, recognising her interests, presented her that Christmas with the poems of Colwyn Phillips, Lord Aberdeen's former A.D.C., who had been killed in May 1915. He also sent her family the latest accounts of heroic deeds at the front and, on one occasion, a copy of the letter from Charles Lister to Lady Desborough on the death of Julian Grenfell. When Pamela herself began writing war poetry Grey was so impressed by her verse "The Blind Soldier" that he secretly arranged for its publication, though she pipped him at the post by getting it printed in *The Queen*. She wrote stories as well, and made enough money to buy clothes. Grey congratulated her on being "the best-dressed young lady in Ireland."

During 1915, Pamela and her mother were able to make periodic trips to Dublin to see the Aberdeens. In September, however, the Viceroy retired and departed, with his wife, and soon the shadow of the war began to impinge on the Hinkson family life. Toby, the older of the two boys, was pressing, despite indifferent health, to be allowed to volunteer. His commission, in the Royal Dublin Fusiliers, came through on 31 December. Later he was assigned to the 1st Battalion, the Royal Irish Rifles and departed for Salonika. The family were very proud of him.

Pamela dreaded the moment when her favourite brother, Pat, would follow the same path. Soon afterwards he took the entrance exam for the Royal Military College, Sandhurst. It was two years before he saw service at the front, partly because of his youth and partly because Sandhurst retained a lengthy training course for regulars, as distinct from the abbreviated version for "temporary gentlemen."

For her, the turning point on "the Ladies' Road" came with the Easter Rising of 1916. News of that momentous upheaval in Irish history filtered slowly through to Mayo. The most immediate anxiety, as rumours flew around, was that the Germans might land on the coast. Farmers lamented being unable to get their pigs to Limerick; and Pat, due at Sandhurst shortly, worried over the trains, which had all been stopped. He got away a week late, and as his ship left harbour, he heard a shot aimed at the soldiers by a lone rebel sniper.

It was only when the family realised the tragedy both of the rebellion and of the ruthless executions following it, that the full horror of the affair dawned on them. It was as though the peaceful progress of the previous thirty years, through the ending of landlordism, through the economic improvements, and through the halting steps towards Home Rule, had all been in vain. The ancient hostility of the English and Irish had been revived. The spectre of the 1798 rebellion and the terrible nightmare of punishment and revenge had come back to haunt the country.

To Pamela, the "Irish problem" before the war had only been a quarrel of the Irish with Protestant Ulster, not with England; and being very young she had known nothing but peace between the two countries she loved. Now the optimism she had so touchingly displayed to Wells was shattered. She could talk and think of nothing else but Easter 1916 and had, as her mother said "taken a grue" – a serious depression. Mrs. Hinkson felt that for her daughter to be alone in the house with one continually busy parent and the other mostly on his travels, could only intensify her gloom. In the end they decided to send her to a boarding school, Mrs. Comerford's, in Wicklow. It was well meant, though it may not have been wise to make her leave her home while she was so vulnerable.

As the war continued, Pamela became preoccupied with what would happen to Pat. He got his commission in the Dublin Fusiliers in May 1917, going off to join the 3rd Battalion in Cork. He was still a year under age for overseas service, and chafed over his enforced inaction – doubly irksome when he had news of his brother Toby being part of Allenby's victorious force in Egypt and Palestine in the autumn of 1917. Toby had already come close to being awarded the M.C. in Macedonia when, on 1 May, his patrol was surrounded, but kept the Bulgarian enemy off with rifles and machine-gun fire for several hours in the darkness. All the talk of danger and death was bad for Pamela, who brooded continually, and because of this and because her mother was finishing a book, it was decided that she had better not come home that Christmas. She stayed with friends.

Her family saw her again in April when she joined them in Dublin to say goodbye to Pat, who was finally departing for the continent. He had four days leave. Before it was time for him to catch the boat, he gave a message for his mother through an acquaintance, who passed it on via Pamela: "Tell her I trust her not to shed a tear." What Pamela did is unrecorded, but she wrote afterwards in *The Ladies' Road*: "Husband and wife, lovers, friends, talked before they parted. But these two were only brother and sister, and closeness lay on them like a weight."

At this point Pamela told her parents that she was giving up school and going to rejoin them, now that both their sons had gone to war. Brookhill, their new home, with its lake teeming with wild duck and overgrown with reeds from wartime neglect, its mysterious woods and its mound where one of the Lambert family, its owners, had been buried long ago, was a far more exciting place than Carradoyne. The house itself was fascinating, full of long low-ceilinged corridors, with unexpected twists and turns, and on the upper floor a "gothick" central hall with a groined roof. A fine, small library in one of the oldest parts of the house led out through a large window on to a flight of steps going down to a tennis lawn. Some visitors spoke of ghosts, but the atmosphere of the house was loved and friendly. Mrs. Hinkson's description of it tallies closely with Pamela's of Cappagh, the Irish house that has a central place in *The Ladies' Road*.

For the Hinksons, above all for Pamela, Pat's departure emphasised the gulf between those at the front and those left behind. In the remote safety of Mayo, she even envied the Londoners because at least from time to time they were bombed. The only way in which the war touched them, as it did all Ireland, was the new threat of conscription, which for political reasons the Irish had hitherto been spared. Desperate for troops to stem the great German push in the spring of 1918, the British government now moved towards enforcing military service on them, a fatal error in the wake of the rebellion. In protest against the measure a national day of silence was declared.

On this very day, just over a week after Pat had gone, Brookhill was reinvigorated by the sudden arrival of large numbers of young people. A brigade of British soldiers came from Claremorris and began to pitch camp in and around the grounds. They were there, it was claimed, because the government had warning that a large consignment of German arms was to be landed on the coast, in cooperation with Irish rebels, the unsubstantiated "German plot," which led the Viceroy, Field-Marshal Sir John French, to arrest many Irish leaders. Some said the troops were there to enforce conscription. Whatever the reason, nothing was actually required of them. They stayed peacefully throughout the year, all the locals nonetheless resenting their presence – all, that is, save the Hinksons. At last, for Pamela, a small part of the war was on her doorstep.

The brigade consisted of battalions of various regiments, including the King's Own Scottish Borderers, the Royal Scots and also a battery of the Royal Artillery. The Royal Scots' commanding officer was the Marquis of Linlithgow, future Viceroy of India, a clever young man of towering stature. His impudent charm immediately captivated Pamela and her mother. It was not long before the officers, and those of their wives who were with them, became part of the Hinkson household. They came and went as they pleased, but were always readily received to play tennis, and in the evenings, bridge. None was more welcome than the brigade commander, the Earl of Shaftesbury, who unwound from the conscientious performance of his duties by singing "Annie Laurie" to Pamela's accompaniment. In the candlelight, and in the light of the turf fire, the soldiers would sit listening to "a tall, gentle, spectacled yeomanry officer . . . who had a gift for playing anything by ear."

Pamela always looked back on that summer of 1918 as a time of extraordinary beauty and romance:

> Those were the very peaceful wartime evenings for men who needed peace . . . with the light fading outside, and the paths between the grass growing paler, in the wide shadowy room presently the firelight had all its own way . . . That light was kind to eyes that still ached from gas and gunfire. No electric light or artificial fire could give one such a memory. When our guests had gone, as in a world half asleep, sleep-walking figures moving to the camp across the dreaming fields, we went up to bed through a house that smelt of an Irish country house in summer, a smell that I have often since tried to

define. Roses — smelling sweeter because sometime to-day
there had been rain on them . . . hay drying or later a rich af-
ter-grass, which the rain had touched too . . . a little mustiness
from the walls about us as we went up the stairs, a smell
which Irish country houses hold all the year round, in varying strength . . . Through these smells and catching them and
mingling them into one, the strongest of them all the rich
heavy sweetness of the turf smoke.

Even so, she could not fully return the romantic feeling that some of
the soldiers felt for her, unspoiled by the war, in their desire to obliterate
their fears through love. There was one young man that summer who
interested her — just a little. When he went off to the front he was
wounded, and wrote to her from hospital. Lord Linlithgow visited him
and wrote to Pamela on 13 November: "I'm glad he's in a fair way to being restored to health and beauty — that's you. Don't forget how smart a
wound stripe looks on a tunic."

These arch hints did not lead anywhere. Pamela was very virginal —
and tense. "A faint personal concern" was all she admitted to and this was
accurate. She was far more bound up with her beloved brother. In every
subaltern she saw a Pat, as he was, or as he might become, with their
boyish or prematurely aged faces. Sometimes her control snapped, as
when she ordered a young Scottish officer out of the room because she
was exasperated at hearing so many complaints about Ireland from his
fellow-countrymen.

After a long, mostly fine summer, the Mayo weather reasserted itself.
In September and October, soldiers, soaked to the skin, would come to
dry themselves in front of the drawing-room fire. Some were still there
after the armistice and there were dances and festivities, including a party
for her birthday, until Christmas.

Meanwhile the Hinksons had heard from Pat, who at last had gone
"over the top" with the 29th Division at Ledegem on a misty October
morning. He was blown over by a shell, but a compass in his pocket
stopped the splinter that might have killed him, and he struggled on to
take part in a successful action against the Prussian Guards. Two days later
his leave came through. The Hinksons were in Dublin in the lounge of

the Shelbourne Hotel one morning, when Pamela spotted him getting out of a car. It was a moment of delirious joy. After he had been swept up briefly into Dublin social life, with reassuring figures like "A.E.," they took him back to Brookhill for ten days. Then he returned to the front and there were two anxious weeks before the war ended and they knew he was safe. He went on, with the British Army of Occupation, into Germany.

Early in 1919, Henry Hinkson died. In her memoirs, his wife expressed less emotion over his passing than she did about their beloved pomeranian dog who died from a surfeit of yew clippings. The immediate material effect was to reduce their income; and there was no further reason to remain in a spot that had chiefly been made tolerable by the recent presence of British troops. For a while she and Pamela led a semi-nomadic existence, staying briefly at different homes, sometimes relying on the hospitality of friends or lodging in boarding houses. Pamela, without the chance of escaping to a university as her intellect deserved, was now trapped at home in the role of devoted daughter. Her mother's crippling neuralgia was reason enough. Pamela could perform the useful function of taking down her mother's deathless words. She became "my faithful Pamela." This did not prevent her from doing her own writing, for her mother encouraged that, and Pamela had determination, as well as a desire to imitate. Emotionally, however, it sapped her independence. Her mother watched her go to society balls with approval, but these functions were not the natural milieu for a clever, penniless girl, haunted by the tragedy of the war and the Irish troubles. Pamela's relationship with her mother was a form of servitude that English daughters, but even more, Irish daughters – and sons – were lucky to escape in those days, as Richard Aldington's *The Colonel's Daughter* painfully illustrates.

During 1919 they were in England, visiting Lord Shaftesbury and Lord Linlithgow and others who had been based at Brookhill during the previous summer; and they revived friendships with prewar companions such as the Meynells. Pat remained in the army and went out to India. Toby came back to see them for the first time since September 1916. He hoped to stay out in the Middle East as a civilian but had to return the next year for health reasons.

Pat was disillusioned – he felt that the great qualities of the fighting days had disappeared. His military career had been less eventful than his brother's, but he had pondered about it, and his patriotic and imaginative views had made a mark on Pamela when she came to write about what soldiers felt. They were the views of a Celtic Catholic, a believer in original sin and the value of suffering, but also in original virtue: "The nearer the men got to the front line the more they appreciated each other at the highest value, and there was a kind of unconscious natural understanding which made men help and rely on one another . . . The most fascinating thing in this world is danger, and beside it everything else is artificial. War may bring out the animal qualities in man: perhaps those qualities are best."

As for the effect of war on the populations that had been invaded, he emphasised what a terrible ordeal it had been for France and Belgium. "Nevertheless, though it is hard on the individual, I think suffering is always good for a nation." That was not a view Pamela could share about Ireland in the years to come.

By June 1920, both brothers were looking for jobs in England. Pamela and her mother went there for a while, then travelled round Europe. Finally they returned to Ireland where, as far as they were concerned, things were falling apart, and the centre, which they represented, was certainly not holding. The British auxiliary forces, the (mostly ex-wartime soldiers) "Black and Tans," supporting the Royal Irish Constabulary, were waging vicious warfare against the Irish republican forces now bent on the ruthless extirpation of the British presence. The I.R.A. terror was remarkably effective. The "Black and Tans," matching killing with killing, burning with burning, failed to gain the mastery. In a year the British government had capitulated. Very seldom did the violence impinge directly on Pamela and her mother. It was, however, the consummation they had feared and for all their Irishness they felt torn to the roots. What seemed to horrify Pamela most, as being symbolic of the great divide, was the burning of Anglo-Irish properties during those years, strongholds, to her, of civilised life now threatened with utter extinction. She never got over that wilful destruction.

To escape from this and the civil war that followed, and to be in a place where their currency would go a long way, her mother decided in 1922 that they should spend a year or two in Cologne, in the Rhineland, still occupied by British forces. They stayed, on and off, till 1925, going for some of the time to France where Pamela worked as a governess.

Mrs. Hinkson had a further reason for choosing Cologne. She was worried about Pamela's marriage prospects and hoped, remembering her wartime romantic interest in the soldiers at Brookhill, that she would find someone in the occupying army.

Her hopes were realised – nearly. Pamela flung herself into the life of the place, remembering her brother Pat's moving letters that he sent to her mother about conditions in postwar Germany and relations between the soldiers and the Rhinelanders. In due course, she formed an attachment to an officer with the undignified nickname of "Pussy," and they became engaged. They never married, however. It was said that Pamela had not found him enough of a gentleman, nor sufficiently romantic. If so, it was not crude snobbery on her part. The trouble was that her view of the male ideal had been formed by worshipping at the shrines of the George Wyndhams, the Lord Elchos, and the Julian Grenfells of Edwardian and wartime mythology. Other males, save Pat, seemed in her eyes rather unimpressive, weak figures, as she had felt her father to be.

By this time Pamela was a practised writer. Following her father's example, she tried her hand at school fiction, of a dated variety, and throughout the twenties turned out stories about a girl called "Victory." In 1922 a book of hers, *Dethronements*, was published – a series of historical portraits in the form of imaginary dialogues. Her first serious novel, *The End of All Dreams*, appeared in 1923. The theme of the book was the destructive tyranny that Irish politics exerted over the men and women who lived there despite the noble sentiments that inspired the struggle for freedom. The main character in it, Denys, an Irish country gentleman who had served on the Western Front with the British, was suspected for his Irish sympathies by his English friends and regarded as an enemy in Ireland because he would not hate the English – the Hinksons' own position. The book ended with incendiarists destroying his home. The novel stated, with impressive maturity and fluency, the view Pamela was to take for the next forty-eight years.

Perhaps because of the criticism she increasingly received on this account in newly independent Ireland, it may have suited her to slip, for several years, into the role of "Peter Deane," and channel her idealism into another sphere in which she felt passionately. Though the true identity of her pseudonym was not kept universally secret – "A. E." wrote her an appreciative letter when *The Victors* was published – reviewers at the time seem to have been taken in.

She was distressed to see how the war had made her brothers and her ex-soldier friends unable to readjust to civilian life. Pat took months before he found a job as correspondent for *The Times* in Buenos Aires. Toby was in despair about getting work until finally, in 1921, he was offered the post of assistant district commissioner in Kenya, where there was a government-sponsored scheme for those who wished to settle. Pamela, concerned that he would be desperately lonely out in the bush, persuaded him, with all the force of her formidable personality, and against his better self-knowledge, to marry a lady they both knew and liked, of impeccable Grattan and Esmonde Anglo-Irish ancestry, so that he would have a companion out there. Sadly, the couple were not compatible, and their marriage ended in divorce.

Outside the family circle, the public spectacle of unemployment was even more distressing. In the winter of 1920-21, when Pamela and her mother were in London, they witnessed maimed war veterans selling worthless toys on Regent Street, wretchedly cold in the icy wind. "The profiteers in the Rolls Royces never saw them, any more than they saw the unemployed collecting boxes," wrote Mrs. Hinkson: "The unemployed were everywhere that winter, marching to a quick-step in all the streets. Not wastrels. Clean, decent-looking ex-soldiers. . . . I remembered how they had gone out to martial music and everyone had cheered them."

Pamela was horrified. At one big London hotel where she was at a New Year party she witnessed people alighting from a huge motor car and dropping two pence into a collecting box for ex-servicemen. She was shocked too by the drunken abandon with which, not the young, but the old and middle-aged rich were disporting themselves, while men who had fought for them wandered in misery through the streets.

Thus "Peter Deane" was born. It was scenes like this that made her decide to put on demobilised men's clothes, as it were, and fight their cause, thus partly assuaging the guilt she had felt during the war about being unable to help them. She felt acutely that war had divided her from her brothers and male friends by a gulf of experience that could never be bridged. At least, however, she could now try to share the pain of their rejection after the war. She had spent the last few years in largely military company on the continent, so that her identification with soldiers went deep. She had considered using her brother Pat's account of his one big day in action as the basis for a novel, but writing about soldiers in civilian life was something she could tackle with more accuracy.

The Victors had an intensity that is akin to the tone of the Pamela Hinkson novels, the same inexorable march towards tragedy. On the other hand it does not seem an especially "feminine" book, as that word was understood at the time. Where she included any detail of military life, acquired through talk and letters, it is authentic.

Her second "Peter Deane" book, *Harvest*, was introduced by no less a figure than Sir Philip Gibbs, the former war correspondent whose experience of contributing to Britain's war propaganda had left him ashamed and determined to campaign against war in the future. Gibbs' own novels, such as *Back to Life* (1920) and *The Middle of The Road* (1923), occupied the same category of war novel as *The Victors* and A. P. Herbert's *Secret Battle* in being written not to record experience but to change attitudes. Without uncovering the author's true identity, Gibbs wrote: "War would not happen so often in the world if like Peter Deane we had pity for the women who do the harvesting." The book was based largely on what Pamela had seen or heard of in the Rhineland – a tragic love affair between a Frenchman in the occupying force and a German girl; a German mother starving to death as a result of the postwar privation; and a girl prostituting herself to avoid the same fate. These and other memorable stories characteristically intermingled the beauty of the country with the sadness of their themes.

When books about the horrors of war were at the height of fashion in 1930, "Peter Deane" launched another impassioned appeal for the unemployed ex-servicemen in the pages of the *Nation and Athenaeum* for 18 October 1930, drawing attention to the tragedy of the living that seemed to her to matter more now than the tragedy of the dead: "The schoolboys who went out between the years 1914 and 1918 had never been anything. When the war was over they had nothing to get back to ... In 1919 every man in power in politics, in business, in journalism, in the professions, was a man who had not left England. It was inevitable and perhaps nobody is to be blamed for it. But it shut out the survivors as completely as though their survival had been a mistake. It might indeed have been that their survival was so unlooked for that no one knew what to do with them."

Thinking, evidently, of those she knew, her brothers, and friends, she went on to say that these young men had been driven abroad, to find employment in the colonies, or had stayed behind, glad to find any menial job. Whatever their occupation they looked with resigned dispassion at the older generation who occupied posts they might have had; the war had created too great a gulf for them even to feel envious. It had detached them, too, from their own country: "This is the country from which they went out as school boys in '16, in '17, in '18," she continued: "'How we loved England then!', I have just been reading, in Stephen Graham's *Life of Wilfrid Ewart*. But a man's home must be where he makes a living, and they leave this country to the old and the very young, and those who stayed at home." She did not add what she felt most bitterly, that the war might not have killed her brothers, but they had been taken away from her nonetheless. The British, she said, had let down the war generation who had once had dreams and aspirations but were broken after the war. In contrast with Mussolini's new Italy, where the Fascist movement united the enthusiasm of the very young with the unique experience of the war generation, she claimed: "We neglect the survivors as though they did not exist, and keep our pity for the dead who have no need of it."

However subjective her view that those who had served largely became a "lost generation" after the war, it was shared by several of her contemporaries among fiction writers, including Warwick Deeping and Oliver Onions and later, in a qualified way, by the historian A. J. P. Taylor. Nonetheless this picture is not wholly an accurate one and while it may have held good, broadly, for the twenties, some more effective members of that generation did take over positions of authority in the next decade: among the leaders of English life in many spheres during the thirties such influential figures as Clement Attlee, Anthony Eden, John Reith, F. R. Leavis, Herbert Read – not to mention many leading names in publishing and the press – were war veterans. Even so, the ground lost in the twenties was striking. Her further assertion that so many ex-servicemen – including, presumably, her brothers – had turned their backs on England is borne out by the views expressed by other writers (including, in this volume, Richard Aldington and Robert Keable). It was a theme also taken up more recently by Professor Paul Fussell in his book *Abroad*.

The image she used, at several points in her 1930 article, of a bridge broken between past and present, had an important place in her subsequent books, under her own name. The second Pamela Hinkson novel, *Wind From The West*, appeared in 1930. It was based on her careful observations while a governess in France.

Like many books of that era – such as David Garnett's *Go She Must* – this novel dealt romantically with the theme of release from constricting old-fashioned values into a new and liberated existence. The book was an elegy for an ancient aristocratic order of French society that was ending. Despite its oversoulful tone, it was perceptive.

It was set shortly after the war, which, by killing off its sons, was shown as an agent of violent change destroying the future of the old Breton noble class. Pamela noticed how the nobility who had been at the front felt weakened and isolated by their experience and missed the brief freedom from family tyranny that, as the heroes of the hour, they had enjoyed during the war. Some of the women among them, recognising that this freedom had gone, decided to complete their wartime self-sacrifice by becoming nuns, leaving the world to the coming generation.

The central drama of the book is the story of Solange de Mauges, a very young girl, who, following the battlefield death of the male heir, is the last of her line. She finds the strength, however, to defy her formidable family's plan to marry her to an aristocrat twice her age, who has shirked military service. Instead, she runs off with a well-bred American (his name is Quincy) symbolic of a fresh new life, liberty, and the pursuit of happiness.

The book, dealing with a traditional ruling class under challenge and its blindness in the face of new, unwelcome realities, linked up with Pamela's novels on Ireland and the war. It presented at the same time the romance of an ancient, rural way of life, with its bigotry, and its tranquillity, mystery, and heroism.

On Good Friday 1931 another powerful regime that had lasted all Pamela's lifetime finally ended when her mother died, at her southwest London home, after years of semiblindness. Inevitably Pamela had felt moments of suffocation, and envied the Solanges of this world for being able to cut loose. Yet the loss was almost overwhelming, simply because "You were everything to her and you both loved being everything to each other," as Pamela's close friend Lady Plymouth, the sister of Lord Elcho, wrote to her.

Her brother Pat returned for a while, revisiting Ireland for the first time in years, painfully groping after childhood memories in a country no longer familiar to him, as Pamela later described. His past began to come back to him at last when he recollected the kitchen at Brookhill while he was still a schoolboy, then a cadet, then a soldier on leave: "I remember coming in from shooting through the yard and kitchen . . . Ellen and Cook sitting by the table on stiff wooden chairs" – or greeting him in the morning on his way to the stables or gun room, with "Any news today, Master Pat?" – news of war or disaster or victory, which was always received appropriately, but with equanimity, in that securest of places.

The stirring up of memory and the shock of her mother's death contributed to the emotional intensity of Pamela's next and most powerful book. *The Ladies' Road* was published in 1932. It is a tale of life in English and Irish country houses before, during, and just after the Great War. A host of characters – guests, retainers, soldiers, and relations – pass before the reader's eyes. The "Irishness" of the old families of the ascendancy is lovingly portrayed: their attachment to the country, their dislike of change, their good intentions never fulfilled, their obliviousness to the hostility of the native population outside their wooded parks.

In the story, Cynthia and Godfrey and their younger brother and sister David and Stella have lost their parents. Stella – the protagonist – and David are close in age and devoted to one another. Their family home, Winds, in the Sussex countryside, is the centre of their life; but they have always spent a part of the year with their uncle and aunt, Hubert and Nancy Creagh, and their sons, at Cappagh in the West of Ireland.

As time goes on, boarding school takes David away from Stella for large parts of the year. Godfrey gets married. When the war comes, the partings are more final. Young men who have stayed at Cappagh before the war are killed, including Godfrey. His wife, Mary, cut off by her grief, no longer feels at home with his family at Winds, which has little meaning to her without him. Hubert Creagh and his elder son lose their lives, while his young son, badly wounded and changed in personality, continually quarrels with his mother. Cynthia makes a wartime marriage, and before she and her husband have come to know one another well, he is taken prisoner and spends two years in Germany. When he returns he is a stranger.

Stella, between the ages of sixteen and seventeen, becomes attached to a succession of young officers quartered near them in Sussex, not so much falling in love with them as identifying them with her brother, David, who has enlisted. All are killed or return changed. Cruellest of all, David himself meets his end in his first military engagement.

At the end of the book, Cappagh is burnt down in the Irish "Troubles," by a local peasantry implacably hostile to British rule. Stella is left feeling cut off from her own past, and all that is most precious to her, by her brother's death, and the destruction of the life at Cappagh. She is isolated from those who have not shared the war's sharpest tragedies; but also finds that grief wraps each sufferer in their own private agony, so that communication at every level is thwarted.

The title, *The Ladies' Road*, reflects the theme of the book – the mental torture that her female characters undergo is the equivalent of the ordeal of war that the men face. There is the further irony that the sector of the French line that David's battalion temporarily occupy in 1918 when he is killed is one known as the Chemin des Dames, from the name of the road along the ridge near Laon at one time used regularly by the daughters of Louis XV ("Mesdames") on journeys to their friend, the Duchess of Narbonne. This "Ladies' Road" was one of the sacred spots of France's wartime struggle and the scene of devastating slaughter, followed by French army mutinies, in the spring of 1917.

Although the family whose story Pamela Hinkson chronicles in *The Ladies' Road* is in most respects different from her own, the book is faithful to her memories of County Mayo and details of her school life. The book demonstrates her obsession with separation and change, which was at its most intense during and just after the war, but which she had felt at every stage in her early life as the family moved from one home to another. The relationship between Stella and David is clearly modelled on her own with her brother Pat. Nancy Creagh's power of sympathy with the young soldiers echoes that of Pamela's mother.

The writing is impressionistic and allusive. The effect is extremely rich. The atmosphere of Cappagh and of Winds are vividly evoked throughout the seasons. On the whole the characters – of dogs and horses no less than humans – are seen as Stella perceives them. They rise to the surface, revealing a face and a mannerism for a moment, then sink down to be replaced by some other half-submerged being. What interests Pamela Hinkson is remembered happiness, apprehension, and grief, as they affect individual characters and Stella in particular. She handles these states of mind with sensitivity and fidelity, though not all the thoughts that go through the youthful Stella's mind are ones she can have had at the time.

The scenes most directly drawn from life are those of Stella's school, and the way the girls are affected when news comes that they have lost a brother or a father, or an admirer. In the latter case there is a degree of irony:

There was a rush downstairs to find the post. Once a girl stood still in the hall, staring blankly at the empty table when everybody snatched their letters.

"Nothing for me."

"Nothing for you." Someone answered cheerfully. "Oh, here, what about this? Funny letter. It's addressed to Felicity, just Felicity. Returned postal packet." She read so much before Felicity snatched it from her. She didn't understand at first.

"He's been killed," she said dully, but no one heard. And she read her own letter, and when she got one the next day, posted before he had gone over, she thought it had been a mistake. But you often got letters now from people when they were dead. She felt it badly for a time while there were no letters for her. But the next term there was a big Australian who had been staying in a neighbouring house during the holidays and who was lonely, he said . . .

Although *The Ladies' Road* conveys the tragedy of war and the resentment that war survivors and the bereaved feel against those who have somehow escaped the worst suffering, it is not a "disenchanted" work in the conventional sense. It had little criticism of war aims or the leaders. It is not pacifist or antimilitary. It simply mourns the effect of all wars – and terrorism – which destroy so many sacred and fundamental relationships with people and places.

Nor does it carry a directly feminist message, as does, for example, Vera Brittain's novel *Honourable Estate* (1936). Although Stella yearns to take part in the war as a nurse or even a soldier, she is not apparently interested in achieving independence. She just cannot bear to be apart from her beloved brother and wants to share his trials (as Vera Brittain, in real life, also did). On the other hand most of the male characters in the book, with the exception of David and the young poet, Edmund Urquart, are irresolute, neurotic, or simple, to be pitied or slightly despised.

When *The Ladies' Road* appeared, reviewers praised its poignancy and delicacy, but interestingly, it had its greatest success fourteen years later, just after the Second World War, when 100,000 copies were sold in the paperback edition. In this it was almost unique among First World War novels, which with very few exceptions evinced no interest at all between 1940 and 1960. Neither the mistakes made by the generals over trench warfare, nor the inspiring messages preached by First War writers such as Robert Keable or Wilfrid Ewart, meant much in 1945. By contrast, Pamela's sensitive handling of the universal problems of separation and personal loss appealed even more strongly a year after the Second World War than when her book first appeared, almost too late to make its full impact, in 1932.

She always considered it by far her best work, a verdict that readers are likely to share. It is also one of the best novels by a woman about the experience of the First World War. Not least, it demonstrated for once and for all that her talent at its best was very much greater than her mother's, for all Katherine Tynan's facility.

Pamela's preoccupation with Ireland and its past continued. After her mother's death, she returned there. Her next book was also about a homecoming. In *The Deeply Rooted*, published in 1934, she expressed, through a rather weak and passionless love story, her own feelings of reconciliation with Ireland. It was full of images familiar in her repertoire: a burnt home; an ex-soldier, reminding the leading character of her brother killed in the war, called, significantly, Pat; roots of friendship reaching back into the past, before the war, that deep divide between a truer, profounder life and the present. Again there were poetical descriptions of Irish countryside: the beech woods, the wild winds, the fallen leaves.

For Pamela in these years, one labour of love was her transcription of the dictated memoirs of the Countess of Fingall, which gave an invaluable and entertaining picture of Anglo-Irish society in the last years of its dominance. The book *Seventy Years Young* came out in 1937 and is in print today.

Although she had little money, and at times accepted financial aid from Pat, Pamela kept up with the high-born acquaintances her mother had made. Her greatest friends included the Esmonde family, and as was the way with many Irish gentry in straitened circumstances at the time, she stayed, often for months on end, as a "personal guest" (self-invited), at their big house in County Tipperary, Drominagh, on the banks of Lough Derg. It was something she had grown accustomed to doing with her mother from the early 1920s. Most of the families she lodged with had a strong tradition of service in the British army. While at Drominagh, she wrote a book, *Irish Gold* (1939), which celebrated the Irish people and countryside and was well received in England, where she was praised as "one of the best living interpreters of the Irish scene."

She also kept up with the Aberdeens and the Linlithgows and it was her reverence for England's colonial overlordship that led her to her next major preoccupation: India, which she visited in 1938, during the declining days of the Raj, when Lord Linlithgow was Viceroy there. Her book, *Indian Harvest*, was one outcome of her trip.

In the Second World War the Hinksons were once more fighting England's battles. Toby rejoined the British army. Pamela was asked by the Ministry of Information in London to give a series of lectures in the United States on the British presence in India ("India through Irish Eyes," "Women and children in India," "The face of India"), and on the historical connection with Ireland. Both subjects needed a favourable gloss in the interests of the newly reviving Anglo-American "Special Relationship." She crossed on the Queen Mary at the height of the German U-boat campaign. In London, during the blitz, she also began writing a novel, *The Golden Rose* (1944). This presented the British way of life in India in quietly heroic terms, and sold well. It was in her most sentimental vein, but as with her best work the atmospheric passages were its main strength.

A fervent patriot for England (she still had her British passport), but nonetheless dedicated to the soul of Ireland, she also took an energetic part throughout the war in the activities of the Shamrock Club, for the welfare of Irishmen in the British armed forces. It was work to which, with her generous nature, she took enthusiastically. It was also one way of paying her debt to the soldiers she had wished to help in the earlier struggle.

In 1946 and 1947 she lectured in Germany, on Irish and British topics, to the British forces and to German audiences. She also broadcast in England, Ireland, and U.S.A. Her writing career continued during the next decade, with contributions to *The Spectator* and *Time and Tide*. Her last novel, *The Lonely Bride*, appeared in 1951. In Ireland, however, where she now resided at Monkstown near Dublin, she was an isolated figure in the world of letters. In sticking defiantly to the Parnellite but pro-English viewpoint her mother had held half a century before, Pamela seemed like some antique survival, though many of her opinions were enlightened – particularly about cruelty to animals, the hypocritical treatment of unmarried mothers, and the anti-British indoctrination that Irish children received. With her reputation for loquacity and her gloomy view of the world, she became, sadly, something of a figure of fun – behind her back. Even those most fond of her found her personality and views at times too strong, complaining that she never allowed them a chance to utter a word. Yet her probity, her loyalty, and above all her acts of kindness still earned praise – and friends. She claimed that friendship was the greatest gift of life and that making friends had been her most satisfying achievement.

Her brothers died before her, Pat in 1958, out in Buenos Aires. Her last twenty years were blighted by illness. She half-expected to die in 1960 when she went into hospital for a spell during that year. Although, in the decades that followed, she never properly organised the huge accretion of papers her mother had left, she made a start: she began to hand over the family's treasures in her possession, among them the portrait of her grandfather by J. B. Yeats, to the Irish National Gallery, then in the charge of the poet Thomas MacGreevy, a veteran of the Great War and hence a trusted ally.

Despite increasing infirmity, she lived on until 1982. At the end her mind began to wander, and she seemed even older than her 82 years: a vestige of Ireland's pre-First War past quite as remote as those great Anglo-Irish family houses whose charred ruins had so long haunted her. Those who saw her in her last year, still smoking, appropriately enough, "like a trooper," but now unable to communicate her thoughts, a jar of cold cream the only concession to femininity in her bleak bedroom, must have longed for that once energetic mind to recall from over the other side of the "broken bridge," a memory: perhaps of when, as a seventeen-year-old girl in the woods at Brookhill, her white dress catching the moonlight, she fled shyly from a soldier who sought her comfort, half-wishing he would go away, half-wishing to help him because all soldiers were, in some degree, her brother Pat.

❧

13

The Generation of the Brokenhearted
Richard Blaker
1893 - 1940

An exile far from home, Richard Blaker is buried in the English plot of the Inglewood Park Cemetery, Los Angeles, amid sweeping lawns and tall conifers reflected in the quiet waters of an artificial lake. His headstone commemorates him, not as the best-selling professional writer he at one time was, but as a soldier and as the author of his most memorable novel, set during the First World War – the war that claimed his life, twenty-two years after its end. The inscription reads:

RICHARD SIDNEY BLAKER

R.F.A.

DEAR HUSBAND OF AGNES MAYO (BIDDY) BLAKER

AUTHOR OF "MEDAL WITHOUT BAR"

DIED FEBRUARY 18 1940, AGED 46 YEARS

It was fitting that *Medal Without Bar* should be on Richard Blaker's gravestone, for it was the book closest to his nature: it concerned itself with friendship, in time of war, within the small, tight-knit group that made up an artillery battery.

When it appeared in January 1930, *Medal Without Bar* was highly praised for its lack of the sensationalism that had shocked many, including ex-servicemen, in recent and vastly successful works such as *All Quiet on the Western Front* and that had a profound influence on uninformed opinion. "You have said in it," one ex-army padre told Richard Blaker, "what I have been trying passionately to say ever since we became flooded with the new type of war book and with the sort of pacifism which thinks it necessary to libel the most gallant fellowship of gallant men the world has ever seen"; an ex-gunner told Richard that the book had conveyed to him "the sense of kinship in times of stress and misery which all of us remember with pride."

The book is slow-moving and very long. In this lies its authenticity. It well conveys the relentless monotony of war. It is mainly autobiographical; but the principal character, the sensible and conventional peacetime soldier, Charles Cartwright, though a mouthpiece for many of the author's thoughts, is not a self-portrait. He is twice as old as Blaker was when he joined the army; nor was Blaker "sensible," nor particularly "conventional" in the generally accepted sense. He was a man of exceptional talents and much of his life was extraordinary. Nor does Cartwright's wife, Dorothy, who is deliberately depicted as prosaic, bear any resemblance to Richard Blaker's own vivid consort.

He was born in Kalka, Punjab, North West India, in March 1893. The Blakers were a large family. In England they had flourished, earning knighthoods and baronetcies; one Dr. Blaker looked after Nelson's Lady Hamilton. Richard Blaker's own branch had settled in India as doctors, soldiers, and administrators in the imperial service. His father, Richard Henry Blaker, was an archivist in the locally recruited "uncovenanted" branch of the Indian Civil Service, less prestigious than that entered through competitive examination in London. Blaker's mother was formerly a Miss Ettie Buckner, the sister of a sergeant in the 9th Royal Lancers.

Richard had jet-black hair and aquiline features. He was dignified, refined, and aristocratic in appearance and manner. As a youth he was handsome, with a sensitive, humorous expression and a gentle demeanour. He possessed a contemplative, though not religious, cast of mind. He was a precocious pupil at his public boarding school, Bishop Cotton's in Simla, and at sixteen gained a Government of India Scholarship, in science, to Oxford. His relations with his parents however – particularly his mother – were troubled. Judging by *Scabby Dichson*, the novel he afterwards based on his own youth, he felt he had been deserted by them; indeed he came to prefer his own company, and that of a few exotic pets, to most of his associates. That book, poetical and evocative, describes a childhood spent for long stretches at Bishop Cotton's. High in the hills, Simla was favoured as a summer retreat for the Viceroy's government because of its cooler climate. In winter it was bitterly cold. The boys at Bishop Cotton's were rough and unsophisticated, and looked forward to careers as traders, soldiers, and "uncovenanted" government officials. Discipline was heavy, though intermittent. *Scabby Dichson* was not straight autobiography, but the leading character "Scabby" had elements of a self-portrait: clever, independent, secretive – a "loner" in one sense, though also popular and respected.

In 1909, at sixteen and a half, not realising that he was still too young to take up his scholarship, he decided to leave home and school. He went over to England, under the wing of a teacher from his school who was going on leave. When he arrived there, he looked up the only relative he could find, one of his uncles, Percy "Stanley" Blaker, a successful paediatrician living in Ealing, which was in the process of becoming a suburb of London.

Stanley Blaker's wife, "Mamie," was the Canadian-born daughter of an adventurous buccaneering businessman who had made various fortunes in fur, timber, and oil. Auburn-haired, with the full-blown beauty of an old-fashioned rose, she had trained as an operatic soprano and performed frequently at the Crystal Palace. Then in her late twenties, she had been married for nine years when Richard Blaker appeared. Her nature, like her father's, was bold and resourceful, but her husband was ten years older than she and had established an uneasy dominance over her. Having married him, at twenty, to escape her own family, she had come to dislike him, as she had come to dislike much that she found snobbish and stuffy in the English character, ever since being bullied about her Canadian accent at school. There were no children from the marriage. It was one of the Edwardian upper-bourgeois households of the "Forsyte Saga" variety in which an ice-capped mountain-mass of public achievement and respectability concealed a fierce emotional magma beneath.

At first she was not much impressed by her husband's young relative, who seemed to her an awkward adolescent, with schoolboy habits and expressions. While he was waiting to take up his scholarship, his uncle found him a job in a bank, but he was so bored by it that he was sacked.

Eventually, in the autumn of 1911, at the age of eighteen, he went up to Queen's College, Oxford; he impressed tutors with his unusual intellectual gifts and they suggested that he should not study science, but read for the prestigious degree of Classics and Litterae Humaniores, "Mods and Greats," a four-year course favoured by many who were ambitious for careers in government service. Though his tutor later described him as one of the most satisfactory pupils he had ever taught, he did poorly in his examinations. He merely took a pass in Mods; while in the "Greats" he only achieved a fourth-class honours, a lowly but useful category usually reserved for peers of the realm, future performing artists, and sons of foreign dignitaries, none of whom were expected to be overdiligent.

Blaker however was never lazy. He flung himself into university life, both social and intellectual, and after war broke out, the O.T.C. The root cause of his undistinguished result was the drama that had by then developed in his adopted home. His arrival in that tense household had a highly disturbing effect. He was young, good-looking, and his heart was easily touched. Mamie was unhappy and trapped. It had taken a tragedy, however, to precipitate the crisis.

In February 1911, Mamie's father, James MacGarvey, then in Grozny, in the Caucasus, drilling oil, had been surprised one night at dinner by brigands who murdered him and left his wife, Julia, for dead. Eighteen months later, in September 1912, Mamie went out to bring her mother back from hospital where she had recovered (apart from a permanently damaged shoulder). Mamie's husband, however, had decided that he could not spare the time to accompany her, so the eighteen-year-old Richard was deputed to take his place at his wife's side. It was a duty too literally interpreted. On that romantic and adventurous journey they fell in love and she was persuaded into an affair. Finding herself pregnant and being far too open-natured to try and conceal matters, she told her husband the whole story.

For the sake of appearances, Stanley did not drive her out of the house. Indeed he became fond of his wife's baby daughter, Betty, but his attitude hardened as time passed. Mamie herself started to visit her nephew regularly at Oxford. Their fates, thereafter, were inextricably intertwined. She had become Richard's lover, the mother of his child, and also a substitute for the mother whom he felt had rejected him. For Mamie, Richard was the means of escape from her marriage. He had all the imagination and sensitivity her husband lacked. He seemed destined for a remarkable future, and they shared a common interest in the arts. Her forte was music, and his literature. Yet in many ways they did not understand one another particularly well. The colonial way of life in India had centred so much on male activities that to Richard women were always mystifying beings. Mamie's warm, headstrong nature at times bewildered him, though he enjoyed her vitality and intelligence, and for years admired her splendid looks. On her part she adored him for his shy, graceful gentleness, and his varied talents. Yet, as later became apparent, she was uneasy with what she felt was his almost promiscuous capacity for friendship, which was extended to many she did not like. The intensity of their relationship and the ordeals through which it had to pass during the years that followed meant also that though they were both, in their different ways, humorous people, there were few jokes between them and relaxed family badinage was unknown in their household. Their life together was complicated too by the fact that Mamie's mother, Julia, lived with them all the time. She was a charming, placid-natured lady; even so, Richard Blaker was always aware that Mamie put her mother before anyone else.

Blaker was popular at Queen's College. Among his friends was Wendell Herrbruck, a tall, thin, drily humorous American, with whom he shared a college room, and a fellow scholar, Louis Golding, from Sycamore Street, in the heart of Jewish Manchester. Both these friendships were to prove of lasting importance in his life. He was greatly attached, also, to a brilliant undergraduate, Edgar Perham, whose devoted sister Margery, later famous as an Imperial historian, was known to Edgar and his Oxford friends as "Midget," though hardly smaller than her brawny brother.

When war broke out Blaker seems to have had no doubts about enlisting straight from the university, like his contemporaries at Queen's, Edgar Perham, Charles Duguid, William Hartley, George Young, Reggie Shaw, William Hanna, A. C. Bender, William Garrard, and George Elliot, none of whom were to return. His patriotic conditioning in India had bred in him an idealism typical of his generation. Instinctively, too, he may have been drawn to the simplicities of an organised all-male society, after the emotional complications of his life. In the summer of 1915 he volunteered for the Honourable Artillery Company and was subsequently commissioned in the Royal Field Artillery like his younger brother Eric, a professional soldier. He trained at Exeter where he was taught the mathematical intricacies of gunnery and learned equitation from athletic noncommissioned officers who had survived the retreat from Mons and the First Battle of Ypres.

Mamie was still legally attached to her husband, Stanley, and continued for a while to live at their house in 37 Creffield Road, Ealing. Stanley himself joined the Indian Medical Service, and later the Royal Army Medical Corps, while she, from the start, busied herself with the national campaign for housing Belgian refugees, raising money for the Belgian Relief Fund through concerts at which she sang under the name of "Helena St. Clemens" alongside George Robey and other stars at the Crystal Palace. Eventually zeppelin raids drove her out of London. She settled with her baby and her mother in Southampton, where Richard Blaker visited the three of them during his leaves. Mamie enrolled as a V.A.D. nurse at a depot where munitions were loaded, and was expected to attend such accidents as crushed feet with little more than a bottle of iodine. She carried on her public singing performances with great success. The poignancy of her songs "She Wandered Down the Mountainside" and "When He Comes Home" caught the emotionally fragile mood of the time, among audiences of soldiers and war-strained civilians all too ready to be moved to tears.

Eventually, in the summer of 1916, Blaker was sent to France, assigned to "D" Battery 58th Brigade R.F.A., part of 11th Division. In the close-knit organisation of an artillery battery, where much depended on an adroit understanding of ballistic principles, his mathematical mind and easy sociability were assets. At this time, a Royal Field Artillery brigade consisted of a major in command of four batteries of four guns (later six) apiece and 33 men per gun, including transport. In Blaker's brigade, three of these batteries, "A," "B," and "C," consisted of 18-pounder field guns, and their crews, who had recently seen service in Gallipoli and Egypt. "D" battery, which had been in Flanders with the Canadians and was therefore treated as "odd man out," was equipped, like other "D" batteries, with the 4.5-in. Quick-firing Field Howitzer.

The battery remained *the* artillery unit in the British army until shortly before the Second World War. "That happy, miserable, elastic family, the battery," as one former signaller later put it, in a letter to Blaker, was the focus of intense loyalty and comradeship. So much depended on a drill, and on the interacting duties of its members, that a well-coordinated battery functioned almost like a single individual. When its controlling spirit, the commander, was absent and a greatly inferior officer took over — as happened at least once in Blaker's experience — there was deep resentment. Heavy losses and rapid replacement by unknown faces could also badly affect its sense of identity. By the time he left it, "D" battery seemed, in Blaker's words, like a small businessman who had attained middle age, worn out by cares, and could only see the business had not failed. That very image, however, attests to a battery's dogged ability to keep going. Despite casualties, it was always held together by the discipline and skill involved in operating its guns and managing its horses, mules, or motor transport.

Originally introduced in 1909, the 4.5-in. howitzer operated by Blaker's battery, that was to give him so much anxiety, was widely claimed in 1914 to be the best field howitzer in the world. It was small, simple, and robustly built, weighing something over a ton and a quarter. It stood on two stout cart-type wheels, and could deliver a 35-lb. shell, on a curved trajectory, to a concealed enemy target over four miles away.

Until their design was modified in 1917, these guns were distinctly dangerous to operate; and indeed, 4.5-in. howitzer batteries were known on the Somme as "suicide clubs," because of their alleged tendency to "prematures" — the premature bursting of the shell in the barrel. All guns were vulnerable to this, since the mass-produced ammunition of the hastily-organised wartime armaments factories could never be checked with the same thoroughness as during the peace; but the 4.5-in. "how" was also found to have a serious fault that had a similar effect. With intense use it developed cracks in the breech, which, at the same time, tended to overheat. When the propellant charge was loaded into the gun after the shell, and the breech was closed, the charge would sometimes explode spontaneously and blow the heavy breech block backwards, killing and mutilating the crew in the gun pit. If a "premcher" [premature] or a block accident occurred, their effects were devastating and batteries where these had occurred were haunted by the fear of a repetition. In the later part of the war, Blaker became obsessed with such a possibility. Such fears were not unique: "I think I was fed up with having so many close shaves," wrote one gunner, Brown, from hospital to Blaker in 1916. "Somehow that day I sort of felt I should not last the day, but I cannot yet get out of my mind the sight of loaders getting killed so near me the same morning."

Though gunners, who were positioned to the rear of the front lines, were normally less exposed and never had to endure the intense ordeal of an infantry attack "over the top," they had far more extended periods of unrelieved activity so that the strain under which they worked could be as destructive in the long run, as Gilbert Frankau described graphically in *Peter Jackson.*

Blaker first caught up with his battery in mid-July 1916, at Agny ("Agony"), in the Dainville Sector, just south of Arras, in what was said to be "a cushy position," the calmest part of the line from Verdun to the sea. The howitzers were in an old chalk quarry, trained on targets about 2,000 yards away over the crest of the ridge behind which they sheltered from the enemy. Though the battery was "in action," the daily allotment of shells for the battery was sometimes only about 60 rounds. It was a relatively gentle initiation for 2nd Lieut. Blaker, who had a quiet month to get to know his fellow officers in the battery. His routine duties at first seemed more alarming to him than the spent bullets that reached them or the sounds of the German shells exploding with a clang in the paved squares of Arras a few kilometres away. "Crashing Christopher," the very heavy hostile trench mortar facing them, was more frightening but its assaults were infrequent.

58th Brigade R.F.A. was under the overall command of Lieut-Col. (later General) Ormonde de L'Epée Winter D.S.O. "Winter's Group," which included "C" Battery, 133rd Brigade, was supporting the 32nd Infantry Brigade; but this lofty figure, whose closer acquaintance Blaker was eventually to make, was less immediately important to him than the commander of his own "D" Battery: Captain Roberts was a robust, efficient, misleadingly scruffy young man in a worn, leather-patched tunic and wrinkled field boots. He made it his business to see that Blaker was immediately integrated into the group: he introduced him ceremoniously to the crews paraded before their guns, and treated him with polite informality that at the same time implied no relaxation of his own authority. An engineer before the war, Roberts had carried his high professional standards over from civilian life. Enjoying as he did the complete confidence of his men, he bore out the widely-held view that battery commanders interpreted their orders with more independence than the commanders of cavalry squadrons or infantry companies.

Blaker usually got on well with his fellow officers, and subsequently, in *Medal Without Bar*, left memorable portraits, some of which were easy for his former comrades-in-arm to identify twelve years later. Steven "Daddy" Waldron ("Whitelaw"), a white-haired, stocky, peacetime businessman, rapidly established himself as a character in "D" Battery when he joined it after the guns moved, for Blaker's first real battle, to a position on the Somme front. Waldron looked like a (rather unkempt) general and had had more raw experience of life than most generals. This gave him confidence when dealing with the military machine, though he remained for a long time a very junior subaltern. He had no time for staff officers and maintained that all colonels were driven by their desire to gain the C.M.G. (Companion of the Most Distinguished Order of St. Michael and St. George – or "Call me God").

Although stalwart and enterprising, Waldron was dominated by a superstitious conviction that one must never tempt fate by volunteering, nor allow another to take one's place. Fate – or orders – must take their course, or death was certain. This doctrine he propounded to his fellow officers and it was seemingly the only symptom he shared of the strain under which they all operated. Otherwise, he was a humorous and reassuring presence. Waldron survived, and was later awarded the M.C. for digging out, while under heavy shell fire, a fellow officer buried beneath debris.

Another officer Blaker seems to have observed closely, and with liking, was Lieut. Hugh Hope M.C., who was the model for "Reynolds" in *Medal Without Bar*. A few years younger than Richard and barely out of his school, Winchester College, he was witty, warm-hearted, and fond of flaunting his classical and Shakespearian learning, an athletic, high-spirited youth from a military background, who was severely wounded and struck off the strength in June 1917. For four years more he lingered on as an invalid, marrying in 1921 and dying tragically a few months later. It was a story that must have haunted Blaker. In his fictional account of his friend, he spared Hope those last unhappy years, making his protagonist Cartwright loosen the tourniquet on Reynolds' thigh (Reynolds was worse mutilated than Hope), in response to the wounded man's murmured pleadings:

> He . . . must still have had wits enough to wonder what
> would be left of Rennie when two legs had gone, one hand

and an eye – for he said again, "Uncle – oh, God, *must* I . . .
Old doctor *had* to talk big . . ."

Blaker wrote other, harsher vignettes: the unloved Brigade Orderly
Officer, "Gaddy" Monks ("Taffy Dolbey") safely in the rear, toadying
to the Colonel: "Dolbey's foulness and meanness in the art of bullying batmen and cooks, signallers, grooms, and even the Regimental-
Sergeant-Major was, since he had neither wit nor sense, stark genius."
Blaker wondered how he had managed to escape murder earlier, while
the Brigade had been at Gallipoli: "At Suvla, for example, while he was
still with a battery, there must have been a hundred opportunities for a
signaller, writhing in petty humiliation, to close his finger over a rifle
trigger behind sights coldly laid on Taffy's ape-like cranium." Survive,
however, "Gaddy" Monks did, ending with Captain's rank and the M.C.
and earning strong commendation from his superiors for his ingenuity
in keeping effective communications open between 58th Brigade and
16th Division Headquarters on the first day of the battle of Messines, in
June 1917. Although he may have been a better man than Blaker reckoned, he was quickly identified from the portrait in *Medal Without Bar.*
    At the end of August 1916, 58th Brigade R.F.A. were moved, inde-
pendently of 11th Division, to new positions east of Auchonvilliers
("Ocean Villas") to face the German trenches at Beaumont Hamel, one
of their principal strongpoints on the Somme front during the great battle that raged there from July to November. They were now attached to
the 29th Division for the pending offensive, which was launched on 3
September. On the first day "no ground whatever was gained with a
considerable loss of personnel," reported Colonel Winter.
    During these operations, "D" battery was detached from the rest of
the Brigade and engaged in "counterbattery" action. As usual the guns
were located to the rear of the front line, out of sight of their targets, the
necessary information being gathered by officers at a forward observation post and relayed back to the gunners by signallers on "D.3" (later
"D.5") telephone wire, reeled out along the ground. Periodically, too,
one of the subalterns in the battery would be sent up by Brigade on liaison duty with the infantry at the front to see how the field artillery was
shooting – accompanied by signallers and weighed down by a drum of
"D.5." In the middle of a battle this involved considerable risk, particu-

larly during an advance through newly captured enemy trenches. Many lost their lives in this way, and not a few, as Hugh Hope was to do shortly, gained the M.C. or the M.M.

In due course Blaker's brigade moved again, near Thiepval on the same front. On 10 September they were bombarding the "Wonder Work," a key German strongpoint captured a few days later. They dug in briefly at Ovillers, formerly held by the enemy, where Blaker encountered for the first time "the unimagined, peculiarly mawkish stench" of death "that in due course became one with the dust and the fog and the drizzle of the autumn and the winter." The fine white powder from the chalk quickly turned into a grey slime in wet weather, on which carriage wheels slipped as "D" battery made its way south, across the road from Albert to Bapaume. Its new position was at one end of "Sausage Valley," an old no-man's-land area taken at the beginning of the offensive.

Later, from 26 to 30 September, they were involved in the fighting round Thiepval. In *Medal Without Bar* Blaker later described going up to the line near Mouquet ("Mucky") Farm, three miles to the north – long frightening, sodden hours, when the infantry gloomily awaited a counterattack and all the fire of the enemy seemed to be concentrated on the trenches where he carried out his observations: "Bangs and bumps; whirls and snarls; the patter of earth flung high and returning again to earth; the hiss of metal in the air, its hot sizzle as it stabbed the cold pulp of the world." Like Tietjens, Ford's hero in *Parade's End*, he perceived that one of the effects of war was to deprive man of his upright posture: "Man's normal gait now was the gait of his ultimate ancestor – bandy-legged and heavy-footed, crouching forward and lurching, the grimy knuckles of hands within easy touch of the ground to give occasional support and restore balance to his cumbersome body. His visage, too, was ancestral; hairy and foul and leathery, his jowls gone puffy and slack, his parched lips sagging apart from the gleam of his set teeth."

In October the battery moved close to the Somme village of Courcelette, "that Hell hole" deluged by shell fire, where the gun pits were cut into the side of a sunken road and camouflaged. The gunners' perilous position made them indifferent to any danger but enemy shells. Cartridge cases and surplus packets of propellant lined the pits, and they thought nothing of having a lighted brazier, fed with wood from the expensive boxes in which the propellant arrived, within feet of these explosives. The fact that the weather was uncomfortably wet made this seem less of a threat. D.58 were involved in cutting wire and in the gas bombardment during late October. They lost a sergeant and a gunner killed, and a junior subaltern shell-shocked. Six others were injured.

Early in November, they were caught up in the final big Somme battle, at Beaumont Hamel, an objective from the very beginning of the campaign that finally fell to the British on the first day of their advance, 13 November. On 16 and 18 November "D" battery lost men when twice they were caught in explosions from "prematures" occurring in the 18-pounder batteries behind them. Thereafter, as the Somme campaign petered out, the battery established themselves to the south-east of Thiepval. They were to have gone into rest billets but were ordered to stay in the line, with the rest of the 11th Division artillery, until late January when they withdrew to Montigny-les-Jongleurs. By that time, the mud was turning to ice, and the force of the exploding shells, instead of being partly absorbed in the soft earth, propelled the hot steel splinters horizontally "with a crack and a sting on the ear drums' across the hard ground, "skimming like the separate particles of a scythe blade," and adding new terrors to their bleak existence.

Early in February, Blaker was transferred from his battery to Brigade H.Q. as Assistant Orderly Officer, a "cushy" job that gave him the dubious pleasure of watching the obsequious "Gaddy" Monks pouring out mineral water at the beck and call of Col. Winter. It is not clear how long Blaker held this post, the man he replaced having been sent home and struck off the strength.

By March the brigade was on the move along cold and boggy roads, as the ice thawed. D.58, now a six-howitzer battery, was once more in action, pursuing the elusive enemy who were withdrawing rapidly to securer positions along their new "Hindenburg Line." The divisional infantry suffered severe losses. Early in April the brigade had established positions on the Arras front, as part of the great Anglo-French spring offensive. During that bitterly cold Easter of 1917 they occupied trenches at the west foot of Vimy Ridge. The Germans were well dug in on the other side, and protected by a thick barrier of wire. The direct impact fuses on the British shells that had been issued were supposed to make them explode before they entered the ground, and tear through this wire – but they proved ineffective, as massed British cavalry formations, supposedly relieving pressure on the infantry in the direction of Monchy-le-Preux on 11 April, found to their cost. Sixty years later Kenneth Davies, one of the gunners in "D" battery, wrote, "I can even now picture the remnants of the cavalry coming back after their failure to find a way through the barrier."

Brigade diaries chronicle the gradual attrition of its numbers. On 10 April one of the howitzers was destroyed by a premature. A major disaster came when Captain Roberts was severely wounded by a shell splinter, after trying to get a gun out of a shell-hole on 16 April. He was awarded the M.C.

Later, during the bombardment of Wytschaete, in Flanders, on 3 June, another howitzer received a direct hit and in the course of the highly successful Messines attack that followed, on 7 June, there was further destruction. A German high-velocity gun inflicted severe damage on brigade wagon lines in the early hours of 20 June and enemy bombs accounted for more casualties on 26 June. Lieut. Hope's disastrous injuries followed a few days later. Meanwhile the battle itself, which seemed a spectacular success, proved a false dawn for the British army. With its guns ranged in a long line, almost wheel to wheel, along the front, the Royal Artillery achieved at Messines a high degree of cooperation with the infantry, to an extent hardly seen since the first months of the war; but the great Flanders campaign that followed the triumph of Messines was one of the most dispiriting and disagreeable the British army ever fought.

At the end of July 58th Brigade R.F.A. were in the thick of the Third Battle of Ypres, occupying old German concrete "pill boxes" on Pilkem Ridge, an exposed position overlooked by the Germans entrenched at Poelcapelle or in their observation balloons. Later the battery's guns were sited on the inundated east bank of the Steenbeck. In that nightmare landscape of mud and shell-holes under a lightless autumn sky, Blaker willingly faced whipping bullets and flying splinters on liaison trips to the front rather than stay in the gun pits where, his fraying nerves told him, he might at any moment meet his end from a shell exploding in a gun barrel. Other symptoms told of his fatigue and the lack of fresh vegetables in the army diet – pyorrhoea of the gums, boils on the buttocks and round the waist, trench fever. He went on leave from the battery and subsequently was posted to Palestine.

Blaker's move east gave a welcome respite, although it separated him from the band of men with whom danger had driven him to forge so close a bond. He was attached to another battery, where he quickly formed friendships, and was sent back with his new unit to France, following the Germans' successful March 1918 offensive that drove the Allied forces back as much as twenty-five miles along the northern French front.

Although the Germans were finally forced into retreat, the last months of the war were some of the toughest. Blaker was gassed more than once and by August his health was once again deteriorating. It never really recovered. At the beginning of October, his battery commander, Hugh Stevenson, released him, still a subaltern, to service in the rear with the Divisional Ammunition Column, paying tribute to the exceptional effort that Blaker had made to keep going. Very soon after, he was sent to a hospital in Southall, close to London but still a rural village surrounded by cornfields. Mamie, her mother, and his daughter Betty, now five years old, all moved nearby, temporarily, and they were able to celebrate the Armistice together. He was demobilised early in 1919. Briefly during that year he returned to digs in Oxford to complete his mandatory residence period at the university, which had been interrupted earlier by his domestic complications.

He now had to support not only Betty and Mamie but also his mother-in-law. Stanley Blaker had decided not to encumber himself with further responsibility for them and had resumed his highly successful career leaving Mamie to her own devices. She had money of her own (£600 a year) from her father, to keep them going, though at a much lower level than either of them desired, until Richard achieved the literary success for which they confidently hoped. He took a job as a schoolteacher in Southampton. He hated it, and gave it up in 1920.

In 1919, Mamie finally divorced Stanley, who, perhaps to spare her from scandal, perhaps to avoid responsibility for Betty, agreed to let her do so, risking his own reputation. However there was an obstacle to her marrying Richard. At the time, a wedding between a nephew and an aunt, even though unconnected by blood, was still illegal. So in 1921 they had to travel to the U.S.A. to marry in Michigan, a state where this law did not apply, in Mount Clemens, which had been the scene of Mamie's parents' wedding many years before. Through his Queen's College friend, the American Wendell Herrbruck, Blaker gained a job as British agent for a surgical glove firm in Canton, Ohio, the Wilson Rubber Company. This brought in income but not happiness. Though a good salesman, Blaker neglected the business, proving a disappointment to Wilson Rubber even after they put him in charge of a new branch factory in Slough. Indeed until the midthirties, when he sold off his interest, it was Mamie who had to deal with emergencies, including a strike (which she quelled). Yet he could not bring himself to admit that she should be given full-time charge of the factory, which would have done much to bolster her increasingly fragile self-esteem.

The truth was that the war had left a profound mark upon both of them. Blaker's health had been undermined. Psychologically too, he was seriously affected, as he immediately came to recognise. In common with his companions, he had suffered the shocks of losing, one after another, those who had been close to him – like Edgar Perham, killed at Delville Wood – and of witnessing horrific incidents that tortured his memory. In *Medal Without Bar* he later described a gunner carrying his forearm, still connected to his shoulder by one strand of nerve and an intact artery, while the rest of his upper arm, bone and flesh, had been torn away by a shell; others, sightless, roasted to the ribcage, or with their brains dripping from open skulls; and an Australian, with a broken back, the inner edge of his thighs burnt away when he was jammed by falling masonry against a red-hot stove. On top of this had been the nervous strain of long months of danger; and, upon return home, the abrupt termination of being one of a brotherhood-in-arms. Blaker instinctively coped with these various violent assaults on his emotional stability by detaching himself. Like others, he had exhausted his capacity to feel intensely: as he said in *Medal Without Bar*, through one of his mouthpieces, the high-strung, heroic young subaltern Reynolds, when the brigade, worn out after the Somme battle, are visited by a powerful nervous reaction:

> "If we get through to the end – out of the other valleys and tribulations as we've got through this lot – there won't be a damned thing left in the world to upset us, and excite us, and make us get the wind up. I dare say we'll be able to smile at

things, now and again; but it'll take a hell of a lot to get a tear out of us . . ." These are they which came out of great tribulation . . . the generation of the broken-hearted.

This gulf of experience separated Mamie from her husband just at the moment when she desperately wanted to be close to him after what she herself had been through during the past years: her father's murder, marital unhappiness, scandal, fear that Richard might be killed. As for him, his ordeal had left him almost unable to face life. In the end, his intellect and her determination saved him. She continued to cope, with enterprise and spirit, but one of the great disappointments of their married life was that she had to put aside her singing ambitions. Her young husband, for all his sensitivity, had no interest in music, and her time was taken up largely with making a home for him and their child. The deep undercurrent of frustration in their relationship might have been eased had he actively encouraged her to revive her musical interests and asserted his own views about where and how they should live. She tended to put these above the needs of his social life. Besides, her nature was to want him more to herself after the deep hurt of the breakup of her first marriage.

Blaker now had to find work and an outlet for his talents. It was not long before he was writing short stories, one of which, "Identity Discs," was accepted by Hilaire Belloc's wartime journal, *Land and Water*, still being published during 1919, the same paper that serialised, in that year, Gilbert Frankau's famous novel of the Royal Artillery, *Peter Jackson, Cigar Merchant*. Through his Queen's College contemporary, Louis Golding, Blaker also made contact with Arnold Bennett, whose welcome encouragement as an eminent literary figure included introducing him to his own literary agent, J. B. Pinker, and to Pinker's son, a former gunner officer. Lieut. Eric Pinker M.C. had been temporarily a special officer with Blaker's brigade H.Q. Eric's long, and later unhappy, professional relationship with Blaker thus had roots in their common wartime experience.

Louis Golding, like Dick, had strong ambitions as a writer. Bad lungs had prevented him from joining the army, but being adventurous and patriotic, he got out to the Western Front and Salonika by working with

the Y.M.C.A. In 1919, he brought out a talented collection of war poems, *Sorrow of War*, which included moving verses about his brother Jack,
killed in the spring of 1918.

When he was nineteen, Golding had made friends in Manchester
with an attractive and cultivated widow, Agnes Louise Owen, and her
young family. She took an interest in his talents, and after they moved to
London in 1917, invited him to live with them there. She had four children of whom the eldest, May, was the same age as Golding. Significantly
for the future, the Owens also became close friends of Blaker. In 1920
"Zzo" (Louis's facetious shortening of "Mrs. Owen") married an Oxford
contemporary of his, the orientalist Neville Whymant. Established in
London, and becoming friendly with a circle that included well-known
figures such as Arnold Bennett and Rebecca West, Golding found an entrée into a successful literary world, which boded well for both his own
and Blaker's prospects as writers.

There was a brief interlude when Richard and Mamie tried living in
Steele's Studios, a nineteenth-century mews converted into artists' quarters in Hampstead, North London. Quite soon, however, Mamie came
to the conclusion that it was too expensive, and that her husband was being distracted from his writing by the social life to which he took so
easily. There was the temptation for him to revert to heavy drinking
habits acquired in the war to cope with strain, and to counteract the evil
furred taste that gas and the smell of death left on the tongue, as *Medal
Without Bar* suggests. Besides, Mamie did not feel at home with many of
their new literary acquaintances, such as John Galsworthy, who seemed
to her both aloof and overcurious about her life story.

This aversion included even Blaker's close friend Louis Golding, who
in her eyes appeared cliquish and dangerously bohemian, with his interest in boxing and boxers and his beer parties at Whipsnade zoo. In fact,
Golding was a far from insensitive or aggressive man. He was memo-
rable-looking, short, burly, and very dark, with thick eyebrows and
piercing brown eyes. His manner was self-deprecating, quiet, and ironical. Though witty and good company, he was a listener rather than a
talker. During the early twenties he suffered a nervous and physical crisis
connected partly with his lung trouble and partly with his family relationships, and his difficulties at that time in trying to become an author,
but also by way of reaction to the intensity and strangeness of the war

years. He was resilient, however, and achieved notable success as a writer. Mamie was not an admirer of his books, which, as they flowed off his pen, he would sometimes read aloud to the Blakers. Richard's devotion to his friend included – a few years later – taking time off to revise the manuscript of his best-selling novel *Magnolia Street*.

Golding's descriptions of Manchester Jewish life were in fact extraordinarily observant, thanks to his obsessive interest in human detail, clothes, mannerisms, and social nuances. In this, his works influenced Blaker. They were painted on a broad canvas, ranging from Russia to the United States, though their central focus was the Cheetham Hill area of Manchester. Like the works of Golding's friend Arnold Bennett, they had an intense sense of local history and atmosphere; there was also a Dickensian quality about the boldly sketched characters and his involvement with them. He was strongly drawn to beauty and charm, in both sexes, as equally he was repelled by the ugliness of greed and intolerance. It was this open partiality and a note of mockery in his highly-flavoured prose that Mamie disliked. This was a legitimate criticism, though such faults were outweighed by his masterly evocation of a world that had already begun to disappear. More memorably than any other English writer (except Henry Williamson and Gordon Stowell, in his novel of Yorkshire and the war, *The History of Button Hill*) Golding has drawn a picture of how the First World War affected a particular local community, with its vignettes of grief, anti-German hatred, worship of local war heroes; shirkers, conscientious objectors, profiteers, wronged soldier husbands, and sailors home from sea.

Personal feelings apart, however, Mamie's main concern was to ensure that her husband led the peaceful existence he needed to write. She herself wrote novels – romantic, quite daring for their time, and poetical – which received good reviews. She looked after Blaker admirably, having a gift for living with a certain style on a small income. Although not domesticated, she was an excellent cook. Soon they moved to the country and cultivated quiet country pursuits. Blaker, when not at work, busied himself with making and repairing furniture, reading, and painting – even earning money as a commercial artist. He was also a proficient golfer and dressed stylishly for the course. His daughter, who grew up happily in these surroundings, enjoyed riding, but he himself never rode or helped with the horses. He had too many painful memories of shooting wounded and terminally exhausted animals during the war. At times his Brigade had operated with as many as 140 animals under strength.

All writers have their quirks. Louis Golding, for example, would go into the garden with a band round his eyes so as to concentrate entirely on what was going on in his head. Blaker used goose quills, which he cut himself, to write his manuscripts in a small, neat, italic hand. He employed the same disciplined approach that he had applied to his gunnery duties: every day he would begin his writing at the same hour, and just before he paused finally, he would indicate, in his last sentences, the direction in which he wished to take the story the next day.

His health steadily improved. Though they had made many friends in their early years of marriage, there were few parties and no drink in the house. Under this new regime he kept sober. In 1930, the arrival of an opinionated seventeen-year-old second cousin, Larry Durrell, while they were living in the New Forest, was more of a nuisance than a diversion. For several weeks Durrell occupied, in unwashed squalor, the caravan where Blaker did his writing, then departed for Corfu without either the toiling Blaker or the future author of the *Alexandria Quartet* doing anything to influence each other. Betty's early relations with her parents were intensely affectionate, and the only sign of tension was Mamie's frequent desire to move house – going from Southampton to Chipping Campden in Gloucestershire, then to New Milton in Hampshire (where they found a good school for Betty), and subsequently, in the early 1930s, to the Slough neighbourhood so as to be near the American glove firm that Blaker was managing.

The first book Blaker offered to a publisher was "The Molehilleer," which he completed in 1920. It revealed defects in his writing that he never altogether cured throughout his career, even in books of greatly superior literary quality. In addition to its obscure title, it was too long, and over influenced, as one friend pointed out, by "the later manner of Arnold Bennett" – the inflation of minor incident and the lack of major incident. Finally it was a little lacking in humour. Pinker urged his friend, "Don't be too serious, old thing, and give your conscience an afternoon off." It was turned down successively by Heinemann, Sidgwick and Jackson, and Mills and Boon. Pinker implored Richard not to despair: "Stick it, the gunners," must be his motto.

His next book, *The Voice in the Wilderness*, was a success, selling over

8,000 copies; but *Geoffrey Castleton, Passenger*, a rewrite of "The Mole-hilleer," which Mamie persuaded Cape to take, sold under a thousand. Cape now had cold feet about paying Blaker a three-year salary for further novels, which he had suggested. Disappointed, he took his next book, *Oh the Brave Music*, to Hodder and Stoughton, who offered a far higher royalty. The book's theme was the postwar career of a captain in the merchant navy. Neither this, nor his subsequent work, *Enter a Messenger* (also about a war veteran, trying to make a fortune in the U.S.A.) did outstandingly well. As before, the money came to the Blakers in dribs and drabs. The fifth book, the oddly named *Scabby Dichson*, his semiautobiographical tale of Indian childhood and youth, had a poignancy and charm lacking in his earlier works and its sales (3,200 in all) disappointed Blaker. However, it attracted fans who looked out eagerly for his next work.

Following *The Umpire's Game* (1929), which suffered a similar fate, came Blaker's first real triumph, *Medal Without Bar* (1930). In addition to tapping his personal store of war memories, he did a great deal of research for this book. He was by inclination an historical scholar with an obsessive concern for detail. In the *Observer*, Louis Golding once described him as "the gadget emperor." Some, indeed, felt that his passion for technical information, like Arnold Bennett's, interfered with his narrative. However this is what makes *Medal Without Bar*, to this day, invaluable to students of the Great War – quite as much as Mottram's *Spanish Farm Trilogy*.

Although written in Blaker's early middle age and dealing with the life of a relatively elderly subaltern, the book is only at first glance a middle-aged view of the war. It is a good deal less dispassionate than Mottram's work. Coming as it did at the height of the antiwar-novel fashion, this is not surprising, though Blaker never concerned himself with questioning the reasons for the war nor decried military virtues. After he launched into writing it, however, there were many who were apprehensive. For example, when, through a friend in the Civil Service, he gained access to official War Office casualty figures for the war, month by month, he was warned that on no account was he to use the information as "materials for any attack on our Army or its leaders, such as has been so commonly made, substantiated by totals of casualties as if battles were lost and won thereby."

Particularly striking were the efforts made by Blaker's publisher, Ralph Hodder-Williams, to purge it of its "disenchanted" elements. Despite the exceptional success of *All Quiet on the Western Front* and *Goodbye to All That*, Hodder-Williams did not want his publishing house to be associated with sensational antiwar literature. Himself a veteran, wounded on the Somme, Hodder-Williams regarded Blaker's Chapter 47 (quoted on p. 356) as "the noblest thing that has been written about the war," and was determined that nobody else, including "Aunt Janes," should think otherwise of the book. First, he got him to trim a few "bloodys" and "Christs" though Blaker refused to go all the way in this direction. "His arse from his elbow" was altered, ingeniously, to "his ears from his elbow." "We are very proud of our reputation," remarked Hodder-Williams when requesting this change. He also persuaded Blaker to remove a contemptuous reference to the author "Sapper" (Cyril McNeile) as the purveyor of a self-consciously tough view of the fighting. "Sapper," said Hodder-Williams, was a friend and might well review the book.

The publisher was disquieted by the antistaff remarks by characters like Whitelaw (Waldron) in the book, complaining that Richard seemed to show personal ill feeling towards everyone who was not in the firing line. Hodder-Williams also disliked the suggestion that soldiers sometimes murdered their officers which Blaker made (see above) with reference to "Taffy" Dolbey. Blaker ignored this objection as well as the query Hodder-Williams raised about another character, the sodden Lieut. "Voo Voo" Parley: "Can you indicate by a parenthesis of some kind that this sort of drunken swine was really extraordinarily rare considering the number of people involved and the strain they were under? You have no idea," he added, referring to R.C. Sherriff's controversial recent play, "what terrible offence *Journey's End* has given – and terrible pain too, which is a great deal more important – I think you will agree that the chronic alcoholic was extraordinarily rare."

He was most upset of all by Blaker's claim that there was little prospect of promotion for long-serving subalterns later in 1918 because hosts of captains and majors whose service had been "years of health-giving rest or rest-giving employments" began to creep out at the end of the war to be "in at the death." "It is by far the bitterest thing you say in the whole book . . . are you sure you are right?" he pleaded. "It would be very hard to imagine anything more bitter. It definitely puts these fellows on a lower moral scale, in my mind, than the conscientious objector, and in my mind – I make no bones about it – the conscientious objector is pretty low." Although Blaker made some modifications, he retained the essence of the passage as it had first been written.

Blaker felt that his first duty was to tell the story of an artilleryman's war truly, as he had experienced it. If his old comrades had said bitter things, then these must be on record. When men were being put to the test in combat it was all too easy to spot those who were making sure they had an easy time, because everyone had *thought* of doing so themselves; and if a general seemed patronising and smug and out of touch, that was not the cruellest or harshest thing that could be said of a fellow-human; General Lamont, whom he portrayed in *Medal Without Bar*, was all these things but was, as Blaker admitted, a kindly and decent sort of fellow. The book is unillusioned, but is not cynical or self-pitying. It is a book for soldiers, expressing the feelings of gunners in the war and stressing their comradeship.

Hodder-Williams, however, begged Richard to look to a wider audience, and he later said that a less specialised approach would have reached a larger slice of the very important female section of the novel-buying public. He may have been right with regard to sales; but Blaker received letters from ex-gunners over the next few years made him feel that he had taken the right course: "May I say that you have 'hit the nail on the head' with regards to the moral contained in *Medal Without Bar*?" wrote one, G. W. Andrews, as late as February 1939. "Such comradeship and self-sacrifice was the one inspiring feature that was shown and could only be shown by the catastrophe of the war." This was typical of many.

For Blaker himself, the purpose of the book went beyond that: its starting point was his own and his comrades' relationship with the normal world after the war. What was left to them? "It is possibly the point of the book that even the remote and dying memory of this sweat and crucifixion places old Cartwright [his protagonist] a little beyond the tears and excitement and alarms and excursions of other souls . . . And of course there is some glamour too." His friend Roy Bower, whom he often consulted, observed that all Blaker's books appeared to have one central theme – of a man saying: "I haven't got what I want, I don't know what I want, I didn't know what I wanted, if I got what I wanted, would I have got anything?" It is probable that the war was one of the origins of this unresolved frame of mind; of his yearning for what was lost and his remoteness, his disengagement from the worst and best of what was there. It is probable, too, that this very state of mind – which he was so anxious to explore – was in part responsible for the real limitation of the book – a lack of intensity, save in the most painful passages, which distances a modern reader from it. One also senses here a defensive armour was forged long before the war, in the conflicts of his childhood, and showed itself in the typically English reticence of his class. It was not the same as serenity, and time was to tell how thin this armour had become. Meanwhile, for the first time he had received enthusiastic critical attention.

Admittedly, the success of *Medal Without Bar* was nothing compared with that of *Way of Revelation*, *Simon Called Peter*, or any of the major sellers examined in this volume. At first it looked as if it would be eclipsed by the other works launched early in 1930, of which the best was *Her Privates We*, an expurgated version of Frederic Manning's *The Middle Parts of Fortune*, which, as has been argued earlier, was the finest British novel about the infantry to emerge from the interwar period. Although without the occasional sentimental passage to be found in Blaker's book, it was written from much the same viewpoint – sceptical, frank, ironical, and loyal to the British soldiery. Neither work has the self-centred quality of, for example, Gilbert Frankau's *Peter Jackson*, though for authentic detail about the artilleryman's war the latter work comes close at times to matching *Medal Without Bar*.

Making a simultaneous appearance was *All Our Yesterdays*, by H. M. Tomlinson, who had been a correspondent on the Western Front. This took a long, detached view of the conflict in its historical context. *Retreat*, by another artilleryman, C. R. Benstead, also came out in 1930, and told the horrifying story of a clergyman's ordeal and breakdown when attached to an artillery brigade during the March 1918 retreat. Reviewers considered its callous tone more shocking and dangerous than that of Blaker's book. These included the Rev. "Tubby" Clayton, the influential founder of "Toc H" (Talbot House) the wartime Anglican organisation for soldiers behind the British lines in the Belgian town of Poperinghe.

Hodder-Williams's initial fears that *Medal Without Bar* would fail proved wrong. The reviews were almost uniformly favourable. They particularly stressed its lack of sensationalism and its emphasis on the companionship among the soldiers. According to *John O'London's* it was "a welcome antidote to the filth and blasphemy." "It will surely live on, when uglier parodies are faded," Tubby Clayton told Blaker: "This is, at last, the comradeship caught on the canvas by a loving and gifted brush."

What Clayton approved of was its tone rather than its content. It actually has more horrific detail than any other account of the First World War. To find passages as blood-curdling one would have to go to books written about the Second World War, like *The Cruel Sea* or *The White Rabbit*. But in the former case the horror is intensified by a sadistic quality in the writer, and this is lacking in Blaker, while in the latter it is compounded by the moral revulsion that any account of the Nazi concentration camps must arouse. Blaker did not shock many people, not even, it would appear, with the contentious passages that Hodder-Williams disliked. Perhaps he did not shock enough. He might have been better remembered if he had.

His sales were satisfying, even if they did not match those of more "antiwar" writers such as Robert Graves or Richard Aldington. With reprints, Blaker's eventually came close to the 15,000 mark. The book did well in the British Empire, and it gained him more fan letters than he received for even his later, better-selling books. Most of the fan mail, naturally, was from ex-servicemen, but *Medal Without Bar* was also enjoyed by clergymen, young people, and women – the latter including the successful writer E. Arnot Robertson. However it was a flop in the U.S.A. – unsurprisingly so, for it was too downbeat in style. Ullstein Verlag, the German publisher of *All Quiet on the Western Front*, refused it.

Blaker's next literary venture was a minutely researched and original novel, *The Needle-Watcher* (1932), based on the true story of the Elizabethan navigator Will Adams, who guided a Dutch merchantman to Japan and laid the foundations of a new Japanese navy. Heinemann accepted it and, before the war, it made a respectable sale of 7,000 copies. Mamie launched *The Needle-Watcher* with a party at the Hotel Rembrandt, London, attended by prominent literary figures and representatives of the Japanese Embassy. Traditionally-dressed Japanese women served *sake*, and there were displays by Japanese swordsmen and wrestlers.

With *Here Lies a Most Beautiful Lady* (1935) Blaker joined the best-selling authors. Based on the life of his mother-in-law, Julia, the novel began, dramatically, with the scenes leading up to her husband's murder in Russia, and then told the story of how Blaker's father-in-law, James MacGarvey ("John Billiter"), had come to marry her and make his fortune in the New World. The central figure was a close – and fond – portrait of Julia MacGarvey. It is easy to see why this was Blaker's most successful book, even though it was not his best. It was fluently written, the subject matter was attractive, and the clichés and embarrassing phrases struck the right popular note for the time. Above all it was a vehicle for his ability to convey historical change. It became a Book Society Choice for 1935, which boosted sales, by 1937, to around twenty-eight and a half thousand. The sequel, *But Beauty Vanishes* (1936), which contained chapters on the war and service in the Royal Garrison Artillery, was also a solid success with around sixteen thousand sold worldwide.

Blaker was by now something of a literary celebrity. As well as the success of his books, he was beginning to gain a niche in a new medium, writing scripts for an English film company, Denham Studios. Psychologically, all this altered his perspective. He was no longer dependent on Mamie. He was confident that he could go on earning a good income. He could give his family what they needed, and in return he felt he could fairly enjoy more liberty and social life. He spent an increasing amount of time in London away from his wife. It was unfortunate that their circle had narrowed since the early years of their marriage when they had seen a good deal of fellow-writers like Thornton Wilder and Laurence Housman – not to mention Louis Golding. By moving away from Gloucestershire because of Betty's schooling, they had effectively cut themselves off for much of the time from the interesting friends who lived there.

Now their marriage was put to the test, and neither proved able to sustain it. Having done much to bring about her husband's success, Mamie had a proprietary interest in it. She was bitterly upset when he said of his work, "The baby's grown up now," feeling that she was being

discarded. Had she been content to let him live more of his life independently, it is likely she would have kept him. For the break, when it came,
was acutely painful to him. It is probable that at this stage he began to
drink heavily again – in secret, mostly. There seems to have been a temporary separation in September 1935 and he was discussing the
possibility of divorce in the spring of 1936.

The break was finally precipitated by his involvement with Louis
Golding's sister by adoption, May Owen. Shy and unselfish, May had
been in love with him for many years. On his part, touched by her devoted friendship, his liking for her developed into feelings of attraction.
She was small, highly intelligent, with an agreeable figure and an appeal-
ing face. Above all she was quiet and made few demands. Socially Blaker
may have been seeking variety, but emotionally he desired a rest. The letters they exchanged showed the depth of their feelings for one another;
but their love was above all gentle and measured.

There were many who felt he had taken a long time to arrive at a
truth that had been all too evident to them for years. These included his
own brother, Eric, as well as Wendell Herrbruck and Louis Golding.
Others, after he left his family, were very distressed and urged him to return. Half of him wished to do so. Though his daughter, Betty, was now
twenty-one, and largely independent, she had been very close to him,
and by his desertion he risked losing her affection too. Besides, Mamie's
devotion and vital influence, whatever others said, had enabled him to
write successfully. With that influence withdrawn, who could say what
would happen? His turmoil after the break made it hard for him to concentrate. Two things, however, prevented any return to his wife: his new
loyalty to May, who had risked a serious rift with her own family over
the affair, and the conviction that if he returned to his wife he would live
forever in an atmosphere of jealousy with less liberty than ever. He did
his wife an injustice, for she had a large nature, but her dread of rejection
made her, now, seem overpossessive.

For a time Blaker achieved a kind of peace in Water Lane Cottage, the
small red-brick sixteenth-century house that he and May rented together. It was in Bovingdon, to the northwest of London, two miles
from Pamela Hinkson's old home at Chipperfield. Now a suburbanised
commuter-land, the village was then in the heart of the wooded Hertfordshire countryside, remote from the nearest railway station.

There, during 1937, Blaker and May gardened, played golf, exercised their beagle, and entertained friends from London. For a time, too, they were *in loco parentis* to two Jewish refugee boys from Germany who were being educated in England, like those described in Louis Golding's *Mr. Emmanuel*, and who subsequently went over to the New World.

Blaker had been under contract with Heinemann since 1935 to produce a book a year, in the next three years, with advances of £400, £200, and £100 respectively; the second and third advances were to be doubled if the first reached its advance, and if it failed to do so, the balance was to be subtracted from the payments for the subsequent books. It was an uncertain arrangement, but the success of *But Beauty Vanishes* (which was also a Book Society Choice – something of a record) gave both publisher and author confidence. Heinemann reissued cheap editions of most of his books.

His next offering, though, did not attract his publisher. It was the fictionalised life of King David, *David of Judah*. It was based on a theory of Blaker's that the tribe of Judah had been a fanatical freebooting mountain people – somewhat similar to Pathan hillmen – who came to political maturity by prolonged warfare with the rich tribes of the plain. He drew on his war experience for his descriptions of the Palestinian landscape and for his vivid accounts of raids against the enemy. Unfortunately, though highly ingenious, the book was too idiosyncratic. He wrote much of it as he would have talked about the subject, racily to Louis Golding, the dedicatee. Goliath and his relatives were described as "a freak family . . . a loutish lot of zanies"; the men of Judah were involved in "a racket"; while King David wondered if he should "spill the beans" to Uriah the Hittite about his affair with Bath-Sheba. There was little of the feeling of romantic remoteness to appeal to readers. The book found a small publisher, Nisbet, in England and, as *Thou Art the Man*, it appeared under an American imprint, both in 1937. Panned by critics, it sank, hardly a copy sold. It was a highly original book, which deserved a better fate.

The next book was almost as much of a disaster. Heinemann accepted *On Pegasus He Rode*, and paid him, in the end, a £400 advance, though they liked neither the book nor the title. The latter was changed, in the English edition, to *Love Went a-Riding*. The sales were poor – some 2,000 to 3,000 in Britain and the U.S.A., when sales of 8,000 were needed to recoup their expenditure. Blaker blamed lack of publicity, and certainly Heinemann did little for the book, but it was not likely to achieve a great success.

Love Went a-Riding was another novel of Blaker's about the long-term effects of the war. The main character was a dashing forty-year-old ex-artillery officer with a glorious war career and a leftover life to kill. Blaker drew Kenneth Cresswell (not unlike an older version of Kenneth Chacey, in Oliver Onions' *Peace in Our Time*) as one of "the generation of the brokenhearted," who found it impossible to engage with anyone at a serious emotional level, and went on occasional, terrifying alcoholic jags – drawn from Blaker's personal experience at the time. The book was an excellent realistic study of alcoholism and its consequences. It contained characters based partly on his daughter, Betty, and on May Owen.

Blaker was bitterly disappointed by its failure. The need to repeat his success of earlier years had become increasingly pressing. He had settled a proportion of all his earnings on Mamie, by creating a "Richard Blaker Trust" to administer on her behalf the funds paid to it. Louis Golding helpfully put up a guarantee of £400. Mamie was entitled to redress if the sums of money paid to her fell below a prescribed minimum and it was not long before she had to use this power, though without result, but Mamie had no intention, at this time, of divorcing him. He and May decided therefore to go to Hollywood. He had long hoped that he could find, like other English writers, rich pickings in the form of script-writing contracts over there. At the same time, he would be able to get a divorce in Reno and marry May. Above all, he wanted to set a distance between himself and Mamie. He believed that if he stayed in England he would fail altogether, "sinking deeper and deeper," as he later wrote, "into misery and sterile desperation."

"Don't let Hollywood 'get you,'" warned his American publisher, Lynn Carrick, however, "I've seen its insidious effect upon a number of otherwise intelligent writing chaps . . . . It's a good place to raid for loot and then make one's escape." In the spring of 1938 they arrived in California.

Blaker's trouble was "that he was too gentle and unselfish not to suffer and be taken advantage of in a pretty rough world," as Eric Pinker, his English agent for nearly twenty years put it. He was well aware that even with an agent working very hard for him he faced formidable competition in films, from many better-known English writers, such as Richard Aldington, Grahame Greene, Somerset Maugham, H. G. Wells, P. G. Wodehouse, and J. B. Priestley.

The divorce in Reno, on grounds of mental cruelty, in January 1938, was quickly enough achieved. It was of course not recognised in Britain, which prevented him from returning, after their marriage, as May's husband. From then on, his path proved increasingly difficult. As it happened, he and Eric Pinker, who was now in charge of the New York offshoot of the Pinker agency, finally fell out over the management of his film affairs, which Blaker wished to put in other hands. He also tried to end his association with the London branch of the agency under Eric's brother Ralph. He had assessed the position rightly. In 1939 Eric Pinker was briefly arrested on suspicion of larceny because he had kept large sums from authors to meet debts, while by 1941 Ralph Pinker, who was in much the same case, was to be declared bankrupt.

Added to Blaker's anxieties about finding employment was the necessity of extending his visitor's permit to the U.S.A. It had never been his intention to stay indefinitely – rather, to make money quickly and build up contacts so that he could return on later occasions with a sure prospect of work. His resources were dwindling. He had to give up the cottage in England. Nothing more could be hoped from *Love Went a-Riding* in Britain, nor were its prospects better in the U.S.A. (despite fan letters from reformed alcoholics). His hopes of film versions of his books had faded, and the script-writing jobs he found were never enough to support him and May. By late spring of 1938, Mamie was receiving no money from him, and was relying for income on the sparse proceeds of a boarding house she ran in Slough. In the last year, Blakey complained in August, he had picked up a mere six months' worth of work. *Strange Family*, his cooperative venture at a play version of *The Voice in the Wilderness*, made him only £12 3s 6d. when it was staged for a week in London that November.

Finally, however, good luck seemed to have arrived when he was given a contract with Selznick International Studios to write the original story for a film of the *Titanic* disaster, to be directed by Alfred Hitchcock. "On promises and verbal inducements, backed up by great publicity, I did twelve weeks of work for £100, which all went, of course, to England," he told his brother. Then, in December 1938, the job was cancelled. David O. Selznick evidently did not much care for Blaker's treatment for the movie; but in any case, as he himself told Blaker, he had decided to give priority to what was to be his own greatest success of all, *Gone With The Wind*.

Blaker was now desperate. His health was deteriorating, "If starvation had been possible we would therefore have starved," he told his brother. 1939 brought no new hope, except that Mamie, hearing he was ill, generously dropped legal proceedings against him: "SICK MANS GRAPES PEACE RECOVER" she telegrammed, adding later, pathetically: "ONLY LOVE HOPING." He had nothing, however, to offer her. The various projects in which he was involved all evaporated. Eric Pinker's arrest threw him into a panic. He tried repeatedly and unsuccessfully to sell short stories and reactivate old ideas such as a "peace pamphlet" he had written months before. His ambitious proposal for a fictionalised life of the Duke of Windsor was also rejected. His best hope was "two unfinished but tremendously attractive nonsenses" he was working into films with the brilliant young humorous actor Robert Morley.

Another actor and writer, Gerald Savory, was helping him to adapt *Love Went a-Riding* as a play. That scheme progressed slowly. Savory was cheerful, and kindly loaned him $750; but he urged him to be patient. Blaker, however, had no mood between optimism and despair. "Everything . . . every damned one thing after another," he told Louis Golding, "seems to have crumpled up and failed." He could not return to England, as May's family were urging: "Coming back face to face with the present thwarted emptiness would set me back – not only financially, but spiritually and artistically – for years if not for a lifetime." He dreaded anything that might spoil his relationship with May ("Biddy") that had grown "more comely every day." All they needed to complete their happiness was a lucky break. As it was she was showing "terrific (even when sometimes, a little wan) courage and good humour and confidence," and had become a loved and welcomed figure in the circles in which they moved.

By August, however, he was once more in despair. He and May were down to their last few dollars. He was completely dependent on a Hollywood writer friend, Bob Lee, for a roof over his head (at Malibu Beach) and daily expenses. He was tortured with guilt about Mamie who had forborne to ask for further money. He was exhausted by "non-stop self-

salesmanship" and churning out short stories without certainty of publication. He suffered from daily headaches, high blood pressure, and
kidney trouble. On top of this he was terrified that "Biddy" would leave
him and return to England to be with her family "in the firing line" now
that war, by August 1939, seemed imminent. He begged Louis Golding
to send him $500 to meet immediate debts, and if his publishers were
unable to subsidise his next book, to finance him to the tune of $250 a
month while it was being written. He felt he ought perhaps to be back
in England serving his country. If he made the trip back, perhaps Louis
would be kind enough to find him a War Office propaganda or writing
job on the strength of *Medal Without Bar* – "for you, laddie," he told
Golding, "will be a very big shot."

These wild pleas were a measure of the fantasy world in which he
now lived. Louis Golding did his best, but as he explained, he was by no
means confident that his good luck as an author would hold and he had
lately been asked by Blaker's banker to honour his guarantee of £400 to
the Richard Blaker Trust. However, he now offered £100 in instalments,
and suggested that Blaker should go and write his novel at the California
farm where May's uncle George lived. He had no influence in the War
Office, and as for Blaker writing "a war book," he was sceptical: "Dick
darling, do you mean about the last war or this war? It's a bloody truth,
but the last war is now considerably deader than mutton" – an assess-
ment that, for publishers, was to prove correct over the next two
decades.

With autumn, hope returned. Blaker signed a contract with his new
American publisher, Morrow, to write "a romantic tale of behind the
scenes" in Reno, entitled "I, Said the Fly." They offered terms that would
free him from the frustrations of soliciting film work while engaged on
the novel.

His health, however, was no better. His lungs, permanently damaged
by gas, were congested, and his self-medication, "crushed lime and soda"
(with the probable addition of gin), was hardly effective. Though still elegantly dressed, he had begun to look old for his forty-six years. Once
again, too, he was faced with the anxiety of renewing his permit to remain in California – and this time he needed to apply for permanent
residence or he would have to leave by March of the following year. He
worked away at the novel while Wendell Herrbruck, who, as a lawyer,

had some influence, tried to persuade the authorities to grant his friend a residence permit. Clearly, however, Blaker was too overwrought to write well. His publishers were disappointed by the early chapters of "I, Said the Fly" – which seemed to be all about England, not Reno, and rambled on in an overleisurely fashion.

Then, in mid-January 1940, he collapsed with hypertensive heart disease. He was rushed into the Good Samaritan Hospital in Los Angeles. His only hope of survival, wrote his doctor, was several months confined to his bed. Taking pity on May, both the physicians who had charge of him told her that there would be no question of asking for a fee until she could find funds. He himself knew that the end was not far away: "There isn't time," he wrote to Louis Golding, "as usual, for much more than a waving of hats & handkerchiefs as the train pulls out."

He lingered on for another month, while May and Louis searched desperately to find means of paying his hospital fees. Back in war-torn England, Blaker's old army friend and fellow artilleryman Col. H. Essex Lewes ("Bunje") threw himself into the search: "It's pretty desperate," he wrote, "to think of poor old Dick hung up on the other side of the world"; but by the time the Officers' Association of the Royal Artillery and the Royal Literary Fund got round to the problem, Blaker had died, on 18 February.

The tragedy was swallowed up in the greater calamity that was engulfing the world. However, friends and local benevolent societies rallied round to rescue May from penury and to give Blaker a fitting burial. Mamie made no further claims on his pitifully small estate. She herself kept going in her usual spirited fashion, running boarding houses and, later, a market garden, while maintaining an appearance of style that was almost heroic. In her sixties, still radiating the afterglow of the romantic charm that had captivated Blaker so many years before, she married again – to a man less than half her age. It did not last, but it renewed her confidence. Her mother, Julia, died finally at 93, and towards the end of her own life, Mamie again became lonely and severely depressed, but after a crisis, she came through to a serene end.

May, meanwhile, had considered returning to England, to her family; but travel over submarine-infested ocean was dangerous and eventually she found work with the British Foreign Office in Washington, D.C., in a top-secret deciphering job, which she held until after the war. Subsequently, back in England, she began her own employment agency. During the last period of her life she tried to keep alive Blaker's name as a writer. Thanks to her efforts, both *Medal Without Bar* and *The Needle-Watcher* were reprinted as library editions in 1963. She died in 1971.

The Needle-Watcher was still selling, in 1994, as an English text in a Japanese edition. Although artistically that book is probably his highest achievement, Richard Blaker's monument remains *Medal Without Bar.* His career and private life were inseparable from the war. It drained him emotionally. Its exceptional demands on his inner resources, together with the effects of gas, had worn him out by 1940. In Hollywood he was still in the trenches. "We just hang on till the last cartridge here," he had told a friend.

During 1941 his headstone, carved by a friend, was placed on the burial place of his ashes in Los Angeles. Beneath his name and other particulars it bore the statement of his moral beliefs from a passage in *The Needle-Watcher*: "There is but one standard of right and wrong among men – benevolence of conduct only" – not an unworthy memorial, but a shade sententious, after the fashion of graveyard inscriptions. Closer to the truth of Blaker's life, in those bitter last months, would have been the lines from Shakespeare's *Henry V*, which he put into the mouth of the young subaltern Reynolds, as, with playful irony, he calmed down an embittered Canadian officer on the point of mutiny – one of the finest moments in *Medal Without Bar*:

> We are but warriors for the working day:
> Our gayness and our gilt are all besmirched
> With rainy marching in the painful field,
> ... and time hath worn us into slovenry.

14

꧁꣸꧂

Afterward: The Personal Record
1892 - 1962

This book has explored the nature of the war and why different authors wrote about it as they did. One important lesson that it teaches us about such writers, all struggling to tell the "truth about the war," is how wrong it is to generalize, how different were people's reactions, and how varied were the routes by which they reached their conclusions, whether hopeful or despairing, about the substance and effects of the First World War. A second is that all these efforts deserve respect even if they failed to be realized in books of lasting power. The reason for any such failure lay of course mainly in relative lack of talent; but so often they were checked, too, by the inhibitions that men of their culture and background in that period felt about expressing their true feelings. Those who fared best, Yeates, Read, Aldington, and Hinkson were better able to release themselves in their writing.

At its outset many, perhaps most, young people were eager to serve their country. This was true of all the authors treated at length in this book, with the exception of the ever-doubtful A. D. Gristwood, and of Herbert Read, an avowed pacifist and internationalist, though both nonetheless volunteered. What this book has shown was how, when, and why such uncomplicated patriotism was shaken or reinforced.

Though there were broadly identifiable fashions in war writing, with "hopeful" novels predominating in the early twenties and "disenchanted" in the later twenties, there were plenty of exceptions to this rule, and very few authors consciously tailored their products to fit a prevailing mood. To please readers, Gilbert Frankau, in 1919, made *Peter*

Jackson end in marital happiness, which did not correspond with his actual experience, his own marriage having collapsed partly because of the war. On the other hand, the patriotic message of the book was genuinely the product of deep conviction. In the absence of a Jewish identity, his whole personality was bound up with being a public-school officer and a patriot.

Henry Williamson, too, in his powerful but limited novel of disenchantment, *The Patriot's Progress*, was another writer who, at first sight might appear to have written to follow a general trend in 1929-30. In a second edition, years later, he implied as much, declaring that he had rejected its viewpoint by the time that he came to write *A Chronicle of Ancient Sunlight* in the 1950s. Looking at his opinions generally in the late twenties, however, it can be seen that though literary fashion may have helped to get an airing for his views in *The Patriot's Progress*, it was not the chief reason for the book's sentiments. "Windy Williamson," as Edmund Blunden unkindly called him at the time, was still dislocated by the war and obsessed by memories of the weeks and months without hope, without liberty – as he put it – that it had cost him.

All of the war books discussed in this volume were complex and contradictory in their inspiration. For Aldington, the failure of love and a sinking poetical reputation account as much for the bitter spirit of *Death of a Hero* as do his vividly described sufferings at the front. Mental illness made Gristwood, in *The Somme*, Ewart, in *Way of Revelation*, and Gurner, in *Pass Guard at Ypres*, paint some of the saddest and darkest pictures of the war, yet only Gristwood took a "pessimistic" line about it. Gurner's book was that of a man divided against himself, determinedly clinging on to his identity as a patriot, but tortured by his memories. Ewart was miserable at the front, yet, with his aristocratic and military background, sincerely believed that the war had vindicated those who lived by the traditional values of duty and service and rejected hedonism. Robert Keable, another "optimist," took almost the reverse view, depicting the war as a vital agent in overturning puritanical attitudes. For him, as for Aldington, his experiences of love – in this case a positive one – determined the tone of his novel. Of the rest, Read loathed war in principle but valued it as a test, while Yeates was bitter against the war for ruining his health, but still proud of his record. Mottram gained confidence from the war, but was appalled by the destruction it wrought – the exact cost of which he had to assess daily for three years – above all to the France he loved; Blaker valued the companionship at the front more than anything else in his life, but recognised how the war could leave a man emotionally drained; it undoubtedly damaged his marriage, as both he and Mamie recognised. Oliver Onions, overage and unable to fight, took pity on those who, having "done their bit" as servicemen, were forgotten, as was their right to decide how the country should be run. Pamela Hinkson's pride in her brothers' wartime prowess turned to indignation when they were forced to live abroad to get work, and her sorrow at the sundering effects of war was compounded by the tragic failure in Anglo-Irish relations after the 1916 Easter Rising.

Complexity is intrinsic to the views of all these novelists and complexity is intrinsic, too, to the motives for tracking down their stories. This book was undertaken not only as an exploration of war and why different writers interpreted it in the way they did, but also to establish a link with that Great War generation, which is now about to vanish altogether. When work on this book began, some of the facts gathered here were still retrievable. They would not have been if the research had been postponed a few years. Both Lady Gurner, Ronald's sister-in-law, and Angela Waddington, Wilfrid Ewart's sister, were over ninety when I met them. It was from Phyllis Gurner that I learnt the full tale of Ronald's childhood and the disappearance of his father. To hear this from her, reaching back to bonfires and snowball fights in Charterhouse Square before the turn of the last century, and to listen to Angela Waddington's ardent and beautifully enunciated pre-1914 voice, went beyond the excitement of scholarly research. Richard Aldington has described the feeling in his memoir, *Life for Life's Sake*. As a young man he went to visit Theodore Watts-Dunton, the poet Swinburne's friend and minder, at "The Pines," Putney Hill. Aside from literary hero-worship, his reason for intruding on the old man, he wrote, "was a sentimental one. Swinburne had known Landor; Landor, Southey; at one time Southey was very friendly with Shelley. The chain was a short one, and I was never likely to get humanly so near to Shelley again. He was only five handclasps away."

I was less ambitious than Aldington; I simply wanted to cross, before it was too late, the ever-widening divide that separated me from the authors of the novels I had read, and the war of which they wrote. The compulsion to find and preserve for posterity the last precious drops of a personal record is hard to explain. It is not exactly an historical instinct, having little to do with considered analysis or a broad view of important tides in the affairs of mankind. It stems more, perhaps, from a desire to bring back an earlier generation, to halt the process of time, and, thereby, to ensure one's own immortality.

This has been a quest that has taken me across the world in search of clues, to Texas and New Haven, to the West Coast of Ireland, to the old battlefields of the Western Front, to the back streets of Croydon, Purley, and Lewisham, to school libraries, hotels, and graveyards. There have been many fascinating dead ends and peculiar coincidences.

At the end of all this, one tantalising conjunction remains in my mind, which concerns Henry Williamson, whose *Chronicle* first inspired my interest in the Great War. One night late in his life, feeling himself close to death, he wandered outside into the Devon countryside, choosing a bush in a wood under which he could die peacefully, like a wild animal. His relations came looking for him, and the moonlight, falling on his thick white hair, betrayed him. He recovered, but later, after further illness, he was taken, very helpless, to Twyford Abbey, on the northern outskirts of London – a former country house in the "gothick" style, which had become an old people's home. On that estate, nearly a hundred years before, the young W. B. Yeats, beloved of Katherine Tynan, had trespassed with friends, hunting for butterflies and rare beetles. There, after a while, Henry Williamson died in the summer of 1977; and such an end seemed to many to be less dignified or romantic than the one he had chosen for himself. Yet if, like Williamson, one believed in "influences," there was a completeness in it. For also at Twyford Abbey, surrounded by mementoes of her Arran and Napier forebears in her little room, lived Angela Waddington, Wilfrid Ewart's sister. Nobody, as she explained to me, told her that Williamson had come: so a meeting that would have moved and consoled the old man never took place. Yet it may be that Angela's proximity in that kindly, though uncheerful, antechamber to purgatory transmitted some unspoken blessing from her long-dead author brother to the dying writer of genius who had passed through the same war and had done his best to keep the name of Wilfrid Ewart alive. Here, in this book at least, they, and others over whom the "Flower of Battle" cast its shade, are brought together.

❧

References

THE FLOWER OF BATTLE

6   *Tolkien:* Tolkien, J. R. R., *The Two Towers,* being the Second Part of *The Lord of the Rings,* London, Geo. Allen & Unwin, 1954, p. 239.

7   *any damn thing one pleases:* Aldington, Richard, *Death of a Hero,* London, Chatto & Windus, 1929, p. x.

    Bottles in the Smoke: London, Longmans Green, 1931.

    Balkan Monastery: London, Ivor Nicholson & Watson, 1936.

    The Dark Forest: London, Rupert Hart-Davis, 1934.

    Tug of War: London, John Hamilton, 1932.

    The Ladies' Road: London, Harmsworth, 1932.

    The Path of Glory: London, Constable, 1929.

    Hollow Sea: London, John Lane, Bodley Head, 1938.

    The Profiteer, a Tale of the Home Front: London, Wright & Brown, 1932.

    Command: 1st pub. 1922, 2nd edn, London, Martin Secker, 1927.

    Dress of the Day: War-and-after Reminiscences of the British Navy, London, Alfred E. Marriott, 1930.

    Biggles: Williams, Piers, ed., *Biggles of the Royal Flying Corps:* London, Purnell, 1978 (stories pub. in 1930s).

    The Other Side of No-man's Land: London, J. M. Dent, 1929.

    Last Men in London: London, Methuen, 1932.

    Grope Carries on: London, Faber & Faber, 1932.

    Patrol: London, Collins, 1927.

    Cousins German: London, Benn, 1930.

    Knight's Gambit: London, J. M. Dent, 1929.

    Roon: London, Hutchinson, 1929.

    "Old Sport": London, Jarrolds, 1919.

    Europa, Europa in Limbo: London, Robert Hale, 1936, 1937.

    Honourable Estate: London, Gollancz, 1936.

    The Just Steward: London, Heinemann, 1922.

Despised and Rejected: 1st pub. C.W. Daniel, 1918; 2nd ed., London, Gay Men's Press, 1988.

The World Went Mad: London, Jonathan Cape, 1934.

A Chronicle of Ancient Sunlight: (War vols) *How Dear is Life, A Fox under My Cloak, The Golden Virgin, Love and the Loveless, A Test to Destruction,* London, Macdonald, 1954, 1955, 1957, 1958, 1960 and revised eds. *How Dear, Fox, Test,* London, Hamilton & Co., 1963, 1963, 1964.

8   *Grey Dawn, Red Night:* London, Gollancz, 1929.

The Middle Parts of Fortune: London, Peter Davies, 1929.

Journey's End: 1st pub., 1929, 1st educ. edn, London, Heinemann Educational Books, 1958.

Peter Jackson, Cigar Merchant: 1st pub. as book, London, Hutchinson, 1920.

Tell England: London, Cassell, 1922.

The Secret Battle: London, Methuen, 1919.

Combed Out: 1st pub. 1920, 2nd ed. London, Travellers' Library, 1929.

Disenchantment: London, Chatto & Windus, 1922.

Rough Justice: London, Chatto & Windus, 1926.

The "Tietjens Tetralogy": Some Do Not, No More Parades, A Man Could Stand Up, Last Post, London, Duckworth, 1924, 1925, 1926, 1928.

The Spanish Farm Trilogy: pub. as a single vol. London, Chatto & Windus, 1927.

These Men Thy Friends: London, Macmillan, 1927.

All Quiet on the Western Front: English edn, tr. A.W. Wheen, London, G. P. Putnam's, 1929.

Journey's End ... recruitment: Bodleian Library Western mss, Richard Blaker papers, mss Eng. Lett. 319, f.138, Ralph Hodder-Williams to Blaker, 18 Nov. 1929; and c.323, f.56–58, Archie White, V.C. to Blaker, 23 July 1930.

9   *The Patriot's Progress: Being the Vicissitudes of Private John Bullock:* 1st edn London, Geoffrey Bles, 1930.

The Sword Falls: London, Geo. Allen & Unwin, 1929.

Generals Die in Bed: London, Noel Douglas, 1930.

The Return of the Brute: London, Mandrake Press, 1929.

All Else Is Folly: a Tale of War and Passion: (with intro by Ford Madox Ford) Toronto, McLelland & Stewart, 1929.

Memoirs of a Fox-Hunting Man: Faber & Faber, 1928.

If Winter Comes: London, Hodder & Stoughton, 1921.

Young Orland: London, Hutchinson, 1927.

Lament for Adonis: London, Ernest Benn, 1932, p. 179.

The Barber of Putney: London, Philip Allan, 1934, pp. ix–x.

10   *The Sunshine Settlers:* pop. edn revised, London, Philip Allan, 1935.

Beaumaroy Home from the War: London, Methuen, 1919.

How They Did It: London, Methuen, 1920.

Not So Quiet: Stepdaughters of War: London, Albert E. Marriott, 1930.

a good war novel: review of *The Case of Sergeant Grischa* in *Life and Letters,* vol. II, no. 10, March 1929, p. 236.

11   *How Young They Died:* London, Collins, 1969.

Victorian Son, an Autobiography 1897-1922: London, Collins, 1972.

The Gambler, an Autobiography, volume II, 1920-1939: London, Collins, 1973.

The Somme: London, Jonathan Cape, 1927.

Desmond MacCarthy: MacCarthy, Desmond, *Memories,* London, MacGibbon & Kee, 1953, p. 141.

12   *curse the wood . . . Dicky:* Sassoon, Siegfried, *The Memoirs of an Infantry Officer,* London, Faber & Faber, 1930, p. 123, permission George Sassoon.

Mr. Ogilby: Williamson, *How Dear Is Life, p. 257.*

13   *Pritchard:* Manning *The Middle Parts of Fortune, Somme & Ancre 1916* (first pub. 1929) 1977 edn., London, Peter Davies, p. 15.

RICHARD ALDINGTON

19   *proclaim their truth:* Temple, F. J., "Words for a Centenarian Young Man" in Blayac, Alain, and Zilboorg, Caroline (eds), *Richard Aldington: Essays in Honour of the Centenary of His Birth,* Université Paul Valéry, Montpellier, 1994, p. x. My warmest thanks to Caroline Zilboorg of Erie College, Ohio, who organised the 1992 Richard Aldington Conference at Montpellier; also at that conference, in particular, Gerald Butler of San Diego State University, Charles Doyle of the University of Victoria, Thomas Nevin of John Carroll University, Ohio, Marie Brunette Spire, of the University of Paris XI[e], and Susan Schreibman, University College, Dublin.

(1929): Aldington, Richard, *Death of a Hero,* London, Chatto & Windus, 1929.

that has been wounded: Temple, op.cit.

great clean sensual beast: see Cournos, John, *Miranda Masters,* New York, Alfred Knopf, 1924, p. 143.

20   *have them bowled:* Lawrence Durrell to Richard Aldington, "before 22 Sept. 1959," in McNiven, Ian S., and Moore, Harry T., (eds), *Literary Lifelines: the Richard Aldington – Lawrence Durrell Correspondence,* London, Faber & Faber, Boston, 1981, p. 102.

Lawrence of Arabia (1955): Aldington, Richard, *Lawrence of Arabia. A Biographical Enquiry,* London, Collins, 1955.

painful subject: Aldington, Richard, *Stepping Heavenward. A Record,* London, Chatto & Windus, 1931, see pp. 57, 60.

ruining his life: as, for example, review of Hogarth Press edn. of *Death of a Hero,* by Kay Dick, 14 September 1984, *The Times.*

21   *heavy drinker:* Zilboorg, Caroline, ed., *Richard Aldington & H.D.: The Later Years in Letters,* Manchester U.P., 1995, pp. 81–82.

Bernard Shaw: Aldington, Richard, *Life for Life's Sake,* 2nd (English) edn, London, Cassell, 1968, p. 54.

poetical inspiration: ibid. p. 56.

Snap loud, parrot: "The Parrot," in Aldington, Richard, *Collected Poems,* London, Geo. Allen & Unwin, 1929, pp. 7–8.

22   *seared my childhood:* ibid. p. 41, "Childhood."

English literature: Life for Life's Sake, chs. 2–5.

23   *on Pound's part:* ibid. p. 125; see also Hughes, Glenn, *Imagism and the Imagists. A Study in Modern Poetry,* Palo Alto, Stanford University Press, 1931, pp. 85–108.

24   *girlish giggles:* see Williams, William Carlos, *Autobiography,* New York, Random

House, 1951, pp. 67–69.

Meleager: Harry Ransom Humanities Research Center, University, see tr. Mackail, J. W., *Select Epigrams from the Greek Anthology,* London, Longman's Green, 1913.

hernia operation: see *Life for Life's Sake,* p. 148.

human nature: Fallas, Carl, *St. Mary's Village, Through the Eyes of an Unknown Soldier Who Lived On,* London, Hodder & Stoughton, 1954.

"Pénis": HRHRC, mss F. S. Flint, Aldington – Flint 27 March 1916.

25   *Whitham: Life for Life's Sake,* pp. 160–162. Aldington refers to Fallas having a low opinion of human nature. This only means that he was not inordinately high-minded. His liking for the human species was not affected by this.

wanted to hear?: HRHRC, mss Flint, Aldington – Flint, 27 March 1916.

fort alléchant: ibid.

bête à deux dos: ibid.

entanglement: see Cournos, op. cit. and Guest, Barbara, *Herself Defined: the Poet H. D. and Her World,* New York, Doubleday, 1984, p. 78.

May 1916: Life for Life's Sake, p. 162.

26   *in an agony of apprehension in England:* HRHRC, mss Flint, Aldington – Flint 12 Nov. 1916.

idiotic and obscene fashion: ibid, Aldington – Flint, 24 July 1916.

to tears: Aldington – Cournos, July, letter, quoted in Zilboorg, Caroline (ed.), *Richard Aldington & H. D. The Early Years in Letters,* Bloomington and Indianapolis, Indiana University Press, 1992, p. 24.

unimaginably low: HRHRC, mss Flint, Aldington – Flint, 16 July 1916.

foul-mouthed animals: ibid. 24 July 1916.

flowers to decorate their tables: ibid. 16 July 1916.

exemption for myself: ibid. 12 Nov. 1916.

27   *parts of a rifle:* ibid. 20 July 1916.

along the shore...: ibid. 19 Nov. 1916.

brisk in these parts: ibid. 22 Jan. 1917.

28   *over in France:* ibid. 31 Jan. 1917.

sans doute: ibid. 3 Jan. 1917.

dull letters from me: 13 Jan. 1917.

not yet terminated: ibid.

gloriously with mine: ibid. 29 Jan. 1917.

29   *We got on splendidly:* ibid.

insult to God: ibid. 2 Feb. 1917.

that's what hurts: ibid. 3 March 1917.

artillery barrage: ibid. 6 Sept. 1917.

30   *not a rifle:* ibid.

youth has gone: Aldington – H. D. 8 Sept. 1918, Zilboorg (ed.), op. cit., p. 138.

British Museum: H. D. (Hilda Doolittle), *Bid Me to Live,* 3rd (Virago) edn, Tiptree, Essex, 1984, pp. 15, 45, 47.

31   *war made impossible:* ibid. p. 46.

Bid Me to Live: ibid. p. 47; see also Yale University, Beinecke Library, mss H. D., series III, Box 48, petitioner's (H.D.'s) statement to High Court of Justice (Divorce Division etc.) 1937.

Lieut. Bate: Wilkinson, David, "Dying at the Word of Command: the Last Days of Richard Aldington's War," in Blayac and Zilboorg (eds), op. cit. See also Bate, H. Roland, "Sixty Years Ago," *Blackwood's Magazine,* vol. 318, Nov. 1975, p. 394.

heartland of Northern France: Public Records Office (PRO), WO 95/2219, War Diary of 9th Royal Sussex Regiment (hence forward shortened to "9 Royal Sussex WD"), March–May 1918.

32   *still living there:* HRHRC, mss Flint, Aldington - Flint, 6 September 1917.

self-inflicted wound: 9 Royal Sussex WD, 2-30 May 1918.

into the trenches: Aldington, *Death of a Hero,* London, Chatto & Windus, 5th printing (cheap edn), p. 421.

put out of action: 9 Royal Sussex WD, 31 May 1918.

two died: Death of a Hero, p. 427.

demobilised in 1919: 9 Royal Sussex WD, Feb. 1919, ref. to 2 Lieut. R. Aldington.

between 11 and 23 June: ibid. May-June 1918.

in the defence: ibid.

33   *very unpopular:* ibid. from April 1918; and Bate, op. cit., pp. 391-2.

and other exploits: 9 Royal Sussex WD. 3, 29 June 1918.

further confidence: ibid. June & July 1918; Wilkinson, op. cit., p. 9; and Aldington - H.D., 2 June 1918, in Zilboorg (ed.) op. cit.

the competence of the generals: see, for example, Aldington - H.D., 28 May, 18 June, 1 July 1918.

proceeded effectively: 9 Royal Sussex WD, Sept. 1918.

sedentary townsmen: HRHRC, mss Flint, Aldington - Flint, 15 Sept. 1918.

34   *zest you never before had:* ibid. 28 Dec. 1917.

more than you need pain: ibid. 2 June 1918.

be a bugger: ibid, 26 Aug. 1918.

clerk's job: ibid. 16 Sept. 1918.

Patrick MacGill (1819-1963, born Donegal, buried at Notre Dame Cemetery, Fall River, Mass.) Served on Western Front, author of *The Great Push* and *The Red Horizon,* toured England advertising the prowess of the British Army. Stayed in the U.S.A. after 1930, when he seems to have put Europe and his war propaganda past behind him.

Paul Nash (1889-1976) Served in France from Feb. 1917 with Hampshires; from October 1917 Official War Artist on the Western Front. He was nearly killed three times in this capacity.

yet written in English: ibid. 7 July 1918.

35   *bitter cup from us:* Aldington, Richard, *Images of War,* London, Geo. Allen & Unwin, 1919, p. 10.

Machine Guns: ibid. p. 34;

Battlefield, ibid. p. 35.

36   *hail and farewell:* ibid. p. 52.

37   *Four years from today?:* ibid. p. 28.

Winterbourne in Death of a Hero: Aldington - H.D., 20 May and 12 July 1918, in Zilboorg (ed.), op. cit., pp. 58, 106.

I desire l'autre: ibid. p. 57.

38   *grass widow:* HRHRC, mss Flint, Aldington - Flint, 22 Jan. 1917.

when I have mine: Aldington - H.D., 12 Aug. 1918 in Zilboorg (ed.), op.cit., p. 126; on Gray, ibid. 4, 5, 21, 31 Aug. 1918, pp. 119-121, 122, 130-131, 134-135.

my Astraea: ibid., 5 Aug. 1918, p. 122.

39   *signals officer:* Wilkinson, op. cit., pp. 10-11; HRHRC, mss Flint, Aldington - Flint, 6 Oct. 1918.

nightmare that would never end: see Wilkinson, op. cit., p. 10; Zilboorg (ed.), op. cit., p. 146; 9 Royal Sussex WD, Oct. 1918.

all our lost comrades: Aldington - Eric Warman, 19 Nov. 1958, in Zilboorg (ed.), op. cit., p. 147.

40   *divine dreams return:* Aldington - H.D., 14 Oct. 1918, Zilboorg (ed.), op.cit., p. 148.

had first gone into action: Bate, op. cit., pp. 393-396.

41   *Perdita Aldington:* see Yale University, the Beinecke Library, mss H.D., series III, box 48; High Court of Justice (Divorce) Division, between Hilda Aldington and Richard Godfree Aldington, respondent; petitioner's statement, 1937. This account by H.D. of the crisis in her marriage must be taken *cum grano,* but it demonstrates the confused state of both partners in 1919.

42   *Eliot's growing reputation:* Doyle, op.cit., pp. 103 & 118.

they don't die: Richard Aldington, *A Dream in the Luxembourg,* special, signed edn of 300, London, Chatto & Windus, 1930, p. 5.

43   *legal action:* see Coleman, Verna, *The Last Exquisite. A Portrait of Frederic Manning,* Melbourne University Press, 1990; and Marwil, Jonathan, *Frederic Manning. An Unfinished Life,* Angus & Robertson, 1988.

found this change a trial: see Doyle, op.cit., ch. 9, "Life for Life's Sake," p. 268.

44   *an aspiring littérateur and interior decorator:* my thanks are due to Mrs. Mary Patmore, Brigit's daughter-in-law, and to the late Cecil Beaton, for information. Mary Patmore's account turned on her mother-in-law's undoubted virtues - her warmth, enthusiasm, and kindness - while Beaton took the view that Brigit was manipulative and out to forward Derek's career. Both views have substance. Brigit's own account of her life, *My Friends When Young,* London, Heinemann, 1968, has a disarming quality. Derek Patmore's *Private History, An Autobiography,* London, Cape, 1960, gives a devoted son's view. Though this must rate as one of the flattest memoirs ever written, it is revealing and not unengaging. H.D.'s opinion of her one-time friend was by 1937 close to that of Beaton and is quite as revealing about herself (Yale, Beinecke Library, mss H.D., Series III, Box 48).

woman who'll rape them?: D.H. Lawrence - Aldous Huxley, Oct./Nov. 1928, in Huxley, Aldous (ed.), *The Letters of D. H. Lawrence,* London, Heinemann, 1932, p. 758.

emotional strain: Patmore, Derek, introduction to Patmore, Brigit, *My Friends When Young* (see above), p. 23.

tears in his eyes: Death of a Hero, pp. 373-374.

47   *extolling military glory: Death of a Hero,* pp. 352-353.

48   *The Return of the Brute:* O'Flaherty, Liam, (1897-1984), pp. 289-290. Irish Guards 1915-18. The novel was published in London, The Mandrake Press, 1929.

the peaks of it are lofty: Bennett, Arnold, in *Evening Standard,* 12 Sept. 1929, in

Mylett, Andrew, (ed.), *Arnold Bennett: The Evening Standard Years, "Books and Persons" 1926-1931,* London, Chatto & Windus, 1974, p. 340; see also Brittain, Vera, in *Time and Tide,* 4 Oct. 1929, p. 1182: "For all its shrieking, scolding, damning and hating, I say unhesitatingly that it is one of the greatest war books that I have so far read."

appeared in 1930: Aldington, Richard, *Roads to Glory,* London, Chatto & Windus, 1930.

Colonel's Daughter: Aldington, Richard, *The Colonel's Daughter. A Novel,* London, Chatto & Windus, 1931.

Enemies: Aldington, Richard, *All Men Are Enemies. A Romance,* London, Chatto & Windus, 1933.

Women Must Work: Aldington, Richard, *Women Must Work. A Novel,* London, Chatto & Windus, 1934.

49 *courting a younger woman:* Patmore, Derek, intro. to Patmore, op. cit.
50 *aged suddenly:* Mary Patmore, information.
national symbol: see generally: Benkovitz, Miriam J. (ed.), *A Passionate Prodigality. Letters to Alan Bird from Richard Aldington, 1949-1962,* New York, New York Public Library, 1975.
51 *desert prostitutes:* see *Death of a Hero,* p. 340; and Aldington, Richard, *Lawrence of Arabia,* London, Four Square, paperback edn 1960, p. 330.

V. M. YEATES

I am indebted to Henry Labouchere of Langham airfield, Norfolk, for giving me a taste of biplane flight in a Tiger Moth.

55 *Johnny Johnson, Fly High, Fly Low,* memoir of Air Commodore J.E. Johnson, C.B.E., D.S.O., D.F.C., extract in mss Yeates (in keeping of Yeates' daughter, Roz Cullinan).
56 *Winged Victory,* London, Jonathan Cape, 1934; reprinted with a preface by Henry Williamson 1934; reissued with new preface & tribute by Williamson, 1961; reprinted 1972; paperback edn, St. Albans, Mayflower Books, 1975.
Lawrence of Arabia: mss Yeates (Cullinan), T.E. Shaw (Lawrence) - Henry Williamson (copy), June (?) 1934.
He did not care: Winged Victory, Mayflower paperback edn (hereinafter the edition cited, as "*WV*"), p. 447.
57 *was born in West Dulwich:* I am greatly indebted to Yeates's children, the late Mary Bardell, Ros Cullinan, Joy Vowles, and Guy Yeates, also Ted Cullinan and Christopher Vowles, for information and help.
Colfe's Grammar School: I am much indebted to Peter M. Heinecke, the Librarian of Colfe's Grammar School, who gave me access to school records including the roll book; see Beardwood, H., (ed.), *The History of Colfe's Grammar School, 1652-1972,* 3rd edn, Christchurch, Hants, Christchurch Times Ltd, 1972.
58 *F.L. Lucas* was an "Apostle" at Cambridge and served in the Great War in the 7th Royal West Kents: see Nicholls, Jonathan, *Cheerful Sacrifice. The Battle of*

Arras, 1917, London, Leo Cooper, 1990, p. 7.

58   *Gayton:* Duncan, Leland, L., (ed.), *Colfe's Grammar School, Lewisham and the Great War 1914-19 with Rolls of Honour and Service,* London, the Blackheath Press 1929, p. 45; Arthur William Gayton, private, 6th City, 11th & 20th Btns. London Regt, joined 19 July 1915.

59   *Special Slackers:* Henry Williamson, introduction, *WV,* p. 8.
      the mediocre half-failures of life: Williamson, Henry, *The Flax of Dream,* London, Faber & Faber, 1936, 2nd part, *Dandelion Days,* ch. 13, p. 366; see also ch. 29, p. 485. *Dandelion Days* was first pub. 1922, revised 1930.
      finding birds' eggs: WV, Williamson intro., p. 8; Williamson, *A Chronicle of Ancient Sunlight* (hereinafter *"Chronicle"*), vol. 3, *Young Phillip Maddison,* ch. 30, "Bag men's Outing," which contains a description of Yeates - "a pale, quiet boy named Cundall"; and mss Yeates (Cullinan), Yeates to Joy Yeates, prob. May 1933.
      small fry socially: Hoys, Dudley, *The Quiet Men,* see war chapter set in Mesopotamia. *WV* pp. 395-6, and Williamson, *Chronicle,* vol. 5, *A Fox Under My Cloak* (Macdonald reprint 1984) ch. 15.

60   *Williamson ... in a letter to his old school:* See *Colfe's Grammar School, Lewisham, and the Great War 1914-19,* pp. 2-3, and also for his army career.
      Richard Jefferies, WV, Williamson intro, p. 8.
      contempt for their motives: information Mary Bardell.

61   *brown eyes:* ibid.
      God's trousers: ibid.
      C. of E.: see PR AIR 1, 1430/204/31/23: "Confidential particulars of officers joining 46 Squadron RFC."
      superficial injuries: For these and other details of his flying career in the pages that follow, his squadron, his crashes, etc. see mss Yeates (Cullinan), Pilot's Flying Log Book, and AIR 1 1430/204/31/23, cited above, and also 1430/204131/26, recommendations for Honours and Awards; and 1429/204/31/18, Squadron record book, giving details of promotion, repostings, sickness, etc.; see also Cole, C., ed., *Royal Air Force 1918,* London, William Kimber, 1968, pp. 57, 63, 95, 99, 148; see also Jones, H. A., *The Official History of the War in the Air,* Oxford, Clarendon Press, 1928, vol. iv, pp. 254, 300-302.
      In that passionless bright void: WV pp. 40-41.

62   *yellow, green and black:* mss Yeates (Cullinan), Yeates - his aunt, 3 March 1918; see also: Munson, Kenneth and Wood, John W., *Fighters 1914-19. Attack and Training Aircraft,* London, Blandford Press, 1968, p. 40.

63   *the stoutest courage: WV* p. 30.
      many of them living well into their eighties: For example, the late Charles O'Brien R.F.C., of Burnham Overy Staithe, Norfolk. Cecil Lewis, the distinguished broadcaster and author of the classic account of air fighting, *Sagittarius Rising,* is alive and living in Corfu at the time of writing this, and has recently published an autobiography, *All My Yesterdays* (Shaftesbury [Dorset], Element, 1993).

64   *élan and stamina.* See *WV;* also Lewis, op.cit. Winter, Denis, *The First of the Few,* London, Alan Lane, 1982 (some of Yeates's articles are quoted in this)
      Manfred von Richthofen: mss. Yeates (Cullinan), Ernest Jupe - Norah Yeates, 11 May 1970, based on Richthofen combat report.

65   *a brave enemy:* see a Second World War example: Duke, Neville, *Test Pilot,* London, Corgi edn, 1955, pp. 80, 87.

Vlasto: mss Yeates (Cullinan), Yeates, pilot's log; Ernest Jupe - Norah Yeates, 11 May 1970, findings based on 46 Squadron combat reports.

conversations . . . highly evocative: ibid. L. Pearce-Gervis - Yeates, 16 Aug. 1934.

not a bad crowd: ibid. Yeates to his aunt, 3 March 1918.

66   *she needs companionship:* Yeates, V.M. "Adjustment," ms novel in keeping of Joy Vowles, 1933 version, pp. 20-21.

not a bad description of the war: WV p. 359.

67   *too profound to be sceptical:* HRHRC mss Yeates, V.M., "Family Life," p. 63.

68   *Morgan three-wheeler:* information Roz Cullinan.

Samuel Butler: The Way of All Flesh, was pub. in 1903, after his death. The passage by Yeates was cut from *WV* but would have appeared on p.170, as the penultimate paragraph of phase 1, ch. 21.

Institution for Airing the Aged: mss Yeates (Cullinan), Yeates - Norah Yeates, undated, from Mistley.

shock guests: information Mary Bardell.

keen to make up for lost time: I am indebted to the late Arthur Payne, who served 1917-18 as a subaltern in 1st Grenadier Guards, for a description of his Oxford University life following the war.

69   *Arthur Dickinson:* Information Mary Bardell.

seriously sick man: ibid. and see mss Yeates, (Cullinan), letters from Yeates to Norah Yeates, 1933-34.

70   *mind-scratching junk:* ibid. 18 April 1934.

cough, cough, cough: ibid. 4 Nov. 1934.

a gas fitter: ibid. 11 May 1933.

on the red tide: ibid. 1 May 1933.

the misfortunate Knebworth: Yeates - Williamson, quoted in Williamson introduction to *WV,* p. 8.

71   *fanatical Fascist beliefs:* see Williamson, *Chronicle,* vol. 12, *The Phoenix Generation.*

excited by its Air Force passages: mss Yeates (Cullinan), typed copy of Williamson "memoir": "Details relating to literary relicts of V. M. Yeates and Henry Williamson," 30 Dec. 1961.

the most difficult moment ... in English publishing: ibid. Huntington - Williamson, 11 July 1933.

72   *conventional drama: Times Literary Supplement,* 12 July 1934; see also *Sunday Times,* 26 August 1934, and *WV,* intro., p. 8.

73   *useless butchery:* HRHRC, Yeates, "Adjustment," 1933 version, p. 162.

Shelley's ghost: Yeates - Williamson, quoted in *WV,* intro., p. 10.

74   *Norah Yeates ... Williamson's political views:* information Mary Bardell.

Hitler was a great poet: Williamson, Henry, *The Flax of Dream,* single vol. edn., London, Faber and Faber, 1936, foreword, p. 7.

scarlet majors: HRHRC, mss H.M. Tomlinson, Williamson - Tomlinson, 12 Feb. 1937, (an example can be seen in *The Flax of Dream,* 1936 edn., pp. 1284-1294).

Einstein: HRHRC., Williamson - Tomlinson, 12 Feb. 1937.

75   *Story of My Heart:* see Williamson, Henry, ed., *Richard Jefferies, Selections of his*

Work, with details of his Life and Circumstances, his death and Immortality, 2nd edn, London, Faber & Faber, 1947, pp. 158-159; The former war correspondent, H. M. Tomlinson, whom Williamson respected, warned him against the book.

correct behaviour: HRHRC, Williamson - Tomlinson, 12 Feb. 1937.

76   *desire to shock:* See Kenneth Young's review in *Sunday Telegraph,* 12 May 1980, of Sewell, Brocard ed., *Henry Williamson. The Man and His Writings,* Padstow, Tabb House, 1980.

an outsider: ibid.

opinions about financiers: see *WV,* p. 59. Here Tom Cundall, who represents, largely, Yeates' view, *disputes* a fellow-airman's proposition that the war was caused by Germany reacting to "the international Jew," admitting that though finance capitalism may be destructive, its practitioners cannot be said to want war or to conspire to make it.

77   *propaganda postcard of Hitler:* information Mary Bardell.

status of a Williamson hero: Williamson, Henry, *Goodbye West Country,* 1st U.S. edn, Boston, Little, Brown, 1938, p. 24.

The Gold Falcon: Williamson, Henry, *The Gold Falcon, or the Haggard of Love, be ing the adventures of Manfred, airman and poet of the world war, and later, husband and father, in search of freedom and personal sunrise, in the city of New York, and of the con summation of his life,* London, Faber and Faber, 1933.

connection with ... The Gold Falcon: mss Yeates (Cullinan), Yeates - Howard (Cape), 27 Feb. 1934.

78   *insisted on calling him a poet:* ibid. "I objected to HW that I would not be adver tised as a poet."

humorous ... in the school magazine: "V.Y.," "Tourists," *The Colfeian,* 1913, p. 8.

sculptured by creative thought: WV, p. 7.

pay back compliments: Yeates mss (Cullinan), Yeates - Norah Yeates, prob. 4 May 1933.

fame and fortune: ibid.

big words about clouds: ibid. undated, May/June? from Colney Hatch.

79   *colour and bias:* WV, p. 9.

Revolt in the Desert: George Jefferson, biographer of Edward Garnett of Cape, letter to author, 20 July 1987.

Nike Pteros: see Yeates mss (Cullinan), Yeates and private Williamson correspon dence with Cape, 1933-34.

80   *smiling fortitude:* ibid. Yeates - Norah Yeates, May 1934.

To Henry Williamson: WV, p. 5.

collaborative effort: Williamson's views can be plainly seen from a study of the typed and handwritten mss of *WV* in HRHRC, mss V.M. Yeates.

the freckled face of the world: WV, p. 9.

T. E. Lawrence ... was full of praise: mss Yeates (Cullinan), copy letter, T. E. Lawrence - Williamson, June (?) 1934.

81   *shoot financiers after the war:* For this and other views of Williamson's that fol low, see HRHRC, mss Yeates, Williamson's comments on *WV* mss (entitled "Wings of Victory"); these comments relate to *WV,* pp. 210-11.

accurate reflection of the war: mss Yeates (Cullinan), press cutting from *Observer,* August 1934.

German attack of March 1918: see *WV,* p. 77.

excessively purple: The cut passage was tacked on in the last para of *WV* p. 392 (edn cited here), and read: "It seemed as if the gods had at length taken notice of the misdoings of men and would overwhelm them with molten mountains when the last rage of the sun melted their bronze."

pullulated: see *WV,* p. 105.

fucking: see *WV,* p. 369 – "this is what your — war does to a man."

ground battles ... from the air: Williamson's suggestion was made about the action described in *WV,* p. 78.

82   *Rittmeister Freiherr:* HRHRC Williamson comments on Yeates mss relate to passages in *WV* on pp. 212-213 (suggestion rubbed out by Yeates) and 436 (refused by Yeates), respectively.

half-starved boys: ibid, *WV,* pp. 428-429.

agonised protest: WV, p. 10.

83   *Then Williamson came in: WV,* p. 438. The evidence of the HRHRC Yeates typed mss p. 597, and the handwritten version pp. 25-27, was that this passage was inserted at a late stage.

did not care: ibid. & *WV,* p. 447.

Cranborne: mss Yeates (Cullinan), Yeates – Norah Yeates, 22 April 1934. On that afternoon, Yeates would have driven close to the home of Wilfrid Ewart's Cecil cousins at Cranborne Manor (where my parents were having lunch on that very day) and to Breamore House, where Ewart's comrade-in-arms, Teddy Hulse, had grown up (where my parents went to a ball the following night).

84   *Ben Ray Redman:* in *The Saturday Review of Literature,* press cutting, mss Yeates (Cullinan), 1934.

Gregory Dunn: See advertisement for *WV,* before its appearance on 9 July 1934, in *Spectator,* press cutting mss Yeates (Cullinan); for Dunn, see Clarke, Stephen Francis (Clearwater Books), Henry Williamson "Spica" Catalogue, 1986, item 145, notes by Clarke; the letters from Yeates from which these notes were taken were lost when Clarke's briefcase was stolen.

James Hilton: Daily Telegraph, 26 June 1934.

Trenchard, Church, Rhys: mss Yeates (Cullinan), Lord Trenchard – Norah Yeates, 4 Jan. 1934; Church, Richard, in *John O'London's Weekly,* cutting in mss Yeates (Cullinan), Llewellyn-Rhys, letter in *John O'London's Weekly* commenting on Jan. 1935 Yeates obituary by Henry Williamson.

sergeant major stuff: ibid. Yeates – Norah Yeates, 27 Nov. 1934.

85   *gave Yeates ... $60:* ibid. Yeates – Norah Yeates, April/May 1934.

Daily Mail, Ypres League: ibid. "R.P." – Williamson, 26 Oct. 1934; and Capt. G. E. de Trafford, Ypres League – Yeates, 26 Nov. 1934.

"Family Life": ms is held in HRHRC, mss Yeates.

I get so sick about myself: mss Yeates (Cullinan), Yeates – Williamson, undated (unsent?).

86   *Wingless Victor: WV,* p. 13.

letter to Dunn: Yeates – Gregory Dunn, 14 Dec. 1934, see Clarke, op.cit. item 145.

Williamson ... obituary: Williamson, Henry, "V. M. Yeates: a personal Tribute," *John O'London's Weekly,* 26 Jan. 1935.

87   *University of Texas:* mss Yeates (Cullinan), Decherd Turner (Director HRHRC,
     Austin) - Mary Wolfard (Bardell), 21 May 1986.
     his literary judgement was sound: ibid. typed copy of Williamson "memoir":
     "Details relating to literary relics of V.M. Yeates and Henry Williamson," 30
     Dec. 1961. In it, Williamson describes how he has kept Yeates in the public eye
     over the years: as in the dedication of *Salar the Salmon,* 1935, in the revised ver-
     sion of "Reality in War Literature," which appeared in the collection of essays
     entitled *A Linhay on the Downs,* in 1934, in *An Anthology of Modern Nature
     Writing* (1936), in his edn of James Farrar's poems, *The Unreturning Spring,* 1950,
     and in *Tonight* T.V. interview with Kenneth Allsop, 27 Oct. 1961.
     new preface and tribute: WV, 7-14.
     another edition ... and the paperback: see mss Yeates, (Cullinan), Graham C. Greene
     (Jonathan Cape) to Norah Yeates, 21 June 1972, and Gaye Poulton (Cape), 4
     Dec. 1972.

A. D. GRISTWOOD

89   *share their knowledge:* Gristwood, A. D., *The Coward* in *The Somme including
     also the The Coward,* London, Jonathan Cape, 1927, pp. 146-7.
     Wells, H. G.: Gristwood, *Somme,* p. 11.
90   *pestilence:* ibid., p. 15.
     bear the burden: Gristwood, *Coward,* pp. 187-8.
91   *the doubter: Coward,* p. 146.
92   *landing at Le Havre:* See W. O. 95/3005, battalion diary of 2/5th London Rifles,
     24 Jan. 1917 & ff.
93   *such trash ... drugged men's minds: Somme,* pp. 24-5.
     delighted prisoner: ibid., p. 43.
     battle is over: ibid. pp. 54-55.
94   *"Weeper" Smart:* Manning, Frederic, *The Middle Parts of Fortune:* Somme &
     Ancre, 1916 Peter Davis, London 1977 edn (1st pub. 1929).
     If ever man had earned gratitude: Somme, p. 86.
96   *allocated to other divisions:* P.R.O. W.O.95/3005, battalion diary of 2/5 London
     Rifles. See also Mitchinson, K. W., *Gentlemen and Officers,* London, I. W. M.,
     1995.
97   *not entirely excellent: Coward,* p. 133.
     Locarno: H. G. Wells papers at the University Library, University of Illinois, Ur-
     bana-Champaign, A. D. Gristwood to H. G. Wells, 4 Nov. 1926. The letters of
     the Gristwood family to Wells at Urbana are almost the only source for the de-
     tails of Gristwood's life, apart from death and birth certificates, and family wills.
     insurance: Urbana, Wells papers, J. A. Gristwood-Wells, 29 Sept. 1929.
     Morley's Academy: see Geoffrey West (Wells, Geoffrey H. - no relation), *H. G.
     Wells, a sketch for a portrait,* London, 1930. The elder Gristwood helped West
     with the school parts of this book, but was not acknowledged in it; and Urbana
     Wells papers, J. A. Gristwood - Wells, Dec. 1929; and Wells' corrective to West's
     account in *Experiment in Autobiography* vol. 1, London Faber & Faber, 1934,
     1984 edn, pp. 85-95.

98   *world of books:* J. A. Gristwood – Wells, 29 Sept. 1926.

two wounds: J. A. Gristwood – Wells, 17 Oct. 1926.

Galsworthy, Ford Madox Ford: see Buitenhuis, Peter, *The Great War of Words,* Vancouver, University of British Columbia Press, 1987, and Smith, David C., *H. G. Wells: Desperately Mortal,* New Haven, Yale University Press, 1986, chs 9, 11; and Field, Frank, *British and French Writers of the First World War: Comparative Studies in Cultural History,* Cambridge University Press, 1991, ch. 5.

99   *ruthless criticism:* Urbana, Wells Papers, A. D. Gristwood – Wells, 4 Nov. 1926.

The Somme: Gristwood, *Somme,* pp. 21-22.

general tone: Urbana, Wells Papers, A. D. Gristwood – Wells, 5 April 1927.

100   *exceptional and unfortunate:* Gristwood, *Somme,* pp. 73-4.

moralising: Urbana, Wells Papers, A. D. Gristwood – Wells, 5 April 1927.

101   *in the machine:* Gristwood, *Somme,* Wells preface, pp. 9-12.

Cyril Falls, War Books: An annotated bibliography of books about the Great War, 2nd, 1989 edn (1st pub. 1930), Greenhill Books, London, p. 276.

future generations: New Statesman, 12 Nov. 1927, p. 146.

Gristwood complained: Urbana, Wells Papers, A. D. Gristwood – Wells 18 Nov. 1927.

amateurish: Urbana, Wells Papers, A. D. Gristwood – Wells, 4 Nov. 1928.

£50: Urbana, Wells Papers, A. D. Gristwood – Wells, 1 October 1929.

102   *horrific impact of war:* ibid.

bitter ... Blettsworthy: Wells, H. G., *Mr. Blettsworthy on Rampole Island,* London, Ernest Benn Ltd, 1928, pp. 249-257 and Gristwood, *Somme,* ch. 3.

actual and terrible: Life and Letters vol. 1, no. 4, September 1928, p. 312.

103   *extremely grateful:* Urbana, Wells papers, A. D. Gristwood – Wells, 1 Oct. 1929.

Guedalla's dog ... father's birthday: see Urbana, Wells Papers, Margaretta Gristwood – Wells, 8 Oct. 1929; A. D. Gristwood – Mrs. (Frank?) Wells, 22 Oct. 1929; and J. A. Gristwood – Wells 27 Oct. 1929.

104   *Sunday Times:* Urbana, Wells Papers, A. D. Gristwood – Wells, 1 Oct. 1932.

105   *verdict of suicide: Dorking and Leatherhead Advertiser,* 26 May 1933, p. 9, cols 3 & 4.

told Wells of the tragedy: Urbana, Wells Papers, J. A. Gristwood – Wells, 26 April 1933, 20 September 1936.

birthday greeting: Urbana, Wells Papers, J. A. Gristwood–Wells.

R. H. MOTTRAM

I am above all indebted to Mrs. Sophia Hankinson, RHM's daughter, for extensive information and help on family history and for editorial suggestions and for permission to quote from RHM's unpublished letters and published writings.

107   *Habits, points of view:* Mottram, R. H., *The Spanish Farm Trilogy,* London, Chatto & Windus, 1927 (vol. 2 *Sixty-four, Ninety-four!* [1st pub. 1925] pp. 42-43).

humanised history: ibid., introduction by John Galsworthy (1924), p. xi.

108   *Prince of Wales:* Mottram, R. H., "The Days of the Top Hat. A Clerk in His Fa-

ther's Bank, *T.P.'s & Cassell's Weekly,* 29 Oct. 1927. (On his early life see also Mottram, R. H., *The Window Seat, or Life Observed,* London, Hutchinson, 1954.)

109   *age of gentility:* ibid. *T.P.'s & Cassell's Weekly.*

horror of the tragic: Norfolk Record Office, mss Mottram, R. H., family letters 1890-1930 (including those from RHM on active service 1914-1918), RHM to Madge Allan, 18 Aug. 1915.

110   *saved my life:* RHM, *Window Seat,* p. 138.

change Ralph's life: on his relations with the Galsworthys, see, in particular, Mottram, R. H., *For Some We Loved, an Intimate Portrait of John and Ada Galsworthy,* London, Hutchinson, 1956; for their friendship see also Marrot, H.V., (ed.), *The Life and letters of John Galsworthy,* London, Heinemann, 1935.

111   *booted and spurred:* Mottram, op. cit. pp. 26-27.

112   *Norfolk Regiment:* RHM, *Window Seat,* p. 215.

pale of face: mss Mottram.

113   *icy rain:* ibid. RHM to his aunt, 9 Feb. 1915.

Roland Aubrey Leighton: ibid. RHM - Fanny Mottram (mother), 14 Feb. 1915 (see also Brittain,Vera, *Testament of Youth, an Autobiographical Story of the Years 1900-1925,* London, Gollancz, 1933).

utterly fatigued: ibid. RHM - Fanny Mottram, 20 Feb. 1915.

none get away: ibid. 6 March 1915 & 30 April 1915.

Montague: Disenchantment, New York, Brentano's (U.S. edn), 1922, p. 10.

114   *soreness out of my heart:* mss Mottram, RHM - Madge Allen, 29 June 1915.

Major tells us so: ibid. RHM - Fanny Mottram, 20 July 1915.

Zeppelin: ibid. 18 Aug. 1915.

115   *close to death:* ibid. RHM - Madge Allen, 6 Oct. 1915.

shells bumping: ibid. 12 Oct. 1915.

end of September: Petre, Brig. Loraine, *The History of the Norfolk Regiment,* Norwich, Jarrold, 1924, vol. 2, ch. 8: "The 9th (service) Battalion in France," p. 251; also Carew, Tim, *The Royal Norfolk Regiment, the 9th Regiment of Foot,* London, Hamish Hamilton, 1967; also PRO, WO 95/1623, War Diary, the 9th btn, the Norfolk Regiment, October 1915.

charming women: mss. Mottram, RHM - Fanny Mottram, 8 Oct. 1915.

116   *cottage chair:* ibid. RHM - Madge Allan, 23 Oct. 1915.

firing line: ibid. RHM - "AJC" 23 Nov. 1915.

he was gone: ibid. RHM - Fanny Mottram, 24 Oct. 1915.

killed around me all day: ibid. RHM - Madge Allan, undated fragment, 1915.

117   *in that sector:* WO 95/1623, 9 Norfolk Regt War Diary.

gibber at each other: mss Mottram, RHM - Fanny Mottram, 13 Nov. 1915.

very awkward: ibid. RHM - Chris Hall, 15 Oct. 1915, copy letter.

Pyrexia: ibid. RHM - Fanny Mottram, 27 Nov. 1915.

118   *run that risk:* ibid. RHM - Madge Allan, 11 Nov. 1915.

Communication Trenches: ibid. RHM - Fred R. (copy), 23 Jan. 1916.

prolonged shell fire: ibid.

119   *treat us to:* ibid. RHM - Chris Hall, 20 Jan. 1916.

miss it for anything: ibid.

instructor's job in England: ibid.

excreta: ibid.

120 *So you see, Darling:* ibid. RHM - Fanny Mottram, 22 Feb. 1916.
had been damaged: For examples of Claims Commission work, see PRO, WO 32/14286.
into his blankets: mss Mottram, RHM - Madge Allan, 6 & 13 March 1916.
121 *France and Germany have:* ibid. RHM - Fanny Mottram, 28 Sept. 1916.
Anglican services: ibid. 18 April 1916.
heaven on earth: ibid. 21 Aug. 1916.
our love: ibid. RHM - Madge Allan, 8 Sept. 1916; also RHM - Fanny Mottram, 31 Aug. & 6 Sept. 1916.
122 *Pickmere:* ibid. RHM - Fanny Mottram, 1 & 11 Oct., 8 Nov., 1916.
wear and tear ... extraordinary: ibid. 18 Oct. 1916.
to bed sleepy: ibid. 15 Nov. 1916.
123 *even today:* ibid. 30 Oct. 1916; and Fanny Mottram - RHM, 27 Oct. and 3 Nov., 1916. *Nor you!:* ibid. 24 Oct. 1916.
I won't boast: mss Mottram, RHM - Fanny Mottram, 22 and 29 Nov. 1916.
Pickmere's violin: ibid. 11 Mar. 1917.
very definite: ibid. 28 April 1917.
124 *rather superfluous:* ibid. 26 May 1917.
she cried dreadfully: ibid. RHM - Madge Allan, 12 Jan. 1917.
château ... spared: ibid. RHM - Fanny Mottram, 16 April, 15 May, 3 June, 1918.
pregnant: ibid. 11 Aug. and 17 Sept. 1918.
125 *slackened:* ibid. 17 Nov. 1918.
theatre: ibid.
not coming home at all: ibid. 28 Nov. 1918.
Burton: ibid. 10 March 1919.
126 *Spanish belfry:* ibid. 22 Feb. 1919.
good already: ibid. Madge (Allan) Mottram - Fanny Mottram, 29 June 1919.
127 *Galsworthy read through his drafts:* R.H. Mottram, *Another Window Seat or Life Observed, 1919-1953,* London, Hutchinson, 1957, ch. 6; and R.H.M. *For Some We Loved,* p. 27.
128 *light-coloured buds: Spanish Farm Trilogy,* pp. 69-70.
fidelity ... brilliance: mss Mottram, RHM - Fanny Mottram, 9 Aug. 1917.
to forget the war: RHM, *Another Window Seat,* p. 52.
La Galette: Spanish Farm Trilogy: pp. 183-234.
129 *thousand English soldiers:* ibid. p. 92.
it was national: ibid. p. 233.
dying stages: ibid. p. 211.
bored and bewildered: ibid. pp. 262-263.
130 *typewriter:* information Sophia Hankinson.
Mr. Norwich: I am indebted to the late Philip Hepworth, of Norwich, for a most helpful account and for the bibliography of RHM's writing, which he prepared for Norwich City Library.
131 *you can imagine:* HRHRC, mss Sassoon, Edmund Blunden - Siegfried Sassoon, 22 April 1926; mss Blunden, Mottram - Blunden, March 1926. On Mottram's other literary friendships, see, for example his letter to H.M. Tomlinson, 20 March 1951 (HRHRC mss Tomlinson) asking to dedicate his latest book to Tomlinson (who had awarded him the Hawthornden Prize).

bellicose than you or I: mss Mottram, RHM - Fanny Mottram, 8 Nov. 1917.

132 *financed ... part of the trip:* see RHM, *Another Window Seat,* pp. 95-103.
   time of intense worry: information Sophia Hankinson.

133 *outpaced those half his age:* notes by Philip Hepworth for Norwich City Library.

WILFRID EWART

137 *Angelina: Excelsior* (Mexico), 3 & 4 Jan. 1923, and Graham, Stephen, *The Life and Last Words of Wilfrid Ewart* (hereinafter "Graham, *Life and Last Words*"), London, G.P. Putnam's Sons, 1924, pp. 257-260.
   Ewart, Wilfrid Herbert Gore, *Way of Revelation. A Novel of Five Years,* London, G.P. Putnam's Sons, 1921.

138 *50,000:* See HRHRC, mss TIF Armstrong (John Gawsworth), Ewart Scrapbook of Ewart cuttings; sales figures given by Rich & Cowan, 1933.
   Henry Williamson, introduction to V.M. Yeates' *Winged Victory,* "Tribute to V.M. Yeates," Mayflower Books, London, 1974, p. 7.
   Clan Maryon: Ewart may possibly have drawn some inspiration for these decadent figures from what he had heard of such prominent bohemians as Ford Madox Ford and his mistress Violet Hunt, whose open affair caused a scandal, and their friend Mary Butts, who experimented with drugs; but no portrait was intended; see Goldring, Douglas, *South Lodge, Reminiscences of Violet Hunt, Ford Madox Ford and the English Review Circle,* London, Constable, 1943.

140 *Nashdom:* information the late Lord David Cecil. For many years, and until later 1987, Nashdom, Burnham, Slough, was an Abbey of the Anglican Benedictine order. Godfrey Stokes O.S.B., Abbot, to author, 2 Jan. 1987.
   psychosomatic illness: diary of Lady Mary Gore, 1877, in the possession of Pamela (Farmer) Thompson, Ewart's niece, to whom I am deeply indebted for information and for permission to quote from his papers.

141 *living in open sin:* Gore, Lady Elizabeth (Betsy): "The Gore Family" (unpub. memoir and family history, set down for the family, 1958), p. 81.
   Greenlands: I am indebted to the late Mrs. Maurice Waddington (Ewart's elder sister), the late Lord David Cecil (Ewart's cousin), and Pamela Thompson for this information.
   Broadleas: Graham, *Life and Last Words,* p. 33. Ewart, Wilfrid, *When Armageddon Came: Studies in Peace and War,* London, Rich & Cowan, 1933, pp. 3-9; and *Love and Strife,* London, Richards, 1936, pp. 261-290. Lady A. Cowdray, information.
   chilliness, desolation: Ewart, *Love and Strife,* p. 17.

142 *Graham Street:* information Pamela Thompson, Angela Waddington, and Mrs. Levy, former member of the congregation of St. Mary's Bourne (Graham Street).

143 *Wyandotte:* HRHRC, mss TIF Armstrong, ms articles by Ewart: see, for example: "The Life History of a Black Wyandotte" (undated) & "Women and Hens" (undated); see also Stephen Graham, op. cit. p. 17; Ewart is listed as a contributor to Brown, J.T. (ed.), *The Encyclopaedia of Poultry,* London, Walter Southwood & Co., 1910.

Wiltshire and Dorset: see mss TIF Armstrong, Ewart, "Tan Hill Fair," ms 17 Sept. 1913.

unoriginal comments: ibid. "The Age of Nonsense," 8 June 1911; "The Flats," prewar, Bottisham Cambridge.

144 *white tie and tails:* ibid. "London Cameos III - The Gay World of London" (undated), and "Early Morning at Covent Garden," 8 April 1914.

relaxed and cheerful: Graham, op, cit., Book I, chs 2 & 7, Book II, ch. 3.

145 *quizzing new acquaintances:* mss TIF Armstrong, Ewart: "The Apaches' Den," 5 Sept. 1912; "The Night City," 7 Nov. 1912.

Sir Edward Grey: ibid. Ewart, W., "England and Germany - a Comparison of Positions" (undated), *Love and Strife,* pp. 34, 51.

no physical standards: Cliff, Norman D., *To Hell and Back with the Guards,* Braunton, Merlin Books, 1988, p. 25.

146 *terrifying odds:* Graham, Stephen, *A Private in the Guards,* London, Macmillan, 1919.

bit of a nuisance: Ewart, Wilfrid, *Scots Guard,* London, Rich & Cowan, 1934, p. 81.

147 *Ruthven admitted:* HRHRC, mss Stephen Graham, Lord Ruthven - Graham, 22 Dec. 1922.

148 *young Prince of Wales: A King's Story. The Memoirs of HRH the Duke of Windsor,* London, Cassell, 1951, p. 120.

Ypres ... Gheluveldt ... Sailly: See PRO WO 95/1657, War Diary of 2nd Btn, the Scots Guards, Oct. 1914-Jan. 1915; see also, Petre, F. Loraine, Ewart, Wilfrid, and Lowther, Maj-Gen. Sir Cecil, *The Scots Guards in the Great War 1914-1918,* London, John Murray, 1925.

149 *Honfleur:* mss TIF Armstrong, letters of Ewart to parents and sister: Ewart - H.B. Ewart & Lady Mary Ewart, 20 Feb. 1915; Ewart, *Scots Guard,* p.16.

Strange twisted figures of trees: Scots Guard, p. 21.

fare worse than his richer: ibid. p. 16; mss Armstrong, Ewart - H.B. Ewart, 24 Feb. 1915.

150 *happily meet together at home:* ibid.: Ewart - parents 2 March 1915; Ewart - Lady M. Ewart, 7 March 1915; and to both parents 9 March 1915.

Estaires ... aviators killed: Scots Guard, pp. 39-47.

151 *hell of muddy fields ... his wound was a blighty:* ibid. pp. 47-68 and WO 95/1657 2 Scots Guards WD, 11 March 1915.

153 *Wyndham ... killed.* Graham, *Life & Last Words,* p. 30.

best writings: see, for example, by Ewart; "Near Blanken by Night," *Spectator,* 28 July 1917; "After Ypres," *Cornhill,* Sept. 1917; "At Neuve Chapelle," *English Review,* June 1915; "Two Mornings," *The Nineteenth Century,* Sept. 1920.

Arkwright: Scots Guard, pp. 70-71 Ewart - parents, 1 Jan. 1915; & WO 95/1223, 2 Scots Guards WD 31 Oct. 1915.

gas bag: mss TIF Armstrong, Ewart - H.B. Ewart, 13 Dec. 1915.

154 *Lonely Post: Scots Guard,* p. 73.

an Englishman's word: WO 95/1657, 2 Scots Guards WD, 25 Dec. 1914, Capt. G. H. Loder's account.

taking prisoners ... very unpopular: Graham, *Private in the Guards,* p. 217.

155 *quaint scene: Scots Guard,* pp. 77-79; and Ewart, "Two Mornings," in *Nineteenth*

Century, Sept. 1920.

All very quiet: WO 95/1223, 2 Scots Guards, WD, 25 Dec. 1915.

156   *haunt the imagination: Scots Guard,* pp. 87–90.

Roger's remedy: mss TIF Armstrong, Ewart - H.B. Ewart, 27 May 1916.

Sir John Spencer Ewart: ibid. 10 June 1916.

neighbouring death: Scots Guard, p. 106.

157   *this waterway:* ibid. pp. 105–106.

leaving the accursed Salient: see "After Ypres," *Cornhill,* Sept. 1917, pp. 294–307.

Jack's grave: Scots Guard, pp. 126–127.

158   *self-confidence:* mss TIF Armstrong, Ewart - H.B. Ewart, 27 Aug. 1916.

affaire de coeur: Ewart, "Three Days" in *When Armageddon Came,* p. 127.

Dollie: I am greatly indebted to Anne (Waddington) Butler, younger daughter of Angela Waddington, and Ewart's niece, for information; see mss TIF Armstrong, Ewart to "Ginger" (his sister Angela), 1 Aug. 1918, re Dollie Rawson.

159   *surcharged emotion:* Ewart, "Some young Women of Modern England," in *Nineteenth Century* May 1919, p. 950.

Toodle-oo: Graham, *The Life & Last Words of Wilfrid Ewart,* p. 58.

Land Rover: I am much indebted to Ursula Wyndham, for information; also Max Egremont, Simon Head, and Victoria Reay.

160   *Deconck ... mud everywhere:* 2 Scots Guards WD 1 Dec. 1916; Ewart, *When Armageddon Came,* p. 131.

Esmond Elliot: Scots Guard, p. 130; *Way of Revelation,* pp. 399–404; *When Armageddon Came,* pp. 148–149.

161   *Goodbye!: When Armageddon Came,* p. 155.

staff job: mss TIF Armstrong, Ewart - H.B. Ewart, 13 Sept. 1917.

Ciro's: Scots Guard, p. 133.

English press: mss TIF Armstrong, Ewart - H.B. Ewart, 13 Sept. 1917.

too dark to read: Scots Guard, pp. 144–145.

162   *New Army discipline:* ibid. p. 146.

tried past endurance: Ewart, "Memory of Bourlon Wood," *National Review,* vol. lxxi, p. 178.

163   *only man left alive besides myself: Scots Guard,* p. 148.

sent home: ibid. p.149.

164   *running for their lives:* ibid. p. 150.

Haig: Sir Douglas Haig, Diary, 4 Dec. 1917, in Robert Blake ed., *The Private Papers of Douglas Haig, 1914-1919,* London, Eyre and Spotiswoode, p. 270.

Good old Mr. Ewitt: Scots Guard, p. 152; mss TIF Armstrong, Ewart - H.B. Ewart, 29 Dec. 1917. *Gavrelle-Roeux: Scots Guard,* p. 153; WO 95/1657 2 Scots Guards WD Jan 1918.

165   *Sandie Ruthven:* mss TIF Armstrong, W. Ewart - H.B. Ewart, 10 Feb. 1918.

M.C.: Scots Guard, pp. 157–160.

vicious antidote: ibid. pp. 160–169; Ewart, "A Vision of Paris," *When Armageddon Came,* pp. 157–178.

Stirling ... introduced: Graham, *Life and Last Words of Wilfrid Ewart,* p. 4.

166   *wanderings after the war:* mss TIF Armstrong, Ewart - Ginger (Angela Waddington), 1 Aug. 1918.

our true calling: Graham, op. cit. p. 7.

I never use my own name: ibid. p. 11.

more effective than any volume of essays: ibid. p. 12.

staff appointment: mss TIF Armstrong, Ewart - H.B. Ewart, 1 Sept. 1918.

No prisoners: ibid. & Scots Guard, p. 173.

knocked unconscious: ibid. and see Graham, *Private in the Guards,* p. 236.

167 *drug-dealing:The Times,* 20 Nov., 14 and 21 Dec. 1918.

ould grey-legs: Scots Guard, p. 194.

silent good feeling: ibid. p. 216; Ewart - G.A.B. Dewar, 6 Sept. 1920.

"The Passing of a Victorian," in *When Armageddon Came,* pp. 3-9.

168 *grey the sky above:* ibid. *"A Pilgrimage,"* p. 243.

under the trees: Scots Guard, pp. 147-150; and Graham, *Life and Last Words of Wilfrid Ewart,* p. 96.

nonsense: Williamson, Henry, introduction to V.M. Yeates' *Winged Victory.*
"Tribute to V.M. Yeates," Mayflower Books edn, p. 7; see "Reality in War Literature" in Williamson, H., *A Linhay on the Downs,* London, Faber & Faber, 1934.

verge of collapse: Ewart, Wilfrid, *A Journey in Ireland in 1921,* London, Putnam's, 1922.

depravity: Imperial War Museum Collections, 75/29/1, 75/29/2. C. Hunting ton (of Putnam's) - Ewart, 10 Sept. 1921; see *Way of Revelation,* p. 521, where Rosemary Meynell is likened to the drugged Parisian prostitute Lola whom Adrian Knoyle has met in an earlier part of the book. In Huntington's correspondence there seems to be a suggestion (he compares the scene to Hauptmann's "Rose Bernt") that Ewart may have contemplated presenting Rosemary as being pregnant by her unsavoury lover Upton. But no extant manuscript version of the novel (there are several) bears out this suggestion.

169 *probably been misled:* HRHRC TIF Armstrong, Ewart: Williamson, Henry, "A Wild Goose Chase with Gawsworth," 1962 - to be put in a festschrift for John Gawsworth, "Gawsworth, Poet-King," on the occasion of his 50th birthday. One of the inaccuracies of this piece was to say that Eric Sinclair in *Way of Revelation* was based on "Percy Wyndham" - when the character derives clearly from Esmond Elliott, with an *element* of George Wyndham.

Santa Fe: See Graham, *Life and Last Words of Wilfrid Ewart,* pp. 153-161.

Indian tribes: Ewart, Wilfrid, "The Dance of the Jemez Indians," Cornhill, Nov. 1923.

170 *tin box ... firing their guns into the air:* Graham, op. cit., book 3, chs 5 & 6.

exit hole: ibid. pp. 257-258.

duelling army officers: see Excelsior, Mexico City, 3 Jan. 1923, and Graham, Stephen, *In Quest of Eldorado,* London, Macmillan, 1924, pp. 295-298.

funeral: Excelsior, Mexico City, 4 Jan. 1923.

Goodhart-Rendel: I am indebted to Fr. Bill Scott, the Vicar of St. Mary's Bourne Street, for information.

171 *Jamie Balfour:* mss TIF Armstrong, Jack Stirling - Wilfrid Ewart (whom he addresses as "Bill") 10 July 1922, and enclosed letter from Victor Mackenzie to Jack Stirling, 6 July 1922.

Zola: Ewart, *When Armageddon Came,* introduction by "G.," p. viii.

collection of articles: care had to be taken in this and a subsequent publication,

Love and Strife, to avoid repetition of episodes, for Ewart often wrote several times about the same incidents in different ways; inevitably there is overlap in the various books and Gawsworth, as editor, was himself sometimes confused by the large number of alternative versions.

dies of consumption: Urquhart was originally called "Knox."

ribbon-developed England: Gawsworth, John, (ed.), Ewart, Wilfrid, *Aspects of England*, London, Richards, 1937. This was based on articles for *The Times, Morning Post, Sunday Times, Country Life, Evening Standard, Evening News, Time & Tide, Graphic, Illustrated Sporting & Dramatic News.*

copies of letters: mss TIF Armstrong, Ewart; H.B. Ewart – John Gawsworth, 13 Oct. 1932, 20, 24 March 1934, 17 Oct. 1935, 5 March 1937.

173 *bibulously, in Fiesole:* Russell Foreman (novelist; close friend of John Gawsworth) to the author, 17 Feb. 1987: "He was that *rara avis* a genuine clown..." Gawsworth actually died in England.

ROBERT KEABLE

174 *first editions:* Mrs. D. Trewolla-Hulme to author, 9 Nov. 1986.

Simon Called Peter: Keable, Robert, *Simon Called Peter*, London, Constable, 1921.

obscene: New York Times, 19 Oct. 1922, p. 2, col. 7.

corpses: New York Times, 17–30 Sept. and 18 Oct. 1922, p. 2.

Gladstone: See Sutherland, John, *Mrs. Humphry Ward, Eminent Victorian, Pre-eminent Edwardian.* Oxford, Clarendon Press, 1990, chs 10–11; also Sadleir, Michael, "In Memoriam Robert Keable," in *Constable's Monthly List,* no. 75, Jan. 1928.

175 *undies: Simon Called Peter,* p. 277.

sidelong glance: Sadleir, op. cit.

care a damn: Keable – Arthur Grimble, 27 Sept. 1921.

176 *Hankey:* Donald Hankey, *A Student in Arms,* London, Andrew Melrose, 1917, pp. 109–115.

177 *reproachfully: Church Times,* 6 May 1921.

Keable replying: ibid. 13 May 1921 and letter from Keable, 7 May 1921.

outlay: Raymond, Ernest, *Tell England,* London, Cassell, 1922.

married twice: Raymond, Ernest, *The Story of My Days: an Autobiography* 1888–1922, London, Cassell, 1968, pp. 182–3; I am indebted to Mrs. Diana Raymond for information; also Leeds University, the Liddle Collection, taped interview with Ernest Raymond.

178 *simply Conservative:* Keable, Robert, *Preadventure,* London, Hurst & Blackett edn, p. 14 (first pub. London, Constable, 1922).

History: The Whitgiftian, Feb. 1928, also Jan. 1971.

180 *spirituality:* Cambridge University, Magdalene College Archive, mss Arthur Benson, Benson Diary and Benson – Keable, 13 and 16 Dec. 1914; also Martindale, Cyril Charles, *The Life of Robert Hugh Benson,* 2 vols, London, Longmans 1916, for example, pp. 19, 35; also Lubbock, Percy (ed.), *The Diary of Arthur Hugh Benson,* London, Hutchinson, p. 223; also Newsome, David, *On the Edge of Paradise, a Life of Arthur C. Benson, from His Diaries,* London, John Murray, 1980,

pp. 173, 267; and Benson, Arthur, *Hugh, Memoirs of a Brother,* London 1915.
Anglican Church: See Forsyth, P.T., "The Reality of God; a Wartime Question"
in *The Hibbert Journal,* no. 64, vol. xvi, 1918.
knows it too: Keable, *Peradventure,* p. 158 & chs 7 & 8 generally, and Martindale,
Benson, pp. 265-274.

181 *Bishop of Zanzibar:* See : Oliver, Roland, *The Missionary Factor in East Africa,* 2nd
ed. 1965; Maynard Smith, Herbert, *Frank, Bishop of Zanzibar, the Life of Frank
Weston, D.D., 1871-1924,* London, S.P.C.K., 1926, pp. 51, 265, and *The Times,*
passim July – December 1913 (on Kikuyu Conference); Hastings, Adrian, *A
History of African Christianity,* p. 45.
mango groves: See Keable, Robert, *City of the Dawn,* London, Nisbet, 1915;
and Oxford University, Rhodes House Library, mss USPG, the Rev. D. Travers,
E.F. Spenton – Travers, 5 July 1912.
kept him from Rome: USPG, Book A1 XVII Weston, 449a, Bishop Frank Weston
to A. J. A. Bullen, 12 Oct. 1923.
simply a Pope: Magdalene, mss A.C. Benson, Benson diary, vol. 143, p. 36.
everyone in the diocese: mss USPG, letters to his mother from Rev. Christopher
Fixsen: f435, 3 Sept. 1911. Fixsen described Weston as "a lovable man ... but he
is a thorough-going autocrat, and as such is bound to have trouble as autocracy
is not episcopacy."
love ... reciprocated: mss USPG Box A1 XVII f 493, Weston – H. Maynard-Smith,
April 1918: "The problem of the day is colour"; Keable, Robert, "African
Priests in France," in *The East and the West. A Quarterly Review for the Study
of Missionary Problems,* vol. XVI, Jan. 1918, p. 53; Keable, R., *City of the Dawn*
ch. 12 (study of old African priest, enumerating faults and virtues); Maynard
Smith, *Frank Bishop of Zanzibar,* p. 262.

182 *spiritual qualities:* mss USPG, box A1 XVII, Weston – Bullen, 12 Oct. 1923.
amazing speed: Keable, Robert, *Darkness or Light. Studies in the History of the Universities' Mission to Central Africa,* 1st ed., 1912.
satisfied!: A City of the Dawn, p. 72.
domineering: Mrs. D. Trewolla-Hulme to author, 9 Nov. 1986. Sybil Keable was
born 3 Feb. 1884, married R.K. 7 June 1915; I am indebted to Sister Mary
Campion of the Convent of the Sacred Heart, Mill Hill, for information on
Sybil Keable.

183 *sexual suppression:* mss A.C. Benson, diary, vol. 175, 6v.
Redemptorist: Hugh Benson – Keable, 15 Sept. 1914, in Martindale, Hugh Benson, p. 373. In this work Keable is not mentioned by name, but can be clearly
identified from the similarities to the detail in his novel *Peradventure,* and
evidently lent the letters for the life of Hugh Benson.
Sekubu: Lewis, Cecil, and Edwards, G.E., *Historical Records of the Church of
the Province of South Africa,* London, SPCK 1934, pp. 471-4; Keable, Robert,
Standing By, London, Nisbet, 1919, ch. 21; Keable, Robert, *Recompence, a
Sequel to Simon Called Peter,* London, Constable, 1924. Dove, Canon R., *Anglican
Pioneers in Lesotho, 1876-1930,* Maseru, 1975, pp. 152-153.
Natal: Magdalene College Magazine, June 1916, p. 38 and see also *Recompence,* chs
6 & 7.

184 *quick succession:* Keable, Robert, *Pilgrim Papers: from the Writing of Francis Thomas*

Wilfrid, Priest, London, Christophers, 1920.

pressed the bishop: Sister Mary Campion, Mrs. Trewolla-Hulme, information.

British rule: Edgar, R.R., "Recruiting, resistance and the South African Native Labour Contingent" in *Mohlomi, Journal of South African Historical Studies,* 1981, pp. 94–108; and *Journal of South African History,* 19, 1978, pp. 68–85.

army chaplain: see *Army List,* 1918 - Overseas Forces, South Africa, chaplains (temp). Keable was commissioned 28.5.17.

died of typhoid: Dr. Anthony Keable-Elliott (Keable's son) to author, 8 Dec. 1990. Henry Keable, Robert's brother, was born 1888, died 1918.

authority: Montague, C.E., *Disenchantment,* London, 1922, ch.5.

185   *for the men:* see Imperial War Museum Collection, IWM 80/22/1, papers of Canon E.C. Crosse D.S.O., M.C. (later Senior Chaplain C. of E., 7th Division), "A History of the Chaplains' Department: War 1914-18," section I, "With an Infantry Brigade at the Front," and IWM, mss Bulstrode, IWM 87/10/1, Rev. R. Bulstrode, "A Parson in Khaki: a Memoir."

rescue the wounded: IWM, Crosse, op. cit.

bad start: Charles E. Raven, Liddle Collection, University of Leeds; see Raven, Charles, *A Wandering Way,* London, Martin Hopkinson, 1928, pp. 156-8; and Dillistone, F.W., *Charles Raven, Naturalist, Historian, Theologian,* London, Hodder & Stoughton, 1975, ch. 4.

primitive lust: Benstead, C.R. (Lieut. C.R. Benstead M.C., R.G.A.), Retreat, London, 1930, p. 313.

Geoffrey Gordon: Oxford University, Bodleian, Western Mss, Eng. lett. R. S. Blaker, c. 317, f 197, Rev. Geoffrey Gordon - Richard Blaker, 8 June 1930; see also, Pym, T.W., and Gordon Geoffrey, *Papers from Picardy,* London, Constable, 1917.

186   *In Mesopotamia:* Thompson, Edward J., *These Men Thy Friends,* London, Macmillan, 1933 (1st pub. 1927). I am indebted to the late Professor E.P. Thompson for information relating to his father.

an informal version: Crosse, op. cit.

deathbed conversion: ibid.

refuses comforts of religion: Simon Called Peter, pp. 159-60.

187   *companionable cigarette:* Crosse, op. cit.

188   *January 1918:* Keable, Robert, in *The East and the West,* vol. XVI, Jan. 1918.

Mr. Keable has chastised…: The Bishop of Zanzibar in *The East and the West,* vol. XVII, 1919, p. 165.

point so openly: Keable, *Standing By,* ch. 5.

189   *whisky and soda:* ibid. pp. 38, 40.

publicans and sinners: ibid. p. 120; *Simon Called Peter,* p. 182.

Hotel Cecil: for this and other family information thanks to Jolie's son, Dr. Anthony Keable-Elliott, and to her sister, the late Lady Knott-Bower; see also Jolie's letters to Robert Keable and Rita and Jack Elliott (Dr. Keable-Elliott).

190   *sacrament of emancipation:* Keable, *Standing By,* pp. 240, 248.

191   *controversial set of essays:* ibid. ch. 19.

"*Wordly*": thanks to Tim Couzens (U. of Witswatersrand) for use of his interview with David Ambrose, 17 May 1992; Sims, J.H., *Basntoland News* 9 May

1961; O'Shea Mary, *Bloomie,* C.T., Dom Nelson, 1977, p. 33.

how to wait: Keable, R., *Pilgrim Papers.*

192 *taking stock of his life:* mss Keable (Dr. Keable-Elliott), Keable - Arthur Grimble, 27 Sept. 1921.

would not visit his parents: Mrs. D. Trewolla-Hulme to author, 9 Nov. 1986 and 24 Oct. 1990.

Voyage to Arcturus: Keable, Robert, *The Mother of All Living: a Novel of Africa,* London, Constable, 1920, p. 289.

God really covers: mss Keable, Keable - Grimble, 27 Sept. 1921.

occult ... life force: Maynard-Smith, *Frank, Bishop of Zanzibar,* p. 115; and Keable, *Mother of All Living,* passim.

193 *thousandfold:* mss Keable, Keable-Grimble, 27 Sept. 1921.

in veiled form to Jolie: "This book is dedicated to JULIE. She never lived, maybe, but it is truer to say she never dies. Nor shall she ever die. One may believe in God, though he is hard to find, and Women, though such as Julie are far to seek."

Gwen Otter: Dr. Keable-Elliott, information; and on Gwen Otter, see Ruck, Berta, *A Smile for the Past,* London, Hutchinson, 1959, p. 226.

194 *Lady Anne Carew:* Keable, Robert, *Lighten Our Darkness,* London, Constable, 1927, pp. 140-1. In the U.S.A. the book was published as *Anne Decides.*

betraying him: ibid, ch. 10.

multum amavit: Keable, Robert, *Numerous Treasure,* London, Constable, 1925; and Keable, Robert, *The Great Galilean,* London, Cassell, 1929.

unfaithful to her: mss Keable, Alta Shapiro (of Brookline, Mass.) to Dr. E.L. Elliott, 23 Feb. 1928.

195 *at odds with the English society:* mss Keable, Keable - Grimble, 27 Sept. 1921; and Mrs. Trewolla-Hulme to author, 9 Nov. 1986.

wanderlust: mss Keable, Keable - Grimble, 27 Sept. 1921.

Cecil Lewis: see, for example, Lewis, Cecil, *Never Look Back: an Attempt at Autobiography,* London, Hutchinson, 1974. Of Tahiti, Lewis wrote: "My memories of the First World War had not left me. In fact, though they had remained underground most of the time, I found they had developed in me a tendency to look for anything which promised even a slim chance of a better way of life" (p. 116); and Muspratt, Eric, *My South Sea Island,* London, Penguin Books edn, 1936: "This South Sea adventure came shortly after the war. It followed a spell of soldiering and a few months of farming, both of which struck me as soul-destroying occupations" (p. 7).

196 *beast to live with:* mss Keable, Keable - Grimble, 27 Sept. 1921.

faint if they knew: ibid. Jolie Keable - Rita Elliott, Nov? 1922, on S. S. *Omar,* leaving Melbourne for Sydney.

teacher for the public: see *Sydney Daily Telegraph,* 4, 8, 9 Nov. 1922.

mere selfishness: ibid. "Non-theologian" letter to, 9 Nov. 1922; and 11 Nov. 1922.

197 *avoid his perils:* mss USPG, Book A1 XVII, 449a, Weston - Bullen 12 Oct. 1923.

Richard Jefferies: Keable - Grimble, 27 Sept. 1921; and see Keable, Robert, *Tahiti, Isle of Dreams,* London, Hutchinson, 1925, ch. 1.

Gauguin's gesture: Keable, *Tahiti,* ch. 5.

198 *£250 a year:* mss Keable, Jolie Keable – "Wuffy" Elliott (Dr. E.L. Elliott's mother), 22 Dec. 1922 and 23 March 1923.
magic that is theirs: Keable, *Tahiti, Isle of Dreams,* pp. 130–1.
small jetty: the house is described in Alec Waugh, *The Early Years of Alec Waugh,* London, 1962, pp. 240–2. See also: Keable, *Numerous Treasure,* ch. 4. The house still stands, with its original interiors: see Kay, Robert F., *Tahiti and French Polynesia, a Travel Survival Kit,* Victoria, Lonely Planet Publications, 2nd ed. 1988, p. 82.

199 *dutiful wife:* mss Keable, Jolie Keable – "Wuffy" Elliott, 22 Dec. 1922 and 23 March 1923.
childbirth with horror: Recompence was finished in March 1923. See ch. 12.
at least four years: mss Keable, Jolie Keable – "Wuffy" Elliot, 21 March 1923.
my cabbage: ibid. Jolie Keable (signed "Betty") – Robert Keable, 26 May 1924.
new novel: ibid. See Jolie Keable, "The Blue Bear" (tale written for Robert Keable to show her husband, suffering from writer's block, how easy it was to write a story), 1924.

200 *told the priest:* ibid. Fr. E. Dowling – Robert Keable, 22 Nov. 1924.
miscalculated the amount: Death Certificate of Jolie Beresford Keable aged 25, 14 Nov. 1924; Dr. A. Keable-Elliott, information.

201 *Magdalene College:* Whitgift School Archive, Will of Robert Keable, 1 Jan. 1925.
sense of obligation: mss Keable, Keable – Rita Elliott, 23 June 1925.
does it matter?: ibid. and see Keable – Rita Elliott, 15 July 1925.
temporary improvement: ibid. Keable – Rita Elliott, 5 March, 28 May, 24 June 1926, 25 May 1927.
losing his touch: ibid. Keable – Rita Elliott, 23 June 1925.

202 *Aldington's Katia:* ibid. Keable – Rita Elliott, 5 March 1926; see also Holmsen, Sverre, *Polynesian Trade Wind,* London, James Barrie, 1949, p. 128.
Robert joked: mss Keable, Keable – E.L. & Rita Elliott, 24 June 1926.
happy one: ibid. Keable – Rita Elliott, 25 May 1927; and Ina Sampson – E.L. and Rita Elliott, 28 Feb., 9 March 1928.

203 *Sunday school treat:* Waugh, Alec, *The Early Years of Alec Waugh,* pp. 240–2.
will die a monk: quoted in: Fr. Bede Jarrett O.P. – Sybil Keable (letter in possession of Mrs. Trewolla-Hulme).
Richard Raynal: Keable, Robert, in *T.P.'s & Cassell's Weekly,* 16 July 1927, p. 382.
transcendent experience: Alec Waugh, op. cit. pp. 268–9.

204 *Monty:* Keable, Robert, *The Madness of Monty,* London, Nisbet, 1928.
some few philosophers: mss Keable, Keable – Rita Elliott, 15 August 1927.
540-lb. swordfish: ibid. 23 July 1927.
in the costume of Eve: ibid. 28 June 1927.
Escadrille Lafayette: see Clune, Frank, *A Tale of Tahiti,* London, Angus & Robertson, 1958, pp. 203–4; and Eggleston, George C., *Tahiti,* London, Travel Book Club, 1952, pp. 24–6.

205 *appeared in 1929:* Keable, *The Great Galilean,* introduction & pp. 156–8.
Isle of Dreams: mss Keable, Keable – E.L. & Rita Elliott, 5 Dec. 1927.
He was forty: James Norman Hall to Rev. R.H. Keable, Vicar of Pavenham, Bedfordshire (father of Robert Keable), 8 Jan. 1928 (I am indebted to Mrs. Brenda Wesley of Pavenham for use of this letter); and mss Keable, James

Norman Hall to E.L. Elliott, 2 Jan. 1928. Hall said nothing to Keable's father about Keable's relationships with Jolie or Ina, which had been kept a secret from his parents.

Catholic rites: information Dr. A. Keable-Elliott.

Papeete Cemetery: James Norman Hall to Rev. R.H. Keable, 8 Jan. 1928.

206 *faded, cooled, were forgotten:* mss Keable, Ina Salmon - E.L. Elliott, 9 March 1928, and Ina Salmon - Rita Elliott, 28 Feb. 1928.

St. Mary's Abbey: Mrs D.Trewolla-Hulme to the author, 9 Nov. 1986; Sister Mary Campion, information.

207 *destructive influence:* see Archibald C. Cowll, letter to the *Referee,* 2 Jan. 1928.

GILBERT FRANKAU

209 *Gilbert Frankau, best-selling author:* information Timothy d'Arch Smith, grandson; more than to anyone else I am indebted to him for memories of his grandfather.

210 *Dispeck:* Newman, Aryeh, "From Exile to Exit":, in the *Jewish Quarterly,* vol. 34, no. 4, (128), 1987, p. 49.

Frank Danby: "Frank Danby" (Frankau, Julia), *Dr. Phillips, a Maida Vale Idyll,* 2nd edn, London, Vizetelly, 1887.

Maida Vale: ibid. and see also Harry J. Greenwall, *I Hate Tomorrow: an Autobiographical Experiment,* London, The Book Club, 1940, ch. 1.

211 *transmit ... Jewish ... heritage:* See Frankau's autobiography, *Gilbert Frankau's Self-Portrait: a Novel of His Own Life,* 2nd edn, London, MacDonald, 1944.

Eton: ibid. I am indebted to the following Eton College staff re Frankau's Eton career: Paul Quarrie, former College Librarian & Keeper of College Collections; Andrew Robinson; Penny Hatfield, Archivist, College Library; see also *Hugh MacNaughten's House Record, Eton, 1899-1920,* pub. Sir Eugene Millington-Drake, limited edn of 200.

Sauce Piquante: Information Timothy d'Arch Smith.

212 *train boys to be men:* Frankau, Gilbert, *Peter Jackson, Cigar Merchant: a Romance of Married Life,* 12th edn, London, Hutchinson, 1920, p. 198. Peter Jackson's name encapsulates Frankau's own divided cultural position, being both an Anglo-Norman name and, in that period, a common adaptation of the name Isaacs.

Hebraic blood: ibid. p. 10.

Anglican until ... middle of ...War: ibid., pp. 23, 160.

213 *bombastic war poetry:* Frankau, Gilbert, "The Song of the Crashing Wing" in *The Judgment of Valhalla,* London, Chatto & Windus, 1918, p. 11.

Swaffer: Information, d'Arch Smith.

litigious: See British Museum 56704, mss Society of Authors, G. Frankau correspondence, for an example of his litigiousness; the file is otherwise without interest.

214 *fine shoulders: Self-Portrait,* p. 104; on Julia Frankau's character see, for example, p. 22.

Disraeli: ibid. p. 54.

215 *Westminster:* see *Self-Portrait;* information d'Arch Smith; I am also indebted to

Elizabeth Eccleshare (Frankau's niece) for memories and views of her family.
my main love: Self-Portrait, p. 98.

216 *a hundred thousand copies:* Frankau, Pamela, *Pen to Paper,* London, Heinemann, 1961, pp. 180-186.
golf course: Self-Portrait, p. 141.
one just does: Peter Jackson, p. 198.
Flatau, Dorota, Yellow English, London, Hutchinson, 1918; on her and her brother, see Gibson, Ashley, *Postscript to Adventure,* London, J. M. Dent, 1930, pp. 95-97: a useful source generally for the pre-First-War journalist's world.

217 *how utterly damnable the infantry job was:* Miller, Patrick (George Gordon MacFarlane), *The Natural Man,* London, Grant Richards, 1924, p. 276.
next to Coates' signature: PRO, WO 95/2197, War Diary of 107th Bde, RFA, 24th Div. Artillery (107 Bde RFA, WD), Jan. 1916, signed by Frankau 1935.

218 *preparedness and professionalism:* ibid. Aug.-Sept.; WO 95/2215, Aug.-Sept. 1915.

219 *High Command still optimistic:* see, for example, Warner, Philip, *The Battle of Loos,* London, William Kimber, 1976; Brigadier General Sir James Edmonds, *Military Operations France and Belgium,* London, Macmillan and HMSO, 1922-49 (1915 vol.); Williamson, Henry, *A Fox Under My Cloak,* revised edn, London, Hamilton, 1963, part 3.

221 *paid ... his respects:* see *Peter Jackson,* pp. 167-169.

222 *unpleasant associations:* Edmund Blunden, review, *Nation & Athenaeum,* 15 July 1929, p. 369.
Menin Road: HRHRC, Austin, Texas, mss Frankau, ms review ("Wipers"), of Sir James Edmonds op. cit., 1914, vol. 1, 1922; the Frankau papers at Austin contain relatively little *correspondence;* most of the documents are his ms novels. I am indebted to Timothy d'Arch Smith and the Humanities Research Center at the University of Texas at Austin for permission to quote from these and other Frankau papers at HRHRC.

223 *new war work: Self-Portrait,* pp. 163-164.
The Wipers Times, a facsimile of extracts from the *Trench Magazine, The Wipers Times, The New Church Times, The Kemmel Times, The Somme Times, & The BEF Times,* London, Herbert Jenkins, 1918, introduction p. vii & passim.
We are the guns: Frankau, Gilbert, "The voice of the Guns," in *The City of Fear and Other Poems,* London, Chatto & Windus, 1917, pp. 46-47.

224 *clap-trap verse:* Frankau, Gilbert, "The Other Side," in *The Judgement of Valhalla,* pp. 49-50.

225 *shrill falsetto: Self-Portrait,* pp. 156-157.

226 *hindered his recovery:* ibid. p. 163 ff.
Judgement of Valhalla: pp. 27-39.

227 *completed the picture: Peter Jackson,* p. 95.

228 *the help that never came:* ibid. Part XV, section 4.

230 *Her breasts were two burning torments:* ibid. p. 349.
great cleansing storm: ibid. p. 9.
pleasures of country life: On his aims in the book generally, see: HRHRC mss Frankau, Gilbert Frankau's handwritten "Scenario of 'Peter Jackson, Cigar Merchant'" - a treatment for his agent or publisher - 14 Sept. 1918.

231 *naked and beastly disorganisation:* ibid.
C.E. Jacomb: *Torment,* London, Andrew Melrose, 1920.
Patrick MacGill: see, Cecil, Hugh, and Mirabel, *Clever Hearts,*
Desmond and Molly MacCarthy, a biography, London, Gollancz, 1990, pp. 155-156.

233 *staunch patriot:* Hutchinson, Arthur Stuart Monteth (1880-1971), *A Year That the Locust –,* London, Ivor Nicholson & Watson, 1935, pp. 13-19, 163-5, 182-5, 189-94.
almost half his age: Deeping, George Warwick (1877–1950), *No Hero This,* London, Cassell, 1935.

234 *experts he consulted:* See, for example, HRHRC, mss Frankau, Gilbert Frankau – Sir Richard Cruise KCVO, 17 April 1936 and Gilbert Frankau – Alan M. Allen of J. H. Lyons & Co., 28 Feb. 1936.
dressing case: Information, d'Arch Smith.

235 *a huge, ramshackle house:* ibid.
particular fancy: See *Self-Portrait,* pp. 290-304.

236 *lunches at the Savoy:* Frankau, Pamela, *I Find Four People,* London, Ivor Nicholson & Watson, 1935, p. 107; see also p. 70 ("They met at that time as unsentimental friends"), p. 155 ("'Money', [Gilbert] ... repeated ... 'has nothing to do with love. Just remember that...'"), p. 157 ("'Have I ... ever failed in generosity towards you?' 'Not exactly ... But you seem to have forgotten my birthday since I was eight, and that has saved you a lot.'"), p. 167 ("'Your father is a Blackshirt, is he not?'").
dealt sympathetically with that problem: Though he was anxious to see her depression as a neurosis rather than a psychosis, Susan Frankau clearly had recurrent problems that indicated a clinical disorder. See Frankau, Gilbert, *Michael's Wife,* London, MacDonald, 1948; and information, d'Arch Smith.
quoting Tennyson: The cemetery is in Fortune Green Road.

237 *weakness of ... the nerves:* See *Michael's Wife,* where this is a recurrent theme.

238 *Royal Field Artillery: Peter Jackson,* p. 399.

RONALD GURNER

I am deeply indebted to the late Lady Gurner (*née* Phyllis Carver, 1895–1991), Ronald Gurner's sister-in-law, for much of the unpublished family information in this chapter. Phyllis Gurner had known the Gurner family from their (and her own) childhood years and furnished me with key information both about Gurner's boyhood and about his death.

239 *To Youth:* Gurner, Stanley Ronald Kershaw, *Pass Guard at Ypres* (hereinafter *"Pass Guard"*), London, J. M. Dent, 1930, p. vii.

240 *holiday chalets:* I am much indebted to Lionel (Leon) Gurner, Ronald Gurner's son, for information.
Worster: See *Pass Guard,* p. 3. I am grateful to Michael Copeland Worster of Hambleden, Oxfordshire, for information about his mother and Ronald Gurner. To Freddie Percy, Archivist of Whitgift School, for information on

Worster and on Whitgift generally, my debt is immense.

243 *THE BROTHERHOOD!: Pass Guard,* pp. 239-241.
answer to Remarque: Freddie Percy, information.
Fahnenjunker Volkenborn: Grabenhorst, Georg, pub. in U.K. as *Zero Hour* (tr. A. Featherstonhaugh), London, Brentano's, 1929.

244 *at the time of ... publication:* See *Daily Telegraph,* 18 May 1939; see also Whitgift School Archive, *Daily Chronicle,* press cutting at time of publication, 1930.
General Vicke: Pass Guard, pp. 127-129.

245 *Gurner was born ... children paid price ... mischievous boy:* Lady Gurner, information.
rugby: ibid. and *The Taylorian* (Merchant Taylors' school magazine), 1908, where Gurner is described as having "plenty of dash, but is too impetuous." In that year he was a regular member of the school XV and weighed 11 stone 6 lb. I am indebted to Miss G. H. Blakewell, Merchant Taylor's Librarian, for assistance.

246 *terrible depression: I Chose Teaching,* London, Dent, 1937, ch. 1.
Norwood: Gurner, Ronald, *I Chose Teaching,* pp. 17-18, and Hill, C. P., *A History of Bristol Grammar School,* London, Pitman, 1951; Norwood, Cyril, *The English Tradition of Education,* London, John Murray, 1929; see also Percy, F. H. G., *The History of Whitgift School,* London, Batsford, 1976, 2nd edn. revised, expanded, Croydon, Whitgift Foundation, 1991.
regime was spartan: See Sorley, Charles (Marlborough 1908-13), "The Song of the Ungirt Runners," quoted in Moore, T. Sturge, *Some Soldier Poets,* London, Grant Richards, 1919, p. 56 and Sydney Sheppard (Marlborough 1919-22), letter to author, 1985.

247 *Rae, Worster:* "E.C.C.," *Keith Rae. A Memoir of Oxford and Marlborough,* Christchurch N.Z., Christchurch Press, 1926. I am indebted to John Jones, in 1985 Dean and Archivist, Balliol College, Oxford, for information on Keith Rae and the Rae Trust; also T.E.K. Rae for booklets on his uncle Keith's life, including the Diary of Lieut. T.K.H. Rae, 1915; also Dr. John Rae (not a close relation), formerly Head Master of Westminster College, for encouragement; information Michael Worster.
twisted ankle: PRO WO95/1895 War Diary of 14th Division Cyclists Coy, & WO 95/792 WD 6th Corps Cyclists Battalion; see WO 95/1895, memo from Capt. Fowler, 7 Nov. 1915.

248 *Ypres was full of meaning: I Chose Teaching,* pp. 35-36.
description of the episode: Lionel Gurner and Lady Gurner both had copies of a document entitled: "Account of Ronald Gurner's last two days at the front that resulted in his wound and award of the Military Cross (as told to his brother Cyril Gurner on 14 Feb. 1921 at Wandsworth)"; see also: WO 95/792, appendix I, report from Maj. R. Westropp, O.C. 6th Corps Cyclists to GOC 11th Bde, 12 April 1917; and: Quarterly Army List for quarter ending 31 Dec. 1917, London HMSO 1918, p. 2725.

251 *When he bathed:* I am indebted to Dr. A.D. Wright of the University of Leeds, for a family recollection of the Gurners bathing.
time of his treatment: I Chose Teaching, p. 50 & ch. 6 passim.; see also Marlborough School Archives, Ronald Gurner to the Head Master, 1918, from Officers'

Hospital, Mornington Lodge, giving a statement of his pay at Marlborough in 1914 and in the army subsequently. I am grateful to G. Kempson, the Archivist of Marlborough College, for his assistance.

his engagement: Lady Gurner, information.

reappearance of his father: ibid.

252   *no doubt crude:* ibid. pp. 233 ff.

253   *regimental crest:* Papers held by Lionel Gurner, Ronald Gurner - Mrs. Walter Gurner (mother), 22 Sept. 1915.

exuberant and humorous: Information Lady Gurner.

Gurner, Ronald, *"The Front Line"* in *War's Echo,* London, T. Fisher Unwin, 1917. See also *The Marlburian, 1914-18* (bound vol. in Marlborough College Library, containing several verses by Gurner; my thanks to William Latham, the Librarian).

254   *Plowman:* Information Lady Gurner. See also: University College London, Library, mss Max Plowman, papers relating to Plowman's resignation (Ronald Gurner's has not survived) and letters from Gurner family, 1921-32; see, on Plowman's resignation, Plowman, Dorothy, (ed.), *Bridge into the Future: Letters of Max Plowman,* London, Andrew Dakers, 1944, pp. 86-131.

appeasement of Hitler: Whitgift School Archive, papers relating to Ronald Gurner's headmastership.

255   *sanctity of one's job: I Chose Teaching,* p. 224.

our petty codes: ibid. p. 228.

Carbury: Gurner, Ronald, *Reconstruction,* London, J. M. Dent, 1931.

256   *sons of our day schools:* Ronald Gurner paper, "The Public Schools and National Life," report of British Association (Education Section) meeting at Oxford, *The Times,* 11 Aug. 1926.

Whitgift O.T.C.; Seven Pillars, T.F. Coade: Lionel Gurner, information.

257   *wandering look:* information G. Kempson, interview 23 July 1985.

Fanner: Whitgift Archive.

his "stare": The late Mrs. Enid Canning, interview, 1 Jan. 1986.

punishment: Sydney Sheppard to author, 1985.

machine-gun fire: Information from Desmond MacCarthy of Wiveton Hall, Norfolk, 1985.

worthy young men: I Chose Teaching, p. 55.

Hadrian: Captain Titchenor B. B., M.B.E., information; I am indebted to the following Old Strandians for their help and/or recollections: A. W. Bates; E. J. Bennett; K. C. Booker; Vernon Butcher; Prof. D. G. Catcheside; Eric Crawshaw; Cyril M. Dark; Charles S. Dunbar; Philip S. Dyer; S. J. Everett; Canon E. W. Eyden; Steven Inglis; Malcolm Parker; Geoffrey Shrubsall; Ernest Todd; John Tooze; C. Turnbull. Only one of these gave an other than favourable account of Gurner's headmastership.

258   *historical investigation:* see Sheffield, G. O., "The Effect of the Great War on Class Relations in Britain: The Career of Major Christopher Stone DSO MC," *War & Society* Vol. 7. 1. May 1989 Univ. of N. S. W.

Goodwin: Information Lady Gurner.

Samurai: See above, Gurner's 1926 paper to British Association. This author recalls Lord James of Rusholme, former High Master of Manchester Grammar

School, voicing a similar view in Nov. 1964.

boots: information F.H.G. Percy. Gurner, Ronald, *The Day-Boy,* London, Grant Richards, 1924.

Edward VII ... School O. T.C.: See *I Chose Teaching* and *Old Edwardians' Association Magazine,* report of A.G.M. of Association, 16 Feb. 1927.

testimonial: Lionel Gurner, papers, Cyril Norwood's testimonial, March 1927.

arrival at Whitgift: Percy, F.H.G., *The History of Whitgift school,* 1st edn, London, Batsford, 1976, ch. 9.

259 *assertive presence ... good leader ... teacher ... stimulating:* information F.H.G. Percy; I am very grateful to John Cummings, former Headmaster of Leyton High School, and mathematics teacher at Whitgift, for information, interview 8 Sept. 1986. I am also grateful to E.A. Warren for information on John Garrett, former headmaster of Bristol Grammar school and friend and colleague of Ronald Gurner at Whitgift.

chaotic and slack: Major the Revd P.C. Blagdon-Gamlen to author, letters 14 Aug., and 12 Sept. 1987. The following Old Whitgiftians have furnished information for this chapter either directly to me or through F.H.G. Percy: Robert Dougall, Dr. E. J. Hewitt, George Labram, Michael Legat, S.V. Pesket.

Staff meetings: Whitgift Archive, "Ronald Gurner & G.E.H. Ellis," communication to F.H.G. Percy by H.E. Parr, 14 Aug. and 4 Sept. 1974.

260 *volcano:* ibid., E.E. Kitchener - E. J. Balley, 11 Dec. 1939.

cruise: information Lionel Gurner.

mortarboard: Whitgift Archive, H. E. Parr, see above.

261 *Rosalie:* information F. H. G. Percy, Lady Gurner, John Cummings.

sexual act: Whitgift Archive, Rosalie Gurner - F. H. G. Percy, 1970.

unsexed woman: Harold Parr, quoting Mrs. Ellis. See also Sharman Prosser, unpublished Leeds University History School undergraduate thesis on shell-shock, 1981, containing the oral evidence of WWI shell-shock victims.

actress: John Cummings information.

widow: Michael Worster information.

262 *Astrid:* Lady Gurner, John Cummings, information.

burden of debt: Whitgift Archive, Rosalie Gurner to F.H.G. Percy; *Daily Telegraph* 22 June 1939; John Cummings information.

Savernake ... Thom: I Chose Teaching, ch. 6; Lady Gurner information; Whitgift Archive, Harold Parr.

263 *Debt ... dogged Gurner:* F. H. G. Percy information; and on Sheffield income, see, for example, *Northern Daily Mail,* 27 May 1926.

Gurner's car, railway in garden: Lionel Gurner information.

jewellery, restaurants: Lady Gurner, information.

Homburg hat: F.H.G. Percy information.

264 *pay cash:* ibid.

coped admirably: Lady Gurner information.

persecution: Whitgift Archive, Harold Parr.

terrible anxiety: ibid.

very quiet: papers in possession of Lady Gurner, diary of Mrs. Walter Gurner, 1 May 1939.

struggled to get straight: Daily Telegraph 22 June 1939; papers in possession of

Lady Gurner, Kathleen Gurner (elder sister of R.G.) - Enid Gurner (younger sister), 22 May 1939.

Mein Kampf: Papers in possession of Lady Gurner, Diary of Mrs. Walter Gurner, 16 May 1939.

265   *Ceylon:* Whitgift Archive, Harold Parr, and F.H.G. Percy commentary.

muscular: Coroner, reported in *Croydon Express,* 22 June 1939.

blackmailer: Whitgift Archive, Harold Parr, and information John Cummings.

papers to the flames: Whitgift Archive, Harold Parr.

war strain: Papers in possession of Lady Gurner, Kathleen Gurner (elder sister of R.G.) - Enid Gurner (younger sister), 17 May 1939.

266   *him and his family:* Menninger, Karl, *Man Against Himself,* London, Rupert Hart-Davis, 1938, p. 19.

MYSTERY FATE: Daily Telegraph, 18 May 1939.

267   *Ypres was dead: Pass Guard at Ypres,* pp. 166-167, 225-226.

church regularly: information Lionel Gurner.

268   *jug on their heads:* Information Mrs. Cuthbert Parker, interviewed Sheffield (where Cuthbert Parker died in 1967), 12 Dec. 1985; I am indebted to her son J. L. Parker for putting me in touch with her and also to members of the congregation of St. James, Clerkenwell, for information on the Rev. Parker. I am grateful to Robert Woods, former Bishop of Lichfield, for information on his father Edward Woods, Bishop of Croydon and friend of Ronald Gurner. The older Woods' papers were destroyed in a forest fire in Australia.

pub-crawling: information Lady Gurner; also P. E. Blagdon-Gamlen to the author, 20 June 1988.

Paul Crowson: Whitgift Archive, Gurner, Paul Crowson - F. H. G. Percy.

269   *Norwood:* F. H. G. Percy, op. cit.

arsenic: Papers of Lionel Gurner, Lady Gurner: "Account of Ronald Gurner's last two days at the front that resulted in his wound and award of the Military Cross, as told to Cyril Gurner 14 Feb. 1921" (see above).

Parker ... key witness: Whitgift Archive, Gurner.

nervous depression: information Mrs. Cuthbert Parker.

270   *Thom ... Enid:* information Lady Gurner.

letter from his mother: Papers of Lady Gurner, Mrs. Walter Gurner to Gurner, 13 June 1926.

Cyril replied: information Lady Gurner.

271   *Grey walls:* "Tryst," quoted in *I Chose Teaching,* p. 37.

HERBERT READ

272   *cold sea:* Read, Herbert, *Annals of Innocence and Experience,* London, Faber & Faber, 1946 edn, p. 141.

indignities of war: Read, Herbert, "Ode II" in *A World Within a War,* London, Faber & Faber, 1944, p. 11.

273   *Happy Warrior:* Read, Herbert, *Naked Warriors,* London, Art & Letters, 1919, p. 26.

274   *golden sparks: Annals of Innocence & Experience,* p. 26.

275   *a wilderness of stone and brick:* See Paraskos, Michael, "Herbert Read and Leeds,"
      in Read, Benedick, and Thistlewood, David, eds, *Herbert Read, a British Vision
      of World Art,* Leeds City Art Gallery, 1993.
      he was a coward: Read, Herbert, "The Raid," in *Annals of Innocence and Expe-
      rience,* ch. 6.
      Evelyn Roff: King, James, *The Last Modern: a Life of Herbert Read,* London,
      Weidenfeld & Nicolson, 1990, ch. 4.
      drastically edited his letters: The letters were published as "A War Diary," in Read,
      Herbert, *The Contrary Experience: Autobiographies,* London, Faber & Faber, 1963.

276   *Nevinson:* see Nevinson, Henry Woodd, *The Fire of Life,* London, Gollancz,
      1935.

277   *I did not hesitate: Annals of Innocence and Experience,* p. 138. For details of
      battalions in which Read served see Wylly, Col. H.C.C.B., *The Green Howards
      in the Great War 1914-1919,* Richmond Yorkshire, 1926, chs. vi, xi, xvii & xviii.
      rungs of the duckboard: "First Blood" in *Ambush,* Criterion Miscellany no. 16,
      London, Faber & Faber, 1930, p. 9.

278   *inherent quality of the person: Annals of Innocence and Experience,* pp. 140-141.
      tree of life: ibid. p. 108.
      the fallen leaves: ibid. p. 148.

279   *an illness Elysium:* "A War Diary," p. 80, 29 Dec. 1916.
      mood of Rupert Brooke: ibid. p. 89.
      Boiry-Becquerelle: PRO, WO 95/2156, 10th Yorkshire Regiment War Diary (10
      Yorkshire Regt WD), April-June 1917.

280   *instincts of the flesh: Annals of Innocence and Experience,* p. 151.
      I am very glad: "A War Diary," p. 99.

281   *a most successful raid:* 10 Yorkshire Regt WD, 31 July 1917.
      his prize, a German officer: ibid., and "A War Diary," pp. 99-102.
      amused him: Naked Warriors, p. 27, "Liedholz."

282   *Kneeshaw:* ibid. p. 9, "Kneeshaw Goes to War."
      Cornelius Vane: ibid. p. 46.
      decency of thought: "A War Diary," p. 97.
      your shattered soul: Naked Warriors, p. 25, "Fear."
      Haig ... ribbons: 10 Yorkshire Regt WD, 9 & 14 Aug., 9 Sept. 1917.

283   *shared these fears: Annals of Innocence and Experience,* p. 151.
      Broodseinde Ridge ... his cheerfulness: 10 Yorkshire Regt WD, 7 Oct. 1917, and "A
      War Diary," pp. 108-11.
      sides of the trenches: 10 Yorkshire Regt WD, 24 Oct. 1917.
      nature so mutilated: "A War Diary," p. 112.

284   *the revolver was too close: Naked Warriors,* pp. 15-16.
      go west: "A War Diary," p. 112.
      damned proud of it we are: ibid. p. 113.

285   *a man of mine: Naked Warriors,* p. 34.

286   *pride of leadership:* ibid. p. 31.
      the root of his anarchism: J.B. Pick to author, summer 1993. The writer John Pick
      took an interest in Read's anarchism during the 1940s and heard him speak
      publicly on the topic. On Read's anarchism, also: "Herbert Read's Anarchism,"

paper – to be published – delivered by David Goodway, at the Herbert Read Conference, Leeds University, 4 Dec. 1993; also see Middleton Murry, John, "The Anarchism of Mr. Herbert Read," in *New Adelphi,* vol. 17, no. 11, Aug. 1941, p. 369.

pacifist opinion: "A War Diary," p. 117.

287 *expansion of heat:* Read, Herbert, *In Retreat,* Criterion Miscellany no. 8, London, Faber & Faber, 1930 (written 1919 & originally issued in Hogarth essays, 1925), p. 24.

risk of their lives: ibid., and PRO WO95/2329, War Diary of 2nd Battalion, the Yorkshire Regiment to April (2 Yorkshire Regt, WD to April), March–April 1918.

288 *anarchism:* ibid. and "A War Diary," pp. 123-133.

abandoned the idea: Annals of Innocence and Experience, p. 190; "A War Diary," p. 141.

Oliver Onions: see this vol. ch. 11.

bourgeois path of marriage: Annals of Innocence and Experience, ch. 8.

289 *jolly open-faced:* "A War Diary," p. 144.

successful novelist: King, op. cit., pp. 25, 92, 150-151.

290 *not a passion:* ibid. pp. 70, 81-2.

unthawed emotionalist: ibid. p. 76.

291 *Mellon Lectures … a knighthood:* ibid. p. 274, and Read, B. & Thistlewood, D. (eds), op. cit. p. 61.

mental health deteriorated: King, op. cit., ch. 7.

one of his finest poems: Read, Herbert, *The End of a War,* London, Faber & Faber, 1933.

292 *Meaurain and Gussigny:* PRO WO 95/1809, War Diary of 2nd Battalion, the Yorkshire Regiment, May 1918 - February 1919.

293 *classical gods:* Read, Herbert, *Ambush,* 1930.

294 *beautiful Green Child:* Read, Herbert, *The Green Child,* London, Heinemann, 1935.

classical erotica: Jünger, Ernst, *Lieutenant Sturm,* (French tr. from German of *Sturm,* first pub. in *Hannoverrischer Kurier* as serial, beginning April 1923, forgotten and "discovered" in 1963).

295 *my reason failing:* Hitler, Adolf, *Mein Kampf,* tr. Ralph Mannheim, intro. D. C. Watt, London, Pimlico edn 1992, pp. 151-152.

four terrible years: Read, Herbert, review of *All Quiet on the Western Front, Nation & Athenaeum,* 27 April 1929.

no visible wounds to lick: Read, Herbert, *A World Within a War,* "Ode II," p. 11.

296 *must be the guide of it:* Miller, Patrick (George Gordon MacFarlane). *The Natural Man,* London, Grant Richards, 1924, p. 318. I am indebted to MacFarlane's nephew John Carswell for information.

collective identity: Col. H.C. Wylly, op. cit.

297 *roman fleuve:* See: Thatcher, David S., ed., "Richard Aldington's Letters to Herbert Read" from letters housed in the Herbert Read collection at the University of Victoria, Canada (copy enclosed with letter to author from Alister Kershaw).

OLIVER ONIONS

301 *so instantaneously could it be assumed:* Onions, George Oliver (1873-1961), *Peace in Our Time,* London, Chapman & Hall, 1923, p. 71.

302 *that noisy company:* see his obituary, *The Times,* 10 April 1967; N. C. Hunter, *The Times,* 15 April 1961; and Ruck, Amy Roberta (Berta), *A Story Teller Tells the Truth. Reminiscences and Notes,* London, Hutchinson, 1935, p. 66.
one vast links: Onions, op. cit., p. 71.

303 *They liked him very much:* information, Onions' son, the late George Arthur Oliver, to whom I am deeply indebted for the background story to *Peace in Our Time.*

> Where are the lads we knew?
> In Piccadilly, in Leicester Square?
> No, not there! No, not there!
> They're taking a trip on the continong,
> With their rifles and their bayonets bright!
> Facing danger gladly,
> Where they're needed badly
> That's where they are tonight!

actual observation of events: Onions, op. cit. p. ix.
poverty-stricken background: see Onions, Oliver, in *T.P.'s Weekly,* 3 Dec. 1927, p. 178: "With a Folio in Fleet Street. How an Out-of-Work Artist Became a Popular Novelist," and see Ruck, *A Story Teller Tells the Truth,* p. 89; information George Arthur Oliver.

304 *hit the pavement:* Onions, *T.P.'s Weekly,* 3 Dec. 1927, "With a Folio in Fleet Street."
Beckoning Fair One: Onions, Oliver, *Widdershins,* London, Martin Secker, 1911, p. 11.

305 *this impenetrable reserve:* quoted from Herbert Read's *Wordsworth* (London, Cape, 1930), in Woodcock, George, *Herbert Read: the Stream and the Source,* London, Faber & Faber, 1972, p. 152.
I'm glad it is "far": Ruck, *A Story Teller Tells the Truth.* p. 66.

306 *he was getting married:* Onions, *T.P.'s Weekly,* op. cit.
vigorous into extreme old age: Berta Ruck's obituary, *The Times,* 12 Aug. 1978.
Maurice Hewlett: 1861-1923, poet, novelist, essayist, author of *The Forest Lovers, The Queen's Quair,* etc. (novels), *The Village Wife's Lament* (poem on theme of war bereavement).

307 *dyed his grey hair and volunteered:* see Elton, Oliver, *C. E. Montague, a Memoir,* London, Chatto & Windus, 1929, p. 107.
W. B. Maxwell: see Maxwell, W. B. *Time gathered,* London, Hutchinson, 1937.
"Old Boys' Corps": Onions' *Times* obituary, 10 April 1967. Arthur Oliver recollects his father being in uniform, "with the two pips just above the cuffs (not on the shoulder straps)" [Arthur Oliver to author 8 Sept. 1987].
new designs for bridges: Work of the Royal Engineers in the European War, 1914-19, Chatham, Kent, R. E. H.Q., 1921.
the narrowed look on OO's face: George Arthur Oliver to author 8 Sept. 1987.

308 *secret intelligence:* George Oliver told me that this was a family legend, never

substantiated; however, see also Ruck, *A Story Teller Tells the Truth*, p. 118, which indicated that Onions was friendly with Admiral Sir Reginald "Blinker" Hall, in charge of "Room 40, OB," the Admiralty Secret Intelligence unit, for which many well-known writers worked.

The New Moon: Onions, Oliver: *The New Moon: a Romance of Reconstruction*, London, Hodder & Stoughton, 1918.

309 *piping in Thessaly:* Montague, *Disenchantment*, U.S. edn, New York, Brentano's, 1922, pp. 279-80.

310 *Cut Flowers:* Onions, Oliver, *Cut Flowers*, Chapman & Hall, London, 1927.

his grim, psychic explorer's heart: in David Lindsay's *A Voyage to Arcturus* (London, Methuen, 1920) the medium Backhouse is described as a man "whose nature was phenomenal – the dividing-wall between himself and the spiritual world was broken in many places." Onions's relations have drawn attention to the uncanny side of his nature, his granddaughter, a television director, even saying, half in jest, that that she could never make a film about him – "he would come back and haunt me." Onions's resemblance to Lindsay's Backhouse has been observed.

Thorgumbald: Onions, Oliver, "Thorgumbald: a Fantasia," in *Pedlar's Pack*, London, Eveleigh Nash, 1908, p. 287.

"Peter Deane": see next chapter.

William Mackay: Ex-Soldier We Are Dead, London, Albert E. Marriott, 1930.

Sorrell and Son: Deeping, George Warwick (1877-1950), *Sorrell and Son*, London, Cassell, 1925.

311 *Seven Men Came Back:* Deeping, Warwick *Seven Men Came Back*, London, Cassell, 1934.

312 *he so sorely needed:* Onions, *Peace in Our Time*, pp. 273-274.

Gwen Otter and others: Ruck, Berta, *A Smile for the Past*, London, Hutchinson, 1959, pp. 193-194; *A Story Teller Tells the Truth*, chs 27, 29.

secretary: information Jane Oliver.

313 *Ragged Robyn:* Onions, Oliver, *The Story of Ragged Robyn*, Harmondsworth, Penguin Books, 1954 (1st pub. 1945).

sandhills on the far side: Darwin, Bernard, in *The Times*, 17 April 1961.

PETER DEANE

315 *road beyond:* Deane, Peter, "The Tragedy of the Survivors" in *The Nation and Athenaeum*, 18 Oct. 1930, p. 102. Peter Deane, *The Victors*, London, Constable, 1925; *Harvest*, London, Hodder and Stoughton, 1926. There is a mysterious link between the book and the celebrated war arist Eric Kennington. The dust jacket of *The Victors* shows a drawing by him, c.1917 or 1918, of a young British officer, but neither the Imperial War Museum Staff nor the artist's son Christopher could identify the subject of the picture, nor was it identified as a portrait of a relation by the nephew of "Peter Deane," nor was Kennington known to be a friend of the author. Eric Kennington's well-known canvas of the Canadian Scottish marching through a devastated landscape, "The Victors," was said by some to be ironically titled, having allegedly been entitled earlier, "The

Victims," and it is possible that the novelist, who was certainly ironical in choice of title, had Kennington's big picture in mind.

316 *Dyett:* See John Terraine's introduction to Herbert, A. P., *The Secret Battle* (first pub. 1919), O.U.P. edn, Oxford, the Clarendon Press, 1982.
Pamela Hinkson: See Obituaries: *The Times,* 2 June 1982; *Irish Times,* 3 June 1982.

317 *conversationalist:* I am indebted to the late Terence de Vere White, Alice Grattan Esmonde, and Alexander Hinkson (Pamela's nephew) for information on her life and personality. Hinkson, Pamela, *The Ladies' Road* (first pub. 1932), paperback edn Harmondsworth, Penguin Books, 1946.

318 *faithful intimates:* See her autobiographical volumes: *Twenty-Five Years,* London, Smith, Elder & Co. Ltd, 1913; *The Middle Years, The Years of the Shadow, The Wandering Years,* London, Constable, 1916, 1919, 1922. I am indebted to Roy Foster, Yeats's biographer, for his comments on Katherine Tynan's relationship with Yeats.
by extension, men in general: I am deeply indebted to Dr. Peter Van de Kamp, Katherine Tynan's biographer, for details of Pamela Hinkson's and her parents' lives. Pamela left papers of her own that are among her mother's papers; these are still not completely sorted and in consequence are not currently available for research.

319 *never failed her: The Ladies' Road,* p. 15.
Dalkey: Hinkson, Pamela, *Irish Gold,* London, Collins, 1939, pp. 267-74.

320 *Russell, Stephens, Colum:* Tynan, K., *The Years of the Shadow,* see for example pp. 87, 94, and chs 3 and 4; see also Boylan, Patricia, *All Cultivated People: a History of the United Arts Club,* Dublin, Gerrard's Cross, Colin Smythe, 1988.
Aberdeens: Tynan, op. cit. pp. 100-110.

321 *Dunsany's home:* ibid. p. 71.
Wells, H. G., Mr. Britling sees It Through, London, Hogarth Press, 1985 (offset from original British 1916 edn), pp. 43-4.

322 *Young Star:* Tynan, Katherine, "Flower of Youth," in *Flower of Youth: poems in wartime,* London, Sidgwick & Jackson, 1915.
profoundly affected: The Years of the Shadow, chs 28, 32.
darkness in winter: ibid. p. 186.

323 *watery sky:* ibid. ch. 27.
best-dressed young lady: ibid. quoted in ch. 20.

324 *rebel sniper:* ibid. p. 194.
taken a grue: ibid. p. 206.
kept ... the Bulgarian enemy off: ibid. p. 277.

325 *not to shed a tear:* ibid. p. 306.
like a weight: The Ladies' Road, p. 175.
Cappagh: The Years of the Shadow, ch. 26. Brookhill, unlike Cappagh in the novel, was not burnt, still stands and, thanks to Dr. Patricia Noone and her husband, is miraculously being restored after years of neglect by previous owners. There is a house, still intact, called Cappagh, close by, but one of the most celebrated neighbouring properties, formerly owned by the writer George Moore, was indeed destroyed by fire.

326 *Linlithgow ... yeomanry officer: The Years of the Shadow,* chs 35, 36; and Pamela

Hinkson, *Irish Gold*, pp. 34-35. My thanks to Simon Head for information on his grandfather, Lord Shaftesbury, at this time.

327   *turf smoke:* Hinkson, op. cit.
      on a tunic: information Peter Van de Kamp.
      faint personal concern: ibid.
      her control snapped: The Years of the Shadow, p. 323.

328   *into Germany:* Tynan, Katherine, *The Wandering Years,* chs 2, 3.

329   *his patriotic and imaginative views:* ibid. pp. 23-4.
      willful destruction: ibid. chs 28-33.

330   *"Pussy":* information Peter Van de Kamp.
      Hinkson, Pamela, *The End of All Dreams,* London, T. Fisher Unwin, 1923.

331   *ended in divorce:* information Alexander Hinkson.
      had cheered them: The Wandering Years, p. 284.
      misery through the streets: ibid.

332   *women who do the harvesting:* see introduction to Harvest.

333   *dead who have no need of it:* Deane, Peter, *The Nation and Athenaeum,* 18 Oct. 1930, pp. 102-3.
      lost generation: see Taylor, A. J. P., *English History 1914-1945,* Oxford, Clarendon Press, 1965.

334   *Abroad:* Fussell, Paul, *Abroad, British Literary Travelling Between the Wars,* Oxford, O.U.P., 1980.
      Hinkson, Pamela, *Wind from the West,* London, Macmillan, 1930.

335   *Lady Plymouth:* information Peter Van de Kamp.
      securest of places: Hinkson, *Irish Gold,* pp. 225-227.

337   *lonely, he said:* The Ladies' Road, p. 81.

338   *Brittain, Vera: Honourable Estate,* London, Gollancz, 1936.
      praised its poignancy: see Brian Roberts in *Life and Letters,* vol. viii, no. 47, Dec. 1932, p. 479; and R. Ellis Roberts in *New Statesman,* 22 Oct. 1932.
      her best work: see *The Ladies' Road,* Penguin edn, biographical note on back cover of book.
      Hinkson, Pamela, The Deeply Rooted: London, Gollancz, 1935.

339   *families she lodged with:* information, Alexander Hinkson.
      interpreters of the Irish scene: see *Times Literary Supplement,* 28 Oct. 1939.

340   *the Shamrock Club:* Ladies' Road, Penguin edn, back cover note.
      Irish children … loquacity … friendship: Obituary *Irish Times;* information Alexander Hinkson, the late Terence de Vere White, Peter Van de Kamp; and Cleeve, Brian, *Dictionary of Irish Writers,* Cork, 1967, vol. 1, p. 61.
      hospital for a spell: Trinity College Dublin Library, MacGreevy Papers, 811 8/ 92, Pamela Hinkson - Thomas MacGreevy, 21 May 1960.

341   *cold cream:* information Peter Van de Kamp.

RICHARD BLAKER

The chief sources for Richard Blaker have been (1) information given by his daughter, Betty Ingleby, his sister-in-law, Mrs. Eric Blaker, and Gareth Owen, the brother of May Owen (May Blaker). To all three I am deeply indebted. (2) The Richard

Blaker Papers at the Bodleian Library, Oxford, (MSS Eng. Lett and Eng. Misc.)
deposited there by Mrs. Ingleby and Mr. Owen. For Louis Golding information and
background, I am also indebted to Lilian Wynne and the Brotherton Library Special
Collections at Leeds University (Christopher Shepherd).

342   *inscription:* see MS. Eng. Lett., R. S. Blaker papers, MS. Eng. Misc.
c557, letters of Louis Golding - May Blaker, f.220, 13 March 1941, and
photographs, and c.326 f.21, arrangements for headstone, 1 Oct. 1941. See also
Reno certificate of marriage to May (D.G. Owen).
Medal Without Bar (hereinafter cited as *MWB*), London, Hodder &
Stoughton, 1930.
ex-army padre: MS Eng. Lett. c318, f.197, Geoffrey Gordon – Blaker, 8 June
1930.

343   *ex-gunner:* ibid. c317 f.8, V. W. Andrews - Blaker, Oct. 1933.
He was born: see notes by Betty Ingleby, 13 Jan. 1986, on Richard Blaker, her fa-
ther, sent to author by her, and also available in the Bodleian. Percy Blaker died
in 1966.
Scabby: Blaker, Richard, *Scabby Dichson* (pub. as "Godfrey Dichson" in U.S.A.),
London, Hodder & Stoughton, 1927.

344   *Mamie:* information Betty Ingleby.

345   *his tutor:* MS Eng. Lett., c323 f.38, E. M. Walker, senior tutor, Queen's College,
15 Jan. 1916, reference for Blaker's commission.
fourth-class: ibid. c321 f.10, H. J. Paton – Blaker, 6 July, 1915, re degree result;
refers to Blaker's "great initial handicaps."
Grozny: see *The Times* 24 Feb., 2 March, 6 July 1911; *Detroit Journal,* 25 Feb.
1911.
the whole story: information Ingleby.

346   *Their life together:* ibid.
Margery Perham ... none to return: Queens' College Record: Oxford University,
Rhodes House, mss Margey Perham, box 2.3, f.19, Blaker - Margery Perham,
21 Sept. 1916.; and Bodleian, MS, Eng. Lett. c321, f.16, Margery Perham -
Blaker, 15 Oct. 1916.

347   *moved to tears:* information Ingleby.
miserable elastic family: MS Eng. Lett. c318, f.216, W. A. Craig-Blaker, 11 Nov.
1930. For direct contact with gunnery practice of a now finally past era, and
having continuity with Blaker's own experience, I am indebted to my cousin
Robert Cranborne, as Parliamentary Under-Secretary for Defence, in getting
me at close quarters to the (relatively obsolete) artillery bombardment drill on
Exercise ST BARBARA (platoon commanders' training) at Warminster on 8
June 1993; thanks also to Maj. Alistair Harvey, R. A. and Capt. Tomlinson, who
looked after me at various phases of the exercise.
small businessman: MWB, p. 470.

348   *4.5-in. howitzer:* see Richard Hogg, I.V., and Thurston, L. F., *British Artillery
Weapons & Ammunition 1914-1918,* London, Ian Allan, 1972, pp. 8-18, 102-
103.
suicide clubs: Cheyne, G.Y., *The Last Great Battle of the Somme. Beaumont Hamel*

1916, Edinburgh, John Donald, 1988, p. 66.

fear of a repetition: Hogg & Thurston, op. cit., Liddle Collection, University of Leeds, K.A. Davies CMG, recollections of battery D58 RFA.

Blaker ... obsessed: MWB, pp. 315, 356, 422, 510-511.

gunner, Brown: MS Eng. Lett., c317 f.285, 89441 Gunner Brown - Blaker, 29 Nov. 1916. Brown seems to have been injured by a premature in an 18-pounder gun behind D 58 battery, 18 Nov. 1916.

349   *strain ... destructive:* see Frankau, Gilbert, *Peter Jackson, Cigar Merchant,* Part 28, "In the Night."

60 rounds: PRO WO 95/1800, War Diary of 58th Bde RFA, July & August 1916; *MWB,* pp. 139-172.

Col ... Winter: See MS Eng. Lett., c321 f.25, Eric Pinker - Blaker, 20 Dec. 1935; and Farndale, Gen. Sir Martin, *The History of the Royal Regiment of Artillery, Western Front, 1914-1918,* London, Royal Artillery Institution, 1986.

Captain Roberts: Roberts is called "Richards" in *MWB* (see pp. 140, 156). See MS Eng. Lett., c323, f.3, Stanley Taylor to Blaker, 4 Feb. 1930 "You have hit Roberts and Daddy Waldron off perfectly," and 319, f.86, Herbert Hirschland - Blaker, 15 Dec. 1930; see also Bidwell, Shelford, *Gunners at War,* London, Arms & Armour Press, 1970, p. 58.

350   *Whitelaw:* MWB pp. 201, 429-431; and MS Eng. Lett., c323 f.36, Stephen Waldron - Blaker 30 Jan. 1930.

Hugh Hope: MWB ch. 41 & pp. 253, 260, 494; MS Eng. Lett., c319 f.86, Hirschland - Blaker, 15 Dec. 1930; WO 95/1800 War Diary of 58th Bde RFA, 14 Sept., 2 Dec. 1916 (when Hope awarded M.C.), and 30 June 1917 (evacuated to England and struck off strength); I am indebted to Gen. Sir Cecil Hugh Blacker (Hope's nephew) and Patrick MacLure, the Wykehamist Society, for information; see *The Wykehamist,* no 535, Nov. 1914, pp. 352-3, Debating Society debate, in which Hope proposed the motion in favour of conscription at the end of the present war; see also will of Hugh Lewis Hope, and death certificate, 19 Oct. 1921).

351   *Gaddy Monks:* MS Eng. Lett., c319, f.86, Hirschland - Blaker, 15 Dec. 1930; MWB pp. 436-37; 58 Bde. RFA WD, 7 June 1917.

reported Colonel Winter: 58 Bde. RFA, WD, XC/9192, "Notes on the engagement of September 3rd 1916," by Lieut. Col. O. Winter RFA.

"counterbattery" action: For this and subsequent information, see 58 Bde RFA, WD and *MWB.* p. 216.

352   *mawkish stench ... cold pulp of the world: MWB,* pp. 241, 303.

man's normal gait: ibid. p. 306.

Hell hole ... lighted brazier: MSS Eng. Lett., c317 f.11, J. E. Bailey, 13 July 1932; and Liddle Collection, Leeds Univ., K.A. Davies, recollections of D battery, 58 Bde RFA.

353   *cutting wire ... Montigny:* 58 Bde RFA, WD.

scythe-blade: MWB, p. 370.

Assistant Orderly Officer: 58 Bde RFA, WD, 4 Feb. 1917.

354   *remnants of cavalry:* ibid. March-April 1917; Liddle Collection, Kenneth Davies.

Messines: 58 Bde RFA, WD.

buttocks: information Ingleby; also Liddle Collection, K. A. Davies, on diet.

355 *Hugh Stevenson:* MS Eng. Lett., d339 f.176, Hugh Stevenson-Blaker, 5 Oct.
1918.
Southall: information Ingleby.
£600 a year ... Mount Clemens: ibid.

356 *surgical glove:* ibid.; MS Eng. Lett., c319, f.30-40, letters from Wendell
Herrbruck - Blaker 1919-23; HRHRC, mss Christopher Morley, Blaker -
Morley, 23. Dec. 1921.
red-hot stove: MWB pp. 356, 499, 535-536.

357 *broken-hearted:* ibid. p. 379.
Arnold Bennett: MS Eng. Lett., c317, f.45, Arnold Bennett - Blaker, 28 May
1919.

358 *Sorrow of War:* Golding, Louis, *Sorrow of War, Poems,* London, Methuen, 1919.
Whymant: information Ingleby; letter D.G.M. Owen to author, 7 June 1994.
Golding: information Ingleby, Lilian Wynne; MS Eng. Misc., c557, f.225, Louis
Golding - May (Owen) Blaker, 29 Oct. 1945 (re *Magnolia Street*); MS Eng.
Lett. c318, letters Golding - Blaker and d339, Alex Shaw - Blaker, Sept. 1938, re
Golding's parties; Special Collections, Brotherton Library, Leeds, mss Thomas
Moult, letters, Louis Golding - Thomas Moult.
Golding, Louis, *Magnolia Street,* London, Gollancz, 1932; *Five Silver Daughters,*
London, Gollancz, 1934.

359 *Mamie's main concern ... horses:* information Ingelby; 58 Bde RFA, WD, 30 Jan.
1917; *MWB,* pp. 192, 253, 346.

360 *italic hand ... Larry Durrell:* information Ingleby.
Mamie's frequent desire: ibid.
Arnold Bennett: MS Eng. Lett., c320, f.222, Dan Nicholson - Blaker, 21 Sept.
1925.
stick it the Gunners: ibid. c. 321 f.62, Eric Pinker - Blaker, 11 Jan. 1921.

361 *gadget emperor:* ibid. c320, f.106, quoted in Gen. H. Essex Lewis - Blaker, 10
July 1932.
casualty figures: ibid. c. 321, f.15-16, B. H. Pearson - Blaker 10 Feb. 1929.

362 *purge disenchanted elements* [and following comments]: ibid. c319, f.134, f.135 et
seq., R. Hodder-Williams - Blaker, 14, 18 Nov. 1929.
suggestions ... Blaker made: see p. 315.
in at the death: MWB, p. 500.

363 *novel-buying public:* MS Eng. Lett., c319, f.171, Hodder-Williams - Blaker, 21
March 1930.
G. W. Andrews: ibid. c317, f.4, G. W. Andrews - Blaker, 22 Feb. 1939.
glamour too: ibid. c318, f.116, Blaker - John Farrar of Doubleday Doran, 14
April 1929.
Roy Bower: ibid. c317, f.277, 25 Jan. 1939.

364 *Tubby Clayton:* MS Eng. Misc. c559, newspaper cuttings, review by Rev. P. B.
Clayton, *Daily Telegraph,* 7 Feb. 1930.

365 *gifted brush:* MS Eng. Lett. c318, f.59, P. B. Clayton - Blaker, 3 Feb. 1930.
sales ... Arnot Robertson: ibid. c319, f.171, Hodder-Williams - Blaker, 21 March
1930; see also c322, f.117, account from printer with sales figures, 22 Sept.
1937.

Verlag Ullstein: ibid. c322, f.13, R. Pinker - Blaker, 15 Feb. 1930.

Japanese: Graphic, April 1932, cutting in possession of Mrs. E. Blaker.

366   *Denham Studios ... interesting friends:* information Ingleby.

baby's grown up: MS Eng. Lett., c322, f.189-93, various letters, undated, Claude Creamer-Roberts - Blaker, 1936?

367   *possibility of divorce:* ibid. c318, f.65, Gilbert Collier - Blaker, 29 Sept. 1935; c319, f.45, Herrbruck - Blaker, 6 April 1936.

overpossessive: information Ingleby; see also MS Eng. Lett., letters of Eric Blaker, Herrbruck, Golding, and Betty (Blaker) Ingleby.

Jewish refugee: ibid. c326, f.174, Kaspar Naegele - May (Owen) Blaker, 26 April 1947. Golding, Louis, *Mr. Emmanuel,* London, Gollancz, 1939; for Bovingdon and Chipperfield at that period, see Tompkins, Herbert W., *Highways and Byways in Hertfordshire,* 1902 and 1926 edns., London, Macmillan, pp. 98-100.

368   *Heinemann:* MS Eng. Lett., c319, f.19, Dwye Evans (Heinemann) - Blaker, 27 June 1935.

Bath-Sheba: Blaker, Richard, *David of Judah,* London, Nisbet, 1937, pp. 142, 372.

Pegasus: Blaker, Richard, *Love Went a-Riding,* London, Heinemann, 1938.

369   *sterile desperation:* MS Eng. Lett., c318, f.188, Blaker - Golding, 3 Aug. 1939.

Carrick: ibid. c317, Lynn Carrick - Blaker, 22 April 1938.

too gentle: ibid. c326, Eric Pinker - May Blaker, 25 Oct. 1941.

better-known English writers: Niven, David, *Bring on the Empty Horses,* London, Hamish Hamilton, 1975.

370   *Pinker ... arrested ... bankrupt:* MS Eng. Lett., c 321, circular from Authors' League of America, 17 March 1939, re E. Pinker's arrest; c322 f.59, Official Receiver's account of bankruptcy of Ralph Pinker, 9 July 1941.

£12 3s 6d: ibid. c. 320, f.142, Blaker - Henrietta Malkiel, 5 Aug. 1938; c318, f.235, summary of box office and subscription takings for *Strange Family* for week beginning 10 Nov. 1938; also, information Ingleby.

Titanic: Blaker - Maj. Eric Blaker (brother), 2 June 1939 (letter in possession of Mrs. E. Blaker).

371   *Gone with the Wind:* MS Eng. Lett., d339, f.157, David O. Selznick - Blaker, 22 Dec. 1938.

starved: Blaker - Major Eric Blaker, 2 June 1939 (Mrs. E. Blaker).

GRAPES ... HOPING: MS Eng. Lett., c317, ff.66, 67, telegs. Mamie Blaker - Blaker, 6, 12 Feb. 1939.

peace pamphlet: ibid. c320, f.118, David Low (cartoonist) - Blaker, 21 Sept. 1937; d339, f.12, Blaker - Philip Conroy, 4 May 1939.

Duke of Windsor: ibid. d339, f.19, Philip Conroy - Blaker, 5 April 1939.

Robert Morley: ibid. d339, f.108, Blaker - Gerald Savory, 23 March 1939; see generally Morley, Sheridan, *Robert My Father,* London, Weidenfeld, 1992, ch. 8.

be patient: ibid. f.109, Gerald Savory - Blaker, March/April 1939. For Savory, in extreme old age, there remains an abiding memory of Blaker's exceptional likeability (conversation with Gerald Savory, 18 Aug. 1994) and Savory to the author, 1991 (from Denville Hall, Northwood, Mx).

for a lifetime: ibid. c318, f.191, Blaker - Golding, 6 May 1939.

372   *very big shot:* ibid. f.188, Blaker - Golding, 3 Aug. 1939.

Dick darling: ibid. f.192, f.194, Golding - Blaker, 4 & 8 Sept. 1939.

Morrow: MS Eng. Lett. c320, f.184, William Morrow contract for novel, 24 Sept. 1939.

publishers ... disappointed: ibid. c326, f.188, Sanders - May Blaker, 19 Jan. 1940.

heart disease: ibid. c323, f.34, medical note by J. O.Vaughan M. D., 19 Jan. 1940. c326 f.93, May Blaker - James Hilton, 2 March 1940.

373   *waving of hats:* MS Eng. Misc. c557, f. 197, Blaker - Golding, 16 Jan. 1940.

poor old Dick: ibid. f.198, H. Essex Lewis - Golding, 13 Feb. 1940.

serene end: information Ingleby.

May: MS Eng. Lett., c326, f.44, re May Blaker's work.

374   *trenches:* ibid. c318, f.166, Blaker - Myddie Fordham, 10 March 1939.

benevolence of conduct: Blaker, Richard, *The Needle Watcher. The Will Adams Story, British Samurai,* 2nd edn Rutland (Vermont) and Tokyo, Charles E.Tuttle, 1973, p. 189 (1st edn London, Heinemann, 1932).

slovenry: MWB, p. 377; Shakespeare, *The Life of King Henry the Fifth,* King Henry's speech, Act IV, scene iii. Reynolds, perhaps deliberately, was misquoting. The original version reads: "We are but *warriors* for the working day."

AFTERWORD - THE PERSONAL RECORD

376   *Windy Williamson:* HRHRC, Mss Sassoon, E. Blunden - Sassoon, 17 Dec. 1928.

377   *Swinburne:* Richard Aldington, *Life for Life's Sake,* p. 44.

378   *die peacefully:* I am grateful to Astrid Garran for this information.

Further details of Williamson's last days are to be found in Daniel Farson's affectionate memoir, *Henry, an Appreciation of Henry Williamson,* London, Michael Joseph, 1982, chs. 13, 14, though family sources indicate that Williamson's state of mind was better than described there. I am grateful to the late Angela Waddington for information about Twyford Abbey.

Select Bibliography

PRINTED ORIGINAL SOURCES

JOURNALS
The Adelphi
The Cornhill
John O'London's Weekly
Life and Letters
The London Mercury
The Nation
The National Review
The New Adelphi
The New Statesman
The Nineteenth Century and After
Time and Tide
T.P.'s & Cassell's Weekly

FICTION
Alverdes, Paul, *Changed Men (Reinhold, oder die Verwandelten)*, London, Secker, 1933.
Blunden, Edmund, ed., *Great Short Stories of the War*, England, France, Germany, America, London, Eyre & Spottiswoode, 1930.
Brophy, John, *The Bitter End*, London, J. M. Dent, 1928.
Grabenhorst, Georg, *Zero Hour*, tr. from the German by A. Featherstonhaugh, London, Brentano's, 1929.
Hope, Thomas Suthren, *The Winding Road Unfolds*, London, Putnam, 1937.
Ingram, Kenneth, *Out of Darkness, a Drama of Flanders*, London, Chatto & Windus, 1927.
Mahon, Terence, *Cold Feet*, London, Chapman & Hall, 1929.
Maxwell, W. B., *We Forget Because We Must*, London, Hutchinson, 1928.
Raymond, Ernest, *Once in England*, London, Cassell, 1932.

"Sapper" (H. Cyril McNeile) *Sapper's War Stories*, collected in one volume, London, Hodder & Stoughton, 1930.

Severn, Mark, *Background*, London, Ernest Benn, 1931.

Sherriff, R. C. and Bartlett, Vernon, *Journey's End* (as novel), London, Gollancz, 1930.

Stone, Christopher, *Valley of Indecision*, London, Collins, 1920.

Thompson, Edward, *In Araby Orion*, London, Ernest Benn, 1930.

Tilsey, W.V., *Other Ranks*, with an introduction by Edmund Blunden, London, Cobden-Sanderson, 1931.

Tynan, Katherine, *The House in the Forest*, London, Ward Lock, 1928.

MEMOIRS, LETTERS

Brabant, F. H., *Neville Stuart Talbot, 1879-1943: a Memoir*, London, S. C. M. Press, 1949.

Burrage, A. M. ("Ex-Private X"), *War is War*, London, Gollancz, 1930.

Carstairs, Carroll, *A Generation Missing*, London, Heinemann, 1930.

Douie, Charles, *The Weary Road: Recollections of a Subaltern of Infantry*, London, John Murray, 1929.

Dunn, Capt. J. C., *The War the Infantry knew*, 2nd edn (intro. Keith Simpson), London, Jane's, 1987.

Eyre, Giles E.M. (Ex-Rifleman R/9885), *Somme Harvest: Memories of a P.B.I. in the Summer of 1916*, London Stamp Exchange, 1991.

Graves, Robert, *Goodbye to All That, an Autobiography*, Jonathan Cape, 1929.

Hart-Davis, Rupert, ed., *Siegfried Sassoon, Diaries 1915-1918*, London, Faber & Faber, 1983.

"Mark VII" (Max Plowman), *Subaltern on the Somme in 1916*, London, J. M. Dent, 1927.

Moseley, Sir Oswald, *My Life*, London, Nelson, 1968.

An "O. E.," *Iron Times with the Guards*, London, John Murray, 1918.

Panichas, George A., *Promise of Greatness: the 1914-18 War* (A memorial volume for the fiftieth anniversary of the Armistice, with foreword by Sir Herbert Read), London, Cassell, 1968.

Plowman, Dorothy L., *Bridge into the Future, Letters of Max Plowman*, London, Andrew Dakers, 1944.

Sassoon, Siegfried, *Siegfried's Journey*, London, Faber & Faber, 1945.

Sheffield, G. D. & Inglis, G. I. S., eds., *From Vimy Ridge to the Rhine: the Great War Letters of Christopher Stone, D. S. O., M. C.*, Ramsbury, Crowood Press, 1989.

Tomlinson, H. M., *Old Junk*, 3rd, pb., edn, Harmondsworth, Penguin, 1940.

Tomlinson, H. M., *Waiting for Daylight*, London, Cassell, 1922.

POETRY

Blunden, Edmund, ed., *The Poems of Wilfred Owen*, 3rd edn, London, Chatto & Windus, 1955.

Powell, Anne, ed., *A Deep Cry: a Literary Pilgimage to the Battlefields and Cemeteries of First World War British Soldier-Poets killed in Northern France and Flanders*, Aberporth, Paladour Books, 1993.

Hibberd, Dominic, and Onions, John, eds, *Poetry of the Great War: an Anthology*, London, Macmillan, 1986.

Sassoon, Siegfried, *Collected Poems*, London, Faber & Faber, 1957.

SECONDARY SOURCES:

BIBLIOGRAPHICAL AND REFERENCE

The Army List for November 1918, 4 vols, reprint from orig. HMSO edn Polstead, Suffolk, J. B. Hayward & Son, 1988.

Enser, A. G. S., *A Subject Bibliography of the First World War: Books in English 1914-1978*. London, André Deutsch, 1979.

Hager, Philip E., and Taylor, Desmond, *The Novels of World War 1: an Annotated Bibliography*, New York, Garland Publishing Inc., 1981.

Kunitz, J., and Haycraft, Howard, *Twentieth Century Authors*, New York, Wilson, 1942, and supplement, New York, Wilson, 1955.

Officers Died in The Great War 1914-1919, new enlarged edn including Indian Army, Polstead, Suffolk, J. B. Hayward, 1988.

Reilly, Catherine W., *English Poetry of the First World War: a Bibliography*, London, George Prior Publishers, 1978.

Rogers, Colin D., *Tracing Missing Persons: an Introduction to Agencies, Methods and Sources in England and Wales*, Manchester University Press, 1986.

LITERARY AND CULTURAL

Bracco, Rosa Maria, *Merchants of Hope, British Middlebrow Writers and the First World War, 1919-1939*, Oxford, Berg, 1993.

Cecil, Hugh, "Edmund Blunden and First World War Writing 1919-36," in *Focus on Robert Graves and His Contemporaries*, vol. 2, no. 1, University of Maryland Press, Spring 1993.

Eksteins, Modris, *Rites of Spring: the Great War and the Birth of the Modern Age*, London, Bantam Press, 1985.

Ellis, G. U., *Twilight on Parnassus: a Survey of Post-War Fiction and Pre-War Criticism*, London, Michael Joseph, 1939.

Fussell, Paul, *The Great War and Modern Memory*, Oxford, O. U. P., 1975.

Harvey, A. D. "'Oh What a Literary War!' An Alternative Version," in *The London Magazine*, Dec. 1993/Jan. 1994.

Hynes, Samuel, *A War Imagined: the First World War and English Culture*, London, The Bodley Head, 1990.

Klein, Holger, ed., *The First World War in Fiction*, 2nd ed, London, Macmillan, 1976.

Onions, John, *English Fiction and Drama of the Great War, 1918-1939*, London, Macmillan, 1990.

Parfitt, George, *Fiction of the First World War: a Study*, London, Faber & Faber, 1988.

Roucoux, Michel, ed., *English Literature of the Great War Revisited: Proceedings of the Symposium on the British Literature of The First World War*, Amiens, Presses de l'Université, Picardie, 1986.

Rutherford, Andrew, *The Literature of War: Studies in Heroic Virtue,* 2nd rev. edn, Macmillan, 1989.

Stephen, Martin, *The Price of Pity,* London, Leo Cooper, 1996.

Swinnerton, Frank, *The Georgian Scene: a Literary Panorama*, New York, Farar & Rinehart, 1934.

Tylee, Claire M., *The Great War and Women's Consciousness: Images of Militarism and Womanhood in Women's Writings, 1914-64*, London, Macmillan, 1990.

Williamson, Henry, "Reality in War Literature," in *The Linhay on the Downs*, London, Faber & Faber, 1934.

MILITARY, WESTERN FRONT

Ashworth, Tony, *Trench Warfare 1914-1918: the Live and Let Live System*, London, Macmillan, 1990.

Baynes, J., *Morale, a study of men and courage: the Second Scottish Rifles at the battle of Neuve Chapelle*, London, Cassell, 1967.

Beckett, Ian, and Simpson, Keith, *A Nation in Arms: a Social Study of the British Army in the First World War*, Manchester University Press, 1985.

Buchan, John, *A History of the Great War*, 4 vols, London, Nelson, 1921-2.

Carew, Tim, *Wipers*, London, Hamish Hamilton, 1974.

Chasseaud, Peter, *Topography of Armageddon: A British Trench Map Atlas of the Western Front 1914-1918*, Mapbooks, 1991.

General Staff, War Office, *Military Engineering (Part IIIb) Military Bridging - Bridges*, London, HMSO 1914.

Haines, M. G. M., *The Rifle Brigade - Militia, Volunteer and Territorial Regiments - the London Rifle Brigade*, notes on an exhibit for the O.M.R.S. Convention, 26 Sept. 1987.

Jeffery, Keith, "The Great War in Modern Irish Memory," in Fraser, T. G. and Jeffery, Keith, eds, *Men, Women and War*, Dublin, Lilliput Press, 1993.

Jones, Nigel H., *The War Walk: A Journey Along the Western Front*, paperback edn, London, Robert Hale, 1991.

Keegan, John, *The Face of Battle*, London, Jonathan Cape, 1976.

Liddle, Peter H., *Home Fires and Foreign Fields, British Social and Military Experience in the First World War*, London, Brassey's, 1985.

Liddle, Peter H., *The Soldier's War 1914-1918*, London, Blandford Press, 1988.

Liddle, Peter H., *The Somme - a Reappraisal*, London, Pen & Sword, Leo Cooper, 1993.

Moran, C. M., (Lord Moran), *The Anatomy of Courage*, London, Constable, 1945.

Nicholls, Jonathan, *Cheerful Sacrifice: the Battle of Arras, 1917*, London, Leo Cooper, 1990.

O'Riordan, C. and others, *A Martial Medley, Fact and Fiction*, London, Eric Partridge at the Scholartis Press, 1931.

Sheffield, G. D. "The Effects of War Service on the 22nd Royal Fusiliers ('Kensingtons'), 1914-1918, with Special Reference to Morale, Discipline and the Officer/Men Relationship," unpub. M. A. thesis, School of History, Leeds University, 1984.

Simkins, Peter, *The Kitchener Armies*, Manchester University Press, London, 1986.

Sparrow, W. Shaw, *The Fifth Army in March 1918* (intro. Gen. Sir Hubert Gough), London, John Lane, 1921.

Terraine, John, *The Smoke and the Fire, Myths and Anti-Myths of War 1861-1945*, London, Sidgwick & Jackson, 1980.

Tuohy, *Occupied 1918-1930: a Postscript to the Western Front,* London, Thornton
  Butterworth, 1931.
Winter, Denis, *Death's Men, Soldiers of the Great War,* London, Lane, 1978.

SOCIETY AT WAR
Parker, Peter, *The Old Lie: The Great War and the Public School Ethos,* London,
  Constable, 1987.
Thompson, Paul, *The Edwardians: the Remaking of British Society,* London, Weidenfeld
  & Nicolson, 1975.
Wilson, Trevor, *The Myriad Faces of War: Britain and the Great War, 1914-1918,*
  Cambridge, Polity Press, 1986.
Winter, J. M., *The Great War and the British People,* London, Macmillan, 1985.

BIOGRAPHY
Goldring, Douglas, *The Last Pre-Raphaelite: a Record of the Life and Writings of Ford
  Madox Ford,* London, Macdonald, 1948.
Green, Robert, *Ford Madox Ford, Prose and Politics,* Cambridge, C. U. P., 1981.
Judd, Alan, *Ford Madox Ford,* London, Collins, 1990.
Lagarde, Francois, de Torwanicki, Frederic, Sagnes, Nora and others, "Dossier, Ernst
  Jünger," in *Magazine Littéraire,* no. 326, Nov. 1994.
Powell, Geoffrey, *Plumer, the Soldiers' General: a biography of Field Marshal Viscount
  Plumer of Messines,* London, Leo Cooper, 1990.
Webb, Barry, *Edmund Blunden: a Biography,* London, Yale University Press, 1990.

RICHARD ALDINGTON
Doolittle, Hilda ("H.D."), *Her,* London, Virago Press, 1984.
Kenner, Hugh, *The Pound Era,* London, Pimlico, 1991.
Kershaw, Alister, *A Bibliography of the Works of Richard Aldington, from 1915 to 1948,*
  intro. Richard Aldington, London, The Quadrant Press, 1950.
Lawrence, D. H., *Kangaroo.*
Tabachnik, Stephen E., and Matheson, Christopher, *Images of Lawrence,* London,
  Jonathan Cape, 1988.

RICHARD BLAKER, GILBERT FRANKAN (ARTILLERY)
Campbell, P. J., *The Ebb and Flow of Battle,* London, Hamish Hamilton, 1977.
Severn, Mark (Franklin Lushington), *The Gambardier: Giving some Account of the
  Heavy and Siege Artillery in France,* London, Ernest Benn, 1930.
Winter, Sir Ormonde, *Winter's Tale, an Autobiography,* London, Richards Press, 1955.

ROBERT KEABLE (PADRES, SOUTH SEAS)
Durrell, Rev. J. C. V., *Whizzbangs and Woodbines: Tales of Work and Play on the Western
  Front,* London, Hodder & Stoughton, 1918.
Eggleston, George, T. *Tahiti: Voyage through Paradise,* London, The Travel Book Club,
  1955.
Grimble, Arthur, *A Pattern of Islands,* London, John Murray, 1952.
Marsh, Edward (ed. with a memoir), *The Collected Poems of Rupert Brooke,* London,
  Sidgwick & Jackson, 1918.

O'Brien, Frederick, *Mystic Isles of the South Seas*, New York, Garden City Publishing Company, Inc., 1921.

Pawson, G. P. H., ed., *Edward Keble Talbot: His Community and Friends*, London, S.P.C.K., 1954.

Talbot, Neville Stuart, *Thoughts on Religion at the Front*, London, Macmillan, 1917.

Tihoti (George Calderon), *Tahiti*, London, Grant Richards, 1921.

HERBERT READ

Treece, Henry, ed., *Herbert Read, an Introduction to His Work by Various Hands*, London, Faber & Faber, 1944.

HENRY WILLIAMSON

Barbusse, Henri, *Under Fire*, London, Dent 1918 (1st edn 1916). (Williamson regarded this as one of the best novels of the war.)

Jefferies, Richard, *The Story of My Heart*, Harmondsworth, Penguin, 1938 edn (1st pub. 1883).

Sewell, Brocard, ed. *Henry Williamson, the Man, the Writings: a Symposium*, Padstow, Tabb House, 1980.

Williamson, Henry, *The Sun in The Sands*, London, Faber & Faber, 1925.

Williamson, Henry, *The Wet Flanders Plain*, London, Faber and Faber, 1929.

Acknowledgments

This book has been written with the help and encouragement of the families of most of the principal authors under study in this book. I wish to thank them for their assistance and also those responsible for family papers for permission to quote from their fathers' and relatives' works and personal documents; in particular: the late Mrs. Eric Blaker, Betty Ingleby, and Gareth Owen (Richard Blaker); Anne Butler, Pamela Thompson, and the late Angela Waddington (Wilfrid Ewart); Elizabeth Eccleshare, Timothy d'Arch Smith (Gilbert Frankau); Leon Gurner, Lynette Sherwood, and the late Lady Gurner (Ronald Gurner); Alexander Hinkson (Pamela Hinkson); Doris Trewolla-Hulme, Tony Keable-Elliott (Robert Keable); Sophia Hankinson (R.H. Mottram); Jane Oliver, Bill Oliver, and the late George Arthur Oliver (Oliver Onions); Benedict Read (Herbert Read); the late Mary Bardell, Roz Cullinan, Joy Vowles, and Guy Yeates (V.M. Yeates). Grateful acknowledgment of their help and of that of others who have helped me in the research for this book is given in the references section. For permissions to quote and other assistance, my thanks to the late Alister Kershaw (Richard Aldington's unpublished letters and published works), the Trustees of H.G. Wells' Literary Estate and A. P. Watt (*Mr. Britling Sees It Through*); Peter van de Kamp (from Pamela Hinkson and for his invaluable help over Pamela Hinkson's life); Mrs. Anthony Hanson (from Pamela Hinkson); George Sassoon (from Siegfried Sassoon's *Memoirs of an Infantry Officer*); Caroline Zilboorg (*Richard Aldington & H. D.: The Early Years in Letters*); Mrs. Edmund Blunden; David Hingham Associates (Herbert Read's poetry and memoirs).

Where I have received author's and literary trustees' permissions to quote, I would like to acknowledge the following publishers: Faber & Faber (Siegfried Sassoon's *Memoirs of an Infantry Officer*); Indiana University Press (from Caroline Zilboorg's edition of *Richard Aldington & H.D.: the Early Years in Letters*); Random Century and Reed Books. Every effort has been made to locate the current holders of copyright in text and illustrations, but I apologize for any omissions and would welcome information so that amendments can be made in future editions.

I also wish to thank the following institutions for permission to print material from the collections in their archives: the Harry Ransom Humanities Research Center at the University of Austin Texas (Fitton Armstrong [Wilfrid Ewart], F.S.

Flint, V.M. Yeates; Gilbert Frankau); Edmund Blunden (R.H. Mottram); The Bei-necke Library, Yale University (Aldington); The Morris Library, Southern Illinois University (Aldington); the Library of the University of Illinois, Champaign-Urbana (Gristwood letters to H.G. Wells); the Liddle Collection (Personal Experience Archive of the First World War); The Bodleian Library, Oxford University (Richard Blaker). I also wish to thank the staff of these libraries, in particular Tom Staley and Cathy Henderson at HRHRC, and Peter Liddle whose archive and enterprise have been an inspiration; and the staff of the following: the Special Collections, the Brotherton Library, Leeds University; The Norfolk Record Office at Norwich Pub-lic Library (the Mottram Papers have survived the fire there last year); the Public Record Office at Kew; the Imperial War Museum, particularly Peter Simkins; Marl-borough College Library; Eton College Library; the New Bodleian Library (Western Mss) particularly Melissa Dalziel; the Rhodes House Library, Oxford Uni-versity; the London Library (where Alan Bell and Douglas Matthews have given invaluable advice); the Library of Trinity College, Dublin.

In addition to those I have thanked in the references for the separate chapters, I wish to thank the following for their interest and help: my colleagues at Leeds Uni-versity, Anthony Wright, Roy Bridge, Edward Spiers, John Gooch, David Goodway, Philip Taylor, Christopher Challis, John Taylor, Keith Wilson, and David Steele. Also Max Egremont; Tim Couzens; Lady Anne Cowdray; Mary Patmore; Simon Head; Paul Binding; Susan Schreibman; John Bourne; Roy Foster; Jonathan Cecil; Jay Win-ter; Brian Bond; Keith Grieves, Patrick Quinn, Gerald Gliddon, Barbara Muir, Sidney Walker, Dick Allison, Lilian Wynne, John Spencer, Robert Blake, Gill Co-leridge, and Ian Whitehead. I am grateful also to Leeds University students over the years whose own research has helped to point me in the right direction: Sally Ack-royd, Jonathan Atkin, Craig Gibson, Maris Irving, Christine Oliver, and many others.

I owe a particular debt of gratitude to Gary Sheffield for checking my manu-script for errors in military history and terminology; if others have crept in since he read it last autumn, these are my mistakes, not his. I also am greatly in the debt of Freddie Percy, the archivist at Whitgift School, who at an early stage in my research inspired me to delve far more deeply into these war novelists' lives than I had earlier planned, and whose thoughts and suggestions for further investigation have deter-mined the character of this book.

I am also indebted to the British Academy who paid for my travel to the U.S.A. and accommodation at Yale University in 1988. I am much indebted to the late Tom Cranfill, William Roger Louis, and Sese and Jim McElwain, for hospitality in Texas on the same research visit.

I wish to thank Anne Dale and Margaret Walkington for the most speedy and impeccable typing, and my wife Mirabel for invaluable editorial advice.

Hugh Cecil,
London, March 1996

Index